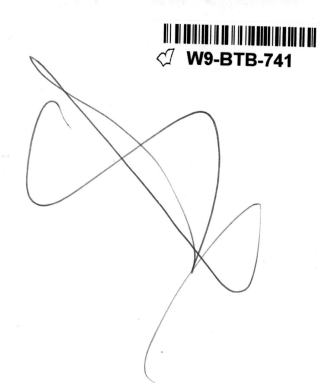

Educational Fund Raising

Educational Fund Raising
Principles and Practice

Edited by Michael J. Worth

Sponsored by Council for Advancement
and Support of Education

AMERICAN COUNCIL
ON EDUCATION
Series on Higher Education
ORYX PRESS
1993

Library of Congress Cataloging-in-Publication Data

Educational fund raising: principles and practice / Michael J. Worth,
  editor.
    p. cm.—(American Council on Education series on higher
education)
    "Council for Advancement and Support of Education."
    Includes bibliographical references and index.
    ISBN 0-89774-814-X
    1. Educational fund raising—United States.   2. Universities and
colleges—United States—Finance.   I. Worth, Michael J.   II. Council
for Advancement and Support of Education.   III. Series: American
Council on Education/Oryx series on higher education.
LB2336.E38   1993   93-16211
378'.02'0973—dc20   CIP

To Christine

Contents

Preface

This book had its genesis in the course I teach on university development in the Higher Education Administration graduate program at George Washington University. When I started offering this course about five years ago, I assigned Francis C. Pray's 1981 *Handbook for Educational Fund Raising* as the "textbook," finding it the most comprehensive volume in the field.

I continued using the Pray book, supplemented by other readings. Other good books on fund raising have appeared, but none I thought covered the subject quite so thoroughly.

Still, as the years went by, I noticed more and more that the *Handbook* was becoming dated. There have been changes in fund-raising practices and in the fund-raising environment over the past decade. The book's descriptions of some practices have become obsolete; more recent trends are not discussed at all.

The *Handbook* has become dated in another way as well. It reflects the anecdotal, experience-based approach that always has characterized fund-raising literature. The past decade has seen an increasing volume of research; now, scholars as well as practitioners have important insights and ideas to contribute.

I want to be clear: I intend no criticism of Pray's work. It was an excellent and important contribution to the field. Its shortcomings today result only from the passage of time and the evolution of the field.

I came to think that it was time for a new book on educational fund raising—one that would reflect the status of the field in the 1990s. I began to discuss the project with others, including Virginia Carter Smith at the Council for Advancement and Support of Education (CASE) and Jim Murray at the American Council on Education. This book evolved from and benefited from those discussions. In important ways, it has turned out different from the book I had initially envisioned, and it is clearly better for the difference. Before discussing what the book is, I need to state a couple of things it is not.

This book is not a revision of Pray's *Handbook*. It includes original writing, by new authors, on different topics—although a few subjects basic to fund raising are of course covered in both books.

Second, this is not a textbook like those you would expect to find in fields such as psychology or economics. Fund raising has not yet established comprehensive and sound "fund-raising theory" based on research. Fund raising remains a blend of science and art. It is still a profession taught by relating experience more than by presenting formulas and graphs. Fund raising is not a "discipline," and, although it has drawn increasing interest from scholars, it is not yet a widely recognized academic field of study.

Third, this is not a book about philanthropy. In recent years, a number of excellent works—most notably those by Robert Payton—have addressed the historical, philosophical, and cultural traditions of philanthropy. These are important traditions; all development officers should be familiar with them, and all fund raisers should understand their role in light of them. The fact that this book does not discuss philanthropy in this sense is not to imply that I dismiss that approach or view fund raising as something removed from philanthropy. But practicality required that this book focus on fund raising rather than philanthropy in order to be more comprehensive in its coverage of the former. There is a need for books on church administration as well as on religion.

Now, to mention some things this book *is*. Like all compilations, it is somewhat inconsistent. The inconsistency reflects in part the differences among the various authors' styles, which manage to survive even the microsurgery of the editor. But the inconsistency also reflects differences among the subjects the authors address. Some fund-raising topics have been examined in research studies and can be discussed in somewhat academic terms. For example, the chapter by Tom Pezzullo and Barbara Brittingham on donor motivations and the chapter by Bruce Loessin and Margaret Duronio on the characteristics of successful fund-raising programs are essentially reviews of research findings.

In other areas of fund raising there has been little research, but practice has become highly standard and systematic. These areas often incorporate a body of knowledge that approaches formal theory, even if it is not research-based. This is evident, for example, in David Dunlop's well-developed thoughts on major gifts.

Still, many aspects of fund raising require a certain "sense," with experience the best teacher. It takes experience and judgment to understand the partnership among trustees, presidents, and development officers that Sara Patton discusses, or the chemistry between consultant and client that George Brakeley emphasizes. And the careful building of relationships described by Michael Adams requires sensitivity as well as, perhaps, some innate talent.

This book reflects the status of the field in the 1990s. It is more than the war stories and anecdotes of seasoned practitioners, but it is far from a statement of some general theory of educational fund raising. Whether the field will move more in the direction of science, or whether it should, is a question beyond the scope of this preface. The diversity of the following chapters demonstrates that fund raising currently stands somewhere between the fields of astrology and astronomy in its rigor.

One element of the inconsistency among chapters is intentional. I wanted to produce a book that would be useful as a guide to practice as well as worthwhile to those who find fund raising an intellectually interesting area. As the book's title implies, the chapters include some—like Connie Clark's on proposal writing—that focus strictly on "how-to" techniques. Others—like Jake Schrum's chapter on ethics—raise issues worthy of the best academic minds. Some chapters are basic introductions to the topic, suitable as orientation for the beginner. My chapter outlining elements of the development program is clearly one of these. Others assume a more sophisticated understanding of both development and higher education.

I hope that this book, as intended, offers something for almost everyone. If not, the responsibility lies with me. If it does, the credit goes to the chapter authors, all of whom are accomplished and respected experts on their topics. I hope this book will make a contribution to the field I have made my life so far, to my colleagues for whom I have such great regard, and to the important institutions we all serve.

Acknowledgments

An effort such as preparing this book involves many people. First, I would cite Virginia Carter Smith, former Senior Vice President of the Council for Advancement and Support of Education (CASE), and James Murray, Director of Advancement, Membership, and Publications at the American Council on Education, for their encouragement and support from the beginning of this work.

Thanks are also due to Ruth Stadius, Director of Publications at CASE, who provided valuable support to the project, and to Teresa Crawford, my executive secretary at George Washington University, for her very capable coordination of my frequent communications with the authors. I am especially grateful to the book editor, Robin Netherton, who worked closely with me and whose brilliant editing is reflected in the quality of the finished product.

Most of all, I thank the chapter authors. All of them are recognized professionals who are both willing and able to share their insights and experiences with others through their writing. Their collective wisdom represents the "state of the art" in educational fund raising.

Contributors

Michael F. Adams (Chapter 12, "How to Solicit a Major Gift") is President of Centre College in Danville, Kentucky.

Robert R. Ashton (Chapter 21, "Fund Raising for Professional Schools within a University") is Vice President and Director of the Capital Campaign at the New School for Social Research in New York City. When he wrote this chapter, he was Associate Dean for External Affairs for the Leonard N. Stern School of Business at New York University in New York City.

James W. Asp II (Chapter 28, "Development and Sponsored Research") is Director of University Development at The George Washington University in Washington, D.C.

Richard B. Boardman (Chapter 24, "Measuring Fund-raising Costs and Results") is Associate Director of Development and Executive Director of the Harvard College Fund in Cambridge, Massachusetts.

George A. Brakeley III (Chapter 14, "The Use of Fund-raising Counsel from Counsel's Perspective") is President of Brakeley, John Price Jones, Inc., a consulting firm based in Stamford, Connecticut.

Barbara E. Brittingham (Chapter 4, "Characteristics of Donors") is Dean of the College of Human Science and Services at the University of Rhode Island in Kingston.

Peter McE. Buchanan (Chapter 33, "Educational Fund Raising as a Profession") is President of the Council for Advancement and Support of Education in Washington, D.C.

Connie Clark (Chapter 9, "How to Prepare a Direct Mail Solicitation") is President of Clark Communications, a consulting firm based in Alexandria, Virginia.

David R. Dunlop (Chapter 10, "Major Gift Programs") is Director of Capital Projects at Cornell University in Ithaca, New York.

Margaret A. Duronio (Chapter 5, "Characteristics of Successful Fund-raising Programs") is Director of Administrative Services in the Office of the Vice Chancellor for Institutional Advancement at the University of Pittsburgh.

Gary A. Evans (Chapter 25, "Organizing the Development Program") is Vice President for Development and College Relations at Lafayette College in Easton, Pennsylvania.

Norman S. Fink (Chapter 35, "Legal Trends Affecting Philanthropy") is Consulting Vice President of Engle, Heald and Associates, Inc., of Chicago. When he wrote this chapter, he was Deputy Vice President of Development and Alumni Relations and Associate General Counsel for Development at Columbia University in New York City.

Sarah Godfrey (Chapter 18, "How to Write a Good Proposal") is Administrator of the Rhonda Fleming Mann Center for Women with Cancer at the University of California, Los Angeles. When she wrote this chapter, she was Associate Director of Development for Health Sciences and Hospitals at the University of California, Los Angeles.

Judy Diane Grace (Chapter 34, "Trends in Fund-raising Research") is Research and Planning Officer for the Council for Advancement and Support of Education in Washington, D.C.

Jeffrey W. Gray (Chapter 20, "Raising Funds for Athletics") is Associate Athletic Director for Advancement at the University of Maryland in College Park.

Royster C. Hedgepeth (Chapter 29, "The Institutionally Related Foundation") is Vice President for University Advancement at Marquette University in Milwaukee, Wisconsin. When he wrote this chapter, he was Senior Vice President for Development at the University of Colorado Foundation in Boulder.

Kathleen A. Kavanagh (Chapter 19, "Raising Funds from Parents") is Vice President for Development at Vassar College in Poughkeepsie, New York.

Bruce A. Loessin (Chapter 5, "Characteristics of Successful Fund-raising Programs") is Vice President for Development and Alumni Affairs at Case Western Reserve University in Cleveland, Ohio. When he wrote this chapter, he was Vice President for University Relations and Development at the University of Pittsburgh.

Ann Gee Louden (Chapter 8, "The Annual Giving Program") is Assistant to the Vice Chancellor for University Advancement at Texas Christian University in Fort Worth.

William P. McGoldrick (Chapter 13, "Campaigning in the Nineties") is Vice President for Institute Relations at Rensselaer Polytechnic Institute in Troy, New York.

Rick Nahm (Chapter 7, "The Role of Institutional Planning in Fund Raising") is Senior Vice President for Planning and Development at the University of Pennsylvania in Philadelphia.

Karen E. Osborne (Chapter 22, "Hiring, Training, and Retaining Development Staff") is Vice President for College Advancement at Trinity College in Hartford, Connecticut.

Sara L. Patton (Chapter 6, "The Roles of Key Individuals") is Vice President for Development at The College of Wooster in Ohio.

Thomas R. Pezzullo (Chapter 4, "Characteristics of Donors") was Vice President for Development and College Relations at Rhode Island College in Providence until his death in March 1992. Tom was an outstanding professional who is missed by colleagues and friends.

Ronald E. Sapp (Chapter 11, "Fundamentals of Planned Giving") is Director of Planned Giving at The Johns Hopkins Institutions.

Jake B. Schrum (Chapter 32, "Ethical Issues in Fund Raising") is President of Texas Wesleyan University in Fort Worth. When he wrote this chapter, he was Vice President for Development and Planning at Emory University in Atlanta, Georgia.

Eric Siegel (Chapter 23, "Operating a Donor Research Office") is Director of Development Operations at the University of California, San Diego.

Joel P. Smith (Chapter 15, "Rethinking the Traditional Capital Campaign") is Vice President for Development-Health Sciences at West Virginia University in Morgantown.

Max G. Smith (Chapter 17, "Obtaining Foundation Support") is Director of Major Gifts at Furman University in Greenville, South Carolina.

Nanette J. Smith (Chapter 31, "Raising Funds for Community Colleges") is Vice President for Planning and Development at Edison Community College in Fort Myers, Florida.

James M. Theisen (Chapter 30, "Raising Funds for Independent Schools") is Director of Development at Phillips Exeter Academy in Exeter, New Hampshire.

Charles H. Webb (Chapter 27, "The Role of Alumni Affairs in Fund Raising") is Executive Director of the Michigan State University Alumni Association in East Lansing, Michigan.

Roger L. Williams (Chapter 26, "The Role of Public Relations in Fund Raising") is Assistant Vice President and Executive Director of University Relations at the Pennsylvania State University in University Park.

D. Chris Withers (Chapter 16, "Obtaining Corporate Support") is Associate Vice President for Development at the University of Richmond in Virginia.

Michael J. Worth (Chapter 1, "Defining Institutional Advancement, Development, and Fund Raising"; Chapter 2, "Elements of the Development Program"; Chapter 3, "The Historical Overview"; Part Twelve, "Current Issues and Concluding Perspectives"; section introductions) is Vice President for Development and Alumni Affairs at The George Washington University in Washington, D.C.

Robert M. Zemsky (Chapter 7, "The Role of Institutional Planning in Fund Raising") is Professor and Director of the Institute for Research on Higher Education at the University of Pennsylvania in Philadelphia.

Educational Fund Raising

Part One
The Development Function

This section establishes the context within which educational fund raising occurs and provides an overview of the elements of the development program. These chapters may be of greater interest to those who are new to the field than to veterans, although I believe that the material also offers some points and questions worthy of consideration by senior development professionals.

Chapter 1 places educational fund raising, or "development," in the broader context of "institutional advancement" and attempts to clarify the definitions of these terms. As Peter Buchanan points out in a later chapter, the establishment of common definitions is one criterion of a profession. The fields of institutional advancement and educational fund raising have yet to achieve such commonality. The discussion in Chapter 1 does not resolve that problem, but it does offer some important distinctions.

One need not be a dictionary buff to be concerned with definitions, since they reflect broader concepts that affect the way we think about and do our jobs. While this book focuses on educational fund raising, it is essential for the development officer to understand that he or she is a member of a professional institutional advancement team and that the institution's success depends upon coordination and integration of the various advancement specialties. I believe this understanding to be so important to the strength of our colleges and universities that it offers an appropriate place to begin the discussion.

Chapter 2 provides an overview that may be particularly helpful to the beginner. It defines the landscape of educational fund raising and how the various elements covered in the balance of the book relate to each other in an integrated whole. While introductory, it offers some principles concerning the allocation of effort and resources that may be helpful reminders to even experienced professionals, particularly at smaller institutions.

Chapter 3 places contemporary educational fund raising in the context of history. It is not a history of philanthropy, a subject with which fund raisers also should be familiar, but rather a brief history of organized educational fund raising in the United States and the evolution of the professional field in which most readers of this book likely work, or plan to work. It is perhaps important to all of us, as professionals as well as individuals, to have some sense of our heritage and genealogy. It affects how we view ourselves and our roles, and ultimately how we perform. Chapter 3 attempts, however briefly, to provide that perspective.

Chapter 1

Defining Institutional Advancement, Development, and Fund Raising

Michael J. Worth

The American system of higher education is the finest in the world, in terms of both quality and diversity. No other nation sends such a significant percentage of its population to college, and none offers such a wide range of institutions and programs to meet individual needs and ambitions. Despite recent criticisms of American colleges and universities, our nation's higher education system remains one of our greatest achievements and strengths.

Steven Muller cites four historical traditions that influenced the development of American higher education and account for its unique status today. First, the earliest colleges were often sponsored by churches, and the principle of separation between church and state kept them independent of government interference. Second, the "commercial character" of American society emphasized the practical value of higher education to the individual and did not treat it as a benefit to be provided by government. Third, the American tradition of philanthropy made it possible to sustain colleges through private gifts. And, fourth, American culture emphasized individual initiative in the public interest and a limited role for government.[1] As a result of these historical traditions, our higher education system developed in a way that provides our colleges and universities with a degree of autonomy generally not found elsewhere in the world.

In most other nations, colleges and universities are owned, operated, and funded by the national government. But in the United States, the responsibility for higher education has been left primarily to private initiative and state government. As Muller notes, the first colleges in the United States were private and were sustained largely through private contributions. Although some received help from state governments from time to time, they remained independent of government control and thus firmly established a tradition of independence early in the nation's history.

When our state universities were created in the nineteenth and twentieth centuries, they were designed to resemble the older private institutions rather than the government-owned universities of other countries. Their boards of regents or trustees, while usually politically appointed, insulate public colleges and universities from direct control by the state government and provide them with the freedom to compete with other institutions, both public and private, in the quest for students, resources, and status.

It is this element of competition among institutions that most distinguishes American higher education from the systems of other nations and that largely accounts for its quality and diversity. As in the economic arena, competition among colleges and universities creates a desire to grow and improve, promoting excellence.

Like their American counterparts, universities in other countries offer academic programs, provide supporting services to students, and perform business and financial management functions. However, American colleges and universities have another important area of activity, that known as *institutional advancement*. As Muller explains, the existence of institutional advancement programs in American colleges and universities is directly related to their diversity and competitive nature:

> The function of institutional advancement in American institutions of higher education is to enable each individual college or university to do well in a competitive environment and to assist the whole sector of higher education to compete effectively for available resources. In a nation that contains such an enormous variety of institutions, each college and university needs to develop and pursue its own distinct strategy for the acquisition of resources. It does so within a society where no effective national policy governs the matter and in which the public policies of the different states, regions, or localities vary significantly. It is primarily the individual institution, rather than the government, that is responsible for its own well-being and even survival.[2]

In recent years, reduced government support for universities in some countries has generated an increasing interest abroad in institutional advancement, and officials of foreign institutions have sought to learn advancement techniques from their American colleagues. But, given its roots in our particular history and culture, institutional advancement on a large scale remains a uniquely American phenomenon.

A. Westley Rowland defines institutional advancement as "all activities and programs undertaken by an institution to develop understanding and support from all its constituencies in order to achieve its goals in securing such resources as students, faculty, and dollars."[3] The activities and programs that generally fall under the institutional advancement banner include alumni relations, internal and external communications, public relations, fund raising, government relations, and enrollment management. The meaning of the term "enrollment management" itself has broadened in recent years to include not only student recruitment but also strategic packaging of financial aid to attract applicants and various programs for retaining currently enrolled students.

As this suggests, the definition of institutional advancement has come to include a wide range of the institution's activities. Indeed, as Rowland notes, "Institutional advancement is something in which the entire institution is involved. . . . Practically everything that happens at or to a college or university makes some contribution to its reputation and its image, good or bad. Each action, program, policy, and performance becomes part of the institution's total institutional advancement program."[4] In its broadest sense, institutional advancement is a state of mind that must pervade all aspects of the institution's life. It is an attitude of optimism and ambition that drives an institution's desire to grow and improve in a competitive environment.

This book is concerned with one important component of institutional advancement: *educational fund raising.* This function includes all the programs and activities by which the college or university seeks gifts and grants from private sources to support its programs and to build long-term strength through improvements to its facilities and additions to its endowment.

The term *development* is usually used interchangeably with "fund raising." According to Robert L. Stuhr, "development" was first used at Northwestern University in the 1920s and originally had a meaning not too different from today's definition of "institutional advancement." Stuhr describes the birth of the term and the concept as follows:

The period just after the first World War was a time of decision for Northwestern. . . . The University had to decide whether to remain what it was or to become a great university in the modern sense. It chose the latter course.

Although the first step in this new direction was the launching of a bold campaign to create a skyscraper metropolitan campus to house the professional schools, the people behind the undertaking realized that greatness would never result from this short-term project alone. They realized that the decision to move forward carried with it an indefinite commitment to the future.

A special department of the university was created to serve in meeting this commitment. . . . Somewhere in the course of discussions and committee meetings, the phrase "Department of Development" was coined.[5]

Stuhr defined the objectives of a development program in a way that resembles Rowland's definition of institutional advancement. Stuhr's objectives included building acceptance for the institution (alumni and public relations), providing the kind and quality of students the institution wants (enrollment management), and obtaining financial support (fund raising). Over the years, however, the meaning of "development" gradually narrowed and the term came to be used synonymously with "fund raising." "Institutional advancement" became the accepted designation for the broader objectives mentioned by Stuhr.

This book follows the contemporary practice; that is, the terms "development" and "fund raising" are used interchangeably and "institutional advancement" is used for the broader effort discussed above. However, I think it may be worthwhile to make a distinction between development and fund raising, at least in concept if not in everyday usage.

Development is a sophisticated *process* that includes several steps or stages. It begins with the institution's academic plan, from which specific financial needs and fund-raising goals are derived. It proceeds to the identification of likely prospects for gifts to support those needs. This step involves using sophisticated research methods and other means, discussed later in this volume, first to identify those financially capable of making gifts and then to learn their particular interests and match them with the institution's needs.

Ideally, the development officer can sensitively mesh the donor's most cherished philanthropic aspirations with the highest goals of the college or university. When this occurs, the gift becomes an enriching and rewarding experience for both parties— a far cry from the opportunistic image the term "fund raising" sometimes brings to the minds of the uninformed.

Once development officers identify donor prospects, they must establish programs to cultivate the prospects' interest in the institution and its specific plans and needs. To be effective, this cultivation must include more than just social contact and providing information. It requires *involving* donor prospects in the institution's planning in a sincere, substantive, and intellectually challenging way, helping to build their identity with, and commitment to, the institution's goals. This involvement is neither superficial nor manipulative. Successful cultivation means giving prospective donors a real and meaningful voice in institutional planning and decision-making, while at the same time protecting the institution's rightful freedom and autonomy. Maintaining this balance requires that both the donors and the institutional leaders have a sophisticated understanding of higher education and its traditions.

Only when these initial steps in the development process have been achieved is the institution ready for fund raising, which in its narrowest sense means solicitation, or simply "asking for gifts." After the gift has been made, there is yet another step in the development process: stewardship. Stewardship includes faithfully and competently carrying out the purposes of the gift and continuing to communicate with the donor regarding the impact of that gift on the achievement of institutional goals. Stewardship is itself an element of cultivation for the next gift, making the development process truly a cycle, in which the donor's involvement and relationship with the institution expands and deepens over time.

In this concept of development, fund raising is but one aspect of a complex process involving the institution, its hopes and goals, and the aspirations of its benefactors. Fund raising is episodic; development is continuous. Fund raising is focused on a particular objective or set of goals; development is a generic and long-term commitment to the financial and physical growth of the institution. Successful fund raising requires a specific set of interpersonal and communicative skills; development requires a broader understanding of the institution and its mission as well as patience, judgment, and sensitivity in building relationships over the long haul. A "fund raiser" is an individual skillful in soliciting gifts; a "development officer" may be a fund raiser, but he or she is also a strategist and manager of the entire development process.

These conceptual distinctions are important. Without them, those who work in development too often fall into simplistic misunderstandings of their own roles, and institutions appoint "development officers" with unrealistic expectations of what the job should and must entail. Failure to understand development as distinct from (and more complex than) merely fund raising deprives development professionals of the respect and regard their considerable skills deserve. As Thomas Broce writes:

> Fund raising as a professional process is best understood when considered in the broader process "development." The latter term encompasses the entire operation from goal identification to gift solicitation. Fund raising should not be confused with "tin cupping." Almost anyone can get token donations. High school band members can sell candy to buy new uniforms. What we are dealing with is the professional process involved in securing significant support.[6]

Again, the terms "development" and "fund raising" are used interchangeably throughout this book, and "institutional advancement" is used for the broader concept of which they are a part. That is current everyday practice, and an effort to continually distinguish these terms would simply complicate the reader's task. However, it may be useful in the future to standardize a different taxonomy that more clearly differentiates institutional advancement, development, and fund raising. Such a differentiation could help to clarify understanding and elevate appreciation of the development function in our colleges and universities. As Robert Payton observes, "Properly understood, fund raising rises to its rightful role as institutional development. The development function integrates with the academic objectives of the institution. It is as honorable and useful and important as any other function in achieving institutional purposes."[7]

NOTES

1. Steven Muller, "The Definition and Philosophy of Institutional Advancement," in *Handbook of Institutional Advancement*, 2nd ed., ed. A. Westley Rowland (San Francisco: Jossey-Bass, 1986), 2-3.

2. Muller, "Definition and Philosophy," 4.

3. Rowland, *Handbook of Institutional Advancement*, xiii.

4. A. Westley Rowland, ed., *Handbook of Institutional Advancement*, 1st ed. (San Francisco: Jossey-Bass, 1977), 523-524.

5. Robert L. Stuhr, ed., *On Development* (Chicago: Gonser Gerber Tinker Stuhr, 1977), 3-4.

6. Thomas E. Broce, *Fund Raising: The Guide to Raising Money From Private Sources* (Norman, Oklahoma: University of Oklahoma Press, 1979), 27.

7. Robert L. Payton, "The Ethics and Values of Fund Raising," in *The President and Fund Raising,* eds. James L. Fisher and Gary H. Quehl (New York: American Council on Education/Macmillan, 1989), 35.

Chapter 2

Elements of the Development Program

Michael J. Worth

To speak of an institution's fund-raising "program," in the singular, is to oversimplify the reality at most colleges and universities today. Most development offices manage a variety of programs, each having somewhat different objectives and each using a particular set of fund-raising tools and techniques.

These various fund-raising programs can look quite different. The excitement and bustle of an annual giving phonathon bears little resemblance to the patient, quiet conversation of a planned giving officer working with a donor's tax adviser. The foundation support specialist sitting at a word processor crafting a detailed proposal is engaged in work quite different from that of the development researcher poring over proxy statements to find alumni able to make major gifts. But these apparently diverse efforts must relate to each other and to the institution's particular needs and circumstances.

This chapter provides a brief overview of the elements of a development program. Later chapters discuss each of these elements in greater detail. While the information in this chapter may seem basic to the experienced development officer, newcomers may find it a useful framework for the more focused chapters that follow.

THE FUND-RAISING PYRAMID

The development program can be represented by a pyramid, as shown in figure 1. The base of the pyramid is the institution's *total constituency*, including all those individuals and organizations that might logically be interested in providing support. The constituency of most colleges and universities includes alumni, faculty and staff, parents of students, corporations, foundations, "friends," and other individuals and groups.

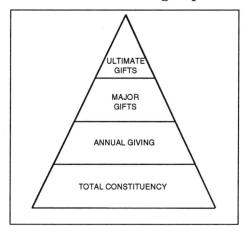

Figure 1. The Fund-raising Pyramid

Some percentage of this constituency supports the *annual giving* program, providing gifts to support the institution's current operating budget. Individuals who participate in annual giving may also be promising prospects for higher levels of support.

A smaller percentage of donors make *major gifts* toward important capital needs of the college or university, usually facilities or endowment. (Some writers use the term "special gifts" instead, reflecting the fact that such gifts are usually for specific projects rather than general support.) A relative few individuals reach the top of the giving pyramid and make what David Dunlop calls *ultimate gifts,* stretching to the limits of their own financial capacity and having a significant impact upon the future of the college or university.[1]

Many major and ultimate gifts are "planned gifts"—long-term commitments established with any of a wide range of financial planning techniques—and are thus arranged in light of the individual's overall financial and estate considerations. Planned giving is not depicted here as a separate element of the fund-raising pyramid or the development program. It is more properly a tool that is used with increasing frequency in major gift fund raising.

The shape of the pyramid represents the number of donors participating in each category, which declines with each successively higher level. But if the pyramid were drawn to represent dollars resulting from gifts at each level it would be inverted. An old fund-raising axiom stated that 80 percent of the dollars comes from 20 percent of the donors. Recent literature has revised this to say that 90 percent of the dollars comes from 10 percent of the donors. Trends suggest the need to revise the formula further to indicate the increasing dependence of colleges and universities on larger and larger gifts from relatively few, very major donors.

Comprehensive development programs aggressively solicit all constituencies and at all levels of the fund-raising pyramid. But the most successful are those that focus on the top of the pyramid, on those major gifts that will produce the largest share of overall support.

CAMPAIGNS

Among the most visible of today's educational fund-raising efforts are the major comprehensive *campaigns,* many having multi-million-dollar goals and extending over a period of five years or longer.

In earlier decades, colleges and universities mounted "capital campaigns" to raise money for specific facilities or endowment needs. Ongoing annual giving and planned gift programs were often run concurrently with, but separately from, the capital campaign. In the 1970s and 1980s, however, it became common practice to combine goals for annual, capital, and planned giving under an overall campaign umbrella. Today's campaigns represent an intensive cranking-up of all elements of the development program.

The campaign itself does not appear in the fund-raising pyramid; it is more accurately described as a fund-raising strategy than as a distinct element of the development program. Today's comprehensive campaigns are designed to enhance the visibility of the institution's needs and increase the urgency for all types and levels of support.

RESEARCH, RECORDS, AND STEWARDSHIP

Some aspects of a development program remain behind the scenes, carried out by development professionals who may never contact a donor or ask for a gift. The "back room" functions of research, records management, and gift stewardship have become increasingly important as development programs have become more comprehensive and intense. Today's development offices include highly specialized, skilled professionals in all of these "support" areas.

Good research is essential to ensure that fund-raising efforts focus on the most promising major gift prospects. Efficient records management and gift accounting is vital to aggressive annual giving programs, which may bring in millions of dollars from thousands of donors each year. And because the best prospects for new gifts are past donors, programs that provide careful stewardship and provide donors with timely information on the impact of their gifts can pay significant dividends in continued support.

Until recent years, stewardship has been a neglected activity in many development programs. Too many donors made gifts only to hear nothing from the institution until the next solicitation. The better development offices have added professional positions with responsibility for stewardship or "donor relations," and continued growth in this area may be a trend of the 1990s.

Systematizing and regularizing communication with donors about their past gifts is more than good fund-raising practice. It should indeed be viewed as part of the responsibility that development officers and their institutions incur when they accept a gift for some purpose. This is a dual responsibility, which includes careful efforts to use the gift as the donor intended as well as keeping the donor informed. Greater attention to stewardship can improve not only fund-raising performance but also the sense of trust and confidence upon which the donor's relationship to an institution must be built.

THE FUND-RAISING TOOL BOX

The fund-raising techniques employed at any particular time depend upon the level of the anticipated gift and the nature of the prospective donor. Annual giving programs, which focus on relatively small gifts from a large number of donors, rely on the devices of mass communication—the mail and the telephone. Modern annual giving programs are as much science as art, using the latest in computer systems and telephone marketing technology. The most successful programs also use personal solicitation, often involving organized cadres of volunteers managed by an annual giving professional.

Annual giving programs often emphasize numbers, aiming for increases in revenues and donor participation. And they tend to downplay specific needs, focusing instead on unrestricted general support.

In contrast, the solicitation of a major gift is more art than science. It is almost always face-to-face and requires a patient, long-term process of communication, education, and relationship-building. Few major gifts are unrestricted or directed to current operating needs. They usually are designated for a specific endowment or facility, reflecting the interests and experiences of the donors. The effective major gift solicitor is therefore well-prepared with a knowledge of both the institution's programs and the prospect. Gifts involving some aspect of planned giving demand that the development officer be expert in not only the art of fund raising but also the science of financial, tax, and estate planning.

FOUNDATION AND CORPORATE SUPPORT

Foundation and corporate donors may participate at any level of the pyramid, although obviously they do not make planned gifts. In practice, while local businesses may support the annual fund, few large corporations or foundations participate in annual giving programs except through employee matching-gift programs.

Foundations and corporations also tend to be reluctant to make major gifts to endowment, preferring instead to support specific projects. That is because they are generally less interested in the welfare of a particular institution than they are in how that institution can help advance their own broader philanthropic goals. While individual donors may have an emotional commitment to the college or university and wish to support it for its own sake, most corporations and foundations are committed first to their particular areas of interest. For corporations, these interests often relate to the firm's business—for instance, computer engineering. Foundation interests usually reflect the concerns of the founding donor or the foundation's traditional mission—say, saving the environment.

Fund raising from corporations and foundations requires a sophisticated understanding of the institution's educational and research strengths, and solicitations often include a written proposal that relates the institution's program to the donor's interests. Because many corporations and foundations establish detailed procedures and deadlines for requests for support, corporate and foundation solicitation requires highly specialized fund-raising skills and knowledge.

The narrowing focus of corporate and foundation giving has blurred the line between fund raising and "grantsmanship." Debates have arisen on some campuses as to which activities properly belong to the development office and which should be handled by a separate office of sponsored research or sponsored programs. This question, of particular interest at research universities, is discussed in a later chapter of this book.

THE FUND-RAISING LIFE CYCLE

A theory in biology proposes that the development of an individual organism reflects the stages in evolution of the species to which it belongs. For example, early in its development, the human embryo has features that resemble gills, which evoke an image of the early forms of life from which we all descend. The growth of other features—and eventually consciousness—come later in the development of the individual fetus, echoing the appearance of these features in the evolutionary history of the human species.

This idea has its analogy in the fund-raising pyramid of figure 1: The growth of an individual donor's giving relationship to an institution parallels the evolution of the institution's overall fund-raising program. Most individuals begin their support of a college or university through participation in the annual fund. As their interest and financial means increase over the years, they may make major gifts in support of particular purposes or campaigns. And in the end, they may designate the institution in their wills to receive the substantial fruits of a lifetime's work.

An institution with a new development program might well follow this same pattern, starting with an annual giving program in order to identify those among its total constituency who have the ability and proclivity to give. Only when the annual giving program has produced a sufficient group of such individuals would the institution begin to consider seeking major gifts from them. And only after these individuals have had the time to develop deeper feelings for the institution would the college introduce a planned giving program to address their estate planning needs.

Robert Stuhr recommends this step-at-a-time approach:

> If an institution is to have a well-rounded program, it is not necessary that
> it immediately build up an enormous development staff and start going
> in all directions at once. Instead, the institution should decide what is
> required to have a complete program, and then move toward its develop-
> ment in an orderly fashion. Each institution can grow into its program,
> just as has been the case with the field of development itself.[2]

DESIGNING THE FUND-RAISING PROGRAM

As explained above, the most successful development programs are those that emphasize major gifts, because the few
donors at the top of the pyramid provide the largest portion of total
support. The definition of a major gift is relative to the institution,
its fund-raising history, and the financial capacities of its constituency. A small institution with a young development program
might consider a $10,000 gift to be major, while a large university
might define major gifts as those of $100,000 or more.

However, the overall design of the institution's development
program should reflect not only its particular characteristics and
needs, but also where it—and its constituents—are in the fund-
raising life cycle. Despite its desire for major gifts, a young
institution with all of its alumni under age 40 might find it futile
and frustrating to invest its resources in a sophisticated planned
giving program while ignoring the annual fund. At the same time,
a venerable college or university that put all its efforts into the
annual fund would deprive itself of those resources most likely to
make a long-term difference in its strength and security.

Similarly, a small liberal arts college, located in a rural
setting far from corporate offices and with little research activity
among its faculty, might be wise to downplay efforts with national
corporations and foundations. This does not mean that it should
totally ignore these sources, but rather that it should allocate
proportionately less effort toward them than it directs toward
alumni, parents, and friends.

The fund-raising program should reflect what the institution
needs most. As Thomas Broce explains:

> When a development program is being started, those persons responsible
> must determine the kinds of gifts needed to meet the institution's
> objectives and the kind of program that will best attract these kinds of
> gifts. . . . Institutions should not spend hard-earned dollars on nonpro-
> ductive programs. Therefore, an institution with a small endowment but

a great need for additional operating support should place its prime emphasis on aggressive annual gifts programs. It also should be active in corporate-support programs with a continuing interest in planned giving programs, but its primary staff and dollar concentration should be on securing operating funds. . . . The institution should also be attracting endowment funds, but that should remain a secondary activity. On the other hand, a research-oriented organization should focus on fund raising from foundations.[3]

Despite this logic, colleges and universities too often strive to replicate programs they observe and admire at very different types of institutions. Stretching their resources to try and do everything results in insufficient effort devoted to those elements of the program most likely to produce revenue or those most relevant to the institution's real needs. Trustees, presidents, and faculty are sometimes culprits in this phenomenon, encouraging development staff to implement programs that they have seen succeed elsewhere, without stopping to consider their appropriateness in a highly different situation.

Many institutions also tend to overemphasize annual giving, with its immediate and tangible returns, at the expense of more long-term efforts to cultivate major gifts. Presidents and deans sometimes overvalue the annual gifts that can help them increase their spending now, while discounting the importance of planned gifts that will benefit their successors.

Again, no element of the development program should be ignored; the key is timing and emphasis. Allocation of staff and budget among the various elements of the program should reflect a careful analysis of the institution's academic programs, needs, and history, as well as the capacities and inclinations of its constituency. The strategic allocation of effort and resources will probably become even more important in the years ahead, as budgetary pressures and demands for accountability continue to increase.

NOTES

1. David R. Dunlop, "Major Gifts," in *The President and Fund Raising*, eds. James L. Fisher and Gary H. Quehl (New York: American Council on Education/Macmillan, 1989), 174.

2. Robert L. Stuhr, ed., *On Development* (Chicago: Gonser Gerber Tinker Stuhr, 1977), 13.

3. Thomas E. Broce, *Fund Raising: The Guide to Raising Money From Private Sources* (Norman, Oklahoma: University of Oklahoma Press, 1979), 20.

Chapter 3

The Historical Overview

Michael J. Worth

In 1641, William Hibbens, Hugh Peter, and Thomas Weld set sail from Boston to London on a mission to solicit gifts for a young American college. Their stated purpose was to raise money enabling the college to "educate the heathen Indian," a cause apparently viewed as worthy by wealthy British citizens of the time.

Weld remained in England, never to return to America. So too, in a manner of speaking, did Peter, who was hanged for crimes committed under British law. Only Hibbens returned to America, a year later, with 500 pounds to support the struggling institution—Harvard College. As historian Scott Cutlip dryly observes, "Such were the rewards of early fund raisers."[1]

The adventures of Hibbens, Peter, and Weld are regarded as the first organized fund-raising activity undertaken for an American college. Throughout the eighteenth and nineteenth centuries, however, fund-raising methods were primitive by today's standards, mostly consisting of "passing the church plate, of staging church suppers or bazaars, and of writing 'begging letters.'"[2] The principal technique was the "begging mission," usually carried out by a trustee, the president of the institution, or a paid agent, who was often given a percentage of the funds raised.

Early colleges were often connected with a sponsoring church, and their fund raising reflected a religious zeal, with gifts being solicited for the purpose of advancing Christianity in a young and uncivilized nation. The blending of religion and higher education was exemplified in the preaching tours of George Whitfield, who raised money for Harvard, Dartmouth, Princeton, and the University of Pennsylvania as well as for "the poor."[3] Even paid agents were often motivated primarily by their religious convictions, and many were principals in the college itself, sometimes playing roles in academic and business affairs in addition to their fund-raising activity.

THE BEGINNINGS OF MODERN TECHNIQUES

Despite their generally primitive methods, early fund-raising efforts do reveal the seeds of modern techniques. On their trip to England in 1641, Hibbens, Peter, and Weld needed "literature," and the first fund-raising brochure was produced. In 1829, a Philadelphia fund raiser, Mathew Carey, introduced the ideas of rated prospect lists and advance promotion of the fund-raising appeal, concepts which Cutlip calls "in embryo, the elements of modern fund raising."[4] Benjamin Franklin's advice to Gilbert Thomas in raising funds for the Presbyterian Church in Philadelphia reflected a strategy that is still employed in today's campaigns:

> In the first place I advise you to apply to all those whom you know will give something; next to those whom you are uncertain whether they will give anything or not, and show them the list of those who have given; and lastly, do not neglect those whom you are sure will give nothing, for in some of them you may be mistaken.[5]

Nevertheless, despite these early beginnings of a systematic approach, fund raising before the twentieth century was generally amateur and personal, a transaction between two individuals, with no role for organization, strategy, or professional managers.

THE START OF THE MODERN ERA

The first organized fund-raising programs in higher education came in the area of alumni annual giving. Alumni interest and loyalty to alma mater was evident as early as 1643, when Harvard alumni began returning to attend commencements and renew old acquaintances. The first formal alumni associations were created in the early 1800s; their primary purpose was to perpetuate memories and intellectual interests. Formal alumni funds also appeared in the 1800s, often promoting the concept of alumni as a "living endowment" for the school.[6] But the most significant revolution in fund raising was to come from outside higher education in the first decade of the twentieth century.

A YMCA executive, Lyman L. Pierce, had begun a campaign in 1902 to raise $300,000 toward construction of a new YMCA in Washington, D.C. With the help of a $50,000 gift from John D. Rockefeller and other gifts, his campaign had come within $80,000 of its goal when it stalled in 1905. Pierce called on Charles Sumner Ward, a fellow YMCA executive from Chicago who had gained attention for his fund-raising skills. Ward came to Washington to help Pierce complete the floundering campaign. As Cutlip recounts:

> The collaboration of Ward and Pierce produced the first modern fund-raising campaign techniques: careful organization, picked leaders spurred on by team competition, prestige leaders, powerful publicity, a large gift to be matched . . . , careful records, report meetings, and a definite time limit.[7]

Ward insisted on a carefully prepared list of prospects and showed prospective donors the names of those who already had given, adopting Benjamin Franklin's advice of more than a century earlier. Ward also introduced what is now called the "campaign clock" or "thermometer," a device to keep the pressure on to reach the goal by the deadline. Although Pierce and Ward collaborated on this historic campaign, Ward became "widely acknowledged as the prime originator" of what became known as the "Ward method" of fund raising.[8]

The first application of the new campaign techniques to higher education occurred when the University of Pittsburgh brought in Ward in 1914 to raise $3 million. Ward recruited others to work on the Pittsburgh campaign, including Carlton and George Ketchum, Arnaud Marts, and others destined to become prominent in educational fund raising.

Ward and his disciples subsequently established some of the best-known consulting firms in the field, several of which survive today. In their role as consultants, they introduced the new campaign methods to universities and other organizations across the country. With further refinements introduced by others over the years, Ward's campaign methods became standard practice in educational fund raising, still evident in today's development programs.

WARD'S CONTRIBUTION: THE BEGINNING OF A DEVELOPMENT PROFESSION

Ward's contribution went beyond the introduction of a new fund-raising method. First, his emphasis on "method" in itself represented a significant change from earlier fund raising, which rested primarily on the personal appeal of charismatic individual solicitors. Second, Ward himself represented a new breed of fund raiser, a fund-raising "professional" who developed strategy and managed the overall enterprise but who was not himself a solicitor of gifts—unlike the paid solicitors or agents who raised funds for the early colleges. The task of solicitation was carried out by volunteers and institutional leaders, with Ward providing the strategy, the method, and overall direction of the campaign. Ward did not personally solicit gifts, yet he raised millions.

Indeed, Ward did not at all possess the personal characteristics associated with so many earlier fund raisers. One of his associates, Carlton Ketchum, described Ward as "an austere and reserved man, very far indeed from any of the campaign types which we all know." Ward's effectiveness, Ketchum said, "was that of the originator of a sane and practical method, and the firmness to insist on its thorough application . . . rather than any personal magnetism."[9]

By creating this new role of a fund-raising strategist and manager, Ward paved the way for the growth of a development profession in the years that followed. In the first chapter of this book, I drew a distinction between "development" as a process and "fund raising" as the more narrow task of soliciting gifts. It was Ward who made this distinction a reality, with his emphasis on system and strategy, in contrast to the "beggar" fund raisers of earlier decades. In that sense, all of us who work as development officers today are truly Ward's descendants.

In the first half of the twentieth century, most college and university campaigns were directed by professionals from consulting firms like those founded by Ward and his contemporaries. Typically, the consulting firm would send a "resident manager," who would work with the institution for a period of months to complete the campaign and then move on to his next assignment at another college or university—all the time remaining an employee of the consulting firm, not the institution. The actual fund raising was performed by the volunteers and institutional leaders, with the consultant providing the strategy and management.

As development programs became more sophisticated, more intense, and more continuous, institutions came to recognize the value of having such a fund-raising professional as a full-time member of the college or university staff and created the position of "director of development." This transition was a gradual one. A survey by the American College Public Relations Association in 1949 found only two members with the title "Director of Development." In 1952, another survey discovered only thirteen.[10] Today, nearly every college and university in the nation—four-year and two-year, private and public—has at least one and in many cases dozens of development professionals on the institutional staff.

Professional consultants have continued to be an important part of the field, and many smaller institutions still use resident managers from consulting firms to direct their major campaigns. As the size and capability of institutional development staffs have grown, however, the trend has been toward using consultants for specialized services and periodic advice rather than full-time campaign management.

It is interesting to observe that the role of the college or university development officer originated in the for-profit consulting world. In the days before development professionals on the college staff became common, the fund-raising professional indeed came from "outside" the academic world and was clearly motivated more by the quest for profit than by loyalty to a particular institution. Alumni secretaries, by contrast, were more often institutional figures and served their colleges or universities for long periods of time.

Although development officers have become almost universally a part of college and university administrations, there continues to be a perceived cultural gap between them and members of the academic community, particularly faculty. Faculty are often suspicious of development professionals, viewing them as apart from the academic world and lacking in institutional commitment. While this view is unjustified in many— perhaps most—cases, it is one probably encouraged by the degree to which development officers continue to follow the patterns of their consultant ancestors. Mobility from institution to institution is high, and it is not uncommon for individuals to move from institutional development positions into consultancies and vice versa. This historical blurring of the for-profit and academic worlds may continue to have implications in the way development is understood and defined in colleges and universities.

EDUCATIONAL FUND RAISING SINCE WORLD WAR II

Three principal trends have marked the evolution of educational fund raising since World War II: first, the increasing professionalization of the field and the expanding role of the development officer within the institution; second, the proliferation of formal development programs at more and different types of institutions, notably state universities and community colleges; and third, ever-higher fund-raising goals.

The Professionalization of Fund Raising

Whether or not fund raising is a bona fide profession in the nature of law or medicine is a subject of some debate. But certainly, development has emerged within the past thirty years as an identifiable field within higher education administration, with its own specialized body of knowledge, standards, training programs, and career patterns. Concomitantly, the development officer or institutional advancement officer has risen to the most senior ranks of college and university administration, with a significant role in the overall management of the institution. In recent years, development even has become a route to the college or university presidency.

A significant event in the history of the educational fund-raising profession occurred in 1958, when representatives of the American Alumni Council (AAC) and the American College Public Relations Association (ACPRA) met at the Greenbrier Hotel in West Virginia. Most members of AAC were development and alumni relations professionals, while ACPRA served campus public relations officers. Prior to the Greenbrier meeting, these two organizations had been rivals, and on most campuses the management of their respective professional areas was fragmented.

The product of that conference, the "Greenbrier Report," gave birth to the contemporary definition and concept of institutional advancement. As Michael Richards and Gerald Sherratt describe it:

> The Greenbrier report was a comprehensive effort to define and improve the management of institutional advancement and its elements, as they were conceived in 1958. . . . The report advised institutions to select an organizing pattern for their programs that would encourage coordination of all advancement functions and that would lighten the responsibilities of the president. The report recommended the appointment of an "administrative coordinator" at each institution who would work in harmony with the president to oversee alumni relations, fund raising, and public relations.[11]

The Greenbrier recommendations gained ascendancy during the 1960s and 1970s, as advancement programs were increasingly placed under the direction of a single administrator, usually at the vice presidential level. With greater responsibilities and an enhanced function in the institution, vice presidents for institutional advancement, development, college relations—or however titled—became key players in the overall management of their colleges and universities as well as direction of their own programs.

In the culmination of the movement initiated at Greenbrier, the AAC and ACPRA merged in 1974 to create the Council for Advancement and Support of Education (CASE), comprising professionals in all institutional advancement specialties. CASE has expanded its programs concurrently with the growth of the field and now offers a variety of services, including more than ninety professional conferences and seminars each year.

In earlier decades, development officers could learn their trade only through experience or the tutelage of a senior practitioner. Francis Pray's experience, when appointed to his first development position in the 1940s, is typical: "When the president of the small college I worked for asked me to 'take over the alumni fund,' I accepted with alacrity, almost instantly afterward realizing that I knew nothing about it, either specifically or generically."[12] Today, programs offered by CASE, the National Society of Fund Raising Executives (NSFRE), and other organizations provide much more systematic training and have greatly improved the professionalism and skill of educational fund raisers. The 1980s have even seen the initiation of degree programs in institutional advancement at several universities and a flourishing of scholarly research on advancement and fund raising.

Educational fund raising or development remains, however, an evolving field. As noted in the previous chapter, confusion continues regarding definitions and roles. The continued high mobility of development officers harms both the institutions they serve and the reputation of the field. On many campuses, there is still a gap in understanding and mutual regard between development officers and their academic colleagues. Despite the general acceptance of the institutional advancement concept over the past twenty years, occasional tension and rivalry exists among the various advancement specialties. The increasing pressure of high dollar goals has given rise to concern with fund-raising ethics and the proper relationship of fund-raising objectives to institutional priorities. In sum, educational fund raising remains an adolescent field, still developing its own identity and place in the broader higher education world.

The Proliferation of Development Programs

As noted earlier, the first American colleges and universities were private institutions, and it was in the private sector that formal development programs originated. Our state universities were created much later, in the nineteenth and twentieth centuries, with financial support coming primarily from state government.

The history of private support for public institutions varies across the country. In the Middle West, state universities were often the first higher education institutions founded, and they enjoyed considerable prestige and support right from the start. For example, the Kansas University Endowment Association was established in 1891 to receive gifts from grateful alumni of the University of Kansas.[13]

In the East, however, state colleges and universities were newcomers in an area dominated by the older private colleges. Their missions were initially limited to agriculture, mechanical arts, and teacher training, often due to political pressure from neighboring private colleges. Moreover, they developed in an era of relatively abundant state budgets and a national climate that placed a high priority on public funding for education. In sum, for many years, most public colleges and universities had neither the ability nor the need to seek significant private support.

The past thirty years have brought significant changes. State universities have flourished, now offering a broad array of educational and research programs and levels of quality comparable to the finest private institutions. Former state teachers' colleges have expanded into comprehensive colleges and small universities. And hundreds of community colleges have appeared across the nation. Public institutions now enroll more than 80 percent of all students in higher education, indicating their importance to society and business.

As the missions and roles of public colleges have expanded, so too have their financial needs. These needs have outstripped the ability of state and local governments to respond, forcing them to seek new sources of support. And they have found such a source in private philanthropy.

Private support for public universities totaled just $356 million in 1971-72, representing 21.6 percent of the total $1.6 billion given to all of higher education.[14] By 1988-89, private support to public institutions had grown to $2.67 billion—nearly a third of all gifts to higher education that year.[15] This dramatic increase in support reflects the mushrooming of development staff and programs at public universities during the 1970s and 1980s. For example, a survey in the early 1980s found that 67 percent of state universities had established private foundations for fund-raising purposes.[16] By 1987, that proportion had increased to 86 percent.[17]

Community colleges have lagged behind four-year institutions in moving into the fund-raising arena. Community colleges responding to a 1987 survey reported that their fund-raising programs were an average of five years old, as compared with an average of twelve years for all public institutions.[18] But their results are not unimpressive given the youth of their programs, with more than $44 million having been contributed to public community colleges in 1988-89.[19]

The growth in private support for public colleges and universities and the increased scope and sophistication of development programs at these institutions are among the most striking changes in educational fund raising over the past twenty years. While the growth in development staffs and programs in public institutions may be expected to level off in the 1990s, a trend began to emerge in the late 1980s that may signal a new area of potential growth: the establishment of fund-raising foundations for public school systems in major cities across the country. Just as public colleges and universities responded to declining public funds in the 1970s and 1980s by building aggressive development programs, the nation's public schools may do likewise in the decade ahead, further expanding competition and the role of educational fund raising in our society.

Ever-higher Goals

Historian Scott Cutlip cites three campaigns run by Harvard University to illustrate the dramatic growth in fund-raising goals in the twentieth century. Harvard's campaign of 1904-05 sought

$2.5 million for faculty salaries. A 1919-20 campaign raised more than $14 million for Harvard's endowment. Writing in 1965, Cutlip described Harvard's 1956-60 campaign as having raised "the staggering sum of $82,775,553."[20]

Nearly thirty years after that, in 1984, Johns Hopkins announced the largest campaign goal ever—$450 million—only to be eclipsed just three years later when Stanford University announced higher education's first billion-dollar campaign. Other universities quickly joined Stanford in the "billion-dollar club," and by 1990, Harvard was rumored to be planning a campaign with a goal in the $2 billion range.

The explosion of fund-raising goals in the 1980s reflected the strong U.S. economy as well as the increasing needs of colleges and universities being called upon to serve a lengthening national agenda. Our colleges and universities are looked upon as vehicles for achieving social justice, enhancing national economic competitiveness, and advancing technological and medical knowledge, among other goals. The costs of needed facilities and equipment has continued to rise, as have faculty salaries, medical insurance costs, and all the other elements of the college or university budget.

At the same time as society is demanding more than ever of its colleges and universities, higher education has come to hold a lower priority for government funds than it did in the decades from World War II through the 1960s. Tuition levels have risen dramatically at both private and public institutions over the past decade, probably pushing the upper limit of what is economically or politically acceptable and thus limiting the colleges' ability to increase revenue in the years ahead. There appears to be no end to the forces driving educational fund raising to the center stage of American higher education and no limit to the goals that development professionals will be called upon to help meet.

Three hundred and fifty years after Hibbens, Peter, and Weld set sail for London, both the rewards and challenges of educational fund raising remain considerable. Contemporary development programs resemble the methods of these three early fund raisers about as much as today's jet planes resemble the sailing ships that took them on their way to England. But private gifts are no less critical to our universities, colleges, and independent schools today than they were in America's earliest years.

NOTES

1. Scott M. Cutlip, *Fund Raising in the United States: Its Role in America's Philanthropy* (New Brunswick, New Jersey: Rutgers University Press, 1965), 4.

2. Ibid., 7.

3. Ibid., 6.

4. Ibid., 8.

5. Ibid., 6.

6. Gary A. Ransdell, "Understanding Professional Roles and Program Mission," in *Handbook of Institutional Advancement,* 2nd ed., ed. A. Westley Rowland (San Francisco: Jossey-Bass, 1986), 374.

7. Cutlip, *Fund Raising in the United States,* 44.

8. Ibid., 40.

9. Ibid., 86.

10. Francis C. Pray, ed., *Handbook for Educational Fund Raising* (San Francisco: Jossey-Bass, 1981), 2.

11. Michael D. Richards and Gerald R. Sherratt, *Institutional Advancement Strategies in Hard Times* (Washington, D.C.: American Association for Higher Education/ERIC Clearinghouse on Higher Education, 1981), 11.

12. Pray, *Handbook for Educational Fund Raising,* 1.

13. Michael J. Worth, ed., *Public College and University Development* (Washington, D.C.: Council for Advancement and Support of Education, 1985), 1.

14. Ibid.

15. *Voluntary Support of Education 1988–1989* (New York: Council for Aid to Education, 1990), 5.

16. Timothy A. Reilly, "State University-Related Foundations," in *Raising Money Through an Institutionally Related Foundation,* ed. Timothy A. Reilley (Washington, D.C.: Council for Advancement and Support of Education, 1985), 9–17.

17. Michael J. Worth, "The Institutionally Related Foundation in Public Colleges and Universities," in *Fund-raising Leadership: A Guide for College and University Boards*, ed. J.W. Pocock (Washington, D.C.: Association of Governing Boards of Universities and Colleges, 1989), 63.

18. Mary Wallace Wheat, "Fund Raising and the Community College," in *Fund-raising Leadership,* ed. Pocock, 86.

19. *Voluntary Support of Education,* 5.

20. Cutlip, *Fund Raising in the United States,* 480.

Part Two

Foundations of Educational Fund Raising

The four chapters in this section attempt to establish a theoretical foundation for the sections that follow by addressing three basic questions: Who makes philanthropic gifts? What institutional characteristics seem to attract those gifts? What are the roles of the key players involved in bringing the donor and the institution together? The fund-raising strategies and programs discussed in the rest of this book reflect our assumptions about these fundamental issues.

Fund raising starts with people. In Chapter 4, Thomas Pezzullo and Barbara Brittingham discuss the characteristics and motivations of those who make gifts to our institutions. Our understanding of these factors reflects the experience and wisdom of seasoned practitioners, supplemented and clarified by an expanding body of recent research.

In Chapter 5, Bruce Loessin and Margaret Duronio review research that has attempted to identify characteristics of institutions successful at raising funds. As they point out, this is not an easy matter, and research findings are often inconclusive. Much work remains to be done.

Still, both research results and the conventional wisdom of experienced development professionals offer clues to the important ingredients of fund-raising success. One commonly cited factor is leadership, along with the establishment of an effective partnership among trustees, the president, and the development staff. Another essential factor, according to both research evidence and the longstanding belief of practitioners, is sound institutional planning.

Consequently, Chapters 6 and 7 are devoted to these two points. In Chapter 6, Sara Patton discusses the roles of the three key players in the effective fund-raising partnership: the trustees, the president, and the development professional. In Chapter 7, Rick Nahm and Robert Zemsky discuss institutional planning as a basis for, and prerequisite to, a development program that successfully addresses institutional needs.

As these chapters demonstrate, educational fund raising is still far from a science. But it is also far from being a random, mindless undertaking. Rather, success depends on a close connection with the broader missions and operations of our institutions.

Chapter 4

Characteristics of Donors

Thomas R. Pezzullo and
Barbara E. Brittingham

Harold J. Seymour said that the business of fund raising is not about money, but about people. And indeed, he devoted the first chapter of his 1966 classic *Designs for Fund-Raising* to "What We Need to Know About People." Knowledge of donor behavior and motivation is crucial to the practicing fund raiser. This knowledge helps determine the timing of solicitations, the types of appeals, and the sizes of requests, among many other things.

The religious roots of early educational institutions suggested that appeals should be charitable; that is, they should offer the donor the chance to give sustenance to the disadvantaged. While often appropriate to health organizations or others whose mission is to relieve suffering, the "charitable" approach has long been abandoned by higher education. Today, colleges and universities use a broader "philanthropic" approach, emphasizing the role of higher education in the long-term improvement of the human condition. Donors respond to that message; as Jerold Panas observed, "Large donors give to heroic, exciting programs rather than to needy institutions."[1]

But philanthropy alone is insufficient to account for giving behavior. Giving may also be motivated by such factors as the desire to buy acclaim and friendship, the need to assuage feelings of guilt, the wish to repay society for advantages received (such as college alumni might want to do), or simply egotism. Some giving may constitute an investment in activities that have indirect utility to the donor (such as support of an institution's research and service activities). And some people give to obtain tangible perquisites (such as an honorary degree or a name on a building).

What exactly do we know about donors? Studies of general giving behavior, some of which draw upon large-scale sources of data, can provide useful insights into who is most likely to give— and who is likely to give most.

By analyzing Gallup, IRS, and Federal Reserve data, and by reviewing prior studies, Christopher Jencks found that giving increases with age, that people who are married or widowed give more than single people, and people with dependent children give more than others, regardless of income level and tax bracket. Further analysis of demographic data suggested that women are more generous than men and that Protestants may give more than Catholics. More important to higher education, estimates indicated that an extra year's schooling adds 5 percent to one's charitable giving, and people who give $500 or more per year make larger average gifts to higher education than to any other type of organization.

Giving patterns differ significantly according to both the circumstances of the donor and the target of the gifts. Overall studies of private giving reveal a U-shaped curve, with the poorest and most affluent giving the largest amounts, measured as a percentage of income. Wealthy respondents tend to give higher proportions of their total charitable gifts to colleges and universities than do less wealthy respondents, whose giving tends to favor religion.

Donors to private colleges and universities are more likely to give to additional colleges and universities than are donors to public institutions. Donors to private institutions also devote a higher proportion of their total charitable giving to higher education. In addition, private institutions receive higher proportions of large gifts; more than three-quarters of their gift income comes from gifts of more than $5,000, compared to about two-thirds of gift income at public institutions.[2]

ALUMNI GIVING

A national survey indicates that about one-quarter of people who have attended college have given at some time to their undergraduate institution. One quarter who have not given indicate they have not been asked! Those who earned a baccalaureate degree give larger amounts than those who did not. Alumni of religious colleges are most likely to give, followed by those of independent colleges and public institutions. Loyalty to one's alma mater is an important factor, especially among those who attended independent institutions. Again, women were slightly more likely to give, and this likelihood increased with income level.[3] Recent, although highly anecdotal, evidence suggests that women's potential is growing more rapidly than men's and that women's motivations for giving are more complex and somewhat different from men's.[4]

A few studies have looked at alumni of distinctive types of institutions. Alumnae of women's colleges, for example, have been shown to be nearly twice as likely to be donors as are graduates of coed institutions, and one study showed their gifts to be 26 percent larger than the gifts of coed college graduates. For the decade ending in 1987, women's colleges showed greater gains than coed colleges in a range of types of private support: average gift, total giving, realized bequests, the share of unrestricted gifts, and corporate matched gifts. These changes may be attributed to a high degree of loyalty, increased earnings and greater financial sophistication among alumnae, increased control over discretionary income, and more effective fund-raising practices among the women's colleges.[5]

Alumni giving to historically black colleges and universities has been quite limited, although current efforts are under way to build expectations and traditions of giving to these institutions. One study found that alumni of historically black colleges had more positive attitudes toward giving if the college president is perceived to be an effective writer and speaker; if the public image of the institution is high; and if the alumni have positive views of the quality and quantity of alumni correspondence, the quality of alumni programs, and their experiences as undergraduate students.[6]

In general, characteristics or behaviors of alumni while they were students—such as patterns of attendance, participation in student organizations, place of residence, choice of major, or grade point average—are not strong predictors of future giving. Findings on financial aid are mixed, with some suggestion that those who either receive no financial aid or who receive scholarships, as opposed to loans, are more likely to give. It may be that students who do not feel that college attendance put them at an economic disadvantage are less reluctant to give later.

The current status, beliefs, and behavior of alumni are somewhat more helpful in predicting their donor behavior toward higher education, but simple demographic variables—such as age, sex, marital status, and children—prove poor predictors. Earning one or more degrees from an institution is a consistent predictor of giving. Occupation is not, although alumni in higher-paying fields may be more likely to give, or to give more.[7]

Perhaps the best predictors of alumni giving are an emotional attachment to the institution, participation in alumni events, and participation in and giving to other volunteer and religious groups. While these variables are the most consistently reported indicators of alumni giving and can be fairly easily measured through survey research, they are not those most likely to be contained in an alumni database. Their utility in selecting alumni likely to give or give more is thus limited.

TAX INCENTIVES AND ECONOMIC CONDITIONS

It is reasonable to believe that philanthropy will rise if more money is available and decline when less is available. Similarly, we can assume that private giving will increase if the "cost" of giving is lower and decrease if that cost rises. The factor that most affects the cost of giving is the deductibility of charitable gifts. Thus, we might conclude that changes in either the general economy or in tax policy should have a direct impact on people's giving.

Both of these ideas were put to the test in recent years, with the tax reforms of 1986 and the stock market crash of late 1987. A rush of private giving to higher education occurred in late 1986, as those who did not expect to itemize their returns in the future made their last deductible gifts. Tax reform also caused the cost of charity to rise. A $1 gift, which before 1987 had a real cost of only 50 cents for those in the highest tax bracket, now costs 67 cents. This change seems to have slightly reduced subsequent gifts to higher education, particularly the types of gifts most susceptible to the reforms—gifts of appreciated property and gifts over $5,000.

As for the October 1987 market crash, several institutions launching campaigns—for example, the Massachusetts Institute of Technology, which began a $550 million campaign in 1988—reported that the event did not diminish progress in any detectable way. But in all, private voluntary support for higher education, which had posted fifteen consecutive years of gains averaging 12 percent annually, faltered in 1987 and 1988. That shift reflects both the rush in late 1986 and the subsequent slowdown, as well as the conservatism resulting from the 1987 market meltdown.

While it is tempting to interpret these gross data and anecdotes, the research on the influence of tax incentives, cost of giving, and economic factors is more illuminating.

Sally Spaid Drachman examined economic trends in relation to giving trends from 1932 to 1974. She concluded that businesses tend to adjust giving to the current economic climate, while individuals—alumni and nonalumni—give without regard to economic conditions.[8]

Several studies of the effect of tax deductibility indicate that tax deductions offer a greater incentive to higher-income individuals; that is, gifts are inversely related to price and directly related to income. Gifts to education and hospitals appear particularly price-sensitive, and eliminating deductibility would thus cut giving to educational institutions and hospitals significantly. However, Jerold Panas reports that many donors of large gifts say that while they report their gifts for the tax advantage, it does not influence their giving.[9]

Christopher Jencks' analysis of Gallup, IRS, and Federal Reserve data suggests two motives for giving: "paying your dues" and "giving away your surplus." Giving to churches is paying your dues; as income rises, giving to churches increases, but not proportionately. Giving to colleges (and hospitals) is more like giving away your surplus. Much alumni giving is to major private institutions, whose graduates tend to do well economically. Much of the total giving to higher education is from nonalumni individuals who give large amounts for such purposes as buildings and endowed chairs.

THE INFLUENCE OF ATHLETICS

The question of whether a successful athletic program increases giving has been studied longer than any other research question in higher education fund raising. For almost seventy years, researchers have looked at this issue from a myriad of viewpoints. Only a handful of studies has detected a positive link between athletic success and fund raising, and almost as many have actually shown a negative effect.[10]

In the face of these findings, some experienced fund raisers argue that success in intercollegiate athletics brings favorable attention and recognition to a college or university, increases pride and bonding among alumni, and hence must have a positive spillover effect on all fund raising at the institution. Others argue that athletic success motivates only a small proportion of alumni and, because it can diminish the academic reputation of a college enjoying athletic success, it can have neutral or deleterious effects on private support.

Still, there is ample evidence that an emotional tie to one's alma mater affects alumni giving, and one highly visible form of that tie is alumni athletic interests. Even though studies show very little link between athletic success and alumni giving, the search for evidence will no doubt continue as long as intuition suggests that the link must exist. Almost nowhere else in the fund-raising research literature is the research more thorough and rigorous, more plentiful, or more convincing. Yet when it comes to the common view of the influence of athletics on donor behavior, a handful of contrary anecdotes seems to outweigh the carefully conducted research.

MOTIVATIONS FOR LARGE GIFTS

As varied as the motivations and circumstances of ordinary giving may be, the psychology of large gifts is "uncommonly complicated," according to Panas, who talked to more than thirty individuals who have given gifts of $1 million or more. Although these donors spoke with enthusiasm, often passion, about their giving and its importance in their lives, Panas concluded that, in the end, their motivation remained incompletely understood, perhaps even by the donors themselves.[11]

He found several common factors, however. Donors of large gifts have developed a habit of generous giving, often over a lifetime. They often describe giving as an important or even essential part of their lives, and several speak candidly of the joy they receive from giving. Seldom responding to "need," these donors are more likely to give to organizations with a mission they support, for opportunities that attract their interest. They participate out of a belief that their gift can make a difference. Large donors, Panas noted, may respond to "dreams and visions that glow," but are unlikely to give where controversy exists, particularly for gifts realized during their lifetimes. While these donors reported they like to make up their own minds and resist being sold, Panas suggests that they respond to being thanked often for their previous gifts.

CORPORATION AND FOUNDATION GIVING

Corporations respond to requests that can best be turned to the corporation's own interests, either directly or indirectly. Corporations tend to give to research that advances the company's work; they also promote education and training of prospective employees. Indirect benefits of corporate giving include enhanced image, improved employee morale, and a sense of corporate social responsibility. Another factor motivating corporate support may be the desire to maintain a climate conducive to free enterprise.

The improvement of a community's quality of life through corporate giving is attractive to new employees and rewarding to continuing ones. But the corporation cannot capture these benefits exclusively for itself; the improvements serve everyone in the city or region, including the corporations that do not make gifts. Consequently, corporations within a given community tend to exert—and respond to—a great deal of peer influence, which leads to a common level of corporate support. This tendency helps explain the enormous differences in giving levels among major cities.

Although foundations, as a group, have been credited with innovations in higher education ranging from faculty pensions to honors programs, individual foundations generally maintain a narrow scope of interest. A foundation's charter, its sponsorship, or its geography usually define its parameters for program funding, thus restricting its influence. Essentially conservative, working with small staffs and voluntary boards, foundations are necessarily wary of risk-taking and new ventures. They prefer to take the well-traveled road and to serve constituencies that are well-defined and, to some views, already advantaged.

Foundations are most likely to support proposals from institutions located in the same state or region, that request unrestricted funds, that have past experience with foundations, that demonstrate sound fiscal management, whose president and administration engender confidence, and that maintain a reputation for academic excellence.[12] This tendency to follow others may be based in part on the conviction that if another foundation has found the cause worthy, a lot of staff time in investigation and evaluation can be saved. (Additional detail on foundation and corporation giving appears in Part VI of this book.)

NOTES

1. Jerold Panas, *Mega Gifts: Who Gives Them, Who Gets Them* (Chicago: Pluribus Press, 1984), 35.

2. Christopher Jencks, "Who Gives to What?," in *The Nonprofit Sector: A Research Handbook,* ed. Walter W. Powell (New Haven: Yale University Press, 1987).

3. For more detail on these points, see Barbara E. Brittingham and Thomas R. Pezzullo, *The Campus Green: Fund Raising in Higher Education,* ASHE-ERIC Higher Education Report no. 1 (Washington, D.C.: George Washington University, 1990), 39–43.

4. Anne Mathews, "Alma Maters Court Their Daughters," *The New York Times Magazine,* April 7, 1991, 40.

5. *Alumnae Giving at Women's Colleges: A Ten-Year Report* (Washington, D.C.: Women's College Coalition, 1988).

6. Jeanette H. Evans, "A Study of the Attitudes of the Alumni of Historically Black Colleges and Universities Towards Financial Giving to Their Alma Maters" (Ed.D. diss., Morgan State University, 1986).

7. Brittingham and Pezzullo, *The Campus Green,* 39–43.

8. Sally Spaid Drachman, "Factors Accounting for Variations in Levels of Private Giving to Higher Education in the United States" (Ph.D. diss., University of Arizona, 1983).

9. Panas, *Mega Gifts,* 141–151.

10. Brittingham and Pezzullo, *The Campus Green,* 45–47.

11. Panas, *Mega Gifts,* 37.

12. William B. Lawson, 1976. "Foundations and Private Institutions of Higher Education: A Merging of Interests or a Parting of the Ways?" (Ph.D. diss., Arizona State University, 1976).

Chapter 5

Characteristics of Successful Fund-raising Programs

Bruce A. Loessin and
Margaret A. Duronio

We began our research on higher education fund raising in 1986 with the intention of creating practical training materials and evaluation guidelines for fund-raising practitioners. We intended to base this work on the example of institutions successful at fund raising, but like many of our fellow practitioners, we were somewhat naive about the complexities involved in measuring fund-raising performance. We knew that good fortune, a successful tradition of fund raising, and institutional wealth and prestige all played a role in fund-raising success, but we also knew that skill and hard work influenced fund-raising results. Lacking research-based models, we thought we could use this "conventional wisdom" as a way to select institutions with excellent fund-raising programs for in-depth study.

We began by looking at data on institutional characteristics and fund-raising results. By "institutional characteristics," we mean quantifiable data such as endowment, educational and general expenditures, and enrollment; we analyzed eight such variables. "Fund-raising results" include not only total voluntary support, but also separate gift totals from alumni, nonalumni individuals, corporations, and foundations. These data, as reported by the institutions themselves, are published annually by the Council for Aid to Education (CFAE) in the report *Voluntary Support of Education.*[1]

At first, we were interested only in research universities such as our own. An initial review of the figures showed that both voluntary support and institutional characteristics varied widely among these research universities. We then reviewed the data for other major categories of higher education institutions and were again startled not only by the vast differences among *types* of institutions, but also by the substantial differences *within* types. From this simple review of descriptive information, we realized that the data did not support the conventional belief that institutions with the greatest institutional resources in wealth and stature raise the most money in voluntary support. Within each type of institution, we found that institutions with high totals in voluntary support were not necessarily those with the highest levels of resources.

We also began to pay more attention to the substantial differences between private and public institutions, both in total voluntary support and in support by separate donor groups. We began to wonder if the same institutional characteristics were equally related to fund-raising success in private and public institutions.

Given these issues, we postponed our initial goal of producing materials and guidelines for fund-raising managers and turned to the more fundamental question of how to measure effective fund raising. We realized that before we could build on the example of successful programs, we had to determine how to identify which programs were successful. With a grant from the Exxon Education Foundation, we set out to discover if there were different models for effective fund-raising programs in dissimilar types of institutions. We continued the work under two additional grants from the Lilly Endowment.

This chapter includes a brief overview of research on institutional characteristics and fund-raising results, followed by a more detailed discussion of our own research, and, finally, a summary of what the research indicates and what course future research should take.

OVERVIEW OF RESEARCH

In 1969, John Leslie conducted the first major study on advancement programs in higher education.[2] This focused on the relationships among fund-raising outcomes, institutional characteristics, and organizational and operational features of fund-raising programs in 105 institutions of several different types. Leslie reported a strong relationship between fund-raising expenditures and gift dollars, noting that the cost of raising money was "approximately fifteen to twenty cents per dollar raised, with a wide range both ways," and that as an institution raised more money, expenditures for advancement programs decreased. Although the study had several methodological flaws, Leslie was the first to argue that empirical research could be used to study fund-raising performance. More notably, he introduced the idea that institutions differ in their potential for successful fund raising and pointed out the need to develop methods to measure potential in order to define and improve effectiveness.

In 1977, William Pickett expanded on Leslie's concept of potential for success in fund raising.[3] Pickett examined fund-raising results in 200 randomly selected private liberal arts colleges. Since gift income in itself provides no information about an institution's potential, he reasoned, judging performance on the basis of gift income alone would make it possible to "confuse a 'fortunate' college with an 'effective' one." To avoid this mistake, he measured fund-raising performance by comparing results with fund-raising potential.

Pickett defined potential as a combination of the financial resources available in a college's geographical environment and the access a college has to these resources. To measure financial resources in the environment, he used four variables: number of alumni, number of families with income over $50,000 in the standard metropolitan statistical area nearest the college, total value of grants made by major foundations in the college's state, and value added by manufacturing in the statistical area. He used eight variables to measure access to financial resources: in-state enrollment, cost of attendance, graduate school attendance of alumni, age of college, value of endowment, federal support for research and development, tenure of president, and enrollment.

Of both sets of variables, only number of alumni, value of endowment, cost of attendance, age of college, in-state enrollment, and graduate school attendance proved important in explaining income from gifts. Using these variables, he conducted multiple regression analyses to predict total voluntary support for each institution. After comparing predicted totals with actual totals for each college, he was able to identify colleges that he defined as overproductive or underproductive in their fund-raising performance. He concluded that it is possible and practical to estimate fund-raising potential in a reliable way and that the geographical location of a college is not as important a factor as is environmental "position"—that is, those factors that determine access to financial resources, such as wealth, size, and perceived

quality. Overproductive institutions, he found, were characterized by strong institutional direction, trustee involvement and
leadership, and greater fund-raising "effort" in terms of budget
and staff.

Several other researchers since Pickett have sought to define
the relationships between various institutional characteristics
and fund-raising results.[4] These studies have documented the
importance of various institutional characteristics to overall fund-
raising success at specific institutions or types of institutions.
However, because of variations in methodology and differences in
study groups, comparisons of research findings across types of
institutions are not appropriate.

A recent study by Larry Leslie and Garey Ramey is one of the
first to analyze institutional characteristics and fund-raising
results for separate donor groups, instead of using total voluntary
support.[5] Although the study covers only research universities, it
clearly documents considerable variation in the relationships
between institutional and environmental characteristics and
fund-raising results for different donor groups. For instance,
Leslie and Ramey determined that while individual donors might
respond favorably to an approach emphasizing institutional need,
corporation and foundation donors are more likely to respond to an
approach that emphasizes institutional capability.[6]

QUANTITATIVE RESEARCH

Our research includes both quantitative and qualitative
studies on ten types of institutions. The quantitative studies are
a series of analyses to describe and compare fund-raising results
and institutional characteristics within and across all major types
of higher education institutions. The purpose of these analyses
was to identify whether institutional characteristics are equally
related to fund-raising results in all donor groups and in each type
of institution. In these studies, we looked at:

- More than 500 private and public institutions, including
  research universities, doctoral universities, comprehensive
  universities, four-year colleges, and two-year colleges;
- Institutional characteristics, including public or private
  status, type of institution, educational and general expenditures, endowment, expenditures per student, tuition, enrollment, alumni of record, and age of institution; and

- Total voluntary support as well as separate totals of gifts from alumni, nonalumni individuals, corporations, and foundations for each institution.

We used three-year averages for institutional characteristics and fund-raising results. Most of the information about institutions was taken from the CFAE reports and the annual editions of the *HEP Higher Education Directory*.[7] The institutions reporting fund-raising results to CFAE each year raise about 85 percent of the total annual voluntary support to higher education. The institutions included in our analyses are representative of all institutions reporting to CFAE and are therefore representative of the institutions raising most of the private support for higher education.

Descriptive Information

A review of the CFAE information for more than 600 institutions for 1987–89 confirms not only that types of institutions vary substantially in dollars raised and in institutional resources for fund raising, but also that there are substantial differences within each type. A small portion of this data—the highest, median, and lowest figures for total voluntary support and endowment for private and public research and comprehensive universities— appears in table 1.

In addition to the substantial variation among and within types, the descriptive information also indicates that:

1. Total voluntary support and institutional resources increase overall as the complexity of the institutions increases—that is, from two-year colleges as least complex to research universities as most complex.
2. Private institutions generally acquire more voluntary support than public institutions of the same type.
3. Although the *types* of institutions with the most resources also receive more voluntary support, *individual institutions* with the most resources are not necessarily those with the highest fund-raising totals. Conversely, individual institutions with the lowest fund-raising totals are not necessarily those with the fewest resources.

The descriptive data alone confirm that comparisons of fund-raising results in institutions across types are highly inappropriate because these institutions operate in vastly different environments. Perhaps even more important, the variance within types suggests that comparing same-type institutions on fund-raising results alone is neither very useful nor very reliable. To achieve more meaningful results, we used two forms of statistical analysis, correlation coefficients and multiple regression procedures, to study the relationships of fund-raising results and institutional resources.

Table 1. Sample of Descriptive Information for Research and Comprehensive Universities (1987–1989)

TOTAL VOLUNTARY SUPPORT			
Type of Institution	*High*	*Median*	*Low*
Private Research	$135,321,436	$69,468,321	$3,471,130
Public Research	65,916,352	34,944,779	6,783,633
Private Comprehensive	14,107,964	2,597,571	180,803
Public Comprehensive	9,844,841	973,228	143,793
ENDOWMENT			
Type of Institution	*High*	*Median*	*Low*
Private Research	$1,972,522,333	$491,283,333	$34,099,560
Public Research	463,876,686	135,216,502	29,216,859
Private Comprehensive	213,177,833	10,404,503	100,000
Public Comprehensive	19,237,023	2,130,177	5,699

Correlations

In general, our analysis of correlations[8] between institutional characteristics and voluntary support indicates that:

1. There is no single or consistent pattern of relationships between institutional characteristics and voluntary support, either across types of institutions or within types. Nor is there a single or consistent pattern between institutional characteristics and fund-raising results for all donor groups. This means that institutions with similar amounts of resources do not always have similar results in fund raising, either for total support or with specific donor groups.

2. When we look at totals—characteristics of all institutions and support from all donor groups—the data strongly support the conventional wisdom that the wealthiest, most prestigious institutions have the most successful fund-raising programs. However, when we sort institutions by type and divide giving by donor group, we find considerably less consistent support for this conventional wisdom.
3. Different types of donors are attracted by different institutional characteristics in different types of institutions.
4. Relationships between institutional characteristics and fund-raising results are different in public and private institutions. Generally, wealth is more of a factor in attracting voluntary support for private institutions; size is more important for public institutions.
5. For both private and public institutions, the statistical relationship between institutional characteristics and fund-raising results is generally stronger for research and doctoral universities than for other institutions. This suggests that particular institutional characteristics may matter less than is generally believed. To use a sports metaphor, characteristics may define the fund-raising league you play in, but they have little to do with whether you win the title.

Multiple Regression Analyses

Sorting institutions by type, we used stepwise regression procedures to predict fund-raising results for each institution within each type and then compared the predicted totals with the actual totals.[9] Regression analysis enabled us to take into account each institution's relative assets in comparison to others of the same type. By comparing predicted and actual totals, we were then able to identify institutions that appeared to be making the best use of their respective resources.

We discovered that some institutions raising amounts that were above average for their institutional type were nevertheless not raising as much money as the statistical procedure predicted they would. We also discovered that some institutions below the average were raising more dollars than predicted, suggesting that these institutions were making more effective use of scarcer resources. These results also confirm that simply ranking institutions by amount raised, even within institutional categories, is not a clear or accurate indicator of fund-raising performance. If we measure fund-raising performance by rank ordering of dollars raised, we would have to assume that the institutions are equal in fund-raising potential. Our analyses indicate that this is not an easy assumption to make.

In summary, our quantitative analysis shows that institutional characteristics alone do not adequately explain why some institutions raise considerably more money in voluntary support than do others with similar resources. The conventional wisdom regarding fund-raising success appears to apply primarily to private research universities and wealthy, private four-year colleges—not to other types of institutions.

QUALITATIVE RESEARCH

If numbers alone are insufficient to identify effective fund-raising programs, we concluded that there must be other factors within each institution that contribute to fund-raising success. One possibility is that fund raisers in more successful institutions are simply doing a better job; another possibility is that fund raisers in successful institutions have institutional resources available to them that are not easily defined by quantitative measures. Some conventional wisdom also suggests that qualitative institutional factors affect fund-raising success, but not much research has been done to document these relationships.

Using the multiple regression analyses from our earlier research, we selected ten institutions—one private and one public for each of the five categories we had analyzed—for which actual dollars raised were higher than statistically predicted.[10] These "effective" institutions varied widely in their institutional resources and gift income. Total voluntary support for the ten institutions ranged from a high of $28.1 million to $322,000; institutional budgets ranged from a high of $165.9 million to $2.8 million.

We visited each institution for one to four days. During our visits, we reviewed materials and documents on fund-raising programs and interviewed more than 100 people, including presidents, chief development officers, and other fund-raising managers and staff. To guide our data collection, we developed a list of qualitative elements believed to contribute to fund-raising effectiveness.[11] This list appears in table 2.

The results of our qualitative research indicate that no single pattern of factors fits all institutions. No institutions were outstanding in all areas studied; some had strengths in only a few. The most commonly found elements in these successful fund-raising programs were presidential leadership, institutional commitment to fund raising, the chief development officer's leadership and role in setting institutional mission, and entrepreneurial fund-raising programs. Less commonly found elements in these successful fund-raising programs were trustees' support and participation, volunteers' roles, emphasis on management, em-

Table 2. Characteristics Commonly Associated with Effective Fund Raising

INSTITUTIONAL CHARACTERISTICS

Presidential leadership
Trustees' participation
Institution's commitment to fund raising
 —Resource allocation
 —Acceptance of need for fund raising
 —Institutional niche and image defined and communicated
 —Institutional fund-raising priorities and policies

FUND-RAISING PROGRAM CHARACTERISTICS

Chief development officer's leadership
Organization of fund-raising function
Fund-raising history
Entrepreneurial fund raising
Volunteers' roles in fund raising
Emphasis on management of fund-raising function
 —Information and communication systems
 —Planning, goal-setting, and evaluation
 —Staff development, training, and evaluation
Staff commitment to institution
Emphasis on constituent relations

phasis on constituent relations, and staff commitment to institution.

Some results were surprising, such as finding that trustees' participation and volunteers' roles were relatively unimportant overall. Overall, results confirm some aspects of the conventional wisdom about fund-raising effectiveness, but they also suggest that the factors underlying fund-raising success are more complex and vary more in individual institutions than the conventional wisdom indicates.

One of the few general rules to be gleaned from this research is that successful fund-raising efforts capitalize on strengths and untapped potential of institutions in direct response to institutional needs and capabilities. The most important factor in making decisions about fund-raising programs may be insight into one's own institution. Furthermore, our qualitative studies illustrate that fund-raising success is, in the end, the result of deliberate, sustained efforts to raise money. Although many of these institutions enjoyed fortuitous circumstances or benefited from fortunate events at some time or another, each institution's general fund-raising success came from sustained and active efforts. None of these institutions was fortunate enough to be able to raise significant amounts of private support simply by being virtuous or worthy.

We do not mean to oversimplify fund-raising success, but it seems apparent that leadership, sustained effort, and a genuine institutional commitment—all of which are anything but simple—are the basics upon which successful fund-raising programs are built.

CONCLUSION

The results of the research to date indicate strongly that institutions with successful fund-raising programs do not necessarily have all the qualities typically associated with fund-raising success. While conventional wisdom gains some support from the research results, those beliefs seem mostly to reflect the circumstances at certain types of institutions, especially private research universities and private four-year colleges. Since these types of institutions have typically been highly successful in fund raising, they have been cited as examples for all institutions. It is certainly clear, however, that these types of institutions cannot serve as models for other, dissimilar institutions.

The results indicate that successful fund-raising programs are those that fully use and build on current institutional strengths. Any institution can improve its fund-raising performance, provided that it spends human, financial, and material resources wisely. If there are not actual prerequisites for fund-raising success, some factors—notably leadership in fund raising at all institutional levels and significant institutional commitment to fund raising—can make a difference, apparently without regard to the institution's wealth and prestige. Factors in success seem to depend more on the nature of the institution rather than on a concrete formula for fund-raising success. For example, strong volunteer or trustee support might not be necessary for some institutions and yet be essential for others.

Overall, the research has provided neither recipe-type instructions nor distinctive, clearly defined models for fund-raising success. The research does indicate that individual institutions vary tremendously in their potential for fund-raising success and that unique individual institutional strengths can be used to good advantage in fund raising. Because of this variation among institutions, we recommend more in-depth multiple case studies of individual institutions. Such studies are needed to provide a more precise understanding of the relationships between institutional characteristics and fund-raising success than we have been able to achieve to date.

NOTES

1. *Voluntary Support of Education 1983-84* (New York: Council for Financial Aid to Education, 1985) and subsequent annual editions.

2. John W. Leslie, *Focus on Understanding and Support: A Study in College Management* (Washington, D.C.: American College Public Relations Association, 1969).

3. William L. Pickett, "An Assessment of the Effectiveness of Fund-raising Policies on Private Undergraduate Colleges" (Ph.D. diss., University of Denver, 1977).

4. These studies include Joseph Oral Dean, Jr. "Educational Fund Raising in Church-affiliated Colleges: A Predictive and Prescriptive Model" (Ph.D. diss., University of Alabama, 1985); Mary Glennon, "Fund Raising in Small Colleges: Strategies for Success," *Planning for Higher Education* 14 (1986):16-29; Bruce A. Mack, "Foundation Fund Raising by Private Liberal Arts Colleges"

(Ph.D. diss., University of Michigan, 1983); Charles H. Webb, "A Policy-relevant Study of Development Programs at Representative Institutions within the State University of New York" (Ph.D. diss., Michigan State University, 1982); and Wesley K. Willmer, *The Small College Advancement Program: Managing for Results* (Washington, D.C.: Council for Advancement and Support of Education, 1981).

5. Larry L. Leslie and Garey Ramey, "Donor Behavior and Voluntary Support for Higher Education Institutions," *Journal of Higher Education* 59 (March/April 1988), 115-132.

6. For a highly readable and insightful review of research on institutional effectiveness and fund raising, see Barbara E. Brittingham and Thomas R. Pezzullo, *The Campus Green: Fund Raising in Higher Education*, ASHE-ERIC Higher Education Report no. 1 (Washington, D.C.: George Washington University, 1990), especially pp. 19-25. The publication of this monograph in the ASHE-ERIC series indicates not only the growth of research in fund raising but also the growth of interest in research results.

7. Constance Healy Torregrosa, ed. *The HEP Higher Education Directory* (Falls Church, Virginia: Higher Education Publications, 1990).

8. Margaret A. Duronio and Bruce A. Loessin, "Fund-raising Outcomes and Institutional Characteristics in Ten Types of Higher Education Institutions," *The Review of Higher Education* 13 (1990):547-551.

9. Ibid., 551-553.

10. For a full discussion of this research, see Margaret A. Duronio and Bruce A. Loessin, *Effective Fund Raising in Higher Education: Ten Success Stories* (San Francisco: Jossey-Bass, 1991) and Loessin and Duronio, "The Role of Planning in Successful Fund Raising in Ten Higher Education Institutions," *Planning for Higher Education* 18 (1989–1990): 45–46.

11. See J. Wade Gilley, Kenneth A. Fulmer, and Sally J. Reithlingshoefer, *Searching for Academic Excellence: Twenty Colleges and Universities on the Move and Their Leaders* (New York: Macmillan, 1986); Glennon, "Fund Raising in Small Colleges"; Philip Kotler and Karen A. Fox, *Strategic Marketing for Educational Institutions* (Englewood Cliffs, New Jersey: Prentice-Hall, 1975); Leslie, *Focus on Understanding and Support;* Pickett, "Assessment of the Effectiveness"; and Willmer, *The Small College Advancement Program.*

Chapter 6

The Roles of Key Individuals

Sara L. Patton

For an institution to realize its fund-raising potential, the key institutional players—the board of trustees, the president, and the chief development officer—must clearly understand and effectively interpret their roles. While some areas of responsibility are and should remain the exclusive domain of the president, the board, or the development staff, many more call for understanding, cooperation, and teamwork among these parties.

William A. Kinnison and Michael J. Ferin make this point in their discussion of the "three-party relationship," in which they discuss how "partnership roles" support and sustain the mission and priorities of the institution. According to Kinnison and Ferin, an institution can effectively set and achieve development goals only if its staff and volunteers know they must act together.[1]

THE ROLE OF TRUSTEES

The environment in which schools, colleges, and universities seek to attract students, faculty members, and financial support has become increasingly competitive. The most successful institutions are those with trustees who involve themselves fully in the planning, execution, and evaluation of development efforts and who can interpret the institution's goals with conviction and understanding within their individual spheres of influence.

One feature unique to the governing board is that its members are responsible for every aspect of the enterprise. As J.W. Pocock states, "The board is the ultimate seat of power and responsibility in the institution." Board members are policy makers, long-term planners, and asset managers; they "hold the assets of the institution in trust for the benefit of the institution, its supporters, and society."[2]

Board members set the standard of volunteer leadership and commitment. At the very top of the hierarchy of volunteers, they are expected to hold a broad view of the institution, to be able to consider it in the context of the larger society, and to be advocates for the particular mission and values of the institutions they serve.

The board also is responsible for maintaining the creative energies and balance of the institution's leadership over time. Trustees should take an active role in identifying, cultivating, and recruiting new trustees, just as they help select and evaluate the institution's president.

Finally, the board bears ultimate responsibility for ensuring the institution's financial strength and vitality.[3] That means giving not only their time, but their resources, in generous measure. Their broad perspective and personal involvement can make them the most effective fund raisers—especially when they themselves are major donors. As Pocock says, "Fund raising is the one major activity in which trustees step beyond their policy and oversight roles and become active players."[4]

This is not to say that every single member of an effective board must be an active solicitor or make one-on-one presentations to major donors. Some trustees, even some who give generously themselves, simply may not be comfortable in this role. They may participate in other ways—perhaps by hosting an off-campus event for alumni and friends or by accompanying the president or development officer on a solicitation visit to a key corporation where the trustee is well known and respected. More important than actually "making the ask" is a trustee's ability to internalize the goals of the institution so that he or she perceives development activity—in a variety of forms—as a necessary and important component of the trustee's service. This perception is especially important when an institution is in a capital campaign; then, trustee involvement becomes not only desirable, but absolutely essential.[5]

Other trustees will relish the opportunity to seek support for a cause in which they are investing time and money themselves. Most boards have a "development committee" whose members are expected to promote development objectives, not only to the institution's various external constituencies, but also to other members of the board. In this sense, the board's development committee serves as a kind of in-house public relations agency for the advancement effort. Individuals with drive, enthusiasm, and the ability to relate to others with empathy—while practicing friendly persuasion—are well suited to this role.

The chair of the development committee at Texas Christian University summed it up this way: "The real responsibility rests with the trustees. We need to give staff the support and resources to do their job. To make the most of what we've got, I ask the (board) chair and the chancellor to appoint to the development committee those with the knowledge and the drive to go out and do the work."[6]

THE ROLE OF THE PRESIDENT

Whole books have been written about the college or university president's role in fund raising.[7] Within the three-way leadership partnership, the president's role is the most complex. The president must be at once the interpreter of the educational environment in general and the standard bearer for his or her institution's unique mission within that environment. The president must take the lead in "defining and articulating the [institution's] mission and priorities."[8] In a capital campaign, these skills help make presidential leadership vital. In the words of Edward Foote, president of the University of Miami, "The campaign is the translation of a vision to the most demanding reality of all, money."[9]

The president must personify the institution's successes and aspirations while balancing various competing needs and special interests. He or she must be both an idealistic visionary and a steely-eyed realist—sometimes in the same half-hour. Since presidents are people, too, they will find some roles fit more naturally than others. As Madeleine Green points out, there is no set formula for successful presidential leadership. "The real issue is . . . a personally authentic approach . . . with a consistent philosophy and value system underpinning it all."[10] This "authenticity" is crucial in fund raising, where the president forges the vital link between trustees and professional development staff.

At most colleges and universities, the president is a member of the board of trustees. The president's involvement in fund raising sets the example for other trustees. If that involvement is positive, enthusiastic, and firmly tied to institutional priorities, trustees are likely to follow suit. If the president is indifferent to development concerns or distant from fund-raising activities, board members are likely to place a lower value on their own participation.

Similarly, the president's relationship with professional development staff, and particularly with the chief development officer, is pivotal. The president sets objectives, monitors the development staff's work, and evaluates the results.[11] The best development work is never an end in itself, but has at its heart the academic mission of the institution. In this regard, the president must be a decisive leader who motivates and educates while giving fund raisers the support they need to attract resources to meet the real needs of the institution.

This support includes such elements as staff, budget, and access to the institution's decision-making structures. The president should also help create opportunities for development professionals to interact with trustees and other key volunteers.[12] Most important of all is the president's systematic dedication of time to assist both trustees and staff in cultivating and soliciting major donors.

THE ROLE OF THE CHIEF DEVELOPMENT OFFICER

The chief development officer (CDO), with other members of the professional development staff, must create specific strategies and action plans to meet fund-raising objectives. He or she must also create a climate of confidence in the staff's integrity and performance by making sure that all players understand and share the institution's short- and long-range goals. An effective development office works as a team to address the many practical tasks that must be undertaken to achieve these goals. J.W. Pocock, then chair of the board of The College of Wooster, explained, "The operational and creative core of the development program is the professional staff, [who] must articulate the program in detail and plan and conduct the overall operation."[13]

A university president observed:

> The senior development officer's post is particularly tough in that it often has more responsibility than it has power and authority. Case, leadership, and constituency are largely the products of actions taken by trustees, president, and faculty, and yet they set the other limits of fundraising's reach. Where the development officer can have maximum impact are the areas of strategy and organization.[14]

The CDO must manage two complementary functions of development activity: creating materials and cultivating donors. The first is mainly internal, and involves producing research, proposals, publications, case statements, operating plans, and the like. The second is an external function that requires the development team's being regularly involved outside the institution in identifying, screening, and cultivating prospective donors and volunteers. Like the trustees and the president, professional staff members must also be persuasive advocates who are able to make the institution's case compelling to diverse audiences.

Above all, it is the CDO's responsibility to facilitate the trustees' and the president's participation in the fund-raising process. Because neither the trustees nor the president can devote full time to development, the time they do give must be used to its fullest advantage. When a capital campaign is in progress, the CDO must also provide effective training for volunteers at every level, including trustees.[15]

And, whether or not in a campaign, the professional staff should give top-level volunteers the best preparation possible for solicitations. That means giving them thorough briefings about a prospective donor's relationship to the institution as well as any written materials or illustrations that would strengthen the presentation. The volunteer who is successful is likely to welcome future assignments; it is in the CDO's best interest to lay the groundwork for continuing volunteer involvement.

CONCLUSION

Board members, with their broad perspectives and high levels of achievement in their fields, can attract strong support for the institutions they serve. As advocates who volunteer their time and interest and resources, they are perhaps the best "authenticators" of an institution's claim of significance in the world beyond academia.

The president must lead the way in defining the institution's mission, making it comprehensible to a diverse constituency. He or she must also demonstrate by personal example, to both trustees and staff, the interactive nature of the fund-raising partnership.

Professional development staff use their practical skills and experience to support and enhance the fund-raising activity of trustees and the president in order to achieve institutional goals and meet educational needs.

The responsibility for an institution's fund-raising efforts is shared among these participants in this "three-party relationship." To be effective, the trustees, the president, and the chief development officer must all support one another's efforts, communicate within their roles, and involve themselves personally in the fund-raising process.[16]

NOTES

1. William A. Kinnison and Michael J. Ferin, "The Three-Party Relationship," in *Fund-raising Leadership: A Guide for College and University Boards,* ed. J.W. Pocock (Washington, D.C.: Association of Governing Boards of Universities and Colleges, 1989), 57-61.

2. Pocock, *Fund-raising Leadership,* 3.

3. At public institutions, fund raising may be the job of institutionally related foundations—private organizations with their own directors or trustees. The members of the university's own governing board may be appointed without regard to their fund-raising abilities or inclinations. In this situation, the interaction between the university regents and foundation trustees is crucial to fund raising. Readers interested in the issue of private foundations and public universities may refer to Chapter 29 of this book, as well as to Michael J. Worth's chapter on "The Institutionally Related Foundation in Public Colleges and Universities" in *Fund-raising Leadership,* ed. Pocock, 63-74.

4. Pocock, *Fund-raising Leadership,* 23.

5. Henry D. Sharpe, Jr., "The Role of the Board of Trustees," in *The Successful Capital Campaign: From Planning to Victory Celebration,* ed. H. Gerald Quigg (Washington, D.C.: Council for Advancement and Support of Education, 1986), 63-72.

6. Malcolm Louden, "Why I Do What I Do," *CASE Currents,* November/December 1989, 24.

7. One such source is *The President and Fund Raising* by James L. Fisher and Gary H. Quehl (New York: American Council on Education/Macmillan, 1989).

8. Kinnison and Ferin, "The Three-Party Relationship," 58.

9. Edward T. Foote II, "The President's Role in a Capital Campaign," in *The Successful Capital Campaign,* ed. Quigg, 73.

10. Madeleine F. Green, "Presidential Leadership: Changes in Style,"*AGB Reports,* January/February 1986, 20.

11. Ivan E. Frick, quoted in "Partners in Development," *Bulletin on Public Relations and Development for Colleges and Universities* (newsletter of Gonser Gerber Tinker Stuhr, Chicago), May 1987, 2.

12. Francis C. Pray, ed., *Handbook for Educational Fund Raising* (San Francisco: Jossey-Bass, 1981), 358.

13. Pocock, *Fund-raising Leadership,* 21.

14. Richard D. Cheshire, quoted in Pray, *Handbook for Educational Fund Raising,* 358.

15. Sara L. Patton, "Solicitation Methods and Training," in *The Successful Capital Campaign,* ed. Quigg, 159–166.

16. Kinnison and Ferin, "The Three-Party Relationship," 58.

Chapter 7

The Role of Institutional Planning in Fund Raising

Rick Nahm and Robert M. Zemsky

Two disturbing maxims are currently making the rounds in higher education development offices. The first holds that "Try as one will, fund raising ends up donor-driven rather than need-driven." In other words, the money that *is* raised is the money that *can be* raised, because alumni, friends, corporations, and foundations are most prepared to support their own priorities. Put simply, when you go hunting where the ducks are, you tend to get the ducks that are available, no matter how odd they might be. The more successful the fund-raising effort—particularly in terms of leadership gifts—the more likely that donor interest, rather than academic need, will determine the future shape of the institution.

The second maxim is no less troubling: "Successful fund-raising programs cost more money than they raise because major donors expect more from the institution." This idea maintains that to please today's donors, fund raising has moved toward "add-ons" and "new ventures." The donor wants to leave his or her mark on the institution, and to that end, is prepared to supply a lead gift: the first dollar, but not the middle or the last. In return, the institution builds buildings and names them for donors who provide less than half of the construction funds and none of the operating funds. It establishes and fills endowed chairs, though the income from the donor's gift may supply less than half of the cost of maintaining a faculty member and none of the "extras" associated with a chair. Some institutions even "discount" chairs: they allow donors to put a down payment on the chair with a promise to pay later, or to finance the gift through devices such as insurance policies and zero-coupon bonds. Payment schedules can stretch over years, even though the chair is filled and costing the institution real money. Any good budget officer will say, "The problem is that you have to pay for fund raising twice: first through the development budget, and second through paying for projects the gifts start but do not finish."

The reality that haunts those most responsible for fund raising—presidents, chief development officers, and board chairs—is that they can't win for losing. They cannot use a focused fund-raising effort either to shift or sharpen institutional priorities. Instead, such an effort is likely to leave the institution with its mission more blurred, more a sum of separate parts, simply because accommodating faculty and student needs with donor interests usually means giving in to all and hoping that enough money will turn up to pay for the promises.

For much the same reason, fund raising cannot become a means of securing the institution's financial future. Fund raising adds commitments, often multiplying the cost of doing business. The escalation of expectations on the part of the entire institution, particularly those areas without ready access to donors, puts added pressure on the budget. The need to keep everyone happy acts as a flywheel, accelerating expenditures throughout the institution.

Institutional leaders are also learning to their dismay that fund raising can raise questions about the institution's management by inadvertently highlighting internal divisions. When separate departments independently market their own programs to the same limited pool of major donors, including the same corporations and foundations, donors cannot help but wonder whether anyone is in charge and whether the institution, as a whole, really knows where it is going. Unseemly disputes over priorities between departments or between faculty and administration only add to the sense of drift. This explains why development officers always advise that faculty be brought into the effort, whatever the cost, as a crucial early step in fund-raising planning. The harshest criticism, however, is reserved for those institutions that announce the successful completion of a campaign on Monday and a major budget crisis on Tuesday. Both the donor and campus communities feel betrayed and are quick to place blame on an administration that clearly did not know what it was doing.

In this climate, most institutional leaders settle for fund-raising programs that avoid major mistakes. When they reach their announced goal, there is little of the euphoria with which they began their campaigns. Glad their ordeal is over, these leaders publicly welcome the chance to spend more time on campus, while privately wondering if this may be the moment to bring their administrations to a successful close.

ALTERNATIVE MODELS

Fund raising in higher education *is* at a crossroads. At stake is not only the character and purpose of fund raising but also the institutional role of development professionals.

One possible response would be to separate fund raising, its purposes as well as its organization, from the general operation of the institution. Under this scenario, the development operation would be like a quasi-independent foundation, serving those parts of the institution that have access to well-defined donor communities and the ability to bear the full cost of intensive fund raising.

The political and financial independence of such a fund-raising foundation would require that supported projects be fully funded, but it would also mean that the objects of this fund raising would be largely independent of institutionally defined goals and priorities. While new buildings would not be started until gift income matched planned construction and projected operating costs, the choice of which buildings to construct would increasingly be that of the foundation and its donor constituency rather than of the institution. Similarly, programs supported through new endowment would be budgeted and planned separately. Under this model, the cost of the fund raising itself would be the responsibility of the client program, department, or school. In this way, fund raising would become "financially responsible," but at the cost of surrendering any claim that the institution as a whole would benefit from the gifts. (Many public universities do conduct their fund raising through separate foundations, and some of these problems have in fact surfaced.)

The preferred, though more difficult, alternative is to solve the institutional problems previously described. To do that, fund raising must be:

• need-driven rather than donor-driven,
• capable of providing relief to the operating budget, and
• designed to integrate the institution's vision.

The challenge is how best to overcome the unrealistic expectations that fund raising unleashes across institutions and how best to control the trends toward add-ons and new programs rather than to funds that support an institution's mission and programs.

Our solution derives largely from our experience in planning and executing a major fund-raising effort for the University of Pennsylvania. We do not suggest that the problems Penn faced are necessarily the same as those of other institutions of different scale and mission. Nor can we say that Penn solved all its problems. We do believe, however, that the basic strategy we put in place has wide applicability for every institution planning a new fund-raising program.

At the core of Penn's strategy was a decision to use the University's academic plan, "Choosing Penn's Future," to structure a major campaign and subsequent fund raising. Every aspect of the campaign, from its concept and organization to its language and symbols, had its roots in this planning process. Penn's academic priorities for the 1990s and beyond became campaign priorities; the cost of funding the plan, the campaign goal. The campaign steering committee did not ask individual schools and programs to submit needs- or wish-lists. Instead they looked to the plan itself to determine the specific objectives of the campaign.

From the outset, organization of the fund-raising effort was a joint effort of the development and planning staffs. As the Vice President for Development and University Relations and the Chief Planning Officer, we served as co-chairs of the operations committee that oversaw campaign planning.

What we learned was that a merger of planning and fund-raising perspectives could result in a major campaign that is need-driven, offers genuine budget relief, and provides a common vision that unites the separate parts of the institution. In the following sections, we present a framework for the effective linking of academic planning and fund raising, based on our experiences in the Campaign for Penn.

THE INSTITUTIONAL PLAN

Academic planning is no longer in vogue—and that's a blessing. It has taken more than a decade, but higher education has at last understood that planning is a craft with neither established theory nor tested methodology. Indeed, the most successful planning is that which is the most simple and straightforward, combining common sense and academic tradition to define institutional priorities.

Good planning involves three elements:

First, a good plan articulates a *vision* of the institution, supplying language and symbols by which an institution collectively comes to understand what it wants to be. Such visions are necessarily more poetic than descriptive, more evocative of aspirations than particulars. Visions are statements of purpose that relate both to current context and long-term expectations. The process of developing such a statement of vision, if successful, helps to draw together the institution in common search of unifying themes.

Second, a good plan is an *agenda;* it answers the question "What do you want to accomplish over the next five years?" In this guise, a good plan is basically a list of proposed actions consistent with the vision on which the plan depends. The items on the agenda should be more about building and establishing educational programs than about administrative or fiscal reform, though the latter are often important preconditions. Each item needs to be cast to allow, after five years, for an unambiguous accounting that plainly notes which of the proposed actions have been accomplished and which have had to be postponed or abandoned.

Third, good plans convey a sense of *scale* and *priority,* in that they propose actions that individually are within the grasp of the institution and that collectively will stretch but not exceed the institution's capacity for change. Hence the proposed agenda cannot be all things to all constituencies. It cannot be a laundry list of every pet project of every member of the community. A plan is about choices, about focused investments in a relatively limited number of ventures that best suit the institution's collective sense of its own future.

The sum of the choices presented in the plan must appear reasonable to both those within and without the institution, particularly when measured against the institution's financial capacity. An academic plan, however, is not the place to describe programs to be closed or services to be eliminated or large-scale reorganizations to limit the autonomy of established entities. Those actions, when necessary, do need to be consistent with the plan. For example, no one wants to propose a new degree program for a department about to be closed or put into administrative receivership. But the rationale and process of such cuts ought to be presented elsewhere, in a manner more supportive of those whose ambitions are being thwarted.

Plans that have these three elements—vision, agenda, and scale—need not be elaborate documents. Indeed, the shorter the better, perhaps with a maximum of 30 double-spaced typed pages. More important than either length or attention to detail is the process by which the plan is developed, vetted, and finally owned by the institution's constituencies: students, staff, faculty, trustees, the relevant state agencies (for public institutions), alumni, and friends. Here two lessons are paramount.

To begin with, the institution's leadership is primarily responsible for drafting the plan. The leaders must cull ideas and proposals from a broad base, and in that sense, a good planning process is "bottom up." Both the vision the plan articulates and the specific agenda it proposes must come from the community. Neither, however, are likely to be the work of a committee. The administration in general, and the president in particular, must first listen carefully to what that community, in its various voices, proposes and then artfully meld those ideas and initiatives into a coherent statement of vision and agenda. Once drafted, that statement must be discussed, amended, and revised, with the administration and president always bearing first responsibility for the new draft.

The resulting academic plan provides the primary text for all institutional discussions. It takes substantial energy on the part of an administration to draft a plan that the entire institution comes to accept as its own. That energy is only possible if the planning discussion itself is at the center of the administration's agenda. The test is simply stated: "If it's worth talking about, it's worth including in the plan." In this sense, the planning process becomes the arbiter of what is and is not important. Over time, the discipline imposed by the injunction to begin and end most institutional discussions by referring to the plan ensures that each constituency sees itself as belonging to the larger whole enunciated by the plan.

The result is an academic plan and planning process that knits together an institution. A successful plan gives substance to a common vision by defining symbols as well as actions that collectively promise to make the institution greater than the simple sum of its parts.

BUILDING FUND RAISING ON THE ACADEMIC PLAN

The promise to make the institution greater than the sum of its parts makes possible an integrated fund-raising effort. Even the most practical items necessary for a smoothly functioning fund-raising program can be derived from a well-formed academic plan shaped by an inclusive planning process. In broad sketch, those "practical items" fall into four specific categories:

1. Developing the message.
2. Setting priorities, including specific gift opportunities.
3. Building the prospect pool, including the cultivation and management of major-gift prospects.
4. Organizing the program, including setting timetables and goals, designating leadership and coordinating groups, and phasing in new projects to be supported by fund raising.

These tasks, when overlaid with and integrated into institutional planning, become keys to success in academic fund raising.

Simply stated, institutional planning examines an institution's mission within the external environment, defines the institution's current position, develops a set of goals and objectives that constitute the institution's new level of ambition, and presents a strategy (including costs) for achieving the goals and objectives. This planning effort then becomes the road map for developing an effective fund-raising program for the institution.

DEVELOPING THE MESSAGE

The crucial first step in implementing a focused fund-raising effort is the development of the case, or rationale for support. This can be as basic as a theme for an annual giving drive or as complex as a case statement for a major campaign. If the fund-raising message derives from the academic plan, it will give potential donors a clear, consistent, well-developed presentation of the institution's priorities. It will not only answer the question, "why us," but also "why now" and "what for." And it will become an educational tool both inside and outside the institution: one that helps move donors toward needs and serves as a scorecard to judge the success of the fund-raising effort.

SETTING PRIORITIES

Like the fund-raising message, the list of priority needs should be compelling, direct, and short—not an endless list of everything anyone within the institution has ever wanted and more. For donors, a long list of apparently unconnected needs becomes a disincentive to giving, fueling a perception that the institution functions as a "black hole," continually swallowing money. It is extremely important to develop priority needs into a concise list of gift opportunities which, when funded, will clearly advance the institutional plan. When fund-raising objectives are presented in this context, needs become opportunities and gifts become investments.

MANAGING PROSPECTS

An important aspect of a prospect management system is the extent to which it is need-driven versus donor-driven. This orientation affects the entire fund-raising program. If the institutional plan provides the guiding principle for prospect management, then it will affect every decision—whether the question involves a policy issue, such as the role of annual giving in a campaign, or a strategy for cultivation, solicitation, and stewardship for one prospective donor.

The charter of an effective system for prospect management contains many clauses. None is more important than the injunction to match identified and cultivated prospects to appropriate needs as defined by the institution's academic plan. Difficult as it is to maintain a need-driven prospect management program, it is impossible without the foundation of an academic plan that can tell donors simply and directly, "You are important to our institution because you understand our needs!" The donor's personal good fortune and success thus become the means through which to achieve well-defined institutional goals and priorities. First comes the donor's loyalty and interest; next comes the plan; and only then is the potential gift defined by placing it in the larger context of that plan.

Prospect management is thus, in essence, a matching process that helps limit both needless competition and mindless gifts. The test used to establish the match is the straightforward question: "Is this prospect best matched with this fund-raising objective or need?" Most issues can be similarly resolved by considering the match—donor to need, priority to vision.

ORGANIZING THE PROGRAM

If the message and priorities for fund raising and the development of prospect management are based on the institutional plan, then basically the overall fund-raising program should be organized in the same manner. Everything from budget and staffing levels to the fund-raising timetable should be guided by the plan's goals and objectives and its strategies for accomplishing them.

In general, the fund-raising plan should take on the same characteristics as the institutional plan. For example, if the institutional plan is entrepreneurial, dynamic, competitive, and marketing-oriented, then the fund-raising plan should have those same elements. The planning and organization of fund raising should be seen as a logical extension of the institution's overall planning and organization.

CARRYING OUT THE PLAN

The ultimate test for success in connecting institutional academic planning with the development of a fund-raising program is the extent to which an institution's governing board embraces the goals and objectives of the plan and actively engages in the fund-raising effort to support the plan. Need-driven investments in an institution, rather than donor-driven gifts, will become the rule only if board members become eager advocates for the processes of institutional planning and strategic fund raising.

Before the board can be expected to "buy in" to the process, an institution's internal constituents, from the faculty to the administration, must believe in the course that has been set and have confidence in the institution's ability to accomplish its stated goals and objectives.

When everything falls into place, the results can be extraordinary. Uniting an institution's vision with its fund-raising capacity to move the institution to new heights or in new directions is the most satisfying activity in institutional advancement. This characteristic is what separates the great programs from the very good ones.

Part Three
Annual Giving

As Chapter 2 points out, the annual giving program is the bedrock of the comprehensive development program. And, as the historical account of Chapter 3 notes, it is the oldest form of organized fund raising in American higher education.

From the perspective of college or university leaders, the annual giving program is sometimes overemphasized and at other times undervalued. Presidents, deans, and other institutional leaders may value the short-run benefits of annual gifts, which enable them to increase spending today, over major gifts to endowment that may take longer to obtain and have less immediate impact on the operating budget. They may argue that an additional $100,000 in annual gifts every year can make a big difference, while $100,000 in endowment produces only $5,000 or so in annual income, which is barely noticed.

Others, however, may see the annual fund as producing relatively little money in relation to the staff effort and resources required to raise it. These people may prefer that the institution concentrate exclusively on major gifts.

Both points of view are shortsighted and unrealistic. In addition to its immediate impact on the current budget, the annual fund is a principal means of involving new donors, identifying those who have a particular interest in the institution, and developing their habit of giving. Over time, the annual giving program can be the incubator for major donors, whose cumulative impact on the institution can be substantial. The annual fund and major gift programs are complementary and necessary components of an ongoing development operation.

In Chapter 8, Ann Gee Louden discusses how to plan, organize, and implement an annual giving program. Such efforts have come a long way from the casual and occasional letters that distinguished the alumni funds of earlier decades. Today's annual giving programs use sophisticated demographic analysis and communications techniques, making the annual fund one of the most "scientific" aspects of the development program.

Despite the introduction of sophisticated techniques, the growing prominence of telephone marketing, and the continuing importance of personal solicitation, the direct mail letter remains the backbone of many annual giving programs. In Chapter 9, communications expert Connie Clark discusses the art of developing effective direct mail appeals.

Chapter 8

The Annual Giving Program

Ann Gee Louden

A newly appointed academic dean asked the institution's director of development: "Why not do away with the annual fund—just ask a few major donors to give enough money to cover the costs, and be done with it? Think how much time your staff spends in planning all those events, cultivating so many small donors, and playing the numbers game to make the goal each year. Surely there's a better way!"

The dean's comment reflected his perception that staff expended too much energy on a program with small returns. His observation was at least half correct. The annual fund does require the energy of staff in the form of an organized campaign effort supported by an operating plan, a budget, and staff resources at each phase of the process. He was wrong on the second count, however. The annual fund produces results that are in no way insignificant.

That's what the development director told the dean. The annual fund, she explained, serves as the foundation for every other fund-raising program. It creates the framework around which capital, major, and planned gifts are raised. And the annual fund identifies an important base of donor and volunteer support.

Too often, those on the outside of the development program believe that only big dollars count. While it is true that almost 90 percent of the total dollars raised comes from 10 percent of the donors, it is also true that the many people involved in an annual fund account for the greatest number of gifts. Said another way, the patterns of giving to institutions of higher education represent a pyramid. At the base of that pyramid is the annual fund.

Without the annual fund, it would be difficult or impossible to:

- promote widespread interest in the institution,
- cultivate volunteer leadership to champion the cause,

- determine who the prospects are for special projects,
- present the case for the institution each and every year,
- measure how your publics feel about your institution,
- create a universal appeal and a sense of immediacy, and
- build an institutional image through solicitation efforts.

WHAT IS THE ANNUAL FUND?

In his oft-quoted reference, *Designs for Fund-raising*, Harold J. Seymour listed the elements an annual fund program must have. He cited the century-old Yale Alumni Fund as first identifying and applying these principles.

1. *Funds received must be directed to unrestricted causes.* The institution usually applies annual fund gifts to support overall operations. In that way, the annual fund becomes another source of yearly revenue for the college or university. Generally, institutions fund their yearly budget mostly through tuition and fees, endowment income, and—for state-supported institutions—tax appropriations. But private gifts make up the balance.
2. *The appeal should go to all constituencies.* By the very nature of an annual fund, everyone who can support the college or university is asked to do so. Obviously, some people are more likely to give than others, and program planning takes that essential point into consideration.
3. *Alumni can be counted upon to be the greatest source of support.* Annual support from alumni is a vote of confidence in their institution and reflects their wish that their alma mater progress. The institution's growth and success enhance the value of their own degrees.
4. *The appeal should be annual.* A yearly solicitation allows donors to develop the habit of giving. They come to expect the annual solicitation and to view giving as an obligation and a continuing responsibility.[1]

These concepts about the nature of the annual fund have not changed, although the techniques involved have become more sophisticated over time.

FINDING PROSPECTS

Because the idea of the annual fund is well established, the chief challenge for development staff today is to identify and solicit prospective donors in the most effective and efficient way. The first step is to identify those from whom you plan to seek funds.

In the early 1970s, the late William E. Sheppard, a founder of the Fund-raising Institute in Ambler, Pennsylvania, developed a system for classifying annual fund support. The "Sheppard Master Plan" divided annual gifts into three groups: (1) support from first-time givers; (2) gifts from those who had previously given; and (3) increased gifts from regular givers. Each of these elements requires a different set of strategies for success. New or young annual giving programs obviously must focus on the first element. Programs with a history of gift support would naturally emphasize the second and third aspects.[2]

You can assume that annual fund donors will be found in seven groups:

- Members of the governing board
- Alumni
- Current and past parents
- Corporations
- Foundations
- Friends
- Church constituency (for church-related institutions)

Without a doubt, the prospects who are hardest to identify and target are those clustered under the amorphous heading of "friend." That group could include individuals who have relatives associated with the institution, those who live near campus, those who may have a nostalgic interest because of particular programs (for instance, a community theater, continuing education seminars, or an athletic team), or simply those who harbor good feelings for your institution.

Identifying corporate or foundation support presents a similar challenge. While you may receive individual gifts from alumni who own small companies or who head family foundations, securing large annual fund gifts from these sources is harder. Obtaining annual fund support from corporations and foundations located outside the college community is also a tough assignment. Given the restrictive gift guidelines of both corporations and foundations, it is simply not realistic to target a major part of your annual fund-raising program toward these groups.

Rather, your best efforts should be directed to the groups with whom you are likely to have the greatest success. For most institutions, that translates into concentrating on trustees, alumni, and parents. These groups have a vested interest in your institution and thus offer the greatest potential as sources of new donors.

SETTING THE DOLLAR GOAL

In *Designs for Fund-raising,* Seymour warns that one of the deadliest games that inexperienced fund raisers play is manipulation of the multiplication tables. For example, for a goal of $1 million, a standard formula recommends asking 10,000 people to give $100 each or 1,000 people to give $1,000 each.

Such schemes invite disaster because they don't recognize that donors are not created equal. Some will be able to give more than others. Seymour's maxim stresses "thoughtful, proportionate giving" based on the varying ability of the givers to give.[3] This principle applies to both annual giving and capital campaigns.

Knowing that each donor is able to give a different amount helps you determine both where to focus your efforts and how much gift income you can reasonably hope to raise. Seymour estimates that among current donors (that is, those who gave last year), 50 percent will give the same amount again; 25 percent will give more; 15 percent will give less; and 10 percent will lapse.[4] You may not be able to determine which individuals will fall into each category, but analyzing gift histories for current donors will give clues and help you prepare strategies. Even before that, however, you can use your annual fund's history to help establish a realistic annual fund goal.

The process of setting a dollar goal begins with a meeting of the key administrators: the chief financial officer, the budget director, the chief development officer, and the director of annual giving. In the most enlightened of settings, the goal is not handed down, but rather negotiated, taking into account the stated need and the possibility of success in raising it. These goal-setting conversations should coincide with the institution's budgeting process. After all, it is typically the projected shortfall in the budget that drives the need for current operating support from the annual fund.

Careful preparation before the meeting—including advance research on national giving trends, comparisons with peer institutions, and your institution's own fund-raising history—will help protect you against the likelihood of being handed an unrealistically high goal. It will also provide better ammunition for staff in the event such a lofty goal must be accepted and attempted.[5]

After the total annual fund goal is identified, it should be approved by the governing board and communicated to the staff. Once the goal is known (preferably six months before the fiscal year commences), staff can get down to the business of constructing a plan.[6]

Sub-goals should be established for every constituency. Prevailing wisdom recommends that the total of these constituency goals should *exceed* the stated overall goal. The reason is obvious: No matter how carefully you draw the plan for each prospect group, there is a good chance that you might not succeed with all of them. Overshooting the goal by sub-groups provides a necessary cushion for the entire effort.

CREATING THE PLAN

J. Richard Wilson, former president of the National Society of Fund Raising Executives, underscored the importance of planning:

> Devote a great deal of time and patience to the planning process. If you are not satisfied with your plan, then you should delay the start of the fund-raising effort. A good plan is essential to fund-raising success. If you don't know where you are going, then you are never going to get there.[7]

The annual fund plan must include four components: (1) the dollars to be raised; (2) the overall objectives of the program; (3) the strategy for soliciting each source group; and (4) the timetable for each solicitation. Based on the dollar goal already identified, you will determine specific objectives, or benchmarks for improving the program. These, in turn, will guide your strategies. For example, if an objective is to improve the support of alumni giving by 10 percent for the coming fiscal year, you must design a strategy that will capture such an increase. This might include creating a challenge gift, developing a class reunion giving program, or doubling the number of class agents.

In turn, you must determine the time you will need for each of these strategies. Activities centered around the best prospects should happen first on the schedule. Tom Broce, consultant and professional fund raiser, noted that "too many annual campaigns . . . reverse the effective order of solicitation. Make sure that your best prospects get the best solicitation."[8] Start with your leadership prospects and work your way from the best to the least likely to give. Thus, if you intend to officially kick off the campaign in September, you should expect to solicit leadership prospects, and secure commitments, before then. Having the top donors' gifts in hand allows you to proceed to secure the many smaller gifts.

During the planning process, you will generate such material as the case for support, assignments for volunteers, a schedule noting when to begin individual tasks, a strategy for soliciting each distinct prospect source, and a method for evaluating success. For example, a plan that focused exclusively on alumni and parent prospects would include the following details:

- The case for the overall annual fund goal
- Dollar goals for each constituency
- An outline of the campaign's volunteer structure
- Job descriptions for each volunteer
- A strategy for personal solicitation for alumni
- A strategy for personal solicitation for parents
- The plan to contact alumni by phone
- The plan to contact parents by phone
- A calendar for alumni mailings
- A calendar for parent mailings
- The schedule for all associated events
- Staff assignments
- The budget
- A list of anticipated support materials
- Questions to answer at the end of the campaign: How did this year compare with last? How many new donors were there? How many increased gifts were received? How effective was the volunteer leadership?

Your task, however, is not just to devise a plan for the year. You must also breathe life into it. The intangible quality of "campaign mentality" makes the difference between simply scheduling a series of events and creating momentum that leads to the final victory. In the vernacular of advertising professionals, the next step is to "market the cause."

MAKING THE CASE

Fund-raising consultant Howard M. Schwartz wrote more than a decade ago:

> I am constantly amazed at the number of significant institutions and organizations that plan and implement fund-raising programs without consideration for, or even understanding of, what I consider to be the essence of the profession—marketing! Fund raising is but the nonprofit world's equivalent of selling, except instead of a physical product to be offered in the marketplace, the offering is of an idea or concept.

Schwartz suggested that most nonprofits make the mistake of assuming that because they are worthy organizations, people will automatically flock to support them. Nothing could be further from the truth. Even educational institutions, which have the luxury of a built-in constituency of alumni, are not exempt from presenting the reasons why they believe donors should give.

Schwartz also proposed that nonprofits could take lessons from business and industry, which long ago learned to appeal to the interests of the consumer. In the nonprofit world, the rules are no different: "Successful programs must be built on a solid base of understanding the prospect (research), developing the right cultivation process (advertising) and effectively evoking support (sales)."[9]

It is wrong to believe that marketing only means pushing the idea of fund raising. For example, the case is *not* made by describing the terms of a challenge gift and asking the donor to give to help meet the challenge. That approach will leave all but the most loyal donors cold. Rather, the case is made by describing what the donor's gift will do to help the institution. Describe the programs, not the dollars that fund the programs. Making the case for annual giving can be especially difficult because the annual fund underwrites hidden needs. Whether you are writing a case statement, visiting a donor, or training your phonathon staff, you must emphasize the impact your institution has on the lives of your donors—and the importance of maintaining that accomplishment.

The development of the case for each segment of the donor base is best done in writing. And you should ask for feedback from members of the groups to whom it will be sent.

The case statement should include these five elements:

- A description of the institution's need for the gift. First-time donors, in particular, may not realize there is a real need for their money.
- A certification of the strength of the institution and the program. Donors want to support a great program, not one that is floundering.
- The plans for the use of the gift. People want to know what their money will buy.
- A reference to progress in the future. Even though the gift may be only for relieving this year's budget, donors want to know they won't regret this year's investment next year.
- The benefits to them for giving. Donors, however altruistic, want to know how the gift helps *them*. The benefit to a donor may be as subtle as a sense of feeling needed or of repaying a debt, but it must be acknowledged. It is not enough to ask people to help; they must be told why it is worth their time and money.[10]

THE USE OF VOLUNTEERS

Inherent in every annual fund program is the dependence upon volunteers. The more volunteers participating in the program, the greater its chances for success.

Volunteers should be recruited for their ability to perform specific assignments. For example, if you need someone to send a solicitation letter to a class, find the person who is best known to that class. If the task calls for soliciting members of the corporate community, recruit a key business executive.

As part of each volunteer's orientation, staff should present and discuss a written job description that spells out the title and duration of the assignment, training required, general and specific duties (including deadlines), staff and other volunteer contacts, and benefits to the volunteer and the institution. As noted in an article on volunteer fund raisers, "Satisfaction comes when volunteer fund raisers feel good about themselves. To feel good, they must do a job well, and that requires thorough training and reinforcement. . . . It's safe to say that there is a direct relationship between the time and money invested in preparing and managing volunteers and the amount of money your program will raise."[11]

Using volunteers has another advantage. The institution knows their level of commitment early. Before the volunteer makes a call, writes a letter, or sets an appointment for a visit, he or she should be asked to make—and should make—a personal gift. This crucial step guarantees that the institution's emissaries have already been sold on the program.

TECHNIQUES

Volunteers typically assist with three types of activities: direct mail campaigns, phonathon programs, and personal solicitation. Each of these techniques serves a different purpose and encompasses a wide range of applications.

Face-to-face contact is always the most effective way to solicit a gift. The telephone is second in effectiveness, and the third and least desirable channel is the mail. Because staff can't possibly handle all the visits or phone calls, it follows that programs with a strong concentration on personal solicitation and phoning also make the greatest commitment to volunteers.

Although personal solicitation and phoning programs take the most time to orchestrate, given the heavy use of volunteers and the associated staff time, they produce more gifts. A fund-raising maxim—which appears to work in practice—holds that in a personal call, the prospect is likely to give at least 50 percent of what was asked 75 percent of the time. In the case of a phone request, the prospective donor will give at least 25 percent of the amount solicited 50 percent of the time. Direct mail results are typically far lower; a good response means 2 to 10 percent of those asked make small gifts.

Remembering the rule that solicitation should begin with the prospects closest to the institution, you must determine which of these strategies to use with your various constituencies. A simple example—which does not consider class reunion gift promotions, challenge gifts, or other special strategies—might be to plan on face-to-face solicitation for trustees, the top 10 percent of alumni and parent donors, top local corporations, foundations that have given before, and friends who have given significantly. Direct mail in conjunction with phone calls might be used for the next tier of prospects—say, other current donors and lapsed donors. Repeated nondonors might receive only mail.

For institutions that can afford to use a combination of phone and mail, the results will probably justify the costs. However, some institutions will choose to employ a direct mail campaign without coordinated phone calls. Either can work. However, it is *never* appropriate for the entire donor pool to receive only mail. At the minimum, the top groups should be treated as personally as possible.

Although most annual fund programs use a combination of personal solicitation, phoning, and direct mail efforts, there remains great latitude in the way individual programs are organized. Your decisions should take into account each technique's advantages, disadvantages, and possible applications.

Direct Mail

We all discover appeals for various causes in our mail boxes each day. Solicitations from institutions in which the individual may be genuinely interested can easily get lost amid the eleven million pounds of advertising mail that goes to U.S. homes daily. The challenge is guaranteeing that your institution's letter will be opened.

In spite of these hurdles, however, direct mail programs will be an important fund-raising technique in annual fund programs for the foreseeable future. One compelling reason is that people judge the credibility of any cause on the fact that printed materials exist to make the case.

The advantages of direct mail include:

* relatively low cost per piece:
* coverage of a wide audience;
* permanence, because the message can be read and re-read;
* minimal requirements on staff and volunteer time;
* the opportunity to enhance institutional image; and
* the chance to showcase names of key participants (through signatures, names on the letterhead, etc.).

Disadvantages include:

* a relatively impersonal approach, even if the letter is personalized;
* no opportunity for immediate feedback;
* difficulty in creating a sense of urgency and excitement;
* the chance it won't be read;

- low rate of return; and
- difficulty in getting an increased gift.

The best direct mail programs use class agents. Long a mainstay of programs at Ivy League institutions, this approach involves identifying a key individual or individuals from each class. Obviously, this will work only if your alumni identify with the class in which they graduated.

The class agent is often chosen by class election in the senior year. Even better, the senior giving chair may become the class agent. Because that person has already directed an organized fund-raising campaign among graduating seniors, he or she is familiar with and appreciative of the annual fund, and class members will identify that name with the cause. If you select class agents yourself, be sure to identify class members who were well liked and respected. Because these people will solicit others, make sure they have the willingness and potential to give themselves. And choose people who live reasonably near campus to make training and supervision easier.[12]

Class agents' duties typically include signing solicitation letters to class members and serving as the titular head of the class in its dealings with the institution. Class agents often also make good chairs for reunion giving programs. Some institutions ask class agents to draft their own letters to their classmates. Most professionals, however, prefer to provide drafts for the agents to edit. This is faster and allows more flexibility and control for the staff managing the program.

Phoning Programs

Although phone solicitation has become somewhat tainted by the abuses of commercial telemarketers, telephone campaigns still reap bountiful results for their institutions. Programs may be conducted by volunteers or paid callers, with phoning sites either on campus or in the offices of alumni located in other regions. Some colleges and universities retain commercial firms, which employ professionals year-round to make the calls from their own centers.

Phoning offers these advantages:

- personal approach;
- instantaneous feedback;
- the chance to push for an increased gift;

- the opportunity to include ancillary announcements (say, to remind alumni about homecoming); and
- coverage of a wide audience.

Disadvantages include:

- relatively high cost, depending on who is called and from what site;
- difficulty reaching donors with answering machines;
- predisposition of some donors to dislike telephone solicitations;
- difficulty in negotiating large gifts; and
- the need to rely on volunteers, who may be imprecise or inarticulate.

For years, fund raisers argued about whether to pay phonathon callers. Today, paid callers are commonplace, and the debate has shifted to whether institutions should hire outside firms to do their calling for them. A sophisticated telemarketing firm can indeed produce results. However, turning your program over to outsiders can create problems of quality control and may sacrifice the spontaneity associated with student callers. Many annual fund directors advocate a mixture of paid and volunteer programs, giving the best prospects to volunteers while sending their toughest names to a telemarketing firm.

You should construct your program to make the most of the cost and time involved. If yours is a one-person office, it may be most efficient to contract your business outside. On the other hand, if your alumni prospect pool is manageable, a group of paid students could handle the program on campus over the course of several weeks.

However you design your phone program, adhering to the following rules will help improve your results:

- Devote the money and time needed to secure all available phone numbers;
- Train callers thoroughly, whether they are paid or volunteer;
- Except in the case of hired telemarketing firms, make sure a staff member is present to act as cheerleader and problem solver;
- Provide as much information as possible to the caller about the prospect, including full name (and maiden name), class

year(s), type of degree(s), student affiliations, names of children who are current students, and giving history;
- Instruct callers to ask for a specific dollar amount;
- Give callers the opportunity to call both donors and nondonors;
- Create an atmosphere conducive to excitement and motivation; and
- Follow up immediately with donors and those who are considering giving.[13]

Personal Solicitation

Given time and an unlimited supply of credible volunteers, personal contact would be the surest solicitation method to employ with every prospective donor. Without question, sitting across from the prospect and making the request personally is most likely to produce a thoughtful response.

Personal solicitation offers the following significant advantages:

- It produces the best results;
- It requires a significant level of involvement on the part of the volunteers, which enhances their own commitment to the cause;
- It is personal;
- It provides for immediate feedback;
- It provides the opportunity to ask for the greatest gift and to make the best case for support; and
- It speaks volumes about the value the institution places on the need for annual fund support.

The disadvantages likewise are easy to identify:

- It requires time-consuming training and preparation for staff and volunteers;
- It is more intimidating to volunteers because of the possibility of being told "no" in person;
- It is more costly than mail or phone programs, which cover more ground in less time; and
- It requires time and energy that few volunteers are willing to spend.

Few institutions can afford to make personal solicitations for gifts under $500. Personal calls are best reserved for the top prospects. However, those who have lapsed in their giving may well deserve more personal attention.

Annual giving professionals use the term LYBUNT to describe a donor who gave "Last Year But Unfortunately Not This" and SYBUNT for one who gives "Some Years But Unfortunately Not This." Sherwood C. Haskins, Jr., the associate director of development at Phillips Exeter Academy, maintains that "saving LYBUNTS for the final stages of the campaign can be risky," adding that once LYBUNTS become SYBUNTS, they tend to be ignored. The desire to bring these donors—particularly those who once made leadership gifts—back into the fold may justify the use of personal solicitation.[14]

SPECIAL PROGRAMS

Whether your program emphasizes personal contacts, direct mail, or phoning, several special tactics can enhance results. Among the most popular are gift clubs and challenge gifts.

Gift clubs offer a means to recognize donors who have achieved certain levels of giving. Donors who increase their gifts become eligible for progressively higher-level clubs. Some clubs offer benefits that range from mention on an "honor roll" to dinners, souvenirs, or special access to campus events.[15]

A club system provides incentive for donors to jump from one gift level to the next, as well as visibility for those who increase their gifts. It also offers a way to incorporate important institutional names into the annual fund tradition, as with the Sorin Society at Notre Dame University. In addition, gift clubs are excellent umbrella organizations through which to sponsor events and communicate with donors.

Challenge gifts are gifts made conditionally, requiring that gifts from other sources be solicited as a match. The purpose of challenge funds is to develop leverage with other donors and motivate them to increase their gifts.

The key to a successful challenge is marketing it appealingly. Donors must be moved by the opportunity not only to make a gift but also to see the challenge give their gifts more impact. For example, if a challenge donor agrees to match any gift increase two to one, a $100 donor who raised his or her gift to $500 would see the institution receive $1,300.

CONCLUSION

Tom Broce described the importance of the annual fund's place in the total development program:

> Annual fund-raising programs are the bread-and-butter programs. . . . They should be consistent in quality and reflect the dynamics and strengths of the institution. Annual campaigns should be continued—and even accelerated—during capital campaigns. Once established, they should never be suspended or postponed. . . . The fund raiser must be aware that in an upward-moving society, the donors' sights are constantly rising, and they expect no less in quality annual giving programs.[16]

Each year's program begins with an assessment of the results of the previous annual fund campaign. After the campaign is concluded, take the time to determine results, not just in terms of total dollars raised, but also on the basis of each component part of the plan. The efforts you expend this year will reap rich dividends for next year's campaign and the ones that follow.

NOTES

1. Harold J. Seymour, *Designs for Fund-raising,* 2nd ed. (Rockville, Maryland: Fund-raising Institute, 1988), 145-146.

2. M. Jane Williams, *The FRI Annual Giving Book* (Ambler, Pennsylvania: Fund-raising Institute, 1981), 87-88.

3. Seymour, *Designs for Fund-raising*, 30-31.

4. Ibid., 54.

5. Scott G. Nichols, "Annual Giving Programs: Responding to New Trends and Realities," in *Handbook of Institutional Advancement*, 2nd ed., ed. A. Westley Rowland (San Francisco: Jossey-Bass, 1986), 255-257.

6. Mitchell L. Moore, "Goals and Strategies," in *Annual Giving Strategies: A Comprehensive Guide to Better Results*, ed. Ann D. Gee (Washington, D.C.: Council for Advancement and Support of Education, 1990), 16-17.

7. Paul H. Schneiter, *The Art of Asking: How to Solicit Philanthropic Gifts*, 2nd ed. (Ambler, Pennsylvania: Fund-raising Institute, 1978), 156.

8. Thomas E. Broce, *Fund Raising: The Guide to Raising Money From Private Sources* (Norman, Oklahoma: University of Oklahoma Press, 1979), 82.

9. Schneiter, *The Art of Asking*, 158.

10. Williams, *FRI Annual Giving Book*, 88-94.

11. Melissa R. Drake and Ray Willemain, "Going First Class: How to Get Alumni to *Like* Fund Raising," *CASE Currents*, November/December 1982, 41.

12. C. Jeffery Wahlstrom, "Small Miracles: Increasing Annual Fund Participation in the Small Shop," *CASE Currents*, April 1989, 34-5.

13. Stanley R. McAnally, "Annual Giving," in *Handbook of Institutional Advancement*, 1st ed., ed. A. Westley Rowland (San Francisco: Jossey-Bass, 1977), 192-193.

14. Sherwood C. Haskins, Jr., "By Hook or By Crook: Recapturing LYBUNTs, SYBUNTs, and never-givers," *CASE Currents*, April 1989, 31.

15. The Internal Revenue Service has questioned the deductibility of charitable gifts for which the donor receives a substantial benefit in exchange. The agency's standards change annually, so development officers should consult their institutions' tax advisers for current rules. For more information, see Mike McNamee, "The Problem with Premiums: How the IRS Views Your Thank-yous to Donors," *CASE Currents*, April 1990, 13-16.

16. Thomas E. Broce, *Fund Raising*, 101-102.

Chapter 9

How to Prepare a Direct Mail Solicitation

Connie Clark

Development professionals faced with preparing a direct mail fund-raising letter can safely assume at least one thing: Even the most welcome fund-raising letter will compete in the recipient's mailbox with other, probably more urgent or more interesting missives. Worse, many who receive it will not welcome it, because it asks them to do something few of us do easily: part with hard-earned money out of the sheer goodness of our hearts.

When we add to these discouraging factors a rise in skepticism among donors, brought on by scandals in the direct mail fund-raising community, it is clear that the direct mail package must overcome intimidating obstacles.

This chapter will explore ways to write effective direct mail fund-raising copy, starting with basic guidelines developed by professionals in direct marketing and direct mail. From these rules, we will move on to learning how to confront the donor's apathy and objections by getting attention, overcoming resistance, and building credibility.

GENERAL GUIDELINES

While direct mail copywriting shares many features of excellent writing in other genres, it has its own particular rules as well. But unlike other forms of writing, direct mail copy is constantly tested; results are concrete and specific, generally measured by the number of replies and the average size of purchase or gift. The writer of a direct mail fund-raising letter would do well to begin with the copywriting guidelines drawn from decades of quantifiable results.

Copy Length

Successful direct mail letters are generally long. Many professional writers object to long letters, saying that no one will bother to read more than a single standard-size page. However, head-to-head testing of short letters versus long letters almost always proves that long letters perform better. Direct marketing experts speculate that, since 95 percent or more of those receiving the package throw it away unopened, the few who *do* open it are in fact highly interested in its contents and thus do not object to reading more than a few paragraphs. Others believe that even interested readers simply glance at the opening, the closing, the P.S., and perhaps a few sentences here and there, and that the rest of the copy is important only in that its very length lends credence to the importance of the message.

Typical lengths for direct mail fund-raising letters fall into the following ranges. "Pages" here refers to standard business size or the slightly smaller monarch size; one page equals one *printed* side of one sheet, so that four-page letter equals two sheets of paper printed on both sides.

- *Prospect mailings* (for those who have not given recently or at all): Four pages and occasionally longer.
- *Donor mailings* (for active givers who are at least somewhat familiar with the institution's mission): Two to four pages.
- *Upgrade mailings* (asking current donors to make a larger gift than before): Two or more pages. Seasoned direct mail fund raisers advise that copy length should increase proportionally with the size of the gift being requested.

While the value of longer copy has been proven in test after test, one caveat must be remembered: Even one paragraph of unimaginative, poorly written copy is too much!

Copy Readability

No matter how educated the audience for a direct mail letter, it is vital to keep the language simple. Avoid jargon and bureaucratic language. Remember that the recipient will be looking for any opportunity to put the letter aside or in the trash. For this reason, the copy should never be a challenge to read; its style should be simple and unintimidating.

It is also important to make the letter nonthreatening visually. Scanning the page, the reader may perceive lengthy, unbroken blocks of copy as "too much work." People overcome this resistance when they must, but direct mail letters are not required reading. Large blocks of dense copy invite the reader to put the letter aside. To avoid this reaction, indent paragraphs and keep them short, preferably five lines long at most. Vary the length of paragraphs. Make sure the letter has adequate margins and that the type is clear and readable.

So, while direct mail authorities advocate sending *long* direct mail letters, they also insist on the efficacy of *short* words, sentences, and paragraphs.

Copy Voice

A letter—even one that is mass-produced in large numbers— is a personal communication. The more a direct mail letter resembles a real personal letter, the more effective it will be. Therefore, the voice, or tone, of the copy should always reflect an "I-you" relationship between writer and reader. When such a relationship does not already exist (as with prospect letters), it should be assumed.

In educational institutions, letter signers are frequently deans or other leaders in the academic community. A common thought is that such individuals should not write a fund-raising letter in a warm, personal style, but this assumption leads to depressed results. Even the most scholarly people can comfortably address their peers in a cordial tone while maintaining their dignity. Certainly prospective donors can be seen as peers to whom a friendly approach is justified!

The letter writer can achieve the right degree of informality, warmth, and emotion by envisioning a typical recipient of the letter to be written: How old is he? How does he speak to his friends? What are her interests? What would a personal letter from her look and sound like? These clues are often within the development officer's easy reach.

A knowledge of how the prospect behaves is very helpful. However, it is also wise not to give much credence to what prospects *say* about direct mail, as this often does not reflect how they behave! For example, most people will say they do not read long direct mail letters; however, as stated above, head-to-head tests almost always prove the long letter more effective.

Package Elements

A typical direct mail fund-raising package for an educational institution includes the following components:

- an outer, or carrier, envelope, often but not always bearing copy (known as "teaser" copy) to entice the recipient to open it;
- a letter;
- a brochure;
- a reply card or form; and
- a reply envelope (sometimes carrying the reply form on the envelope flap).

Of all these elements, the carrier envelope and the letter are by far the most important—the envelope because it must convince the recipient to open the envelope, and the letter because it bears the fund-raising proposition. A frequent mistake is to lavish attention on the brochure; it should be noted that in many direct mail fund-raising packages, removing the brochure entirely will not adversely affect the results. In fact, the decision to save money by skipping the brochure can make the difference between an unprofitable package and a profitable one.

To avoid the brochure-centered approach, consider these guidelines:

- *Lavish attention on the letter.* Include in it any points you would normally put in a brochure.
- *Labor over the teaser copy.* If you choose to use teaser copy, it should be irresistible.
- *Next, focus on the reply device.* This often-neglected piece should briefly recap the fund-raising proposition and provide an easy-to-use return vehicle for the donor's gift.
- *Consider including other elements.* The list of possibilities for package enclosures goes far beyond the standard brochure. Examples are a "lift" letter (an additional, shorter letter from someone other than the main letter signer); a photograph with writing on the back; a certificate of appreciation to loyal donors; or architect's plans for your new building.

Keeping these stylistic guidelines in mind, we now move on to consider how to get the recipient's attention, involve him or her emotionally, and prove an institution's credibility—all essential steps in procuring a gift.

GETTING THE DONOR'S ATTENTION

The single most important factor in getting a direct mail package opened is the appearance of the carrier envelope. The copywriter must carefully consider how to make the envelope look different, fascinating, promising—somehow irresistible. Fundraising expert Jerry Huntsinger, among others, claims the best envelope option is a hand-typed, closed-face (as opposed to window) envelope with a commemorative stamp and no teaser copy, because it most closely resembles a personal letter. While such a carrier often justifies the higher cost involved in producing it, it is not usually profitable for mailings to new prospects or to low-dollar or inactive donors.

Copywriters often must work within the constraints of a window envelope, which is obviously not a personal communication and thus by its very nature is at a disadvantage in the mailbox. You can overcome this disadvantage in several ways:

- *Design.* A striking, unusual, even offbeat design, if not too expensive, can catch the recipient's eye. However, it is important that the envelope still resemble a bona fide communication from one person to another and not take on the look of a postcard or brochure.
- *Copy that mystifies.* Teaser copy can draw the reader into the envelope with a statement that seems strange, shocking, or fascinating. The reader opens the envelope to find out more.
- *Copy that promises.* If the direct mail letter offers a gift, special news, or an invitation of some kind, mention this offer on the envelope to imply that it might be foolhardy to throw the letter away. Also in this category is the use of a famous letter-signer's name on the return address. For years, Planned Parenthood had great success using Katharine Hepburn's name in this way.
- *Copy that demands attention.* If your institution is facing a true emergency, call attention to this crisis on the carrier envelope. (This technique has been overused, often with emergencies that appear less than truly urgent; take care in presenting the emergency so that it is easily believable.)

Once you have created acceptable teaser copy, you must be sure that two parts of the letter grab the reader's attention just as effectively as the outer envelope. These are the letter's opening and its close.

Studies have shown that most people receiving a direct mail letter scan the salutation and first line or so, then skip to the end of the letter. The *lead*—consisting of the salutation and the opening paragraph, and sometimes a "Johnson box" (a few lines of copy, perhaps framed in a box, above the salutation) —should elaborate on the theme of the outer envelope copy, if any. It should also keep up the tension, mystery, or drama created by the envelope teaser or appearance. The *close*— consisting of the last paragraph, signature block, and P.S.—should recapitulate the theme of the teaser copy and the lead, while also urging the reader, in the boldest possible terms, to act now. The P.S. is an essential component of a good direct mail letter because many people read it first, or second, after opening the envelope.

You can also pique the reader's interest by adding a *premium* to the package. Typical direct mail premiums include name-and-address labels, decals, bookmarks, calendars, and booklets, to name just a few. Premiums are expensive, but often their use boosts response enough to justify the added cost. Fund raisers should select premiums somehow related to their cause. For educational institutions, items bearing the college or university logo are ideal. Premiums seem to work for two reasons: First, they make the carrier envelope stand out in the mailbox and seem enticing, especially if the teaser copy calls attention to something free within. Second, they make the donor feel obligated to send a gift in return.

Premiums can be "front-end" (sent before a gift is made) or "back-end" (sent later to fulfill a promise made in the direct mail letter). Experience suggests that front-end premiums have the strongest response-boosting power. Back-end premiums some-times work well as inducements to current donors to upgrade their level of giving.

Overcoming Resistance

Why do people give money? While that question has no definitive answer, two major factors are evident: A desire to help other people, and a desire to gain a sense of belonging, prestige, or identity.

The Importance of Emotion

"People only give to people," says development expert and Funding Center founder Barry J. Nickelsberg. By this he means that they do not give to a nonprofit organization to advance an abstract cause or to build a building for its own sake. Rather, people are motivated to give in order to help other individuals with whom they empathize. The direct mail letter must translate a mission statement into human terms so that the donor can relate emotionally to the people who are served by the organization.

To give an example, a college might send an annual fund letter that lists the institution's recent accomplishments and major plans for the near future. This is a good idea, but *how* it is done is crucial. You should show how the recent accomplishments have benefited students, preferably by telling about specific people. The importance of the plans to individual students will make the ideas come alive. Of course, if you can show that the college's accomplishments and plans will have an impact on the *donor's* life, too, all the better. This could be done by exciting the donor's desire to keep the college's reputation at its current excellent level.

Many successful fund-raising letters stress what will happen to one individual—or several or many—if sufficient money is not raised. This excellent technique forces the donor to think about possible negative consequences for specific individuals. It is much harder to say "no" to a brilliant young student who desperately needs scholarship assistance than it is to say "no" to an unknown dean who asks for help in meeting general operating expenses. The more clearly the writer can draw the individuals to be helped, the more effective the letter will be. The personalities and situations of these people should leap off the page.

One important point about general operating support: You can ask for funds for specific needs (scholarships, for example) and still use the funds raised to cover general expenses. The letter must include copy to that effect: for example, "Your support of Oakwood College's Annual Fund helps cover our operating expenses and enables us to give scholarships to worthy students like Sarah, Bill, and Jenny."

Once you have motivated the donor by describing the need in human terms, you must "close the sale." There should be absolutely no ambiguity or confusion about what the writer wants the donor's response to be.

Three steps will help move the donor to the point of actually writing the check:

First, ask specifically for the gift, preferably for the exact amount you hope to get (with a suitable range of options, such as $100, $150, or perhaps as much as $200).

Second, give the donor a deadline by which his or her reply is needed—the more believable, the better. Ideally, a deadline should be four to six weeks from the date a letter is mailed.

Third, tell the donor to use the enclosed reply card or contribution form, and the enclosed reply envelope, to return his or her gift. If the gift can be made by phone with a credit card, explain how.

An Opportunity to Belong

Richard P. Trenbeth, fund-raising consultant and author of *The Membership Mystique,* believes many people are hungry for a feeling of belonging and a sense of meaning. He cites these hungers as major forces behind the phenomenal growth of membership organizations in recent years.

When it comes to fulfilling this longing, educational institutions have a built-in advantage: Many among their natural constituency, alumni, already feel a strong loyalty to their alma mater. Copywriters can make the most of this advantage by using certain techniques that capitalize on this sense of belonging.

- *Thank the active donor.* Many nonprofit organizations fail to thank their donors adequately. In direct mail, frequent thanks are vital. Every solicitation letter to an active donor should include references to what has been accomplished thanks to the donor's help and personal expressions of gratitude from the suitably important letter signer. This helps create a warm, personal tone in the copy and demonstrates that the donor's actions have definite, positive consequences that are actively recognized.
- *Praise the prospective donor.* For prospects, or inactive donors, you can kindle a sense of loyalty and belonging by praising the prospect simply for being affiliated with the institution. For example, "As an alumnus of Oakwood College, you have a different perspective on life. The fine liberal arts education you enjoyed here gives you a unique vantage point on today's problems—and on the challenges facing our college."

- *Appeal to memory.* Use the institution's unique ability to invoke memories. Help the donor recall his or her time on campus. Referring to campus landmarks, traditional events, or well-known symbols reminds the donor of a shared history. Few techniques are more effective in building a sense of belonging.
- *Appeal to a sense of prestige.* Every institution has its well-known accomplishments and its good reputation for one or several things. These should be rallying points in direct mail copy. Chances are good that alumni take pride in being affiliated with the institution because of these positive factors. Make a practice of referring to at least one point of pride in each letter.
- *Point out that the donor belongs to a special club.* By virtue of having attended the institution, the donor is already part of the family. This may seem too obvious to state, but most successful membership acquisition and appeal letters state it very obviously indeed.

In addition, applying the basic rules of copywriting outlined earlier in this chapter will make your copy warm and personal, implying a sense of belonging by its very tone.

BUILDING CREDIBILITY

You now have the donor's attention. You have made a strong, specific, emotionally appealing case for the gift. Throughout the letter, you have made references to the donor's special place in the institutional family. You have explained specifically how and when to make the gift. Only one possible roadblock remains. The donor may wonder, "Will my money *really* be used wisely and well?"

Generally, an alumnus will not scrutinize the balance sheets or call the Better Business Bureau to verify that the institution's business practices are sound. However, in a day where fraud and abuse of donors' dollars have been sadly common, we cannot overlook the need to establish an institution's credibility. The direct mail copywriter can use these methods to enhance credibility and to build a strong sense of trust in the donor:

- *Explain how past contributions have been spent.* Naturally, this cannot be done in detail. However, it is possible to outline recent major accomplishments and to stress the link between donor support and the achievement of goals.

- *Establish the solidity of the institution's reputation.* Mention major accomplishments and recognitions (for example, a faculty member winning a Nobel Prize). Include quotes by prominent speakers or writers about the institution, if available.

- *Explain, in as much detail as possible, how the donor's contribution will be used.* When asking for general operating support, list a number of high-priority goals. When asking for support for a special project, give a budget breakdown. Including dollars *and* cents in cost estimates is by no means too detailed: Such specifics dramatically increase the credibility of the funding request.

- *Use well-known alumni or university leaders as letter signers.* The value of the celebrity signer is mentioned above. The success of a fund-raising letter is rarely dependent solely on the strength of the signer's reputation. However, this can give a tremendous boost not only in getting attention but also in building credibility.

Effective direct mail fund-raising copy may seem overly emotional, lengthy, and even pushy. But it should be remembered that good direct mail copy seeks to incite action. As such, it must be powerfully persuasive, more like a sermon or political speech than a policy statement or article. With good direct mail copy, today's fund raisers can overcome increasing challenges, including spiraling postal rates and production costs as well as overcrowded mailboxes. When copy is clear, simple, warm, and personal, when it calls the donor's emotions into play, and when it demonstrates the trustworthiness of the organization, the educational fund raiser can realistically expect excellent results from direct mail.

Part Four
Major Gifts

Among the most tried and true of fund-raising axioms is the rule that 80 percent of the dollars will come from 20 percent of the donors. This axiom has been revised in recent years to say that 90 percent of the dollars come from 10 percent of the donors. And some suggest that a further revision—to 95 percent and 5 percent—would better reflect today's reality.

Whatever the exact percentages, there is no question that the successful development programs are those that focus on major gifts and that such gifts have a significant, lasting impact on the institution.

In Chapter 10, David Dunlop provides a thoughtful overview of principles and practice in the major gifts field. As Dunlop emphasizes, the essence of successful major gift fund raising is the nurturing of relationships between donors and institutions. While the techniques for doing this have become quite sophisticated, it is essential to avoid even the perception that the process is manipulative. Such a perception is both inappropriate and likely to be offensive to major donor prospects. We must remember that a major gift represents the donor's heartfelt expression of commitment to an educational purpose and not a response to fund-raising techniques. As Si Seymour reminds us, "Nobody ever buys a Buick just because General Motors needs the money."

At the same time, major gifts are simply too vital to the futures of our institutions to be sought in a casual or random manner. Our responsibilities to our institutions require that we manage our major gift programs in a professional, systematic manner in order to maximize the support we get from our constituencies.

Planned giving offers a tool box of financial instruments for major giving. Ron Sapp provides an overview of these methods in Chapter 11, but the subject is a complex one; anyone wishing to specialize in planned giving surely will need to go far beyond this introductory discussion. Readers also should be aware that tax laws do change, and some revisions in laws described in this chapter are in fact under discussion even as this book goes into publication.

As with the larger major gifts effort, it is important to keep planned giving in perspective. No donor makes a gift exclusively or even primarily for financial or tax reasons. Planned giving provides a way for the donor who already wishes to support the cause to do so in the most financially sound manner. Unfortunately, the literature of some institutions appears to emphasize the techniques of planned giving over the purposes and needs such gifts are intended to address. This is an approach unlikely to inspire serious donors. Nevertheless, in the proper context of a thoughtful major gifts programs, planned giving is an essential tool for every development officer in today's complex financial world.

Major gift fund raising eventually comes down to one individual looking another individual in the eye and asking for the gift. The face-to-face solicitation is the culmination of the development process and is the only effective method for obtaining a major gift. Surprisingly, it is an aspect of fund raising that is too often neglected in the professional literature. As Michael Adams notes in Chapter 12, the face-to-face solicitation can cause stuttering, stammering, and wincing, or it can be "invigorating." And, as Adams explains, the difference lies primarily in perspective and preparation.

Chapter 10

Major Gift Programs

David R. Dunlop

The largest gifts an institution hopes to receive require a special kind of fund raising and a development program specifically tailored to this effort. These programs are sometimes known as *leadership gift* programs, *principal gift* programs, or *special gift* programs, but most frequently they are called *major gift* programs. Most major gift programs are directed toward individual givers, although these individuals might choose to make their gifts from companies they own, from foundations they have established, or from their personal resources.

There is no precise dollar figure that defines a major gift; each institution must determine for itself the size of gift toward which it directs its top level of fund raising. The most sophisticated and successful major gift programs are concerned with several kinds of gifts. In turn, they often employ several different methods of fund raising to encourage them. To understand major gift fund raising, you must first understand the different kinds of gifts people give and the different methods used to encourage them.

KINDS OF GIFTS

Let us first consider the characteristics that distinguish the different kinds of gifts that people make. These characteristics reflect the perspective of the giver, rather than the perspective of the institution.

Regular Gifts

These are the gifts people make to their church every week, to their public television station every quarter, or to the United Way, Cancer Crusade, or their college every year. The timing of these gifts is dictated by the calendar. Although such gifts are often called "annual gifts," it seems more appropriate to call them regular gifts, because it is their *regularity,* not their interval, that has implications for both the giver and the solicitor.

For example, because the giver has been moved to make a similar gift to the same cause many times before, the solicitor does not have to ask for the gift in the same way he or she would ask for a first-time gift. Also, the amount of the gift reflects the fact that the giver anticipates making a similar gift to the same cause next week, next quarter, or next year. While regular gifts rarely fall into the category of "major gifts," they are of concern to the major gifts programs, as they help to build the habits of giving essential to developing the sense of commitment upon which major gifts are based.

Special Gifts

When an institution has a special need, it naturally turns for help to the friends who have supported it regularly. The resulting special gifts are often paid over several years. A giver's special gifts are often five to ten times larger than the same person's regular gifts to the same cause. Their timing reflects the needs of the institution.

It used to be said that people give annual gifts out of income, to support operations, and capital gifts out of accumulated capital, to support capital needs. That no longer appears to be true, if it ever was. Many people make gifts to capital purposes out of current income, and some may make annual gifts from capital. Many special gifts are large enough to be considered "major gifts."

Ultimate Gifts

Whether we call the first two kinds of gifts regular and special or annual and capital, we must also recognize a third kind of gift on the spectrum of giving. I call this the ultimate gift—not because it will be a person's last philanthropic act, but because it is the largest gift that the person is ultimately capable of giving. Ultimate gifts are often 1,000 to 10,000 times larger than the gifts the same person gives on a regular basis to the same institution. Ultimate gifts almost always assume "major" proportions.

Usually people decide to commit a significant portion of their wealth to a cause or causes only after they have a sense of the wealth they will ultimately have available. Ultimate gifts usually are made late in life; they often take the form of a trust or bequest.

You might ask if we are really talking about planned or deferred giving when we speak of ultimate gifts. Often we are. But the terms *planned gift* and *deferred gift* imply methods of giving. The significance of a person's ultimate gift lies not in the method used to implement it, but in its being an individual's greatest and most significant philanthropic expression.

And not all ultimate gifts are planned or deferred gifts; wealthy people can give a large share of their resources away during their lifetimes and continue to live comfortably while they witness the results of their giving.

METHODS OF FUND RAISING

Just as the gifts people make can be viewed in light of a spectrum of different kinds of gifts, so too can the various fund-raising methods used to encourage them. I find it helpful to divide the spectrum of fund-raising methods into three major areas: speculative fund raising, campaign/project fund raising, and nurturing fund raising. A comparison of these methods appears in table 1.

Speculative fund raising focuses on broad-based asking on the *speculation* that enough prospects will respond positively to make the whole effort worthwhile. In this kind of fund raising only a small portion of all the effort involved is invested in cultivating the individual prospects—that is, in preparing them to want to make a gift. Almost all the effort involves the processes of asking. Examples of speculative fund raising include direct mail appeals, phonathons, telethons, and those face-to-face solicitations in which the solicitor asks the prospects to give without knowing their readiness to do so.

Speculative fund raising is typically used for regular gifts, such as a college annual fund seeking unrestricted funds for current operations. Or it may be used for special gifts, such as funds for scholarships. Whatever the case, it is primarily project-oriented, not prospect-oriented. People doing this kind of fund raising are charged with raising funds for a specific objective, and they gauge their success by the total number and dollar amount of gifts the institution receives toward that objective over a regular interval, typically a year.

Although the word "speculative" can carry negative meanings, I do not use it pejoratively. Done well, speculative fund raising can help form the foundation upon which lifetime habits of giving are built. Rarely, however, is it used to solicit major gifts.

Campaign/project fund raising emphasizes both preparing the individual prospective giver and asking for the gift. In this kind of fund raising, as much as half the time and resources involved are invested in building the prospect's understanding of and commitment to the purpose for which the gift is sought.

For example, when a college seeks to raise funds to build a new wing on its library, it might invite carefully selected major gift prospects to campus to meet with librarians, faculty members, and members of the administration and to see first hand the conditions that prompt the plans for the new wing. While they may not be asked for their gift toward the new library until after they return home, the visit is still an important part of the fund-raising effort.

Campaign/project fund raising is mostly used as a way to encourage special gifts, either as part of a fund-raising campaign or as part of a sustained development effort. It also may be used to encourage regular gifts. Like speculative fund raising, campaign/project fund raising is primarily project-oriented, as fund raisers endeavor to find prospects who will support their project. Evaluation is tied to the period during which the campaign or project is conducted. At the end of that period the number and amount of gifts made will tell whether the effort has succeeded.

Nurturing fund raising is most often reserved for the individuals from whom an institution hopes to receive its largest

Table 1. Methods of Fund Raising

	SPECULATIVE	CAMPAIGN/PROJECT	NURTURING
Primary gift type and size	Regular $1X	Special 5X - 10X	Ultimate 1,000X - 10,000X
Emphasis	Focus on asking, little on preparing prospect	Half on preparing prospect, half on asking	Focus on preparing prospect, little on asking
Basis of timing	Calendar	Institution's needs	Prospect's life and circumstances
Period for bottom-line evaluation	Annual	Duration of campaign or project	Lifetime of prospect
Orientation	Project-oriented		Prospect-oriented
Programs typically involved	Annual fund, capital campaign, and special project programs		Major gift program

gifts. Almost all the time, talent, and other resources invested in this type of fund raising focus on nurturing the prospective givers' sense of commitment to the institution and to the purpose for which their gifts are sought. While nurturing fund raising is intended to yield very large special gifts or ultimate gifts, it will also yield a stream of regular gifts.

Only a small portion of the resources involved in nurturing fund raising are invested in the process of asking. This is because the timing of ultimate gifts is linked more to the life and circumstances of the givers than it is to institutional need. Given appropriate attention, the givers themselves will decide when they wish to give.

Nurturing fund raising is much more prospect-oriented than project-oriented. Those who do nurturing fund raising focus primarily on the prospects with whom they are concerned and, as a consequence of each prospect's interests, focus secondarily on projects and purposes for which the institution seeks gifts. Their success cannot be gauged at the end of a year or the end of a campaign, but only at the end of the life of the givers whose friendship they have nurtured. While nurturing fund raising is very costly in time and effort, the gifts it encourages usually cost far less per dollar raised than any other method of fund raising.

ORGANIZATION AND ORIENTATION

However an institution organizes its speculative, campaign/project, and nurturing fund raising, these efforts should be integrated, coordinated, and complementary. In deciding how to conduct our speculative fund raising for regular gifts, we must also consider how those decisions will affect the longer-term objectives of campaign fund raising and nurturing fund raising. When we recognize that an institution's interests in fund raising go beyond the processes of asking and include processes to develop a sense of commitment, the focus of our planning shifts from raising dollars and cents to building attitudes.

Too often, an institution's various fund-raising efforts are segmented, independent, and competitive. For example, an institution may find it easy or efficient to use its development staff to solicit gifts for a campaign or to pay students to make calls at a phonathon. But doing so means discarding priceless opportunities to involve regular and special gift prospects as fund-raising volunteers. Volunteer involvement is an ideal way to develop prospects' awareness, understanding, and sense of commitment—essential steps on the path to ultimate giving.

When people first encounter an institution, they view its people and projects in the third person, in terms of "they," "them," and "those." Before they can become prospects for significant giving, that perspective must change to the first person: They must speak, think, and feel in terms of "we," "us," and "our." Few experiences are as effective in fostering this shift in perspective and attitude as the task of asking another person to make a gift. At that moment, volunteer solicitors become the voice of the institution. They will have prepared themselves with the reasons such a gift is important and why it should be made now. They will have examined how their own values and beliefs align with the values and purposes for which the institution stands. The people they solicit will view them as representing the institution, reinforcing the volunteers' feeling that they are indeed part of it. They very likely will become friends with the staff and faculty of the institution in the process. Yet the opportunity to use volunteers to help solicit gifts is often discarded for the sake of efficiency.

A major gift program should be concerned with more than one kind of gift and more than one method of fund raising. Certainly it should be oriented toward nurturing fund raising for ultimate gifts. However, to be successful in raising ultimate gifts we must also encourage regular and special gifts through which the habits of giving to the institution are developed. Because separate fund-raising programs within the institution may be responsible for different kinds of gifts, it is essential that all these programs be integrated, coordinated, and complementary.

THE PROCESS THAT LEADS TO LARGE GIFTS

While each giver's experiences will be unique, the types of experiences that lead a person to make an ultimate gift follow a common path. All givers of ultimate gifts whom I have known had some experience that first developed their *awareness* of the institution and the purpose within the institution to which they later made their gift. Other experiences then developed their *understanding* of the institution and the purpose for which they gave their gift. Also necessary were experiences that developed a sense of *caring* and provided opportunities for *involvement*. In addition, people were offered a variety of opportunities to express the *commitment* they felt. These were not limited to financial expressions of commitment; prospects were allowed to express their personal, political, moral, and spiritual support of the institution as well.

One of our nation's greatest fund raisers, G.T. "Buck" Smith, sees the process of fund raising as a cycle illustrated in figure 1. Note that the figure is drawn in the form of a circle to suggest the repetitive character of the process. In theory, after each gift, the cycle repeats itself, leading to still another gift. In practice, the sequence of initiatives is not quite this predictable. Nevertheless, these diagrams provide a useful perspective from which to consider the type of initiative that would be most helpful with a prospect.

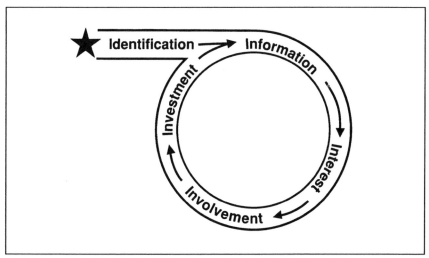

Figure 1. Smith's Fund-raising Cycle

As we focus more on nurturing relationships from which we hope will develop ultimate gifts, it may be helpful to refine Smith's concepts to look like the cycle illustrated in figure 2.

Let's look at the steps in this cycle in more detail.

Identifying Prospects

Three criteria should be used in selecting prospects for nurturing fund raising:

• financial capacity,
• interest or potential interest, and

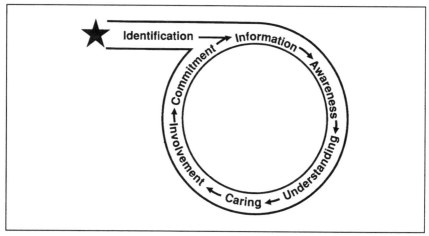

Figure 2. The Nurturing Fund-raising Cycle

• charitable nature.

Of these three, the signs of wealth and interest are easiest to discern. Yet much of your efficiency and effectiveness will depend on your ability to recognize those who have a charitable nature as well as capacity and interest. But take care: Prospects who lack a history of large gifts do not necessarily lack a charitable nature. Many generous people need their capital for as long as they remain in business and so postpone making major gifts until after they retire.

Getting Information

You can draw on three types of sources for the information you will need to use in nurturing fund raising:

• public sources,
• peers of the prospect, and
• the prospect.

Public sources of information are the sources on which development research traditionally relies. Chapter 23 of this book provides more information for drawing on these sources.

Information from a prospect's peers is often more reliable, helpful, and current than information from public sources. In seeking such information you may appear to be prying into private affairs. The type of information you seek and how you go about securing it can increase or decrease that risk. Asking about people because you want to welcome them into the life of your institution is entirely different from asking because you are just seeking a way to separate them from their money without regard for their own desires.

As you begin your work with the prospect, you will not need detailed information about that person's wealth. The information that will be most helpful is the common currency of any friendship. Look for shared values and shared interests that can provide the basis for involving the prospect in the life of the institution.

The information a prospect offers willingly is almost always the most helpful, reliable, and current. Regrettably, this third and best source of information is the source most often neglected. Some of the most valuable information will come only after the prospect trusts you completely. Recognize that a prospect may not share sensitive information unless there's a need for you to know it.

The habits of speculative fund raising often prompt solicitors to ask for gifts and even prepare elaborate proposals for major gifts based on assumptions and conjecture rather than on knowledge of the prospect's interests, capabilities, circumstances, and values. One of the distinguishing characteristics of nurturing fund raising is that it depends more on information from the prospects themselves than does either speculative or campaign/project fund raising.

When you pursue personal sources of information (either from peers or the prospect), keep in mind the following guidelines: (1) follow the Golden Rule and treat your subjects as you would want to be treated; (2) be open and honest about what you intend to do with the information you receive; and (3) make sure the information you seek is appropriate to your need to know at the time.

Building Awareness, Understanding, Caring, and Involvement

Initiatives to build awareness, understanding, caring, and involvement fall into two categories. The first includes initiatives that are conceived, planned, and executed with a specific prospect in mind. I call these *foreground initiatives.* Here are some examples of foreground initiatives taken to bring a prospect closer to a college:

- Setting up a meeting with the dean
- Reporting on the impact of a gift from the prospect

- Having a faculty member call to express thanks
- Asking a student scholarship recipient to write a thank-you letter
- Offering congratulations on a promotion or other personal event
- Requesting advice
- Arranging special seating at a college event
- Inviting the prospect to a private dinner with faculty
- Scheduling a visit from the president
- Using the prospect's home for a college reception
- Borrowing art from the prospect for a show on campus
- Borrowing the prospect's private plane to bring VIPs to campus
- Presenting a distinguished service award
- Holding a testimonial dinner in the prospect's honor
- Naming a campus garden after the prospect

The second type of initiatives are those that are conceived, planned, and executed not for an individual prospect, but for a group that includes one or more prospects. I call these *background initiatives*. Examples include:

- Alumni magazines
- Newsletters
- Annual reports
- Brochures
- Films and slide shows
- Alumni class activities
- Reunions
- Alumni club activities
- Visiting committees
- Advisory councils
- Campus tours
- Sports events
- Groundbreakings
- Dedications
- Commencement ceremonies
- Presidential inaugurations

Background initiatives are often developed by others at your institution for purposes unrelated, or barely related, to fund raising. It is up to you, the fund raiser, to use them wisely. Both foreground and background initiatives play important roles in nurturing the relationship with the friends whose sense of commitment you want to develop.

Expressions of Commitment

Earlier we noted that expressions of commitment are not limited to monetary gifts. We must provide opportunities for our friends to give their personal, moral, political, and spiritual support, along with their financial support. The chance to express feelings of caring plays an integral part in developing the sense of commitment so essential to giving very large gifts.

In the process of nurturing a person's sense of commitment, the moments of asking for regular or special gifts have a special place. These are the moments when you and your prospects discuss their beliefs, values, and giving capabilities. The information shared in these discussions can help you to select future initiatives to build the prospect's awareness, understanding, caring, and involvement.

In nurturing fund raising, written proposals should rarely be used to ask for a gift. The decision to give, the purposes for which a gift is to be given, the amount of the gift, the method(s) used to fund the gift, as well as how the gift will be recognized and administered are best developed in discussions with the giver. The written proposal, if used at all, is used to summarize and record an agreement.

You may, however, draft a letter of commitment for the convenience of the giver. In a way, such letters are used in place of the proposal to record the terms and purposes of the commitment. The giver can then send the letter to the institution's chief executive officer, who signs it in a space provided at the bottom to indicate the institution's acceptance of the terms. A copy is then returned to the giver.

PARTNERS IN THE PROCESS

To create experiences that build your prospects' awareness, understanding, caring, involvement, and commitment, you will need assistance. That means deciding who is in the best position to help you do this work. Years ago, Buck Smith, then vice president for development at the College of Wooster in Ohio, pointed out three roles to be played in this work. He called them the *prime,* the *secondaries,* and the *staff manager.*

While solicitors are enlisted or assigned, primes and secondaries are discovered. These are people who are naturally involved in a prospect's relationship with your institution. These may be faculty, trustees, students, neighbors, classmates, officers of your institution, staff—almost anyone who knows and cares about both the prospect and the institution. From among these natural partners, the one who is in the best position to help you nurture the relationship between your institution and the prospect is the prime. The other natural partners are secondaries.

I would suggest that you not use the terms prime and secondary with those who fill those roles. They will most likely think of themselves as simply helping you, their friend, and the institution.

Many institutions enlist volunteers who help with major gift fund raising to serve on a "major gifts committee." Valuable as these groups are, I advise you to proceed slowly in taking this step. Once formed, a major gifts committee will demand time and attention. Often the same benefits can be gained while operating informally without having to invest in organizing and staffing such a committee.

The primes and secondaries you enlist to help plan and carry out both foreground and background initiatives with your top prospects need a staff manager to support and assist them in their work. It will be the staff manager who brings discipline to the process and stimulates activity. Every few weeks—certainly no less than once a month—the staff manager should review the prospect's relationship with your institution. Working with the prime and secondaries, the staff manager should:

1. review what has transpired,
2. plan the next initiative(s),
3. coordinate with others involved,
4. implement the initiative(s),
5. evaluate the initiative(s), and
6. report and record the result(s).

ESSENTIALS FOR SUCCESS

You could invest a great deal of your own and your institution's resources to create a system of nurturing fund raising for large gifts and yet gain very little unless you give careful attention to three essentials for success. These are the *quality, frequency,* and *continuity* of the initiatives taken with each prospect.

The quality of the initiatives you take should be appropriate to the prospect's relationship with your institution. You don't want your efforts to seem like the birthday cards I receive from an insurance salesperson who wouldn't recognize me if he saw me on the street. Let your friendships grow naturally. Don't assume familiarity that is not based on the experience of your relationship with the prospect. The best way I have found to judge the appropriateness of initiatives is to apply the same standards you use in your personal friendships.

If your institution does not enter the life and consciousness of a major gift prospect every few weeks, other charitable interests that do will receive priority for that person's ultimate gift. If the initiatives you take do not build on one another to create the necessary awareness, understanding, caring, involvement, and sense of commitment, the likelihood of your institution's receiving a prospect's ultimate gift is diminished. Thus, the *frequency* and *continuity* of initiatives are essential for your success.

NECESSARY TOOLS

You will need several tools to conduct nurturing fund raising. These include *prospect files,* an *information system,* and a *prospect tracking system.* The form these take may differ depending on the number of prospects you are addressing, the size and complexity of your institution, and the number of primes, secondaries, and staff managers involved.

Prospect Files

You will need a file for each prospect containing copies of relevant correspondence, memos, news clippings, and reports. These files will become the primary repository for prospect information. Because of the personal character of the information they contain, these files must be treated confidentially.

Information Systems

Your institution probably has a system in place to keep track of a wide range of constituent information. That system should be able to identify your major gift prospects, as well as the prime, secondaries, and staff manager involved in your nurturing fund raising. This ensures that others who use the system are alerted to the institution's special investment in these individuals and that they can easily identify the proper person to consult.

You will want to be able to include or exclude these prospects in special mailings and other communications. Much of your institution's communication with constituents will be based on your information system, so you should periodically check to make sure the information in this system is complete, correct, and up-to-date.

Prospect Tracking System

You will also need to keep track of initiatives planned and taken with each of your major gift prospects. If you are attending to only a few prospects, a simple piece of paper in the front of each prospect's file may suffice. Draw a line down the middle. On the left record the date and description of each initiative planned for that prospect and who is responsible for it. On the right record the date and description of each initiative that occurs. This simple record will provide a convenient summary of the initiatives taken and a chronological index to the more detailed documents in the file.

The more prospects you have and the more people involved with the prospect, the more likely it is that you will need a computer to track initiatives planned and taken. The best computer-based tracking systems clearly identify the prime, secondaries, and staff manager for each prospect and record information about the overall strategy, recent history, and upcoming initiatives planned for each prospect. The system should use plain language, without limit on the number of characters used. Those systems that use codes to record information ignore the subtleties of relationship building.

Many tracking systems include a tickler function that reminds the user automatically of initiatives to be taken. The system should be able to print paper reports that can be distributed on a regular basis to the staff managers and selected primes and secondaries so that those people remain up-to-date on the prospects with whom they are personally involved. There will undoubtedly be many primes and secondaries for whom such computer-generated reports are inappropriate. The staff manager will instead need to consult with these natural partners by phone, letter, or personal visit.

The best prospect tracking systems do far more than simply help manage initiatives. The information they disseminate on a confidential, need-to-know basis also enhances communication and coordination among a select group of people close to each prospect. Tracking systems stimulate activity and help guide those who are involved in nurturing fund raising for the first time. They give a new dean or faculty member a real-life view of what leads people they know to make major gifts to their institution.

It takes time to develop a computer-based prospect tracking system and to develop and train the users. At first users will feel that it is an unnecessary administrative burden. Once they become experienced with the system, however, they will consider it their indispensable servant.

GETTING STARTED

If you are just beginning a program of nurturing fund raising, the following steps will get you started.

1. *Select five or ten prospects.* Begin with a small number of prospects. These should be individuals who are capable of giving the largest gifts your institution hopes to receive, who are closest to your institution, and whom you know the best. Later, you can add more.
2. *Plan time on your calendar.* You cannot do successful nurturing fund raising by investing only the time that is left after you have met all the other demands that are placed on you. To ensure the quality, frequency, and continuity of initiatives that are essential for success you will have to block out time on your calendar every week. The amount of time needed will depend on the number of prospects you are addressing and the depth of your institution's involvement with them.
3. *Create a file for each prospect.*
4. *Research the public sources of information.*
5. *Identify each prospect's natural partners.* Begin by reading the correspondence people at your institution have had with each prospect and examining the results of the research about them.

6. *Consult the natural partners.* Your conversations with friends of the prospect will disclose additional information and identify others you should consult.

7. *Select a prime and secondaries for each prospect.* Not everyone who knows the prospect well will be in a position to help you nurture their relationship with the institution. Select those who are willing and able to help in the process. Their selection does not mean that you have to ask them formally "to serve." But you do have to ascertain their willingness to help foster a satisfying relationship between your institution and their friend.

8. *Organize biographical information.* Develop a standard format to record and display the biographical information you will need for your work. By putting it in a standard format you can more easily recognize gaps you will need to fill.

9. *Establish a tracking system.* That divided piece of paper at the front of your file will probably suffice as you get some practice with the first 5 or 10 prospects. Only after you develop a feel for conducting this type of nurturing fund raising should you attempt to develop or select a computer-based prospect tracking system.

10. *Identify gift objectives.* Set some objectives—even tentative ones—for each prospect's next major gift. These objectives should include amount, purpose, timing, and means of giving (outright gift, bequest, trust, gift in kind, etc.). Be prepared to refine and revise these objectives as you learn more about the prospect. Having tentative objectives in place will help stimulate initiatives that should lead to their revision or accomplishment.

11. *Factor background activities into the planning.* Think through the functions and events your institution has planned for the year ahead and arrange for your prospects to be included when appropriate.

12. *Keep track of the distribution of initiatives among your prospects.* If you are like most staff managers, you will find it easier to take initiatives with the prospects with whom you are most comfortable and most familiar. As a result, there may be a tendency to direct a disproportionate amount of time and attention to them and give less to the others. To avoid this, keep a simple record of the number of initiatives you take with each prospect each month. A page with each month listed

across the top and each prospect's name listed down the left margin will serve to record the number of initiatives taken each month for each prospect. A glance at such a record will tell you to whom you should be directing more attention.

13. *Perform the six-step cycle for each prospect each month.* In the time you have scheduled on your calendar for nurturing fund raising make sure that no less frequently than once a month you have gone through the six-step cycle described earlier: reviewing past events, planning the next initiative, coordinating with others, implementing the initiative, evaluating the initiative, and reporting and recording the results.

14. *Add prospects.* As you gain experience and begin to feel comfortable with nurturing fund raising, you will find you are ready to add more prospects. Select only a few at a time. Make sure they are the best available, taking into account their financial capacity, interest or potential interest, and charitable nature. Forget about practicing on the less-promising prospects. Give preference to the prospects who are closest to your institution. They are likely to be most productive.

15. *Evaluate the program annually.* The next section examines this step in more detail.

THE ANNUAL CHECKUP

At least once a year, step back from the day-to-day work of your major gift program and ask yourself:

1. Are the initiatives the program generates consistent with your institution's strategic plan?
2. Has each prospect been asked for an annual gift?
3. Has each prospect received a desirable quality, quantity, frequency, and continuity of initiatives?
4. Have initiatives been distributed appropriately among the prospects?
5. Are you working with the right number of prospects?
6. Are the prospects selected the right ones?
7. Does each prospect have the most appropriate prime and secondaries?
8. Is staffing and budget appropriate to the giving potential of the prospects your program is addressing?

If your consideration of the last question leaves you convinced that more should be invested in the program, work through the appropriate channels to secure the additional staffing and budget you believe is warranted by the potential. Provide those who must make these decisions with the information that convinced you the increases you propose are prudent investments. Once the decision is made on the program's resources for the year ahead, cheerfully work with the resources provided to do the best job possible.

Because you undoubtedly will be working with your institution's leading benefactors, some of whom may be trustees of your institution, you may be tempted to appeal to them for help in getting additional support for your program. Avoid doing this. No team can tolerate an end run on a matter as vital as the allocation of resources.

ANTICIPATING PROBLEMS

Major gift fund raisers must be especially alert for situations in which the priorities of the major gift program may compete with other people and projects. Knowing where such competition is most likely to crop up will help you anticipate—and avoid—problems.

Earlier in this chapter I noted that people come to the work of fund raising with different orientations. Some fund raisers are assigned a project for which to raise funds. Other fund raisers' assignments center on methods of giving. Still others focus their efforts on a particular group of prospective givers.

It is not hard to imagine a situation in which these orientations compete with one another. For example, an institution may have an athletics department fund raiser (project-oriented) who wants to solicit Mr. Jones for funds to send the baseball team on a southern tour to play ten games over spring break. The college also has a planned giving officer (method-oriented) who recognizes the advantages that a charitable remainder trust has for a person in Mr. Jones's circumstances and wants to discuss a considerably larger charitable remainder trust gift with him. The director of major gifts (prospect-oriented) is concerned that the timing for either of these approaches is not right because Mr. Jones only six months ago made a generous gift to endow the Jones Scholarship Fund and just last month made a generous gift to the annual fund. How these differences are resolved will have an effect on Mr.

Jones. How they are resolved will also affect the staff's feelings and morale, as well as the culture and spirit of the institution.

You must also watch for competition among the various people you involve as primes, secondaries, and staff managers, who may have different gift objectives in mind for the same prospect. Your institution's relationship with prospects will be stronger, and the likelihood of their giving ultimate gifts will be greater, if the prospects have a relationship with and commitment to several parts of your institution. And the more successful you are in developing primes and secondaries to build and sustain those relationships, the more they will be concerned about who gets to ask "their prospect" for what.

Whether competing orientations and purposes have a positive or negative effect hinges on three things: (1) Whether values are shared by all who are working with prospects for the good of the institution, (2) the degree of care taken in planning, and (3) the degree of communication.

It is not enough simply to designate an arbiter to decide who gets to ask whom for what. Nurturing fund raising requires energetic communication among all the partners key to the prospect's relationship with your institution. No one expects his or her opinion to prevail all of the time, but people who make an investment in building relationships for the institution do expect their opinions to be considered and to be informed of the decisions.

The system you devise for deciding who gets to ask whom for what should be guided by the following principles:

1. It should balance donor interest with institutional priorities.
2. It should be information-based rather than authority-based and should solicit information and opinions from the prime, secondaries, and staff who have a stake in the prospect's relationship with the institution.
3. It should minimize the personality factor by involving more than one person in difficult and controversial decisions.
4. It should ensure that the appropriate prime, secondaries, and staff are promptly informed of any decision made regarding their prospect.
5. It should provide opportunity for a decision to be appealed if a participant believes it is wrong.

The level of communication these guidelines require was next to impossible only a few years ago. With computer-aided communication we now can routinely share with the natural partners the information they need and solicit the information and advice they can provide. This level of communication is costly in the time and effort it requires. Because it is so demanding it should necessarily be reserved for your top prospects.

SUMMARY

In this chapter we defined three different kinds of gifts from the giver's perspective: *regular, special,* and *ultimate.* These different kinds of gifts are encouraged by different methods of fund raising we have called *speculative, campaign / project,* and *nurturing.* While a major gift program must certainly be oriented toward nurturing fund raising for ultimate gifts, to be successful it must also ensure that its prospects have opportunities to make regular and special gifts through which the habits of giving are developed.

We noted that those who make ultimate gifts generally have certain types of experiences that lead them to those gifts. It is therefore appropriate for a major gift program to foster the same type of experiences with others from whom it hopes to secure ultimate and other very large gifts. These experiences develop each prospect's *awareness, understanding, caring, involvement,* and *commitment* to the institution and to the purpose for which their gift is sought.

We saw that both background and foreground initiatives accomplish these objectives. The natural partners in each prospect's relationship with the institution—whom we call *prime* and *secondaries*—can help carry out these initiatives. We defined a six-step check list to bring discipline to the process of generating initiatives no less frequently than once a month. This process requires a staff manager working with the prime and secondaries for each prospect to ensure the quality, frequency, and continuity that is crucial to the success of nurturing fund raising.

With the concepts of nurturing fund raising your major gift program can hold out a welcoming hand to those whose gifts can transform your institution from what it is today to what it hopes to be. It can invite them to become full partners in the great work of placing knowledge at the service of humanity.

Chapter 11

Fundamentals of Planned Giving

Ronald E. Sapp

In years past, charitable giving that made use of financial planning methods was called "trust and estate planning" or "deferred giving." Today, we refer to it as "planned giving," and occasionally (and more accurately) as "charitable gift planning." These changes in terminology reflect the movement of planned giving programs from a technical orientation to a "donor friendly" orientation—a shift that has helped make planned giving programs successful.

We can define planned giving as a way for a donor to give an *asset* (cash, stock, bonds, real estate, family business, antiques, etc.) by using a *method* (unitrust, bequest, deed, contract, etc.) that will provide *benefits* to both the donor (in the form of charitable fulfillment, tax savings, income, asset management, family protection, etc.) and to the institution (in the form of funds now or in the future). With the wide variety and flexibility that planned giving offers, donors never before thought of as major gift prospects are able to make major gifts.

Becoming knowledgeable about planned giving is a long-term task. Part of the task is mastering the tax rules and regulations that encourage charitable gifts. Part is developing the financial acumen to understand and handle assets. And another part is knowing the various gift instruments—the forms planned gifts can take.

This chapter will cover some basics of tax rules, assets, and instruments. It is essential to remember, however, that the mechanics of planned giving are always secondary; the basis of every major gift is charitable intent. Donors give because they want to support a certain cause or purpose. How the gift is structured proceeds from that important starting point.

Planned giving, then, integrates "how" people give with "why" people give. The skilled fund raiser learns enough about each donor's assets and needs to be able to suggest a planned giving arrangement appropriate to the individual's situation. At its best, planned giving can help donors to increase the value of a gift by reducing tax costs, to use cumbersome assets easily, and to enjoy financial planning benefits.

TAX RULES AFFECTING PLANNED GIFTS

Certain rules of the Internal Revenue Service (IRS) Code can make charitable giving an attractive option for a donor. To understand what sorts of planned gifts will be to the donor's advantage, the fund raiser needs to be familiar with tax rules. A few basic points follow.

Tax Deduction Limits on Charitable Contributions

The extent to which an individual is allowed an income tax deduction for charitable contributions is limited, based on the donor's contribution base. For the great majority of donors, contribution base is their Adjusted Gross Income (AGI). When planning a major charitable gift, the fund raiser must understand the deduction limits in order to properly evaluate the financial benefits to the donor.

The most generous limitation, which is 50 percent of a taxpayer's contribution base, applies to contributions to organizations that fall under Section 170(b)(1)(A) of the Internal Revenue Code. These include colleges, universities, museums, private schools, religious organizations, and hospitals, as well as the foundations and endowment funds established by these organizations.

A gift of cash entitles the donor to a charitable income tax deduction that is limited, in the year of the gift, to 50 percent of contribution base. A gift of appreciated property—for example, securities or real estate—is deductible at fair market value and limited to 30 percent of contribution base. Gift value in excess of these limits may be carried over for up to five additional years.

For gifts of appreciated property, the capital gain is included in calculations for alternative minimum tax (AMT). The AMT, which is figured according to a different formula than normally used for income tax, is designed to ensure that taxpayers with substantial income do not avoid paying income taxes through the unlimited use of exclusions, special deductions, and credits. Those few donors with income high enough to bring the AMT into play may enjoy less tax benefit from their gift. In such cases, the donors should consult their tax adviser.

Valuation of Non-cash Gifts

The Tax Reform Act of 1984 led to new rules affecting non-cash charitable gifts. The rules require donors to follow certain procedures in order to claim a charitable tax deduction. The recipient organization must also meet particular reporting requirements. These rules become especially important when gifts involve assets such as securities, real estate, and tangible personal property.

Donors of non-cash charitable gifts worth more than $500 must complete IRS form 8283. Non-cash gifts worth more than $5,000 also require an appraisal by a qualified appraiser. Securities are an exception: nonpublicly traded securities (closely held stock) require an appraisal only if the value exceeds $10,000, and publicly traded securities do not require an appraisal at all.

For non-cash gifts requiring appraisals, the recipient organization is required to sign the donor's IRS form 8283. Then, if the organization sells, exchanges, or otherwise disposes of the property within two years of the date of the gift, it files IRS form 8282 with the IRS to report the amount received from the transaction.

ASSETS

Cash is only one of the many assets donors can use to make gifts. Other assets—including securities, real estate and other tangible property, and even life insurance policies—can form all or a part of a gift. Often, a donor can realize significant tax benefits by giving the asset itself, which may enable the donor to increase the value of the gift. Fund raisers who are familiar with these options, and who suggest them to donors who can benefit, can help both the donor and the institution.

Gifts of Appreciated Securities

Donors who hold long-term appreciated securities—publicly traded common stocks and bonds as well as nonpublic securities—can realize two important tax advantages from giving them to an institution. First, the donor is entitled to a charitable income tax deduction based on the fair market value of the securities, provided the donor has owned them for more than a year. In addition, the donor avoids paying tax on the capital gain that would be realized if the donor sold the securities.

A donor can give securities outright or transfer them to create a life income gift (as described later in this chapter). The transfer of publicly traded securities must follow certain rules in order to provide the donor with all of the tax benefits available.

Securities that have depreciated in value should not be donated directly to the institution. It is to the donor's advantage to sell the securities to establish a tax-deductible loss and then donate the cash proceeds.

Gifts of nonpublic securities can provide the same tax benefits as publicly traded securities, but this type of stock requires special handling. The significant difference is the lack of a ready market for the institution to sell the stock and convert it to cash. Various methods exist for converting closely held stock to cash, but all require caution. Institutions and donors should rely on the advice of qualified legal and tax advisers.

Gifts of Real Estate

Many donors have enjoyed significant tax benefits by making gifts of real estate. Gifts of real estate can consist of almost any type of property—a primary residence or a vacation home, a farm or ranch, a commercial building, subdivision lots, or an undeveloped parcel. The gift can be the entire property or a partial interest in the property. Real estate subject to debt presents special problems that need to be carefully considered when structuring a charitable gift; legal and tax advisers can help in such cases.

The donor's financial needs and philanthropic objectives determine which of the various methods of donating real estate is most appropriate. Options include the following:

- *An outright gift.* The donor can deed the property to the institution, which sells it unless there is a special investment reason for holding it.
- *A bargain sale.* The donor can sell the property to the institution for a price below its fair market value. The difference between the bargain sale price and the fair market price is a charitable gift. The institution can then sell the property at full value.

- *A life income gift.* The property may be transferred to a special trust (called a "charitable remainder unitrust") and then sold. The proceeds are then invested to produce income for life to the donor and, if desired, to a second beneficiary. After the last income beneficiary dies, the trust assets pass to the institution. Another method for receiving income is for the donor to deed the property to the institution in exchange for a gift annuity contract. (More detail on these income-producing arrangements appears later in this chapter.)
- *A gift with lifetime use.* If the property is being used as a residence or farm, the donor may transfer ownership to the institution while retaining the right to use the property for life. At death, the life estate ends and the institution takes full possession of the property. Under certain conditions, an income for life can be provided to the donor as well, using the remainder value (an actuarially calculated partial value) of the property as the funding basis for a gift annuity contract.
- *An undivided partial interest in real estate.* An undivided portion of real property can be conveyed outright. For example, the donor can make the institution a co-owner by giving a one-half undivided interest in a residence, vacation home, commercial property, or farm or ranch. When the property is sold, the donor and the institution share proportionately in the proceeds. Or, as with the preceding options, the donor can receive income by transferring a partial interest to a unitrust or exchanging it for a gift annuity contract.
- *A bequest.* The donor may leave real estate to the institution in his or her will.

Gifts of Tangible Personal Property

The term "tangible personal property" refers to physical assets other than real property and financial instruments. Examples include art, antiques, collections, manuscripts, books, vehicles, and boats.

Donors can give tangible personal property for charitable purposes, but the tax value of the gift depends on the purposes of the charity. If the property can be used in a manner related to the charity's tax-exempt purpose, then the donor may claim a tax deduction based on the fair market value of the donated asset. If the property is unrelated to the charity's exempt purpose, the donor's charitable income tax deduction is limited to the property's cost basis—that is, the original price or appraised value at the time it was inherited—or the fair market value if that is lower.

The related use test does not apply in the case of tangible personal property gifts bequeathed in a will. All such property given by will is fully deductible for estate tax purposes.

Gifts of Life Insurance

Life insurance policies provide a means for making future gifts. There are several ways to use life insurance for charitable purposes:

- *Donate an existing policy.* A donor can designate the institution as the owner and beneficiary of an existing policy that is not fully paid up. The donor is then entitled to a charitable deduction for the "present value" of the policy (approximately the cash surrender value or the cost basis, whichever is less). The donor can then continue to pay the premiums to maintain the policy in force and be entitled to deduct the premium payments each year as a charitable contribution.
- *Establish a new policy.* A donor can establish a new policy, designating the recipient as the owner and beneficiary. The donor may then deduct the premiums as a charitable contribution.
- *Asset replacement.* Life insurance can be used as a "replacement" asset. A donor gives appreciated property to the institution and replaces the dollar value of the asset with life insurance payable to family members. The income tax savings from the gift may be sufficient to pay for the "replacement" insurance. The insurance premiums are not a charitable contribution, however.
- *Establish a unitrust.* A donor can use life insurance to fund a charitable remainder unitrust for a beneficiary. The unitrust provides income for the beneficiary after the death of the donor. At the beneficiary's death, the trust principal becomes the property of the institution.

- *Convert to cash.* A donor can liquidate a policy no longer needed for family protection and donate the cash value to the institution as a tax-deductible charitable gift.

GIFTS THAT PROVIDE INCOME

Of the many methods by which a donor can make a planned gift, a few share a particularly attractive benefit: They provide continuing income to the donors or to one or more beneficiaries of the donors' choosing.

Loss of income is a frequent barrier to giving. Some individuals would like to make gifts but cannot afford to give up the annual income they draw from the assets that would form the gift. Potential donors often assume that the only alternative is to provide for a future gift in their will. This need not be the case. Special provisions in the tax code allow donors to make a charitable gift while retaining the right to income during their lives.

This type of charitable gift arrangement—called a "life income gift"—has been in existence in one form or another for most of this century, but it did not come into wide use until the enactment of the Tax Reform Act of 1969, which introduced charitable remainder trusts (annuity trusts, unitrusts, and pooled income funds). One other life income gift instrument, the charitable gift annuity, predates that law and is still in use.

The features and legal basis of these arrangements vary, but they all provide the following benefits:

- Income for life to the donor(s) and/or another beneficiary.
- An immediate federal income tax deduction for a portion of the value of the gift.
- Elimination or reduction of capital gains tax if the gift is in the form of an appreciated asset.
- In the case of charitable remainder trusts, transfer of the gift remainder to the institution at the death of the last beneficiary.

While the various life income gift arrangements share these characteristics, they each have unique features that allow them to be used creatively to meet the requirements of both the donor and the recipient. Important factors to consider in setting up these arrangements include the approximate size of the gift being considered by the donor, the type of asset to be donated, income

requirements, the term of payments, investment risk, and beneficiary selection. Also, for a charitable remainder unitrust or
annuity trust, the donor must name a trustee. In some cases, the
institution may fulfill that role.

Annuity Trusts

A charitable remainder annuity trust is a life income plan
that pays a fixed dollar amount (annuity) to one or more named
beneficiaries. The payments may continue for life, for a term of up
to 20 years, or some combination of these options. When the
beneficiary dies or the term is up, what is left in the trust—the
"remainder"—goes to the institution.

The annuity payment is a fixed dollar amount, equal to at
least 5 percent of the initial fair market value of the trust's assets.
The annuity, once set, cannot change, and no additional contributions can be made to the annuity trust after the initial transfer of
assets. If the invested assets produce more income than needed to
pay the annuity, the excess is added to principal, thereby increasing the amount ultimately payable to the institution. If the
annuity trust's income is less than required to meet the annuity
payment, the difference is taken from the principal, thereby
reducing the amount that will ultimately go to the institution.

When the annuity trust is established, the IRS requires an
actuarial test, called the "5 percent probability test," to evaluate
the possibility that the trust will be depleted before the end of its
natural term. If the test determines there is a greater than 5
percent probability the charity will not receive the remainder, the
donor may not take a charitable deduction.

The charitable deduction is calculated based on the annuity
rate, the initial value of the assets transferred to the trust, the
date of transfer, the age and number of beneficiaries and/or the
term of years, the initial payment date and frequency thereafter,
and IRS tables for remainder values. This calculation, as well as
the 5 percent probability test, can be done manually or with
computer software.

A significant factor affecting the charitable deduction is the
annuity rate. A higher rate—which means more money paid out
over the trust's life—produces a smaller deduction than does a
lower rate. Age is also significant, in that younger beneficiaries,
who stand to receive more payments over time, produce a lower
charitable deduction than do older beneficiaries.

Taxes on the annuity income paid to the beneficiaries depends on the type of income earned and accumulated by the trust. Space does not permit a full discussion of this point, but details are available in IRS publications and other planned giving guides.

Unitrusts

The charitable remainder unitrust has many features in common with the charitable remainder annuity trust, but there are important differences. The chief difference is the method of determining the payment. The unitrust, like the annuity trust, is required to pay at least 5 percent of the trust's fair market value. But while the annuity trust payment remains fixed, based on the trust's *initial* value, the unitrust payment is recalculated annually based on the current value of the unitrust. Thus, while the percentage remains the same, the payment increases or decreases each year as the unitrust's value changes over time.

A standard or "straight" unitrust draws the payment from the trust's income when possible, and from principal when income is not sufficient. Or the donor may select a variation called an "income-only" unitrust, which limits payments to the stated percentage rate or to the actual income earned, whichever is less. This variation, which leaves principal and appreciation intact for the life of the unitrust, is especially useful when funding a unitrust with non-liquid assets that are earning little or no income. For example, if the donor funds the trust with real estate, the income-only provision allows time for the trustee to sell the real estate and reinvest the proceeds, free of any obligation to make payments before income is available.

A further variation is an income-only unitrust that is allowed to recoup deficiencies in payments. This "income-only unitrust with make-up" uses income earned in excess of the stipulated annual payment to make up for shortfalls earlier in the life of the unitrust. This variation of the unitrust is useful in retirement planning when the objective is to use low-income-growth investments to minimize payments in early years and shift to high-yield investments to produce increased payments in later years.

None of the unitrusts are subject to the 5 percent probability test required for an annuity trust. Donors may also make additions to a unitrust, which enhances its use as a long-term financial planning instrument.

Pooled Income Funds

Charitable remainder annuity trusts and unitrusts are self-contained fiscal entities and by their nature require a minimum size that may preclude some donors from making this type of gift. Fortunately, there are two alternatives suitable for smaller donors: pooled income funds and charitable gift annuities.

A pooled income fund is a type of charitable remainder trust that operates like a mutual fund. A donor's gift to a pooled income fund, along with similar gifts from other donors, is invested by the institution, acting as trustee (or by a bank or trust company designated as trustee by the institution). In return, the donor or a designated beneficiary receives income for life, typically in quarterly payments. Payments vary depending on the beneficiary's share of the income earned by the fund. When the beneficiary dies, the corresponding share of the fund's principal goes to the institution, to be used as directed by the donor at the time of the original arrangement.

An important feature of a pooled income fund is the combination of many donors' gifts in a single trust, which spreads administrative costs as well as investment risk. As a result, each gift can be considerably smaller than would be necessary for a stand-alone unitrust or annuity trust. Institutions that establish pooled income funds usually set the initial gift minimum at $5,000 or $10,000, with additional gifts set at a lower level. Pooled income funds generally accept gifts of cash and publicly traded securities. Real estate is not prohibited, but most funds prefer not to accept an asset that is not readily convertible to an income-producing investment.

Pooled income funds can be a particularly useful fund-raising tool because institutions can structure the fund to appeal to certain types of prospective donors. A plan might seek to achieve a high rate of income (a high-yield fund). Or it might be designed to achieve a balance of income as well as growth in value over time (a balanced fund). Or it might be invested primarily to achieve growth and, to a lesser extent, income (a growth fund).

A pooled income fund donor is entitled to a charitable deduction for a portion of the value of the gift transferred to the trust. The deduction amount is based on IRS tables, the age of the beneficiary, and the rate of investment return. The beneficiary must report all of the income as ordinary income for federal tax purposes.

Charitable Gift Annuities

The charitable gift annuity, a popular form of charitable giving, has been in existence for most of the twentieth century. It differs from the charitable remainder trusts and pooled income funds in that the actual agreement is a contract between the institution and the donor.

A charitable gift annuity is part gift and part annuity. A donor makes a gift to the institution and, in doing so, purchases a fixed income for one or two beneficiaries for life. The income amount can commence within the year the contract is made (immediate annuity) or it can be specified to commence at a date a year or more in the future (deferred annuity).

Like a charitable remainder annuity trust, a gift annuity contract requires payment of a fixed income. However, the payment obligation differs. An annuity trust can pay the annuity income only to the extent of the trust assets. If the trust assets run out, the annuity ends. A gift annuity is a binding contract, obligating the institution to pay the annuity from its general assets. This contractual guarantee is one reason for the popularity of charitable gift annuities.

The amount of the annuity payment is usually based on the ages of the beneficiary or beneficiaries. The Committee on Gift Annuities, a Dallas-based volunteer association of more than 1,000 charitable organizations, publishes recommended annuity rates; charities are not required to use these rates, but they are broadly accepted. These uniform rates serve to discourage the use of unrealistic annuity rates and also to provide a degree of self-regulation among charities.

A gift annuity donor is entitled to a charitable income tax deduction for a portion of the value transferred. The calculation is based on the age of the beneficiaries, payment frequency, annuity rate, and IRS tables. It is worth noting that a charitable gift annuity and an annuity trust using identical actuarial factors of age, annuity rate, frequency, and IRS tables result in an identical charitable deduction. However, taxation of the annuity payments differs.

Payments from a gift annuity funded with cash are taxed in part as ordinary income and in part as a tax-free return of the donors' original investment. If the annuity is funded with appreciated securities, part of the long-term capital gain is spread over the annuity payments and taxed as capital gain income, thereby reducing the tax-free portion. The tax-free portion, and the capital gain portion, if any, continue for the actuarial life expectancy of the donor. Should the donor outlive expectations, all of the income becomes fully taxable as ordinary income.

In addition to cash and securities, real estate and tangible personal property are sometimes suitable assets to exchange for a gift annuity. However, in some states insurance regulations prohibit such transactions.

Part of the popularity of gift annuities with institutions is the ease with which they can be established. Unlike the other life income arrangements described above, gift annuities do not require a trustee. However, the institution must carefully consider the legal responsibility as well as administrative responsibility of a contractual obligation of this type.

Like pooled income funds, gift annuities offer an economy of scale that permits gifts as low as $5,000. But small size is not a requirement; gift annuities and pooled income funds also work well with large gifts of trust size. In fact, many planned giving programs direct large gifts to their pooled income funds or gift annuity program, recommending annuity trusts and unitrusts only when the donor's unique requirements call for a custom-designed life income plan.

OTHER PLANNED GIVING INSTRUMENTS

In addition to the methods that provide life income, other planned giving arrangements exist. These options increase the fund raiser's planned giving menu even further to suit donors' individual needs.

Charitable Lead Trusts

The charitable lead trust works like a life income gift in reverse. Income from this trust goes first to the institution; when the trust terminates, the remainder transfers to the donor or another beneficiary. Generally, a lead trust provides one of two benefits to the donor. If the trust is a "grantor lead trust" (that is, the trust assets revert to the donor), the donor can advance income tax deductions for future income payments to the institution into the year in which the gift is made. If the trust is a "non-grantor lead trust" (the trust assets do not revert to the donor), the donor's tax benefit is a reduction of gift and estate taxes that would otherwise apply to the trust property passed to heirs.

The use of lead trusts has diminished steadily through the 1980s due to changes in tax rules. Given the current limitations, charitable lead trusts are used far less than the life income plans described above. Its best place is in planning a sizable estate, with help from legal and tax advisers experienced in using lead trusts in estate planning.

Charitable Bequests

A charitable bequest is a legal provision made by will, naming a charitable organization as the recipient of all or part of the donor's estate. The bequest may be in the form of cash, real estate, securities, or other property as specified in the will. Testamentary giving enjoys special tax benefits allowed by the federal and state estate tax laws. The estate tax laws are generous in allowing the donor to pass assets to charity free of estate taxes and of many of the limitations that normally apply to gifts.

The most common method of testamentary giving is an outright transfer at the time of death. When given outright, the entire estate of a donor can be donated to charity and qualify for a charitable deduction. The property transferred can include tangible property, capital gain property, ordinary income property, and more, without regard to the charity's exempt purpose and without percentage limitations.

The tax deductibility of a gift by will reduces its cost to the donor's estate. The cost of gifts by will varies with the size of the taxable estate and the applicable tax bracket. For example, if a donor whose estate is taxed in the 50 percent bracket makes a bequest of $100,000, the real cost of the gift to his estate is only $50,000—because the other $50,000 would have been lost in estate taxes had the gift not been made.

Bequests can take various forms depending on the donors' wishes for heirs and for other charitable organizations.

- *Specific bequest.* The institution receives a specific dollar amount or specific assets such as securities, real estate, or personal property.
- *Residuary bequest.* The institution receives all or a percentage of the estate remaining after the payment of expenses and any specific amounts designated to other beneficiaries.
- *Contingent bequest.* The institution receives a bequest only in the event that a named beneficiary predeceases the donor.

A will is an important legal instrument that should be prepared by the donor's attorney. In some cases, the institution has the opportunity to provide sample language for a new will or a codicil for an existing will.

In addition to outright transfer, bequests can also be used to create life income gifts. The gift must be in the form of a charitable remainder trust, pooled income funds, or charitable gift annuity.

THE TIME FOR PLANNED GIVING

Planned giving has come of age, due in large part to the innovative tools and creative strategies that fund raisers and others have developed in recent years. The result has been to provide valuable financial and estate planning benefits to donors while at the same time achieving generous support for charitable organizations.

To advance this effort, today's fund raiser needs to know the planned giving basics. But to truly succeed, it is essential to be able to communicate the benefits of planned giving to donors in ways they can understand. Achieving that objective will result in major gifts from which everyone will benefit both now and in the future.

Chapter 12
How to Solicit a Major Gift

Michael F. Adams

Rare is the professional fund raiser, even a senior one, who has not driven around the block working up an extra ounce of courage before entering a donor prospect's office to ask for a major gift. Perhaps no process is more important to the future of American higher education, and less written about and understood, than the "simple process" of one person sitting down and asking another to give resources to support a particular cause. Over the last twenty years I have seen scores of successful business people and professional fund raisers stutter, stammer, and wince during an official "ask." College and university trustees—including some who have developed reputations as tough business negotiators—often wilt like a rose in the noonday heat when placed in the situation of asking someone, perhaps a respected colleague, to give.

On the other hand, I know a small circle of extremely successful fund raisers across the country who find solicitation so invigorating that they recommend it wholeheartedly to any educational professional who will listen. One is led to wonder about the nature of a process that reduces some sophisticated and caring adults to bumbling children and at the same time encourages others to a degree of involvement in philanthropy that provides an exultant high over and over again.

That so many fund-raising "asks" are muddled in one way or another would be humorous if it were not so devastating. The fact remains that more than 70 percent of the money given to American higher education comes from individuals, and most of that largess is a direct result of one interested party asking another for support. There is no more important process in educational development than face-to-face solicitation.

A comprehensive study of the literature, coupled with personal experience in both political and educational fund raising, have convinced me that success in person-to-person fund raising is linked to four key concepts.

1. The solicitor's perspective on asking;
2. The solicitor's preparation for the ask;
3. The donor's relationship to the institution and its people; and
4. The solicitor's technique.

Inadequate attention to any one of these four areas will almost always render the solicitation meaningless and a waste of time for both the fund raiser and the prospect. Let's look at each area in detail.

THE SOLICITOR'S PERSPECTIVE

The process of giving is neither dispassionate nor unemotional. Robert Payton, formerly of the Exxon Foundation and now a scholar of philanthropy at Indiana University, points out that philanthropy has at its base the Greek word "philos," meaning love for one's brother. The very best fund raisers I have known are people who simply love other people and who love their cause. These people share three common beliefs.

First, they recognize that they are asking for support of a cause larger than any one person. In other words, they know that they are not asking for themselves. This attitude not only gives credibility to the solicitation, but it also serves to reduce some of the tension often felt before a fund-raising call. I have been helped many times by thinking of a particular student who made it through school, an edifice that was erected, or a professorship that was endowed because someone was willing to ask another party for money. Only when a fund raiser begins to develop a solicitation perspective that is rooted in concern for others, rather than worry about personal success or failure, does real philanthropy begin.

Second, the individual solicitor has to believe that he or she is treating the donor prospect properly. I genuinely believe I have helped make many people much happier by helping them redirect some of their resources. Some of the happiest people I know are those who have made major commitments to colleges and universities, often in the prime of life, and have then stood back to see the benefit of their philanthropy. Those who view the donor prospect as merely prey to be hunted have overlooked one of the real joys of participation in this process; some of my dearest friends are people from whom I have solicited large sums of money for causes I represented.

Stories about people making major bequests to colleges and universities and then living well into their eighties and nineties are a regular joke in fund-raising circles. I do not believe that such instances are coincidence. Time and again I have witnessed donors make sound financial plans and develop a "sense of peace" that literally extends their lives. I do not have the research to prove it, but I truly believe people who make major philanthropic commitments tend to live longer. The good solicitor develops the perspective that the donor, as well as the cause, will benefit.

Third, a proper solicitation perspective increasingly demands that the solicitor understand that he or she is a part of a fund-raising team, not a lone miracle worker. The most successful fund raisers recognize the myriad of activity that goes into the preparation for a major gift. Fund raising is founded on teamwork; those who ignore this reality do so to their own detriment.

At a typical college or university, most major gifts are the result of a long courtship. This usually begins with the kind treatment some individual received from a caring professor when attending the institution. A thoughtful and appropriate article in the college publication may nurture the feeling. The institution's academic, athletic, or artistic success may touch the person's heartstrings. And an expression of warmth from a student, staff member, or senior college official may be enough to generate and solidify the person's commitment to the cause. Individuals have told me that the thoughts that sparked their gifts were as diverse as "The students looked nice and smiled at me while I was on campus" to "I really like the way you keep the buildings and grounds here; it shows a care and concern that I admire." Who would argue that the one fund raiser who has the privilege of representing the institution for the ask is the person responsible for that institution's success?

To be successful, then, those who ask for money must develop a positive solicitation perspective. They must recognize that they are not asking for themselves. They must truly believe there is benefit to the donor and to the cause. And they must recognize that success in acquiring a gift most often depends upon preparation, nourishment, concern, or empowerment generated by people other than themselves.

THE SOLICITOR'S PREPARATION

Preparation for a major fund-raising call begins months or even years in advance. This usually entails not only years of personal experience but also three key elements: sound financial research; a detailed knowledge of the person's likes and dislikes, habits, family relationships, and hobbies; and a great willingness to listen.

Prospect research has received much attention in recent years. Most colleges and universities with strong development operations have at least one person responsible for informing the fund-raising team of a prospect's financial capacity. While there are important ethical considerations involved with current donor research methods, I will leave that subject to others. The fact is that the solicitor needs to know not only the prospect's net worth, but also the prospect's giving capacity—the resources that person has available and the form those resources take. Everyone knows stories of people who were "extremely wealthy" in the 1980s because of large real estate or land holdings, who are not so wealthy in the 1990s because the market has changed dramatically.

In addition to understanding prospects' giving capacity, the solicitor must know their giving orientation. The solicitor's preparation often includes many hours spent with prospects, during which the solicitor comes to know their habits, likes and dislikes, family situation, favorable and unfavorable impressions of the institution, and perhaps most of all, donor intent. The same person who will support an endowed chair or scholarship will not necessarily support a campaign for a new president's home or a weight-lifting room for the football team.

Perhaps most important, the effective fund raiser spends a considerable amount of time listening to prospects before ever approaching them about a gift. Seemingly insignificant bits of knowledge gained from such listening can prove important. For example, a prospect who says "I hated physics in college" and "I especially enjoyed Professor Smith's analysis of Elizabeth Barrett Browning's poetry" is obviously more likely to endow an English chair than one in physics, although the institution may clearly need both.

In short, the best preparation for solicitation involves solid donor research, an intimate knowledge of the prospect that leads to a sixth sense about the prospect's likes and desires, and an unusual capacity to listen.

THE DONOR'S RELATIONSHIP

Jerold Panas suggests in his book *Mega Gifts* that the average cultivation period for a truly significant gift is about seven years. While relationship building between individuals and institutions differs from case to case, the fact remains that people do give to institutions and causes in which they believe. The process of building that relationship may be the most important process in fund raising.

It can take many forms. At Harvard, it might be engendered by the sense of quality and history that envelops the institution. At Wheaton College it might relate to a commitment to evangelical Christianity. At Pepperdine University it might be stimulated by the excitement and beauty of the Malibu campus. At my institution, Centre College, it's the result of 175 years of quality and a sense of membership in America's most loyal alumni body.

Relationships are built over quiet dinners, at frenetic football finishes, in somber lecture halls, or amid the excitement of a laboratory discovery. Whatever the case, virtually every major gift donor has a long-standing, carefully nurtured relationship with the institution or cause—and, by extension, the people who represent it.

In that regard, let me note one major barrier to relationship building. High turnover of development personnel is clearly epidemic today and perhaps borders on the unethical. Successful development people are in such demand that the capacity to leapfrog from one job to the next is virtually unlimited. I would encourage professionals to spend six or eight or ten years, or more, with a single cause or institution. It is in such situations that the kind of relationship leading to major gifts is most likely to be built.

Institutions must pay increasing attention to maintaining a critical mass of personnel known by the prospect community. During my seven-and-a-half years as a vice president at Pepperdine, I found that each year was exponentially more successful than the one before. This was not due to any change in me or my approach, but simply to the fact that important relationships developed and grew during that time. When search committees began to contact me about presidencies, one of my major concerns was the prospect of going somewhere I could create and maintain roots for a considerable period of time. Relationship building is not just technique. It takes a significant investment of time to succeed.

SOLICITATION TECHNIQUES

While techniques are important, I am convinced that they are overrated as a factor in fund-raising success. The solicitor's perspective, preparation, and relationship to the donor often, if not always, are more important than the particular solicitation techniques that he or she uses. But techniques do matter as well; improperly handled fund-raising calls can ruin years of relationship building.

As with any skill, there is no one correct method. Mickey Mantle and Ted Williams used radically different stances for hitting a baseball, but both were successful. While the following techniques may not be the right ones for each person reading this chapter, they are the ones I usually employ, and I believe they will provide an appropriate framework for many different personal approaches.

That framework involves six major steps: the call, the statement of a vision, the ask, a description of the amount needed, the thank-you, and the follow-up. When each of these six areas is handled appropriately in direct conversation with a donor prospect, the likelihood of success increases dramatically. All of this, of course, assumes that adequate attention has been given to the solicitor's perspective and preparation as well as the donor's relationship to the institution or cause.

The Call

It is often more difficult to get an appointment with a prospect than to get the money. This is especially true of prospects who are still actively engaged in business pursuits. These are very busy people to whom time is precious. Often an indication to them of your seriousness is the way you use their time and yours.

If at all possible, place the call for an appointment yourself. Get the donor prospect on the line. After you complete the initial short niceties of polite conversation, say something like "John, Board Chair Lee Brown and I would like to come see you and Mary next Tuesday to talk about a major commitment to the 'Save Old

Main' campaign. Would you be available to talk with us at 10 a.m. in your office on that day?"

Major donor developments rarely occur when a solicitor "sneaks up" on the donor. Most donors know exactly what your purpose is and where your commitment lies. If they share your perspective, then at least half your job is already done. If not, the prospect is probably not yet ready for a major appeal.

The Vision

Shortly after the formalities of friendly conversation are completed, a person among the fund-raising group should paint a quick and succinct vision of the institution and what it is trying to accomplish. The successful fund raiser will use language that is poignant and real, yet sometimes emotional. He or she will portray a clear vision of what the institution will become and how it has already progressed because of the support of people like the prospect. Much of this depends on a leader already having articulated a vision for the institution; research on institutional presidents shows over and over again that the truly effective leader is a bit of a dreamer or missionary or visionary.

My own experience has confirmed what Jerold Panas found in his research about major donors: Those who are most likely to give are those who understand the institutional vision. This seems especially true at colleges and universities where people have a strong "identity of place." For many people, the college campus evokes some of the warmest memories of their lives. This is the place where many have met and courted their spouses, discovered their capabilities and truths about themselves, engaged in numerous good times, savored athletic triumphs, and developed lifelong friendships. Colleges and universities play a major role in calling all of us to a higher vision of ourselves.

The Ask Itself

Immediately after painting the picture of the institution's vision, the fund raiser needs to move directly to the purpose. It is at this point that many fund raising opportunities break down, due to the solicitor's own reluctance or ill preparation or unease with the cause.

The effective fund raiser proceeds immediately to the point at hand, using friendly, direct language, and a cordial but businesslike manner. "John and Mary, you know why we are here. One of the hospital's greatest needs is its proposed cardiology unit. You have been a part of the meetings where that need and the fund-raising plan were discussed. We would like for you to make a commitment of $2 million to that fund raising effort, which would be matched by other hospital donors to complete the $4 million campaign for cardiology."

At that point the solicitor must stop and wait. Most donors are fully capable of responding on their own. Numerous fund-raising calls fail because, after making the ask, the solicitor nervously continues to talk. You should simply be quiet and listen.

Donor responses can range all the way from a simple "yes" or "no" to "I'll think about it" to "I need to discuss this with my accountant" (or spouse, or lawyer, or business partner). Some donors have told me simply, "You guys are certainly not bashful."

Use real numbers as a part of your request—not only during the ask itself, but throughout the process. Rarely have I been questioned about the efficacy of the project or the fund-raising plan during the actual fund-raising call. Barring unseen or unusual difficulties, project costs can be approximated. Any figure should include a 10 percent to 15 percent contingency price above the total estimated cost.

Most successful campaigns can acquire 50 percent or more of the cost from a single source. Just as what used to be the 80-20 rule has become the 90-10 rule (90 percent of your funds will come from 10 percent of your supporters), so too has the oft-used rule of "30 percent in hand before a campaign is announced" moved near the 40 or 50 percent level.

In short, be direct. Use real numbers. Be able to justify the ask you are making. But leave the verdict to the donors. They serve as both judge and jury.

The Thank-you

Whatever the donors' response, I thank them for both their commitment to the institution or cause and their willingness to share their time with us. Nothing more is necessary. I don't thank them for considering the proposal. I don't thank them for their most recent gift. I don't acknowledge their long-standing relationship with the institution. Such niceties should have been handled previously. You are indebted to them on this day for two things:

their commitment to the institution, which got you there to begin with, and their most precious commodity, their time, which they have chosen to share with you.

While most such calls have a businesslike formality about them, I have found most to be cordial and encouraging relationship-building experiences to be savored, rather than traumatic experiences to be feared. Most donors have high regard for those of us who are trying to move a cause forward. This is all the more true if the donor is committed to the cause.

Follow-up

Follow-up is necessary regardless of the outcome of the direct meeting. Often too much time is left between the ask and the follow-up. I usually find about a week to ten days to be the outside limit. Follow-up can be as simple as a quick and cordial telephone call to the donors, to acknowledge once again their commitment and thank them, or to inquire how an accountant, spouse, or business associate reacted to the proposal. Does the prospect have any further questions about the material that we shared with him or her? If you promise additional information, provide it right away.

WHAT NOT TO DO

Those who are new to the field, as well as veterans, should remember a few "don'ts" on the solicitation process. These points may seem obvious, but they are important.

- *Don't stake the donor's relationship to the institution on this one ask.* Most people who do not respond favorably have legitimate, and often private, reasons for so doing. The fund raiser who says "John, we know that you voted for expansion of the engineering school at the last Board of Trustees meeting, and therefore knew you would want to back that up with a gift for the new building," is shopping for trouble. Most trustees know they are expected to give. While this donor may believe the university needs a new engineering school, and hence voted for it, his personal commitment might rather be to the fine arts or to some other need. Donor responses are often a judgment of priorities, not a test of anyone's commitment.

- *Don't overstate the case.* Most institutions will exist next week and next month whether the fund-raising call is successful or not. High-pressure sales techniques have no place in educational fund raising. The needs are real. The benefits are legitimate. Rarely, however, are we talking about life-and-death matters.

  One of my favorite stories tells of the college president who went on fund-raising calls among supporting churches, saying that if supporters did not "give this year" that the students would be cold and freezing in the dorms during the winter. Fifteen years and two presidents later, the new president tells me that when he returns to some of the same places, the first question he hears is, "Are you keeping those students warm in the dorms?" The need was compelling, but it was stated so strongly that fifteen years down the road, it undercut legitimate fund-raising efforts for the institution.

- *Don't win the battle and lose the war.* Both you and the donor will likely "live to ride again." Just as your best donor prospects are those who have given previously to the institution, so too are the best fund raisers those who can go to the same funding source time and again. Your approach, your manner, your ethics, and your sensitivity will be remembered long after the specific request is accepted or turned down.

All in all, almost no human experience is as exciting and exhilarating as a successful fund-raising call. This, however, grows out of many months or years of trust, respect, and relationship building. Techniques only become important when the solicitor has a healthy perspective of his or her role, is adequately prepared, and has watched carefully (if not managed) the donor prospect's relationship to the institution.

Part Five
The Campaign

The most visible educational fund-raising programs today are the major college and university campaigns. Once called "capital campaigns" because they focused primarily on raising funds for facilities projects, most campaigns today are "comprehensive," including annual, capital, and planned giving in their overall goals. The increasing size of campaign goals has led to the introduction of a new term, "mega-campaign." Goals in the hundreds of millions now are common, and a few universities have announced comprehensive campaign goals of $1 billion or more.

Mega-campaigns have become an issue in recent years, and some of the criticisms are discussed in the concluding section of this book. But the campaign model, developed early in the twentieth century and refined over the decades, remains one of the most effective and time-tested of fund-raising strategies.

Since the advent of the campaign, there have been those who argued against it, preferring an ongoing major gifts program as the way to raise the most dollars over the long run and to appropriately match philanthropic support with institutional needs. However, I believe that the overwhelming majority of fund-raising professionals think there is simply no better way for an institution to raise large amounts of money for defined purposes within a limited period of time.

In Chapter 13, William McGoldrick provides an overview of campaign principles and the campaign process from start to finish. This chapter will provide a valuable introduction to campaigns for development newcomers. But I think even seasoned professionals benefit from occasionally touching base with campaign basics. While creativity is important, this is one area where "sticking to the book" is almost always the best approach.

As George Brakeley points out in Chapter 14, colleges and universities use professional fund-raising consultants in a variety of situations. But it is in the campaign that the consultant's role is particularly important. Indeed, the role of the consultant in a campaign goes beyond merely giving advice; counsel often is an integral part of the entire process and a part of the campaign team along with the president, development staff, and volunteer leaders. As a consultant, Brakeley understandably makes the case for the use of counsel. The reader should bear in mind that there are negative aspects to use of professional counsel, including substantial expense.

As I said above, campaign goals have become a subject of controversy. Many of the points raised in the current debate about campaign goals echo the broad concerns expressed by Joel Smith a decade ago in his thoughtful and perceptive chapter, "Rethinking the Traditional Capital Campaign," in Pray's *Handbook for Educational Fund Raising*. Now a development consultant, Smith was vice president for development at Stanford University when he wrote this essay.

Smith's prediction of billion-dollar campaign goals has, of course, been fulfilled in the intervening decade. But the points raised in this seminal essay are as relevant today as they were in 1981. For this reason, Smith's essay is reprinted, with permission, as Chapter 15 of this book.

Chapter 13

Campaigning in the Nineties

William P. McGoldrick

Is there a college, university, or independent school in the United States or Canada that is not at this moment considering a major campaign, involved in a campaign, or completing a campaign? Probably not. On nearly every campus—be it an elite and wealthy Ivy League university, a small and struggling church-related independent school, a publicly supported land-grant university, or an urban community college—the idea of fund raising and the words "capital campaign" are ubiquitous.

Trustees hire presidents they think can lead campaigns. Presidents hire vice presidents with "campaign experience." Vice presidents call colleagues everywhere looking for a major gifts officer who can persuade wealthy donors to support Old Siwash. The campaign has become one of the most important programs on American and Canadian campuses and recently on campuses abroad, including Oxford and Cambridge.

In the 1950s, universities debated whether to begin campaigns. In the 1970s, they debated how often to begin campaigns. In the 1990s, they debate how large the campaign goal can be.

In that time, the campaign itself has undergone changes. The "capital" campaign of the early part of this century has been generally transformed into a "comprehensive" development campaign. The comprehensive campaign counts in its totals all gifts to the university. It often includes bequest expectancies and sometimes includes government support and other revenues from nongift sources.

Campaigns once were relatively short; today, they are planned to extend over five or more years. Once, campaign gifts were solicited by volunteers who were encouraged by a small staff on campus; today, large professional staffs are the primary major gift solicitors in many campaigns.

This chapter will help you understand the choices you must make before recommending plans for a major campaign to your institution's board of trustees. It outlines the phases through which every campaign passes, the roles of the people who can make it happen, and some specific issues you will need to address along the way.

WHAT IS A CAMPAIGN?

A campaign is an organized and intense effort to secure extraordinary gift commitments during a defined period of time to meet specific needs that are crucial to the mission and goals of an institution.

As discussed in Chapter 3, fund-raising efforts for American education started not long after the founding of Harvard in 1636. But the "campaign" as we know it today was born in the early 1900s when the YMCA movement introduced the concept of specific goals and fixed time limits for fund raising. The American Red Cross followed with campaign efforts during World War I that included the solicitation of corporate support.

Until after World War I, the solicitation of support for American higher education most often fell to the president alone. And while a few colleges and universities began organized efforts in the first half of this century, it was not until the 1950s that broad and massive efforts to support education emerged.

During the 1960s, Harvard completed an $82 million campaign and several other universities demonstrated that $100 million efforts could succeed. As the 1970s came to a close, Stanford University raised the stakes of campaigning with a successful $300 million program. And on February 10, 1987, Stanford's announcement of a $1.1 *billion*, five-year campaign ushered in the era of the mega-campaign.

Today, campaigns at even the smallest colleges and universities seek millions and tens of millions of dollars, while large institutions chase goals of hundreds of millions, even billions of dollars.

BEGINNING A CAMPAIGN

The financial threats to the American system of higher education—aging facilities, spiraling tuition, a declining population of college-aged students, the increasing demand for financial aid—have increased the pressure to secure philanthropic support. But pressure is what campaigns are about. They are not easy to plan. They are not easy to carry out. They are highly visible. And their progress is judged differently by various constituencies.

Like military campaigns, they involve leadership, planning, logistics, volunteers, execution, and persistence. The planning often takes months, even years, to complete. There are considerable risks associated with campaigning, and your institution must make the decision to move forward very carefully.

Six key tests will help you decide if your campus is ready to campaign. They are all vital to an informed decision. (It may be helpful to involve outside counsel in answering these questions. The use of counsel in a campaign is discussed in Chapter 14.)

1. *Does your institution have a clearly understood and easily recognized mission?* Is the mission written and widely shared with volunteers and donors? Donors want to be certain that they understand your university's role in society, how you differentiate your role from the role of other institutions, and what impact your institution has upon its constituents. This mission is the foundation for all the plans and goals you develop.

2. *Is there a written long-range plan?* The entire campus must understand and endorse your strategic plan. The plan should contain measurable milestones and present a clear vision of what your institution will look like when the plan is executed successfully. It must state the academic, financial, administrative, and admissions goals for your campus over at least a five-year period. It must demonstrate great aspirations centered on your mission. From this document will come the clear, concise, and compelling document we call a case statement.

3. *Is campus and volunteer leadership strong and capable?* The role of the president and the trustees in campaign success cannot be overstated. Campaign activities may require as much as 50 percent of the president's time. Is the president prepared to cultivate and solicit key donors? Does the president plan to remain in office through the completion of the campaign?

Are the trustees eager to begin a campaign? Do they understand the need for a campaign, and are they willing to commit their time to development activities? Are the trustees committed to their personal leadership roles and prepared to make generous financial contributions to the campaign?

Are there volunteer leaders who are ready to assume key campaign roles, including campaign chair and chairs of volunteer committees?

Without strong and dedicated leadership, a campaign cannot succeed. If you cannot honestly answer these questions in the affirmative, your institution is not ready to launch a campaign.

4. *Is there compelling urgency to campaign now?* As the internal planning and discussion of a campaign proceeds over several months, the campus begins to believe in the need and the urgency for greater resources. Too often, trustees and key volunteers are brought into this process far too late. The campus is off and running (or wants to be) and cannot understand why trustees, key volunteers, and top donors have not "bought in" to a major campaign.

The skill with which the president and the chief advancement officer inform and involve the volunteer leadership in the planning process will prepare them for the timely decision of campaign readiness.

5. *Are there potential donors?* More campaigns fail for lack of donors than for any other reason. That is not profound, but it is true.

Have you tested your market? A market survey, or feasibility study, is crucial to understanding the ability and willingness of donors to support your university. This study will help you set an aggressive but realistic campaign goal and will also help you understand which campus needs are perceived as attractive gift opportunities by donors.

6. *Are the elements of a campaign plan present?* With a strategic plan, an eager president, a committed board, an experienced staff, an aggressive campaign chair, a flashy case statement, and a ready list of potential donors, you're ready to go. Right? Wrong!

The chief advancement officer is responsible for the written campaign plan. This business plan sets timetables, outlines philosophical approaches, states campaign accounting rules, discusses the roles of each major campus and volunteer player, outlines the roles of public relations and alumni relations in the campaign, and covers the myriad details that enter into such a major effort. The outline for such a plan should be in place so that details can be incorporated during campaign planning discussions.

With these six questions answered, you and your campus leadership can decide if you are prepared to campaign. Since the entire university—strengths, weaknesses, people, and programs—is exposed to public scrutiny during a campaign, the risks are great. But the rewards can ensure the health of your institution for many years to come.

THE SIX PHASES OF A CAMPAIGN

While it is easy to oversimplify complex topics such as campaigning, it is also easy to overcomplicate them. Every campaign passes through six successive phases. While following the steps outlined here does not guarantee success, understanding the importance of each phase is essential to reaching your goal.

Phase 1: Pre-campaign Planning

Pre-campaign planning is that period during which the institution's officers develop a strategic plan, define needs and priorities, and test the feasibility of a campaign among important constituents. This period might last from six to eighteen months. In this time, the president and vice president must determine whether to recommend to the board that a campaign should commence.

During this phase, you and your team must:,

- complete the institutional strategic plan,
- define the institution's needs and priorities,
- complete a market survey (feasibility study),
- begin donor research and evaluation,
- define the campaign program and priorities,
- write a campaign rationale,
- enlist four to six key volunteers,
- determine the role of alumni relations staff in the campaign,
- involve public relations staff in writing a communications plan,

- develop gift tables,
- determine a rough budget and possible funding sources,
- determine the current base of gift support, and
- determine a possible campaign starting date.

You should not proceed to Phase 2 until all the elements of this phase are complete.

A few of these tasks deserve further discussion here. When determining the current base of support for the university, don't look just at last year's total giving or the highest total the university has achieved. To determine the true base of support, average the total giving to your institution over the last three to five years, after eliminating any extraordinary major gifts that greatly skew your totals.

Preparing the campaign rationale involves writing down succinctly why this campaign is needed for the university and why it is needed now. If you are not able to create a compelling case for urgent support, you are not ready to begin major gift discussions with your donors.

During this period, you must address campaign staffing and budget very directly. Can you execute the campaign with current staff or will you need additional staff? How will you pay for the campaign—out of the university's operating budget? from unrestricted gifts? from a tax on all gifts? To avoid great unhappiness later, solve these problems early.

Phase 2: Campaign Planning

Phase 2 is a short and relatively intense period of three to six months. During this time, you must build support with important opinion leaders on and off campus. During this phase, you and your team must:

- refine the analysis of needs and priorities,
- write the formal case statement,
- intensify research of the top 100 to 500 potential donors,
- write a detailed campaign plan,
- determine the goal of the nucleus fund, and
- prepare a smooth budget and determine the funding sources.

By this time, there is a real possibility that someone will want to jump the gun and "just start the campaign." Resist that temptation. Each planning step must be well-executed, and the president and volunteer leadership must possess confidence in the plan. Their enthusiasm will depend upon the confidence of success that a well-formulated plan provides.

Even as you prepare your plan, you will be working on another document essential to establishing the credibility of your campaign. This involves translating your institution's needs and aspirations into a clear concise statement of your objectives, relating those objectives directly to the campaign's monetary goals, and supporting the credibility of those goals with a realistic plan to succeed. The document that does this is the case statement.

Harold J. Seymour called the case statement "the one definitive piece of the whole campaign. It tells all that needs to be told, answers all the important questions, reviews the arguments for support, explains the proposed plan for raising the money, and shows how gifts may be made and who the people are who vouch for the project and will give it leadership and direction."[1]

Phase 3: The Nucleus Fund

Few campaigns are announced publicly before enlisting the commitment of several key donors who, by their statement of generous support, bring credibility to the campaign, its goals, and its leadership.

Nucleus donors are often well-recognized board members, alumni, and key major donors of long standing. Since these donors are usually the most knowledgeable and most involved in the university's life, their willingness to back the campaign is invaluable evidence of their belief in your cause, your plans, and your leadership. Such commitments, far more than verbal endorsements, demonstrate the generous financial commitment of the university's leadership.

This stage of "quiet" or "private" campaigning may take one to two years. Generally, when a campaign is publicly launched, the nucleus total is announced along with the names of the key donors and the purposes that their gifts will serve.

During this phase, you and your team must:

- enlist a cadre of volunteers,
- solicit the first gifts to the campaign,
- build campaign enthusiasm among volunteer leadership,

- begin to cultivate the next group of major donors,
- analyze success and recommend a campaign goal, and
- complete all targeted nucleus fund solicitations.

One purpose of the nucleus phase is to convince those most important major donors to make large commitments that will set the sights of other donors at a high level. With this start, you can then seek support from the next group of leadership donors. Years ago, I heard George Brakeley, Jr., former chair of the campaign consulting firm Brakeley, John Price Jones, refer to this process as "sequential fund raising." He meant that one should approach those capable of making the largest gifts early in the campaign and move through the list of potential donors to smaller gifts. This approach makes sense, because major donors often need the time to organize their affairs to make a large commitment and the flexibility to pay their commitment over time. Also, generous gifts tend to encourage others to give generously.

Because major donors, properly approached during this phase, may surprise you with gifts ten times, 100 times, or even 1,000 times greater than their previous largest gifts, it is worth being patient before announcing a public goal. Until now, you will have proceeded with a "working goal" for the campaign. Understanding the base of support your university has had historically, adding to that the gifts from successful nucleus fund solicitations, and analyzing the ability of your remaining donor pool, you are now able to intelligently recommend a public campaign goal. (Later in this chapter we will discuss how to set that goal.)

Phase 4: The Kickoff

Balloons, parties, and gala celebrations often accompany the announcement of a major campaign. It is important that all potential donors be aware that the campaign is under way and that they will be approached. The kickoff may be as short as a day or as long as a year, depending on whether you are planning one celebration on campus or a series of celebrations all across the country.

During this phase, you and your team must:

- announce the campaign goal and nucleus fund success,
- introduce the campaign volunteer leadership,
- present the case statement,

- demonstrate the president's clear leadership of the campaign,
- expand the volunteer base,
- continue to solicit the "critical few" donors who are able to make major gifts, and
- begin cultivation activities for the several hundred to several thousand donors who are able to support the campaign at levels below your "major gift" level.

Prolonging the enthusiasm of the kickoff with alumni events and publications is crucial to the ongoing credibility and success of the campaign. Success, in turn, will maintain enthusiasm. Staff and volunteers should thus be prepared and trained to solicit and close gifts early.

In this phase, you should still be focusing most of your energy and resources on the "critical few" prospects who are able to make major gifts. Once there was a rule that said 80 percent of the giving to a campaign came from 20 percent of the donors. Later the rule was amended to say that 90 percent of the giving came from 10 percent of the donors. Today, many universities find that 95 percent of the giving comes from 5 percent or fewer of the donors.

This is not surprising considering the immense goals of our campaigns and the distribution of wealth in America. Very, very few people can give $1 million to support our universities; fewer still can give $5 million or more. Yet more and more goals require gifts of $5 million, $10 million, or more to succeed.

The "critical few" capable of such gifts must receive the appropriate attention from the president and the campaign leadership early in the campaign. They need information germane to their interests and to the goals of the campaign, as well as the opportunity to learn how their support will make an important difference to the future of the institution.

Phase 5: The Plateau of Fatigue

Not everyone agrees with the name of this phase of the campaign. Some feel it is too negative and that the label becomes a self-fulfilling prophecy. But the experience of many veteran campaigners indicates that every campaign that stretches its goals and pushes its programs beyond "business as usual" eventually runs into problems.

At this stage, the enthusiasm of the kickoff has worn down. Donors are not responding enthusiastically to each solicitation. Volunteers are not completing their assignments as quickly as you suggested. And staff are more than a little frustrated by their inability to move their programs forward according to the wonderful plan the vice president wrote quite some time earlier.

Careful planning can help to minimize the negative effects of this phase of the campaign. This is the one- to three-year period of hard work that will ultimately determine whether the campaign succeeds in reaching all it goals and whether it heightens or lowers the morale of volunteers.

During this phase, you and your team must:

- continue the programs of cultivation and stewardship,
- continue the solicitation of leadership donors,
- begin the active solicitation of donors who were newly identified during the early phases of the campaign,
- assess the results of each program,
- adjust plans as you understand donor response to requests and new campus needs,
- overcome volunteer and staff burnout, and
- analyze cash flow.

Regional programs, discussed later in this chapter, are most apt to suffer the effects of fatigue because they are frequently used to target first-time major gift candidates—a difficult prospect group—and because they often employ volunteers who have little or no experience with major gift solicitations.

Development professionals must take positive steps to maintain the campaign's momentum. The mental toughness of the vice president, director of development, and staff will often determine the attitude of the president, volunteer leadership, and volunteers. Plan on activities to rebuild enthusiasm.

Phase 6: The Home Stretch

During the last twelve to eighteen months of the campaign, you will be able to demonstrate the successes achieved to date in the campaign. You will also have the opportunity to highlight goals that have not yet been achieved and to focus on their completion.

People give to winners. As your campaign begins to accomplish major objectives and you celebrate these achievements, people who have considered giving but have not yet made their commitment will step forward to be part of the success. Recognizing this phenomenon and planning to capitalize on it can help your campaign reach or exceed its goal.

During this phase, you and your team must:

- celebrate goal achievements,
- recognize the generosity of many donors,
- thank and honor volunteers,
- if appropriate, resolicit donors who are now ready to give again,
- communicate actively with all donors to thank them, and
- begin the strategic planning for post-campaign activities.

Recognition events for major donors are also cultivation events for donors who have not yet made commitments. Be certain that you pay close attention to a potential donor's reaction to the thanks you publicly offer to committed donors.

Resolicitation of donors is a very tricky process. Be certain that you carefully examine the donor's past giving, potential for support, and present attitude toward the campaign, the campaign leadership, and the unmet goals. Rarely do donors with outstanding payments due on pledges increase their commitment before completing their initial pledges. Donors who have completed their commitments should be examined carefully.

By this time, the president and vice president should already be discussing the plan for post-campaign development activities. When will the university be ready for its next campaign? When will the president be ready? The volunteers? The staff? The donors?

A new written plan should be in the works to avoid the post-campaign blues. Without careful planning, volunteers will move on to other causes, staff will move on to other jobs, and the program built so carefully will become shaky.

THE PEOPLE WHO MAKE IT HAPPEN

Although raising money is the object of every campaign, you must never lose sight of the fact that it is people who will achieve the goal. Campaign leaders must be thoroughly convinced of the importance of the campaign and be able to inspire others to adopt the cause. Staff and volunteers must know their contributions are important and feel their work is valued and appreciated. It takes many people, each fulfilling a specific role, to make a campaign successful.

The President

People give to people. And people make extraordinary gifts to leaders who convey great vision, aspirations, conviction, and the ability to succeed. The role of the president of the institution is central to the success of any campaign. No one will carry a greater burden of public responsibility.

Since the campaign is the outgrowth of strategic planning, this immense responsibility of the president makes sense. According to Edward T. Foote II, president of the University of Miami, "The campaign is the translation of a vision to the most demanding reality of all, money. The president is both the principal author of the vision and, as the university's chief advocate, the ultimate asker for big money."[2]

Today, presidents are being selected not only for scholarship, vision, and leadership, but also for their perceived ability to raise great sums of money. In March 1991, the *New York Times* announced the selection of Neil Rudenstein as president of Harvard; among the most important challenges enunciated for his administration was the launching of an expected $2 billion campaign.

The Vice President

The vice president is responsible for preparing the campaign strategy, executing campaign plans, and organizing the time and activities the president and trustees devote to the campaign.

The timely execution of the campaign plan is crucial to its success. This time-limited activity exemplifies the simple concept, "When you're ahead, you're ahead; when you're behind, you're behind." Once a campaign begins to lose momentum, it is very difficult to get it back on schedule.

The vice president is the conductor who sees that every player knows and carries out his or her part. The vice president directs the activities of the staff, the deans, the faculty, and the volunteers. In large campaigns, there are obviously many staff members, each performing specific assignments. But it is the vice president who is ultimately responsible to the president and to the board for all campaign logistics.

The Campaign Chair

The campaign chair is the role model for all other volunteers. This person will commit untold hours to working with the president, the vice president, and key volunteers. He or she will play a major role in articulating the importance of the campaign, in setting an example for personal giving, and for actively soliciting major donors.

Because people give to people who also give, the campaign chair and trustees will be called upon for leadership giving early in the campaign. Without their generous financial commitments, the campaign will falter quickly. Since people volunteer when they are asked by other volunteers, the campaign chair and key lieutenants will set the pace for volunteerism in the campaign. Their belief in campaign goals will inspire others. Their commitment of time to visit potential donors will encourage others to join them in this activity. Their oversight of campaign progress will require staff to remain aggressive in their daily activities.

Alumni and Public Relations

Those planning and executing major campaigns often fail to employ the advice and participation of alumni relations and public relations professionals. Their experience working with volunteers, publications, and the media can help you understand and communicate effectively with your constituents.

Involve your alumni relations and public relations leadership from the beginning and delegate to them the roles they must assume to make your campaign effective. Alumni officials can ensure appropriate alumni programming during the campaign and help you gain the personal support of alumni leaders. The PR staff can provide the publications and media relations support you need.

IMPORTANT STEPS

Some of the tasks mentioned above deserve additional discussion here. The way you go about these steps will affect the nature of the entire campaign.

Setting the Campaign Goal

The campaign goal is often a matter of considerable debate on campus and among volunteers. Some people advocate goals based upon need alone. Others believe that whatever goal the president desires is right. Some feel a modest goal will ensure success. Others point out that low expectations will never produce great accomplishments. And some may believe that campaign goals are determined by local psychics or on a Ouija board. But only accurate information and sound advice will help you determine your campaign goal.

In setting the goal, institutional decision-makers should consider the priority needs of the university, the identified potential of prospective donors, the institution's past experience in development, and the effectiveness of your campaign plan. As mentioned earlier, a feasibility study will provide additional information about the reaction of important donors to proposed campaign objectives.

While it is dangerous to use mathematical formulas to set campaign goals, it is highly unlikely that a college raising $1 million per year will be successful in a $50 million campaign. A random look at several recent comprehensive campaigns indicates that goals of eight to ten times the most recent year's total are common. As goals get larger, the length of campaigns typically extends to five years or more, and accounting periods for receiving payments often extend beyond ten years.

By postponing announcement of the official goal until well into the nucleus phase of the campaign, you will be able to make a more informed decision based on the total raised during the nucleus phase, the number of identified donors "used" to reach that total, and the number and potential of donors remaining in the major gift pool. If more than half of the known potential major gift donors have made commitments and the total of their gifts reaches only 30 percent of the hoped-for goal of the campaign, that goal is probably unrealistic. Conversely, if only 10 percent of the known potential major givers are committed and their gifts total 75 percent of the planned goal, the goal is too conservative.

From 30 to 40 percent of your goal should be accumulated during the nucleus phase of your campaign. The thinking is that most of your most important donors will make commitments during this period and their gifts will often be among your largest. If your nucleus total is considerably less that 30 percent, examine your goal carefully before proceeding.

Keep in mind that these rules are poetry, not science. Nevertheless, they are based on experience and should help you calibrate your campaign goal.

Setting the Campaign Budget

Like every other budget, the campaign budget is a political as well as a practical issue. Certainly the budget determines how much is available to be spent for each particular campaign purpose. It also is a statement of the confidence of the institution in the campaign director's personal leadership and professional credibility.

There is no recipe for what a campaign should cost. It will greatly depend on your own circumstances. Is this your institution's first campaign? Can you depend on having a substantial volunteer effort? If your ongoing development program already possesses a reasonable budget, the incremental amount needed for a campaign may be a very small percentage of the campaign goal.

In a recent study of sixty-five universities, total development costs averaged 16 cents per dollar raised. The report cautioned, however, that such a figure, taken alone, may badly mislead, and that costs reflect the unique characteristics of each institution.[3]

Develop your budget in considerable detail. Document your assumptions and your budget needs thoroughly. Share it widely with other institutional officers and encourage their suggestions and questions. Account for your spending regularly. Remember, you will develop the budget; you will be responsible for its use.

Conducting Regional Campaigns

Most comprehensive campaigns are a combination of many smaller campaigns. Sometimes these campaigns are organized around specific purposes. Sometimes they are organized by alumni classes and incorporate reunion giving. But often they are organized geographically, as a practical means of reaching hundreds or thousands of potential donors.

The regional campaign is a brief, intense microcosm of the overall campaign executed on a local basis, with local leadership, local volunteers, and a local goal. Events to kick off and to support regional campaigns provide momentum and importance. Solicitation of attendees should begin rapidly following such events to capitalize on their effect.

Such campaigns succeed best when they are completed within three to six months. If a region is large enough to necessitate a longer campaign, it may be wise to divide the region into smaller areas that can be managed more quickly.

The relatively swift nature of these efforts enables volunteers to accomplish their tasks efficiently, permits many rapid successes for the campaign, and maintains a sense of momentum for the greater campaign effort. When regional campaigns founder, however, morale deteriorates, momentum is lost, and the fatigue of campaigning overwhelms volunteers and professionals alike.[4]

CONCLUSION

The campaign will be under as great a pressure to change during the last decade of this century as it was during the first decade. Some critics say that mega-campaigns have focused our efforts on how many dollars we seek rather than the purposes for which we seek funds, that billion-dollar goals cause even million-dollar donors to question the impact of their support, and that annual fund donors feel lost among the hoopla we create for major donors.

Our imagination and our skill as professionals will be tested during the 1990s, which have begun with a far less optimistic economic environment than did the 1980s. As professional advancement officers, we must provide optimism and confidence, reality and pragmatism. We are often the source of our donors' imagination and vision and our volunteers' energy and enthusiasm. We will be the architects of a new era of campaigning.

Education's need for philanthropic support will not diminish. Our challenge will be to understand and react to the changes required and to lead our institutions to success.

NOTES

1. Harold J. Seymour, *Designs for Fund-raising* (New York: McGraw-Hill, 1966), 42-43. Other excellent discussions of the case statement can be found in Richard D. Chamberlain's chapter in *The Successful Capital Campaign: From Planning to Victory Celebration*, ed. H. Gerald Quigg (Washington, D.C.: Council for Advancement and Support of Education, 1986) and in Kent Dove's *Conducting A Successful Capital Campaign* (San Francisco: Jossey-Bass, 1988).

2. Edward T. Foote II, "The President's Role in a Capital Campaign," in *The Successful Capital Campaign*, ed. Quigg, 73.

3. Council for Advancement and Support of Education and National Association of College and University Business Officers, *Expenditures in Fund Raising, Alumni Relations, and other Constituent (Public) Relations* (Washington, D.C.: Council for Advancement and Support of Education, 1990).

4. Kent E. Dove's *Conducting A Successful Capital Campaign* contains an excellent plan for regional campaigning.

Chapter 14

The Use of Fund-raising Counsel from Counsel's Perspective

George A. Brakeley III

America is overflowing with human needs. Our population is growing, along with illiteracy, drug use, poverty, crime. At the same time, nonprofits of all types are suffering from tightened budgets, reductions in funding, disincentives for charitable gifts, and unprecedented competition for the philanthropic dollar.

The result is a collision between harder-to-get dollars on the one hand and increasing needs on the other. Nonprofits, including colleges and universities, are caught in the unfortunate middle—and are feeling the impact.

A fiscal squeeze such as this means either havoc or haven for fund-raising consultants, who find themselves sometimes sought out and sometimes cut out. Yet counsel exists primarily for times like these: times that require knowing what to do and what not to do; times that require strategy, creative solutions, and the synergy of good ideas.

If your institution is seeking out, not ruling out, professional counsel, be assured that this does not signify inadequacy or incompetency on your part. One might think that the primary market for counsel would be neophyte professionals or fledgling development operations, but not so. Instead, it is the more seasoned and sophisticated development professionals—not the least—who most appreciate the value of an objective, outside view. It is they who see the need for breadth of comparable experience from which to develop astute strategies.

And experienced professionals are not intimidated by counsel. As my colleague Robert Roche has written:

Insecure people and departments are not generally interested in having us around. The development officer whose continued employment and influence depend (in his opinion) on building and maintaining an image of personal infallibility is not likely to invite a consultant within his walls. Presumably the fear of being shown up, or wanting in some respect, outweighs the expectation that something of value might be imparted that would add additional luster to his activities.[1]

THE CLIENT/COUNSEL RELATIONSHIP

Let's assume that you are about to make formal inquiries into retaining counsel. Perhaps your first question is, "What exactly are we getting into? How does this client/counsel partnership actually work?"

For openers, it helps to clarify the *purpose* of counsel. A consultant's role is quite different from that of people who run day-to-day operations. I like to think of counsel's purpose as twofold: The consultant is *active* in offering new ideas and suggesting new initiatives, and *reactive* in observing, listening, analyzing, and responding to the circumstances of the moment.

The client/counsel relationship is most effective when:

- *It is, in fact, a partnership joining "insiders" and "outsiders" to blend the best of what each has to give.* A primary role of counsel is to introduce the "outside viewpoint" to internal problems and decisions. This includes reacting objectively to the performance of volunteer leadership, supporting institutional staff and the overall fund-raising operation, and providing some measure of assessment of new ideas— as well as generating some of those ideas.
- *It includes counsel throughout the process.* This means in planning and formulating policies, strategies, and procedures, and, later, in coordinating and implementing those plans.
- *It allows counsel to tread where staff may (rightfully) fear to go.* Counsel can be forthright and candid at all levels—from the trustees down—and can prod leadership in ways that in-house staff cannot.
- *It maximizes the use of counsel in planning strategies for principal gift prospects.* Counsel can be an enormous help in identifying new donor prospects—or, as is often the case, in providing new perspectives or new information about prospects already known to the institution. Solicitation strategy is probably the most valuable by-product of any client/counsel relationship.

WHEN COUNSEL CAN HELP

An institution might turn to counsel at almost any time. Most typically, however, this occurs at one of three junctures: before a comprehensive campaign, during a campaign, or between campaigns.

Counsel is not necessarily synonymous with campaigns; sometimes an institution can benefit from an objective evaluation of its ongoing development operations. Counsel is often retained for short-term or part-time assistance in such areas as direct mail, computer applications, annual giving, long-term planning, and planned giving—as well as periodic consulting to assist in enhancing development programs more broadly.

Before a Campaign

Often an institution seeks counsel when it is thinking about beginning a campaign or when it wants to find out whether it can, in fact, expect success in such a venture. A normal practice is to retain counsel to assist in institutional strategic planning and get the institution up to speed for a formal pre-campaign feasibility study. Campaign planners rely upon such a study in much the same way a surgeon relies upon X rays; both are diagnostic tools. Feasibility studies can also be undertaken to assess the practicality of short-term projects or programs.

In effect, the study is the client's insurance policy against misguided and unplanned action. Although its primary focus is usually the feasibility of the envisioned campaign, it also assesses the total fund-raising environment. The process yields an evaluation, not just of the proposed campaign, but also of the other operations associated with the institution's fund-raising function—such areas as alumni or community relations, annual giving, public relations, publicity, and publications.

During a Campaign

An institution may turn to counsel after it has decided to embark on a campaign—either because the effort is beyond the capacity of its in-house operation, or because institutional leaders feel that the institution and the campaign would benefit from the perspective of an objective third party. This is no reflection on the quality of the development staff; more accurately, it reflects the need for extraordinary attention to achieving such ambitious goals.

The results of the feasibility study should help determine the role counsel should play during the campaign itself. Different consultants provide different types of service, and a full-service consulting firm may offer any of several consulting arrangements during a campaign.

At one end of the spectrum is part-time consulting, perhaps arranged for as little as two or three days per month. The consultant serves as observer, sounding board, reviewer of policy and strategy, and the like.

At the other end is full-time resident management, which may take one of several configurations. Resident management might provide everything from A to Z in a self-sufficient operation that does not rely on the institution's own staffing resources. It might complement in-house staff, working with and through existing development staffers rather than independently. Or it might take the form of a resident counselor, whose purpose is to develop a trained campaign staff and campaign plans, procedures, and policies, but who is not responsible for managing the campaign on a day-to-day basis.

Other variations include half-time management or even "on-call" arrangements for occasional consulting on selected or perplexing questions.

Between Campaigns

Whether a campaign is the institution's first or fourteenth, it is likely to enjoy some spectacular successes as well as suffer some notable failures and frustrations. Through the post-campaign audit, counsel can provide an objective evaluation of the campaign to identify both ends of the spectrum, determine how they came about, and recommend actions to address the questions left unanswered.

Counsel also can—and ought to—participate in the planning of the *next* campaign, whether it is five or ten years down the road, capitalizing on the lessons learned and the building blocks created during the just-completed campaign.

Finally, counsel can help the institution address its ongoing development, alumni relations, and other constituency-related activities and programs. Often, there is a role for counsel even if the institution is not considering a campaign in the foreseeable future. Many times, the institution has only short-term, special-project needs. Examples of work that can be subcontracted include long-range planning, audits of development departments, executive searches, annual giving planning, direct mail programs, planned giving counseling, development of written materials, design of computer applications for fund raising, and prospect research.

ADVANTAGES OF COUNSEL

Many institutional officials are hesitant about retaining counsel. Most of their concerns are not valid, however. One misconception appears in the oft-heard statement, "We're unique—a consultant could not possibly understand us." Good consultants are chameleons; they are skilled at becoming one with the institution in a hurry. Besides, a consultant who is truly "just like us" may lack objectivity, which is one important quality for which the client is paying.

Another common—but unfounded—fear is that institutional memory will leave when the consultant leaves. Good consultants document their activities and seek other ways to transfer relationships and information over to in-house staff. Their fundamental mission is to work themselves out of a job by bringing staff along as fast as possible to the point of running the campaign without help. Also, conscientious counselors remain available to the institution for occasional advice long after the relationship has formally ended.

Some institutions simply do not want advice that disagrees with what they have already decided to do. Such institutions view retaining a consultant as merely an insurance policy; the consultant's assignment, implicitly or explicitly, is only to validate the undertaking and not to rock the boat, even gently. The ethical consultant faces a dilemma in such instances, and I believe the institution is best served in the long run by the consultant's taking a strongly proactive stance, even if this puts the relationship at risk.

On the other hand are the horror stories of not using counsel. For instance, it is not at all uncommon for an institution to set a campaign goal that reflects its funding needs, with no reference whatsoever to the philanthropic marketplace. The error is often compounded by a refusal to invest in a precampaign feasibilty study or by total lack of interest in retaining a consultant who might bring some reality to the situation. The result is a campaign that is doomed to failure.

There can be down sides to using a consultant. One obvious concern is the cost. Another is the fact that many experienced professionals are now available who could be brought onto the full-time staff.

But used intelligently, counsel can be a cost-effective alternative to permanent staff additions. Counsel can provide campaign staff for a precise amount of time and in the precise areas of expertise required. This custom-tailored approach enables the client to avoid the costs of hiring, training, and providing benefits. It also accelerates the fund-raising effort by eliminating the need to suffer through a learning curve that can be expensive both in terms of dollars and of lost credibility and momentum. And counsel also acts as a catalyst; the mere presence of a consultant automatically imparts a certain sense of urgency.

In addition, counsel has the advantage of being able to provide a level of objectivity that cannot be found internally. Starting as early as the feasibility study, counsel tends to hear things that people inside the institution have not been told. In interviews, counsel can draw out how people really feel (as opposed to how the client thinks or assumes they may feel). A consultant's objectivity also ensures that the institution's "case" is conveyed in language free of the internal jargon that is meaningless to prospects outside the institution.

Last but not least, counsel can provide "instant expertise." The experience of counsel is based on a variety of campaigns. That breadth is helpful in keeping progress on course while avoiding pitfalls along the way. Through counsel, the client acquires that cumulative experience. This equates to high-caliber advice on such matters as timing, techniques, prospects, trends in philanthropy, and the mechanics of running effective development operations.

HOW TO CHOOSE A CONSULTANT

The process of selecting counsel from a vast array can be daunting. One must not lose sight of the top priority: rapport.

A colleague of mine has the most peculiar way of asking for my time. She peeks into my office and says, "I need access to your brain." That concept—access to a brain—fairly sums up what I consider to be the ideal client/counsel relationship. It is a *dialogue* based on trust in one another; it is the *meeting* of minds; it is a *partnership* that provides the institution with the extra hands and extra brains it needs to achieve ambitious fund-raising goals.

If indeed the ideal client/counsel relationship is a partnership, then chemistry, or rapport, is essential to success. There needs to be mutual respect, mutual trust, and the ability to sit down together and figure out challenging and puzzling situations.

There is probably no test for rapport other than listening to your own insides. But your institution will benefit if you ask at least a few tangible questions of the firms you are considering. For example:

- How many campaigns of this nature (or projects of this type) has the firm handled in the last five years?
- Of those, were there any in which the goal was not achieved?
- What has the firm done in situations similar to ours?
- How long will all this take?
- How much will all this cost?
- What about travel and other costs? How can we control those?
- Can the firm provide appropriate references?

The interviews should produce a clear idea as to the level of competence and costs—and an effective means of comparing candidate firms. Your goal is to select the consultant who will best understand and mesh with your constituents, who will be the most flexible in responding to change as the effort develops, and who will provide the candor and forthrightness required for an effective client/counsel partnership.

There is much more to the process of choosing counsel—so much more that my late colleague Arthur Raybin wrote an entire book on the subject.[2] Suffice it to say that this one chapter can treat the subject only in summary.

Most consulting services are provided on a fixed-fee basis, in accordance with the Fair Practice Code of the American Association of Fund-Raising Counsel, Inc. Fees are generally based on the level of professional requirements involved, without relation to the financial goal of the campaign or project. This ensures that the long-range interests of the institution will be protected, with strategy based on what is best for the institution rather than on what will make the biggest impact on the consultant's bottom line.

THE PROFESSIONAL'S PROFESSIONAL

In whatever form counsel is retained, its purpose is essentially the same: to augment the in-house fund-raising team and to serve its members in virtually every conceivable capacity—as sounding board, change agent, checkpoint, amateur psychiatrist, catalyst, orchestrator, even gadfly. The best consultant is perhaps characterized by certain telling traits—echoed by similar characteristics on the part of the client.

The best consultant . . .	*The best client . . .*
Is unquestionably experienced in fund raising	Has a good program, is confident, and does not fear counsel
Is action-oriented	Places high priority on fund raising
Is a creative strategist	Institutes sound planning
Is an accomplished manager	Employs capable staff
Efficiently uses own time and that of others	Helps the institution focus on fund raising
Is a good arbiter	Listens to and acts on professional advice
Has excellent judgment	Has institutional integrity
Has high-level contacts	Demonstrates gratitude to volunteers and donors
Is fast of foot and mind	Is fast of foot and mind
Brings fun to fund raising	Has fun with fund raising

NOTES

1. Robert P. Roche, writing in Maurice G. Gurin's *What Volunteers Should Know for Successful Fund Raising* (New York: Stein and Day, 1981), 141.

2. Arthur D. Raybin, *How to Hire the Right Fund-raising Consultant* (Washington, D.C.: The Taft Group, 1985).

Chapter 15

Rethinking the Traditional Capital Campaign

Joel P. Smith

For the past three decades, capital campaigns have been the centerpieces of most college fund-raising programs. By *capital campaigns* I mean concentrated, full-throttled efforts to achieve predetermined dollar goals for a variety of purposes during a specified period of time. According to the conventional wisdom, these campaigns are exceedingly valuable. Indeed, that view is so widely accepted that success in fund raising, more often than not, is measured by the frequency and magnitude with which colleges undertake capital campaigns—and meet their goals.

I have grown skeptical of that conventional wisdom. It is not that I have concluded that all campaigns are a mistake—distinctly not. But increasingly I question their universal utility as a fund-raising technique, and my purpose here is to raise some new questions about what they are intended to accomplish and the extent to which they succeed.

CAPITAL CAMPAIGNS IN CONTEXT

En route to examining the arguments for and against capital campaigns, it will be helpful to review some basic points about the nature and character of fund raising itself, particularly its purposes and limitations.

The first point, obvious but nonetheless important, is that fund raising is more art than science and is likely to remain so. No matter how hard we try to be analytical and systematic, we cannot gainsay the fact that ours is a profession based on transactions among human beings; for that reason, among others, it is impossible to subject the basic causal relationships in fund raising to

Reprinted with permission from *Handbook for Educational Fund Raising*, ed. Francis C. Pray (San Francisco: Jossey-Bass, 1981).

rational analysis. In the case of many large gifts, for example, the gestation period takes years and the causal chains are intricate. Almost always they include some factors that we cannot know or do not understand and others that, although we may perceive them more or less clearly, we cannot influence. Even with relatively small gifts, such as those that constitute annual giving, the motivations of donors are much too diverse to permit us to be certain that one kind of appeal is better than another. Because we are uncertain about which causes bring about which results, it is difficult to be systematic.

Another fundamental point in the art-science equation is that fund raising is charged with emotion. That is not to deny that there are rational components in the decisions donors make but rather to say that almost always powerful emotional factors are also involved—so powerful that almost every major gift transaction is *sui generis*. Very few generalizations about them will stand up, either in describing what occurred or in predicting what might happen.

Finally, not only are the gifts of donors voluntary but so too are the commitments of the volunteers, who are vital to fund-raising programs. Their relationships with the institutions they care about are not employment relationships; they are based, rather, on allegiance and enthusiasm, and it follows that they lack the structure and discipline inherent in the relationships between employers and employees. I do not mean to criticize volunteers. It would be naive to underestimate the importance of volunteers to the success of an ambitious fund-raising program, but it would also be naive not to understand that with voluntary activity there are delays and lapses to cope with. More often than not, such problems must be handled artfully rather than authoritatively. With volunteers we must encourage and inspire, but rarely may we direct and instruct. That is yet another reason, returning to the art-science equation, why it is difficult to be systematic.

THE STATE OF THE PROFESSION

Having stated that fund raising has to be more art than science and believing that to be a very basic observation, I must nonetheless confess to disappointment in precisely those terms about the current state of our profession. Within the limitations I have stipulated for rigor and system, I think there is much too little emphasis today on those elements. Although the causal relationships are often dimly perceived, it does not follow that we cannot see them at all; it also does not follow that because fund-raising transactions involve emotion, reason has no role to play. And even though many crucially important relationships with individuals beyond our institutions are voluntary, that fact does not negate the importance of planning and self-discipline by measuring our accomplishments according to well-considered schedules and objectives; indeed, it makes those measurements all the more important.

Fund raising will more successfully serve our institutions only when we fund raisers perceive more clearly that sustained success depends on penetrating some of these limits: (1) making increasingly informed judgments about causes and effects, so that we may plan better; (2) realizing that donors' decisions can often be significantly influenced by reasoned argument based on an understanding of institutional need; and (3) recognizing that the contribution of volunteers depends largely on the ability of staff to find ways that enhance the probability that volunteers will be successful and, in the process, will derive greater enjoyment and satisfaction from what they are doing.

IMPROVING THE STATE OF THE PROFESSION

Now, more than ever, it is lamentable that fund raising is not as advanced as we would wish, because increased gift support is essential to the quality of most colleges and to the survival of some. What would make the profession better? What would permit colleges to be more confident that their return on the investment they make in fund raising will provide a margin of support that will truly make a difference during this difficult period? How can we calculate more confidently what it makes sense to do and not to do and determine which strategies are sound and which are wishful thinking?

There are many answers to these questions, I am sure, but two themes among them, in my judgment, are overwhelmingly important: The first is the need for greater professionalism among fund raisers; the second is the need to do a much better job of identifying institutional needs and then translating those needs into fund-raising objectives. The two, of course, are inextricably intertwined.

When I say that we need to be more professional, what I mean most of all is that we need to get beyond the excessive reliance on emotional allegiances and a faith in happy accidents that unfortunately characterize many fund-raising programs. Professionalism demands mastery of a body of knowledge, such as the tax aspects of charitable giving and the general principles of institutional as well as individual finance, which permits fund raisers to provide sophisticated assistance to donors and their counselors. And perforce it includes respect for the tenets and values of academic life, as well as thorough knowledge of the history and character and aspirations of the institutions we represent. Without that knowledge and without a truly profound understanding of our institutions, sophisticated fund raising, worthy of being called professional, is virtually impossible.

Professionalism also places a premium on some particular personal talents and attributes. For example, it requires determination as well as patience, for there is always much to be discouraged by in fund raising, just as there is always much to be in a hurry about. To blend determination with patience is not easy, but that blend is almost always present in outstanding fund raisers. They are able to live comfortably and work creatively with a dilemma that is at the center of fund raising: The two most frequent errors are to ask too hastily and to fail to ask at all.

With an appropriate emphasis on that knowledge and those personal attributes, our profession would have higher standards, and we, as individual fund raisers, would have a more solid claim to professional respect. Ironically, the emergence of professionalism has, perhaps more than any other single factor, promoted mobility, and fund raisers are too mobile. Fund raising is now more dependent on code and craft and less on personal enthusiasm for a particular institution. But we must be careful: Code and craft are crucial but so too is a deep, personal understanding of the people who care about a particular place. No short course can provide such understanding. It is acquired only over time.

THE INSTITUTIONAL AGENDA

Defining institutional needs and translating them into specific and readily understood fund-raising objectives seems a simple enough proposition, at least in the sense that it states an obviously desirable objective. But the simplicity is deceptive, for few places have this kind of agenda. This failure is not primarily the fault of fund raisers. It is the consequence of the extraordinary complexity of the decision-making process in academic institutions, which so disproportionately favors participation over authority and therefore so conspicuously features discussion rather than decisiveness. But whose fault it is, or, indeed, whether fault ought to be ascribed, is largely beside the point. What matters is that most academic institutions do not have an institutional agenda, and without it, fund raising is destined to be more random than rational—an amateurish activity around which serendipitous events will occasionally occur, but by which they are rarely caused.

Is my judgment too harsh? After all, in almost every college hundreds and hundreds of hours are committed to long-range planning every year. However, the product of those exercises, when there is a product, is commonly a statement of aspiration, which is not what I mean by an institutional agenda. What I have in mind begins with aspiration—with vision and hope and dreams—but it goes way beyond those to include: (1) reducing aspirations to needs, and translating those needs into fund-raising objectives; (2) ranking those objectives in their relative order of importance so that the many people who participate in fund raising at a particular place understand its priorities; and, crucially, (3) grounding the entire process in financial reality—that is, facing the fact that dollars raised ought to be an integral part of the institution's financial plan rather than something unplanned and therefore extra.

My prescription is a tall order, but there is no alternative if we want fund raising to make a major difference to our institutions, for it is possible to serve the most important institutional objectives only if those objectives are understood. That means, in turn, that some gifts are more important than others; in fact, there is rather dramatic differential utility among gifts. An institutional agenda is the *sine qua non* of a strong fund-raising program because without it we cannot make intelligent judgments about relative utility.

Fund raisers cannot formulate the institutional agenda, which is properly the responsibility of trustees, faculty-student committees, and preeminently the president and senior academic officers. But fund raisers can urge to the point of insistence that it be done, and in that urging they are armed with the unassailable argument that fund raising without an agenda will necessarily be less than it otherwise could be.

There is something else fund raisers can do. They can discourage the notion that the success of a fund-raising program ought to be judged by a big number on the bottom line. That fascination with larger and larger numbers is shortsighted and superficial; it ignores the entire subject of utility. How regrettable it is, then, that so many fund raisers and the institutional leaders who employ them are preoccupied by big numbers instead of promoting an understanding of which gifts are the most useful, which the least, and what is the approximate order of the many that fall between those extremes.

CAPITAL CAMPAIGNS

Given those observations about fund raising in general, what about capital campaigns? The conventional wisdom about capital campaigns is that they are virtually essential in a successful program, a conclusion based on this set of propositions:

- Campaigns are a valuable discipline. Within the institution, they force attention to institutional planning; beyond the institution, they provide the impetus for strengthening the organization of volunteers by imposing systems, objectives, and deadlines.
- Campaigns challenge donors to make larger commitments than would happen in the ordinary course—in order, in part, to be involved in the larger cause and, when successful, in the larger victory.
- Campaigns have a longer-term effect. They raise standards of giving during the period of intense activity and have a follow-through effect so that regular donors tend to give at higher levels following a campaign.
- Campaigns provide valuable experience for staff members. The intensity and variety of activity at least encourages and perhaps even forces professional development, which, as with higher standards of giving, has beneficial consequences long after the campaign is completed.
- Finally, it is widely assumed that the enthusiasm and momentum of a campaign make it possible to set and to meet goals that could not otherwise be accomplished. This arrangement recognizes that the spiritual aspects of fund

raising are more than a little important, and it claims that the esprit of a campaign—its enthusiasm and sense of urgency—creates a dynamic that takes the program further than would otherwise be possible.

Each of these claims has some merit, and, taken together, they accumulate as a rather persuasive case. The most significant point, I believe, is the impact of campaigns on volunteers, in terms not just of esprit but also of providing structure and discipline, so that during these periods, when there are plans, schedules, and meetings, there is an opportunity to manage by objective, which, as I view human activity, is usually the preferred managerial method.

I think it is important to challenge the conventional wisdom, not because I am certain that it is wrong but rather because I believe there are increasingly persuasive reasons to be skeptical. These reasons derive principally from the two areas needing improvement that I discussed earlier: greater professionalism and a better understanding of utility. It is not at all obvious that capital campaigns always, or even often, promote these objectives.

First, consider professionalism. It is true that a few institutions entering campaigns with relatively strong staffs have been able to increase their professional competence during those efforts, but for most places that is not true. On the contrary, most institutions, because they do not know how to undertake a campaign or lack the requisite confidence to get it done, turn to consultants and not infrequently to short-term hired hands. That approach is understandable; moreover, there are many able and honorable people who serve colleges well in those capacities. The point, however, is that reliance on outsiders more often than not reduces the probability of professional growth within the institution, and instead of coming out of a campaign with a stronger staff, some places actually lose ground.

Another reason why campaigns tend to discourage professional fund raising is that they are inherently episodic, whereas sophisticated fund raising is patient, subtle, and sustained. It is not that campaigns force individuals to cut corners, in the sense of doing dishonorable things, but rather that they force them to hurry, to claim present commitments at the expense of the longer view, so that, again and again, the emphasis is on large numbers—large numbers now. If that is the standard by which fund raising is judged, it is not at all likely that professionalism can be effectively nourished. The probable result, instead, is haste and waste, a lot of relatively indiscriminate activity that may produce apparently impressive results. But when such results are more carefully analyzed, they can be soberly disappointing.

Campaigns also encourage neglect of the all-important subject of utility. This point may seem contradictory, for one of the most popular claims on behalf of campaigns is that they force attention to institutional priorities, which ought to be acknowledged as valuable even if not undertaken in the name of utility. In most campaigns, utility gets short shrift.

It is true that planning committees are commissioned and case statements are prepared, so that many campaigns create the appearance of an institutional agenda. However, the difference between appearance and reality is disturbing. What the committees tend to decide (often, to be sure, with much thought and imagination) is what it would be desirable to have. They formulate an institutional wish-list, commonly prefaced by a suitably platitudinous discussion of institutional merits and needs in the context of institutional history and nostalgia. And the entire exercise is significantly influenced by preoccupation with big numbers.

Such a statement is not an institutional agenda. The agenda will emerge only from a much tighter process, disciplined by trading off the relative importance of programmatic objectives and permeated by rigorous financial planning. Without that discipline, hard choices are too easily avoided, and fund raisers pursue additional and often cosmetic objectives, rather than the basic institutional needs. As a result, the most that fund raising does in those situations is to provide occasional symptomatic relief rather than a continuing contribution to fundamental health.

Evidence that the preparation for campaigns is often insufficient is seen in the frequency with which they are permitted severely to damage well-developed annual giving programs. Unrestricted funds, which come predominately from annual support, have the highest utility of all gifts, by definition. It is, therefore, a bad bargain for a college to trade significant sums of unrestricted annual support for larger amounts of restricted support, unless that restricted support is designated for fundamentally important purposes, which rarely happens.

What capital are we talking about when we refer to capital campaigns? When the idea of campaigns became popular in the late 1950s and early 1960s, many colleges were expanding, and the capital they sought was primarily for facilities—not for endowment, which provides support for faculty salaries, scholarships, libraries, and other basic objectives. Today those proportions are dramatically different. Many colleges need to renovate or replace facilities, but few are building extensively; and almost all ought to be concerned about strengthening their endowments, provided that gifts for endowment, if restricted, are restricted to basic purposes. However, fund raising for endowment is a subtle business. This is particularly true for larger gifts; when they are sought with an appropriate concern about utility, subtlety and sophistication are required—in short, the key components of professionalism. I am not arguing that campaigns automatically cancel the possibility of that kind of subtle and sophisticated fund raising, but I am suggesting that, primarily because of the emphasis on haste and the preoccupation with big numbers, they all too frequently promote it.

Another serious concern about campaigns derives from what happens at their conclusion. When they end there is usually a respite—a respite, it is argued, that has been earned by the extraordinary effort of the campaign and, in any event, is required because a campaign necessarily exhausts the system by claiming virtually all available gifts and by demanding so much of volunteers. That decision to wind down for a while is usually a mistake. In a campaign of any duration, some donors and volunteers exhaust their resources as well as themselves to the point that they deserve to be left alone for the nonce. But many others during the campaign begin to develop or expand their interest in the institution, both as donors and as volunteers, and it is regrettable if the campaign's conclusion means that those new allegiances are neglected and that the opportunities they represent are forfeited.

One of the trade-offs, therefore, in a campaign followed by a respite is that between the discipline which forces as many gifts as possible within the specified period of time, and the loss of attention to those individuals and those transactions which, for any number of reasons, may not fit into the prescribed period. Increasingly, I suspect that we overrate the benefit of the discipline and worry too little about the lost opportunities. However, if activity is to be sustained at an intense level, then a strong professional competence within the institution is imperative because there will almost certainly be some fatigue and many changes among volunteer leaders following a campaign. But that competence is rarely there. On the contrary, when campaigns rely on consultants and hired hands who leave at the end, there is no alternative to a respite.

Finally, I worry not just about the preoccupation with larger and larger numbers—which is extremely damaging because it neglects the importance of utility—but I also worry about how large objectives have become and how much larger they will become in this time of inflation if we continue to conduct comprehensive, full-throttled campaigns. It is not far-fetched to predict that small colleges will be setting targets of $100 million and more, and some major university will soon boldly announce the first billion-dollar effort.[1] Perhaps those numbers will have the classically presumed effect of increasing the standards of prospective donors and thus of improving the flow of gifts to those institutions, but I doubt it. The much more probable result is that their constituents will be put off, that they will perceive those programs as reaching way beyond what even the most faithful among them thought of as a legitimate realm of need—in short, as grasping for all that they can get.

Donors, we ought to understand, are increasingly sophisticated, and fund raising is increasingly competitive. I am quite certain that donors will request, with growing determination, persuasive statements of why their help is needed—not just general statements that these are parlous times for institutions of our kind but specific statements as to what difference, what crucial margin of difference, their gifts will make in well-led, well-managed, well-disciplined institutions. I am highly skeptical about conveying those messages in the context of campaigns that emphasize the number on the bottom line.

IF NOT CAMPAIGNS, WHAT?

Many colleges and universities will continue to conduct campaigns in the established mode; of that we may be certain. We may be reasonably sure that some will do reasonably well, and a few—particularly those with strong campaign experience and very strong staffs—may excel in at least one more all-out effort. But for the reasons I have summarized, I think that many colleges and universities will be well advised to consider the alternatives to conventional capital campaigns. The elements of a preferred alternative are not difficult to identify:

- Work continually to refine the institutional agenda, so that it is possible to go to individuals who care about the institution with clear, cogent statements of the crucial difference their support will make.
- Assemble a professional fund-raising staff that is able to assert that agenda to volunteers and donors day after day.
- Care more about utility and less about large numbers.
- Integrate financial planning and fund raising.
- Understand that staff work, sometimes rigorous, sometimes artful, can be at least as helpful in enabling volunteers to be effective as the enthusiasm and esprit of a campaign.
- Avoid the fallacy of thinking of the institutions' constituency as fixed, as a closed circle of faithful friends who may be asked for support and then given a respite. In fact the constituency changes continuously, an important reason why fund raising ought to be sustained rather than episodic.

Will that kind of sustained program yield as many dollars as campaigns? Maybe, maybe not. But the point I wish to make is that we ought to be asking a different question: Which pattern will provide more support year-in, year-out for the most important objectives of the institution? The answer cannot be a generalization. Each place will find its own way, and for some that will surely include campaigns. What I hope is that when campaigns are conducted, they will be built upon an understanding of utility; promote, rather than discourage, professionalism; and be selective, rather than comprehensive, so that the total dollar objectives inspire rather than offend donors.

Finally, I urge tolerance, indeed respect, for those places that, after careful consideration, elect not to conduct campaigns. In the past such a decision has been interpreted as evidence of institutional timidity. In the future it may well be evidence of superior judgment.

NOTE

1. Editor's note: Smith's prediction has come true in the decade since he wrote this chapter in 1981.

Part Six

Corporate and Foundation Support

Corporations and foundations—important sources of support for higher education—differ from individual donors in significant ways. This means that the corporate or foundation development officer must possess specialized knowledge and skills.

Corporate support increased significantly in the first half of the 1980s but has leveled off since the middle of the decade. As I write this, the national economy is in the grips of a recession that is tightening corporate giving, at least temporarily, and creating a highly competitive situation for corporate fund-seekers. In addition, trends in the giving patterns of corporations are requiring new and carefully targeted strategies for solicitation.

While foundations always have provided a relatively small percentage of total support for most institutions, they are the most logical source for certain kinds of needs. In addition, gifts and grants from foundations have a "prestige value" that makes them highly desired by colleges and universities. As with corporate giving, the patterns of foundation support have changed, and development officers must be aware of these trends when assessing foundations as possible sources of support.

In Chapter 16, Chris Withers summarizes trends in corporate giving and describes strategies for cultivating corporate interest and soliciting support. In Chapter 17, Max Smith provides a companion analysis of the types of foundations, patterns in foundation giving, and methods for managing foundation relations programs.

Giving programs at many corporations and foundations are highly professional and require formal approaches. Funding decisions typically involve committees, or at least more than one individual. Often, this means the grantseeker must prepare a written proposal. In the final chapter of this section, Sarah Godfrey offers guidelines on how to write an effective request for corporate or foundation support. As Godfrey emphasizes, success depends not only on the quality of the proposal as a writing project, but also on the degree to which the writer can put himself or herself in the place of the grantmaker and relate the proposed project to the corporation's or foundation's own objectives. As an old fund-raising adage says, "The case must be larger than the institution."

Chapter 16
Obtaining Corporate Support

D. Chris Withers

"Times have changed," a colleague recently said to me. "Gone are the days when we could be sure of getting significant corporate support simply by muscling our way in to see the CEO. Now, they're requiring that we go through channels. Our case has got to be much tighter. As the competition for dollars gets more intense, most of us in the nonprofit sector will face a tough task in trying to expand corporate support."

It is quite true that competition for the corporate dollar has increased, while corporate giving has leveled off and even declined slightly in the last few years. According to the consulting firm Barnes & Roche, Inc., a poll of more than 300 of the nation's largest corporations indicated that

> their contributions to nonprofit organizations increased annually at rates from 13 percent to 26 percent between 1977 and 1984. Since 1985, however, that growth has dropped to between 3 percent and 7 percent annually . . . in some years not even keeping pace with inflation. Meanwhile, the number of nonprofit organizations competing for the eroding share of corporate contributions has risen by nearly 100,000 in the last seven years![1]

Times *have* changed. Rather than simply responding to pressured requests for $50,000 here or $50,000 there, as in previous years, corporations today are far, far more interested in *quid pro quo*—what is in it for them. Today, the sophisticated corporate relations program is a carefully systematic plan involving both institutional and corporate objectives, programs, needs, visibility, and resources.

These trends are quite recent. Corporate giving as a distinct activity did not begin until the early 1920s, although some of the earliest examples of corporate giving to higher education date back to the first two decades of this century. Tax deductions for such contributions were not allowed until 1935, and the legality of these gifts was not established until the 1950s. These two developments stimulated the growth of corporate support in the following years.[2]

In a 1980 article in *Foundation News*, Frank Koch, then the community affairs director for Syntex, made three predictions for the future of corporate giving: (1) Corporate gifts will continue to rise to 2 percent of corporate pre-tax earnings—a level recommended in 1975 by the Filer Commission, a privately initiated and funded citizens' panel created two years earlier to study philanthropy and volunteerism in the United States. (2) Corporations will require educational institutions to provide more clearly defined guidelines about how the gifts will be spent. (3) Cooperation will increase among nonprofit organizations seeking resources within the same city.

Koch was correct. The 5 percent limit on charitable deductions for corporations, imposed by the IRS in 1935, has not been a hotly debated issue because aggregate figures show that corporate charity amounts to only about 1.5 percent of corporate net income. A few corporations give amounts approaching the 5 percent limit, but most give considerably less; thus, encouraging corporations to reach the 2 percent level is still an important goal for nonprofits.[3]

PROSPECTS AND GIFTS

Different types of companies require different approaches for gifts. A proposal to a local family-owned bank, for example, is quite different from a proposal to a major national corporation; fund raising on the local level requires a far more personal approach.

Whether on a national, regional, or local level, you should build your list of prospects as a series of concentric circles, beginning with those corporations or businesses most closely associated with the institution and then working outward. Categories in such a list might include:

1. Companies already supporting your institution.
2. Companies operating in the local or regional area.
3. Distantly owned companies having facilities and large numbers of employees in the area.
4. Companies standing to benefit directly or indirectly from current or projected research, teaching seminars, or other projects at the institution.
5. Companies having large and profitable sales volume in the area.

6. Companies successfully recruiting graduates and/or employing large numbers of alumni.
7. Companies selling a large volume of goods to the institution on a regular basis, who have thus become loyal vendors.
8. Companies having alumni, parents, or other friends as directors, CEO's, or other officers.
9. Companies vulnerable to undeniable requests by prominently placed friends or alumni of the institution.
10. Companies that have relationships with faculty members (who serve as consultants, for example).

Creative thinkers can find many other routes to corporate dollars in addition to those on this list. These approaches, for example, might involve getting support from the corporate operating budget from such areas as sales, marketing promotions, senior management, discretionary funds, and research and development. This is a more focused, targeted approach. Corporations tend to be more eager today to sponsor individual programs, arrange for loaned executives, or swap corporate market research or access to an individual marketing group in lieu of giving cash outright.

Corporations generally give five different kinds of gifts:

1. *Annual gifts.* These gifts provide direct budget relief. They are most often unrestricted and less than $10,000.
2. *Matching gifts.* Many companies match gifts by employees— and sometimes retirees and directors—to designated types of nonprofits.[4] Individual donors initiate a match by including a form from the company with their gift; the institution completes the form and sends it to the company for processing. Some corporations offer matches of two or more times the size of the original gift. Most limit the number or size of matches per employee or per year. Many institutions, seeing matches as an easy way to multiply gifts from alumni and other individual donors, work hard to encourage eligible donors to request matches. Some will match up to $10,000.
3. *Capital gifts.* These are generally multi-year pledges, often secured during a major campaign, and typically designated for a specific purpose, such as a facility, scholarship, chair, or endowed fund. They range from several thousand dollars to several million dollars. Many corporations have giving policies that determine the size of their capital gifts as a percentage of

the total campaign goal. This has led to a disturbing trend, however, as some institutions set their campaign goals unjustifiably high simply to attract larger corporate gifts.

4. *Gifts-in-kind.* Corporations seem to be offering increasing amounts of support in forms other than cash. For example, C&S Bank in Atlanta and Eli Lilly each gave over $3 million in noncash support in 1987, while McDonnell-Douglas, NCR, and Scott Paper each gave around $2 million. Gifts-in-kind can take the form of equipment, books, or other noncash items that can be used for the educational mission of the institution. Institutions can benefit from gifts-in-kind, but only if the materials or services given truly meet institutional needs.

5. *Consulting or contractual services.* Corporations often provide money in exchange for faculty expertise in services or research. While such funds may not be gift dollars, they may still represent a source of important income from corporations to the institution or its faculty members. And these relationships may eventually lead to outright gifts that will directly support the operating budget or campaign needs.

GUIDELINES FOR SEEKING CORPORATE SUPPORT

Several years ago, John Bacon, then assistant secretary and director of corporate contributions for RJR, Inc., addressed a gathering of nonprofit agencies in North Carolina sponsored by the Donor's Forum of Winston-Salem. In that speech, Bacon identified eleven commandments of corporate fund raising. Corporate fund raisers would do well to heed them:

1. *Thou shalt not send a form letter to a corporation.* Companies get literally dozens of these every day. If you don't care enough to do your homework and personalize your appeal, it is not going to get a reading. Form letters are easy to turn down—and they *are* turned down.

2. *Thou shalt not send a letter to the chief executive officer of a company.* It will not be read. Find out the name of the individual who handles contributions and communicate with that person directly. (There are some exceptions here, but they are rare.)

3. *Thou shalt not send a contributions officer a blind letter.* You will do better if you call that person first, explaining briefly who you are and what your organization is trying to accomplish.

Then, when this person gets your letter, he or she will have some idea of what it is all about.

4. *Thou shalt not go too far from home.* Charity begins at home, and it usually ends there. For instance, Bacon noted, RJR gives a third in North Carolina and probably 80 percent in communities in which it has operations.

5. *Thou shalt not send five cubits of documentation with your first letter.* The easiest way for a contributions executive to make a dent in his or her pile is to throw it away.

6. *Thou shalt not call today and expect shekels tomorrow.* Everyone but your neighborhood merchant works on an annual contribution budget. Plan ahead and get your proposal in early.

7. *Thou shalt, if at all possible, find someone who knows the company to make the first call.* The chances of this person opening the door are greater than if it is a cold call. Recruit business people to call on business people.

8. *Thou shalt, if thou art clever, get the potential donor to do some of thy work.* If you have a basic idea that appeals to the contributions professional, talk with that person about how to best package it. The chances of approval are almost assured if you can get the contributions officer to work with you.

9. *Thou shalt remember that big companies like big projects, those with elements they can call their own.* The company can publicize its involvement in such projects to employees, shareholders, and the community.

10. *Thou shalt learn patience.* The company that says "no" this year might be a donor next year if you come back with a better idea. Once you get a corporate gift, you stand a chance of staying on the company's contributions list.

11. *Finally, thou shalt say thank you.* The best way to say it is to tell the donor what has been accomplished with the gift. Business people, maybe more than most, expect something to happen when they invest, so tell them.

FIVE STEPS TO A GIFT

As you plan and carry out corporate solicitations, it helps to follow a specific series of steps. These include developing a case, identifying your institution's links with the prospect company, cultivating your institution's relationship with the prospect, soliciting the gift, and recognizing the gift appropriately.

Developing Your Case

You must be able to answer any company's obvious question: Why should we give to you? For companies with interests in your city or region—your most important corporate prospects—you can best show your institution's worth by documenting its positive effect upon the community and the state.

The case should describe your institution's economic impact and show how the institution ranks, in payroll and number of employees, as a local employer. What kind of expenditures, both operating and capital, does the institution make in the community? What kinds of expenditures do students and institutional visitors make?

Be certain to document the impact of trustees, directors, and alumni. How many alumni live within the institution's community? How many are attorneys, physicians, or other professionals? How many alumni serve as officials in the legislature or in other government positions? How many chair major businesses? How many are educators, clergy, teachers, accountants?

Look also at the impact of your institution's cultural and athletic programs. List, for example, the number of concerts, plays, art exhibits, football games, basketball games, and so on offered each year. How many community members attend these events?

Research educational, social, and religious impact. How many people are enrolled in continuing education or special programs? What about library usage by local residents? Does the institution keep records of who visits the campus, particularly its museums, hospitals, and other branches?

Making Your Connection

Next, you should identify the impact of your institution upon the particular corporation being solicited. Document the number and positions of alumni employed by that corporation and the number of corporate employees enrolled in your institution's courses. Compile a list of faculty who serve as consultants to the corporation.

How much business does the institution do with that corporation each year? Translate this into dollars expended for goods and services. Is the corporation a past donor? Note the effect of those earlier gifts.

Cultivating a Relationship

Work over time to build on your relationships with the company. Keep a file of news clippings on the company; send congratulatory notices to alumni and institutional friends who receive promotions in the company. Visit corporate contributions officers and regularly review your organization's latest plans with them. Send copies of annual reports, the institution's magazine or tabloid, and other pertinent information. Consider developing a newsletter for corporate prospects, illustrating and documenting the institution's ties with the business community.

Consider scheduling "corporate days" on campus. Many institutions set up special days that bring together representatives of one or more companies with students and faculty members specializing in areas related to those companies' work.

Some institutions bring together business executives for programs geared especially to their needs. At the University of Richmond, for example, we offer a bimonthly breakfast lecture series for representatives of smaller businesses (those with fewer than 100 employees). Businesses that have given gifts of at least $1,000 also receive complimentary use of our Business Information and Research Center, the Office of Career Planning and Placement, and a one-day seminar at our Management Institute.

Soliciting a Gift

As you develop your strategy and write your proposal, try to determine where the target corporation ranks in the pecking order of similar corporations in the community. Many organizations have had success in securing a very large commitment from a third- or fourth-ranked company and then using that gift to stimulate higher-ranked corporations to raise their sights.

It's often wise to consult with the corporation's giving officer before presenting an official proposal or making a formal solicitation visit. Find out when the corporate funding committee accepts proposals and what form the company prefers for requests. You might review your proposal privately with the corporate giving officer, eliminating any surprise questions during the full presentation. And you might precede the formal visit with a "chemistry" meeting between the corporate CEO and your institution's president.

The old adage of having the right person calling on the right person for the right amount is still a good guide to success. Draw on both volunteers and staff. Suggest that two or three people make the call. For example, the campaign chair can give an overview of the campaign, the president can provide the institutional perspective, a staff member can review the proposal, and the campaign chair can present the proposal and close. A more elaborate presentation might be a talk with visuals charting relationships between your institution and the corporation. It may be necessary to present the request, in different forms, to different people or groups—for example, the CEO and the board.

Once the actual presentation has been completed, be sure to follow up. Encourage members of the solicitation team and your institution's boards to write letters of appreciation.

Do not expect a decision at the time of the presentation. A firm decision often comes first by phone to a trustee or the president and then in writing shortly afterward. Corporate funding decisions are rarely rapid, but you should hear within 90 days. If not, ask your closest high-level contact to the company to follow up.

Providing Recognition

Corporations require prompt, accurate reports on how their funds were used and what results were achieved. They often request special additional documentation. This might be presented in brochure format or in a form modeled on a corporate shareholders' report.

Some institutions list corporate givers in a regular newsletter—sometimes called a "campaign flash"—to its trustees, volunteer leaders, and alumni or friends who are leaders in the business community. Those who receive the newsletter are asked to send follow-up words of gratitude to the donor company's officers and directors.

Be sure to recognize the corporation's gift publicly in an appropriate way. Recognition can take many forms—honor roll listings, plaques, publications. For large gifts, many institutions provide opportunities for a donor company to place its name on the project it has funded. The naming of a building, laboratory, or other facility generally requires a contribution of 50 percent of the actual cost of the project. Naming a professorship, scholarship, or other endowment usually requires a gift of $50,000 or more.

In any case, keep cultivating even *after* a gift is received. Repeat gifts—from corporations with whom your institution has well-established relationships—are much easier to obtain than new gifts.

CORPORATE SELF-INTEREST

Corporate philanthropy has become more businesslike in recent years. Companies are working consciously to align their giving with specific corporate objectives, to be accountable to management and shareholders for their giving choices, and to maximize return on their gift "investment." For obvious reasons, corporations seek to support causes that will reflect well on them or will give them some advantage in return. We can make our institutions attractive candidates for a company's dollars only if we understand what the company wants to accomplish with its charitable giving.

We can see this merger of business interests and charitable intent with the recent increase in *cause-related marketing*. This typically refers to a company's efforts to link its promotion of its products to its charitable giving to causes or institutions—for example, when the company advertises that it will donate to a given cause some percentage of its profit from each sale. Such arrangements have more than tripled in the last few years; today, more than 3,000 companies are pumping out $1.5 billion annually in promotional expenditures.[5] Corporations are increasingly combining their giving with other functions such as community relations, government affairs, or public relations. The idea is to consolidate management responsibility and to focus the giving program more directly on company interest as well as community interest.

What are the implications of this trend for institutional development officers? First, you must research potential donor companies thoroughly and choose your prospects carefully, using a rifle-shot approach rather than a shotgun. Second, you must document what makes your institution unique from the one next door or down the street or across the nation. Third, you must justify the corporate investment in your institution in terms of the company's management goals and programs. Finally, you should seek opportunities to collaborate with neighboring institutions;

by coordinating facilities and programs, you may become more attractive, as a team, to corporate prospects.

At the outset of this chapter, I stated that times have changed. That *is* true in part because of the recession affecting the country as I write this chapter in 1991. This is not a good time to seek major corporate support. Should we believe that eventually corporations will again increase their support of our institutions? I believe they will, because they will *have* to. Corporations depend on higher education to provide trained, talented personnel. They value the pluralistic system of higher education. They need continuing research. They want to be perceived as good corporate citizens for their stockholders. The coffers may be temporarily low, but U.S. corporations are not going to go out of business. We can still expect substantial corporate support in the future.

But our institutions will need to be more accountable for the corporate contributions we receive. It will be vitally important for us to constantly remind corporate boards, shareholders, and contributions committees "what is in it for them." Why should they support your institution versus another? Your case will need to be solid and justifiable. Corporations are no longer responsive to emotional appeals. They will not be won over by war stories, worn-out jokes, football tickets, or parking privileges.

Instead, corporate cultivation and solicitation programs will need to be sophisticated. Whatever the state of the economy, your success or failure depends upon how well you do your homework and how well you adjust to changing corporate interests.

NOTES

1. "Strategies for Increasing Corporate Support," *Directions in Development: A Periodic Bulletin of Information and Comment on Philanthropy* (newsletter of Barnes & Roche, Rosemont, Pennsylvania), June 1989, 1.

2. D. Chris Withers, "Generating Corporate Support," in *Handbook of Institutional Advancement,* 2nd ed., ed. A. Westley Rowland (San Francisco: Jossey-Bass, 1986), 268.

3. F. Koch, "Corporate Philanthropy in the 1980s," *Foundation News* 21 (December 1980):17-21.

4. The Council for Advancement and Support of Education (CASE), which operates a national clearinghouse for information on matching gift programs, maintains lists of companies that match gifts to various kinds of educational institutions, cultural organizations, and health and welfare agencies.

5. "Corporate Giving Changes, Trends, Special Considerations," *Bulletin on Public Relations and Development for Colleges and Universities* (newsletter of Gonser Gerber Tinker Stuhr, Naperville, Illinois), January 1987, 2.

Chapter 17

Obtaining Foundation Support

Max G. Smith

Private foundations are receiving more grant requests from higher education institutions than ever before. But since fewer than 10 percent of those applications receive funding, success requires a high level of skill and unusual persistence. The adage "the rich get richer" is perhaps truer in the area of foundation support than any other area of educational fund raising: Institutions winning foundation support usually have earned it before.

It is the job of the foundation development officer (FDO), as the in-house specialist, to energize, activate, and focus the institution's resources in an aggressive foundation program. The FDO must have a basic understanding of the various kinds of foundations as well as trends in their funding patterns.

TYPES OF FOUNDATIONS

Of the more than 30,000 active grantmaking foundations, the ones offering the most grants to higher education are those classified as *independent foundations*. These foundations—typically created by an individual, a family, or group of individuals—may be operated under the direction of the donor or members of the donor's family, or they may have an independent board of directors. Their mission may be as broad as benefiting humanity everywhere or as narrow as research on schistosomiasis. In addition to giving for a wide range of specific needs, they often award grants for general support of institutions or programs. Depending on the nature of their giving, independent foundations may also be known as "general purpose" or "special purpose" foundations.

Large independent foundations, such as Ford, Kellogg, Rockefeller, Kresge, and Sloan, are looked upon as leaders and pacesetters in the foundation field.[1] Easily recognized by their high visibility and national or statewide programs, they usually have substantial assets, professional staffs, and clearly defined programs. They tend to see their money as experimental—a means to bring about change or move society toward the future. They often lend their support to solving basic problems through grants for special programs, demonstration projects, or research. Every few years, they step back and evaluate their role in their fields of activity before reaffirming or modifying program emphases.

Some independent foundations function entirely under the direction of family members and are thus referred to as "family foundations." Because most of these are small and tend to operate with little or no staff, little is known about many of them. They offer great opportunity, however, for institutions that establish a good relationship with the donor or the foundation.[2]

By contrast, *corporate foundations*—such as the Procter & Gamble Fund, the Minnesota Mining and Manufacturing Foundation, and the Hallmark Corporate Foundation—are instruments of company giving. Whereas grants by an independent foundation may range broadly over many types of institutions and charitable organizations, giving by corporate foundations tends to relate to the company's field of endeavor. Corporate foundation funding typically goes to research and educational projects in fields related to company activities and is often restricted to communities with company operations. Although these foundations' governing boards are usually composed of officials of the sponsoring company, local plant managers and officials often participate in grantmaking and policy decisions. Company contributions to corporate foundations represented nearly one-third of the $3.7 billion increase in assets reported for 1987 by the 7,582 foundations listed in the 1991 *Foundation Directory.*[3]

A third category, *community foundations,* has grown noticeably in number and assets in recent years. These locally sponsored foundations—such as the New York Community Trust, the Cleveland Foundation, and the Minneapolis Foundation—typically consist of many individual trusts administered under one managerial roof. Members of the board are usually prominent local citizens, and funds usually come from many local donors. Grants are made for social, educational, religious, or other charitable purposes within the foundation's locality or region.

Finally, there are *operating foundations,* which use their resources to operate specific programs for research, social welfare, or other charitable causes. Their assets are usually derived from a single source and decisions are made by an independent board of directors. Examples are the J. Paul Getty Trust, the Charles F. Kettering Foundation, and the Russell Sage Foundation. For example, the Getty Trust funds only eight programs and centers, the most prominent of which is the Getty Museum in Los Angeles. Operating foundations rarely make grants to outside organizations.

TRENDS IN FOUNDATION GIVING

Foundation giving has undergone some changes in the past decade. Some of the larger foundations have shown increasing interest in international activities, especially in South Africa, South America, and most recently Eastern Europe.[4] With this broadening world view has come a more pronounced emphasis on protecting the environment, animals, and wildlife. Giving for health has shifted from medical care to public health and preventive medicine. Minority programs have received increased funding, with issues such as race relations, minority education, and equality very much in the forefront. Further, the share of funds for children and youth has doubled since 1983, and support for primary and secondary education is expected to rise.[5]

Higher education continues to be of strong interest to grantmakers. Education funding dropped off suddenly in the early 1980s, when government cuts in social programs increased demand for private funding for social-service projects. But that trend was short-lived. In 1989 foundation giving for education showed substantial growth, increasing slightly more than the cost of living. At $1.74 billion, it constituted almost 20 percent of private contributions to higher education.[6]

Some redistribution of funding between private and public institutions has occurred. Before 1983, private institutions received three times as much as public ones; now they receive less than twice as much. The size of the largest grants has increased, and the number of grants of $5 million or above, as well as those in the $2.5 million to $5 million range, has doubled since 1983. In 1989, however, despite fund-raising campaigns with unprecedented goals, no single grant for higher education was reported in excess of $5 million.

From 1984 to 1988, the proportion of higher education grants going to program support increased from 27 percent to 38 percent of the total. Research grants grew to 22 percent. Capital grants for such purposes as buildings, equipment, computer systems, land acquisition, and debt reduction increased slightly to 21 percent.

While endowment grants to colleges and universities represented a relatively small portion of the total in 1989, the awards themselves tended to be comparatively large, made on a one-time basis to specific institutions. More than half of the grant support for student aid in 1989 was for graduate or postgraduate fellowships.[7]

A practice that continues to grow in popularity with grantmakers is awarding *challenge grants,* which require recipients to secure matching funds from other sources. Some large foundations, such as the Kresge Foundation, have used challenge grants to inspire recipients to more vigorous fund-raising efforts.[8] Also, many foundations are participating in cooperative efforts in which funding for a given project is shared with other foundations or funding sources.

We may gain insight into what to expect in the future from a recent survey by the Foundation Center.[9] Twenty-two leading independent foundations active in the field of education were asked what they planned to support and why. Minority education—a focal point today for many foundations that support higher education—received strong interest, with grantmakers citing projects to strengthen historically black colleges, increase access for minorities, and prepare minority teachers and scientists.

Other causes receiving a high rate of response were strengthening science education and encouraging international education in different fields. The foundations also expressed interest in interdisciplinary scholarship, linking fields such as economics and political science with cultural and regional studies as well as with international studies.

Other areas favored were liberal arts colleges, humanistic scholarship in non-Western cultures and American pluralism, women's studies, university libraries, and improving campus facilities. Respondents also mentioned social-science scholarship on world peace, leadership development, and programs to advance the status of women.

THE FOUNDATION DEVELOPMENT OFFICER

While the foundation development officer must have a broad knowledge of foundations and their grantmaking practices, learning about foundations is only half the battle. The FDO must also have comprehensive knowledge of his or her institution and its various divisions and programs. Foundation officials can ask penetrating questions on every aspect of the institution, including finances, budgets, students, faculty, academic programs, alumni, and long-range plans.

Because foundations tend to fund projects that help them achieve their goals, one of the FDO's most important tasks is to identify and articulate the interests that a foundation and the institution share. The FDO also must work to build long-term relationships because, as in other areas of philanthropy, people tend to give to people they know and trust. As with individual prospective donors, every effort should be made to involve the foundation prospect in the life of the institution.

While development usually deals with external relations, internal relations—that is, managing processes and people—are equally important to success in gaining foundation support. The FDO is like a broker trying to arrange a marriage between the project and the foundation. Since the processes often entail working behind the scenes, the FDO must develop an unusual mixture of aggressiveness and deference.[10]

Specifically, the FDO acts as a catalyst, making faculty and administrative leaders aware of grant opportunities and suggesting ideas for proposals, particularly for new or developing programs within the institution. The FDO helps faculty and others with such matters as the preferred manner of presentation, timing of the approach, coordination with other university grant requests, and mechanics of proposal preparation. While the faculty or staff member in charge of the program may be primarily responsible for the actual drafting of a proposal, the FDO should be available for editorial and technical assistance.

FDOs wishing to expand their skills can take advantage of workshops on foundation support offered by several organizations. These include year-round comprehensive training programs presented by the Grantsmanship Center, conferences sponsored by the Council for Advancement and Support of Education (CASE), and periodic seminars given by the Foundation Center.

RESEARCHING FOUNDATION PROSPECTS

As a rule, foundation research involves two phases. The first is to identify the overall target group for the institution's foundation grants program. First on the list should be those foundations that have contributed in the past. For identifying additional prospects, references such as *Comsearch Printouts* (the Foundation Center's series of guides to foundation giving on a wide range of topics) and the *Grants Index* are particularly helpful. The most important element in singling out a foundation as a good prospect is its grantmaking record.[11]

While the total number of foundation prospects for each institution will vary, the average liberal arts college will probably have only 40 to 60 real prospects that warrant significant attention and time. For major universities, the number may be as high as 100 or more.[12]

After determining the target group, the second phase of research involves examining them individually and intensively. Two chief sources of information on a foundation are its annual report and its IRS Form 990-PF, which provides detailed information on its assets and grantmaking. Among the many items to consider when gathering information on a foundation are the scope of its interests, geographic preferences, restrictions, application procedures, and possible deadlines. In-depth information on many larger foundations is available in *Source Book Profiles,* published annually by the Foundation Center, and the *Taft Foundation Reporter,* published annually by the Taft Group.

The Foundation Center has the nation's largest collection of information on foundations. Its libraries in New York, Washington, Cleveland, and San Francisco maintain vertical files, IRS 990 forms on microfilm, and a reference book collection. The organization maintains a network of more than 170 funding information centers throughout the United States and offers a wide range of publications. Most of this information is available to the public. Individuals wanting frequent access may pay an annual fee for telephone and mail services, custom searches of computer files, and a library research service.

Several of the Foundation Center's publications deserve mention here. The *Foundation Directory* gives information on foundations with assets of more than $1 million or whose annual grants total $100,000 or more. The 6,615 foundations listed in the

1991 edition accounted for 96 percent of the assets and 93 percent of the grantmaking in 1987.[13] About one-fourth of these publish brochures, grants lists, or other documents to inform the public of their operations, and many publish an annual report. The recently published *Foundation Directory, Part 2* (1991-92 edition) offers similar information on many smaller foundations.

The annual *Grants Index* is a cumulative listing of grants of $5,000 or more by many foundations, including the top 100 in assets. Since it is the most thorough source available on the actual grants of many of the major foundations, the *Grants Index* provides a good barometer of current foundation interests and giving patterns.

The *National Data Book* contains basic data on the more than 30,000 grant-making foundations in the United States. Information provided in the two volumes (one arranged alphabetically, the other geographically) includes name, address, principal officer, financial data, and annual report information.

Finally, the Foundation Center's database is available for on-line retrieval by computer. The database includes information on funding sources, philanthropic giving, grant application guidelines, and the financial status of foundations.

In addition to larger foundations, universities often discover grant prospects among foundations located in their own or in nearby states. Information on these can be found in a growing number of state directories of foundations. Although the information in these directories may be minimal, they can be at least a starting point for preliminary research. Their advantage, of course, is that some of the foundations included in them may not be identified elsewhere.

For keeping abreast of foundation grant activity, such publications as *Foundation Giving Watch Newsletter, Foundation Grants Index Bimonthly, The Chronicle of Higher Education, The Chronicle of Philanthropy, Foundation News,* and *Philanthropic Digest* are excellent sources. They afford a current picture of foundation funding on a regular basis.

THE GRANT-GETTING PROCESS

By studying the pertinent information on a foundation's personnel, programs, and purposes, the FDO can gain a "feel" for the foundation prospect. This will enable the FDO to formulate an appropriate plan of action for pursuing the foundation. Patience is essential, as an institution must often cultivate a foundation for several years before its proposals receive serious consideration.

The actual process of submitting a proposal may involve only a fraction of the time required to carry out the total grant-seeking endeavor, and occurs only after a series of other steps. The process, which begins with identification of key prospects and preliminary research on them, proceeds with preliminary contacts by letter and telephone and informal visits. Then comes cultivation through further calls, letters, or exchange of information.

During the cultivation process, the FDO may find it helpful to have a succinct institutional profile to present to prospects. This written statement should emphasize the distinctiveness of the institution. What is it that sets this college or university apart and makes it different from others? What are its strengths, unusual programs, or notable achievements? What is the institution's vision of its future and how does that vision relate to the foundation's interests? It must be obvious that the institution has its priorities in order.

As the FDO works toward a proposal, he or she may wish to send a pre-proposal letter to explore the foundation's interest in a specific project. Successful development officers wait to submit a full proposal until a serious foundation prospect invites them to do so. Some foundations prefer visits prior to proposal submission; others require that a proposal be under review before an appointment is scheduled. After submitting a detailed proposal, the FDO should keep in touch with the foundation and provide any additional material it needs. Whenever possible, the FDO should arrange for foundation personnel to visit campus.

If a submitted proposal is not funded, often the rejection can serve as an opportunity to further the relationship and plan the next approach. If the proposal succeeds, the grant money should be used not just wisely, but so well that the foundation will be interested in providing additional funding in the future.

Whatever the decision, the FDO should maintain contact with a foundation on a continuing basis, not simply when the institution is seeking a grant. For example, the FDO should call or write when there is good news to report or a special announcement of interest.

FUNDING WORTH SEEKING

Most philanthropic dollars to colleges and universities come from sources other than private foundations. Yet there is no boost to an institution quite like a significant foundation grant. It is a vote of confidence—not only in that program, but also in the institution's overall leadership, mission, and future.

Stalking the elusive foundation dollar requires knowledge, skill, courage, patience, endurance, and limitless energy. All grant-seekers must go through the same mill. There are no short cuts; persistence often wins.[14]

Those who prevail will know the satisfaction expressed by a chemistry professor to a group of colleagues at a recent national meeting. "This was our eighth time to apply to this foundation," he said. "This time we made it."

NOTES

1. *Foundations Today*, 5th ed. (New York: The Foundation Center, 1988), 4.

2. J. David Ross, ed., *Understanding and Increasing Foundation Support* (San Francisco: Jossey-Bass, 1981), 67.

3. *Foundation Directory*, 1991 ed. (New York: The Foundation Center, 1991), xxiv.

4. Loren Renz, director of research of the Foundation Center (presentation at the national meeting of the National Council of Research Administrators, Washington, D.C., November 5, 1991).

5. Renz (presentation at the Conference on Corporate and Foundation Support, sponsored by the Council for Advancement and Support of Education, Washington, D.C., May 12, 1990).

6. *Research Report* (New York: Council for Aid to Education, 1990), 1.

7. Statistics in the preceding three paragraphs come from the 1990-91 edition of the *Grants Index* (New York: The Foundation Center, 1991), xv-xviii.

8. Mary Kay Murphy, ed., *Cultivating Foundation Support for Education* (Washington, D.C.: Council for Advancement and Support of Education, 1989), 166.

9. Renz, May 12, 1990.

10. Murphy, *Cultivating Foundation Support*, 194.

11. Virginia P. White, *Grants: How to Find Out About Them and What to Do Next* (New York: Plenum Press, 1975), 128.

12. Murphy, *Cultivating Foundation Support*, 106.

13. *Foundation Directory*, 1991 ed., v.

14. Murphy, *Cultivating Foundation Support*, 111.

Chapter 18
How to Write a Good Proposal

Sarah Godfrey

Securing corporate and foundation support often depends on presenting a well-written, persuasive proposal. The proposal's winning edge lies in its ability to show how the institution and the foundation or corporation can form a partnership that will benefit both. The most innovative and exemplary program will not be funded unless the proposal explains how the program will fulfill the grantmaker's objectives.

Virtually every foundation and corporation has a set of goals and objectives that it wishes to meet through its philanthropic activity. These objectives may be as broad as "to improve the quality of education in the United States" or as narrow as "to decrease the dropout rate among high-school students in Smith County." A grantmaker cannot accomplish its objectives without the participation of the institutions it funds—such as schools, colleges, and universities. The grantmaker and the grant recipient act in partnership to carry out programs and projects that fulfill a shared mission.

This notion of partnership is fundamental to the preparation of a good proposal. Seen in this light, the proposal's purpose is to explain how the foundation's or corporation's dollars can combine with the institution's resources to bring about changes that both parties desire.

A well-written proposal covers all the pertinent information in a concise, logical, and compelling manner. The development of such a proposal typically follows a certain series of steps and addresses a standard set of questions.

RESEARCHING GOALS AND OBJECTIVES

The first step in preparing a successful proposal is to identify those foundations or corporations whose objectives appear to match those of your institution's particular project. Directories such as those published by the Foundation Center and the Taft Corporation offer extensive information on the philanthropic activity of the nation's grantmakers and often provide specific categories of interest. A search through these directories helps in developing a list of possible funding sources and in eliminating those foundations and corporations whose interests are not likely to match yours.

You must then carefully research those prospects to identify those whose past grants most closely match the grant you seek, both in program content and dollar amount. The best sources for this information are the annual reports and other printed information distributed by the grantmakers. Read these publications carefully. What is the foundation or corporation's philosophy of giving? What does it hope to accomplish through its grantmaking? What types of projects has it recently funded that seem to exemplify these objectives?

As you conduct this research and consider your own project, keep in mind the fundamental difference in motivation between foundation giving and corporate giving. Most foundations are altruistic in their grantmaking and seek to bring about a change in society. Corporations, however, are accountable to employees and stockholders. Their motivation is *quid pro quo:* They seek programs and projects that will directly benefit the corporation and the community it serves.

Be sure to review your own files: A foundation or corporation that has supported your institution in the past may be an excellent source for your new project. Perhaps a faculty member has been in contact recently with a particular foundation or corporation. What can he or she add to the profile you are developing? Board members, trustees, and other key volunteers frequently are good sources of information, particularly when they have a personal or professional contact with the grantmaker in question.

After you have developed a profile of a foundation or corporation you believe to be a good match, call and ask to speak to the program officer responsible for the area in which you are interested. Describe your project briefly and ask if it is consistent with the grantmaker's objectives. Can the program officer provide you with additional information or advice? You may not always be able to have an extensive discussion, but it is worth your effort to call.

The information you gather inevitably will save time for both you and the program officer.

DEFINING THE LARGER PROBLEM

As you move forward with identifying an appropriate source of support, it may help to take a second look at your project or program. Try to evaluate its general purpose through the eyes of a grantmaker.

Almost every project arises out of a need that extends beyond the campus walls. Amid daily pressures and the rush to secure funding, we may lose sight of the larger significance of the projects for which we seek support. We view our projects from the "we need" perspective: "We need a new language laboratory"; "We need a new gym"; "We need remedial reading programs." We see our projects as ends unto themselves, not as ways to address problems that affect all of higher education or society.

Grantmakers look at the larger picture and then evaluate how our projects may help improve that picture. They regard our projects as the means to accomplish broader objectives: to prepare students to live in the global village; to encourage healthy exercise as a means of disease prevention; to lower the adult illiteracy rate.

Before you begin to write a proposal, you must understand the greater problem that your project will address. Ask yourself, "Why would XYZ Foundation want to fund this project?" The answer is probably not, "To make Ivy College a better place." The XYZ Foundation does not particularly care that Ivy College's science laboratories are scattered across campus and suffer from twenty years of deferred maintenance. It may be interested, however, in the ways in which Ivy College proposes to address the national decline in science education by creating a centralized environment for scientific learning.

Keep in mind that a program officer may review up to 100 proposals each week and most likely will have to give clear justification for selecting yours for further consideration. That justification lies in the degree to which your project's objectives match those of the foundation. This shift in perspective from your need to the grantmaker's objectives is crucial. If the larger issue inherent in your project is not clear to you, go back to the faculty and administrators involved and ask them to address the issue.

DETERMINING THE CONTENT

Understanding the ways in which your project will help fulfill a grantmaker's goals is the key to tailoring your proposal to a particular recipient. It should be obvious that the "shotgun" or "boilerplate" method—sending identical proposals to a list of foundations and corporations—is not effective. Each proposal should be written for a specific audience and should reflect a clear understanding of the ways in which a partnership can be created.

As you prepare a proposal, you should follow the grantmaker's specifications. When the grantmaker does not provide guidelines, or when the specifications indicate only maximum page length, be sure the proposal answers the following questions:[1]

1. What is the issue to be addressed?
2. Why is your institution the best place to address it?
3. What changes will the project bring about?
4. How will you accomplish these changes?
5. What do you need (time, funding, people) to do it?
6. How will you gauge your success?
7. Why are you sending this particular proposal? Can you make a special appeal to this source?

WRITING THE PROPOSAL

In general, proposals can take any of three formats: a letter-proposal (one to two pages); a standard proposal (three to five pages) with a cover letter; and a longer proposal (over six pages) with a cover letter and an executive summary. Most foundations and corporations now specify which format they wish to receive. Because of the ever-increasing volume of applications, the trend is toward the letter-proposal, especially for initial inquiries. All three formats should contain information that addresses the seven questions above.

The structure of a standard proposal or a longer proposal generally should follow this outline:

I. Introduction
   A. The issue
   B. Your institution's plan to address the issue
   C. The amount of your request and the foundation/corporation from which you are requesting it

II. Project Description
  A. More about the issue
    1. What needs to be changed or improved? How do you know?
    2. Why is it important to address this issue?
  B. How does your institution plan to address this issue?
    1. What do you propose to do?
    2. What have others done?
    3. Why is your institution's approach better?
  C. What will it take to address the issue?
    1. People
    2. Other resources (space, equipment, etc.)
    3. Funding
  D. How will you know that you have successfully addressed the issue?
    1. What do you wish to accomplish?
    2. What will your next steps be?
    3. How will the project continue after the conclusion of the grant period?
  E. Why is your institution an excellent place to address the issue?
    1. What have you done in the past that has prepared you to address the issue?
    2. What is happening at your institution now to enhance your position?
    3. What resources are you contributing (talent, time, space, money)?
    4. What financial resources, if any, are you getting from extramural sources?
  F. Why would a grant from this foundation/corporation to your institution for this project be especially appropriate?
    1. Mutual rewards
    2. Relationship—appreciation of past support from this grantmaker
III. Conclusion
  A. Summary, including amount of request
  B. Thanks
IV. Appendices
  A. Budget and budget narrative

B. Specific information pertaining to the project
C. Pertinent general information, such as background on your institution
D. Curricula vitae of faculty members and other key people involved in the project

Following are some guidelines you should keep in mind as you write.

The Introduction

As you prepare your proposal, remember that the person who will review it may have 10 to 20 other proposals to read that day. The reviewer usually does not have quantities of time to spend on each proposal, nor can he or she take time to try to decipher what it is you are requesting. You can make your proposal more competitive by stating at the outset what it is that your institution proposes to do. Begin your proposal with a concise introductory paragraph that, in a few sentences, states the name of your institution, what it proposes to do, and the amount of funding you are seeking. Do not make the reviewer read through three or four pages to determine why you are writing.

The Body

You should construct the body of your proposal with short paragraphs that present the material clearly and logically. Avoid the temptation to tell everything you know about the subject; include only the information that supports your case. Put yourself in the position of the reviewer, and consider the volumes of material that he or she may have to read each day. Your proposal will be easier to assess if you include only the important information.

Keep in mind, also, that the decision-makers at many foundations and corporations never actually read the proposal that you submit. They read, instead, a synopsis—an evaluation sheet or a check list prepared by a staff member who reviews your proposal. These formats present only the essential information. It is to your institution's advantage to make this information easily discernable in your proposal. If a proposal longer than three to five pages is necessary, include a one-page executive summary to give the reviewer an immediate understanding of the key elements.

Tone

The tone of a good proposal should err on the side of understatement. Let the facts about your institution and the plans for your project speak for themselves. Remember that you are presenting your institution as a candidate for an important partnership. Avoid a tone that is self-satisfied or condescending. Avoid, as well, the other extreme; a proposal that grovels or shows a sense of inferiority will not be attractive to the reader. If you have done your homework and you know why your project is a good match with the grantmaker's objectives, you should not have to explain the reasons you provide for why your proposal should be funded. Do not tell the grantmaker how to make its grants.

Involvement of Others

Many proposals come about because of personal relationships that you institution's faculty, administrators, and volunteers develop with board or staff members at a foundation or corporation. These contacts are invaluable, and it is usually appropriate to mention them in the cover letter or in the body of a letter-proposal. You must maintain a fine balance so that you do not sound presumptuous. Often, you can mention people by thanking them for their help. If you mention an individual other than the person to whom you address the proposal, send a copy to that person.

Appendices

Select with care the appendices to your proposal. Generally, information that supports your case or further explains a specific point should be included in an appendix. Detailed budgets and budget narratives often appear as appendices because their inclusion in the text of the proposal would interrupt its flow. Curricula vitae of the faculty involved in the project usually belong as appendices, as do histories of your institution and general descriptions of academic and extracurricular strengths. Most foundations and corporations require copies of your institution's tax-exempt status, a list of names of trustees, and a recent audited financial statement. These and similar documents should appear as appendices.

FINAL STEPS

Wonderful proposals can lose much of their strength in the editing process, particularly if several individuals review the copy. The proposal may lose clarity, continuity, and its sense of urgency. It is important to have one final reader to read the proposal to make sure that it makes sense, it presents its material logically, and it maintains a consistent tone and style. Often the most effective reader at this point is someone who has not been involved in preparing the proposal. This "outside eye" can point out weaknesses and tell you whether the proposal is logical and compelling.

The institution's highest-ranking administrator should sign the proposal-letter or the cover letter, as evidence of institutional endorsement. If a trustee or another volunteer has played an important role in bringing the proposal to the attention of a particular foundation or corporation, note that you are sending a copy to this individual.

The most effective packaging of your proposal lies in its content, not in a slick presentation. Recipients often discard fancy bindings because they are cumbersome. Many reviewers also put stock in the adage, "the glossier the presentation, the weaker the content." Unless the guidelines indicate otherwise, the best presentation is to type the proposal neatly and bind it simply.

SUMMARY

The key to a good proposal is its ability to establish a partnership between your institution and the grantmaker. To write a successful proposal, you must understand the funding objectives of a particular foundation or corporation and be able to explain the ways in which your project will help meet those objectives. If you present information in a style that is clear and compelling, you will enhance the case for this partnership and give your proposal a competitive edge.

NOTE

1. These questions and the outline following them were developed over several years, with the help of many experts, for the "Writing Winning Proposals" workshop conducted by the Council for Advancement and Support of Education.

Part Seven
Special Constituencies

Most colleges and universities work with a variety of constituencies, each defined by the nature of its relationship to the institution. These groups include faculty and staff, parents, alumni, friends, and students as well as corporations, foundations, and other organizations.

In addition, we can define constituencies according to their primary interest in the institution. Some constituents may be most interested in the arts, or in athletics, or in the programs of a particular department or discipline. Particularly in large universities, alumni and others often find it difficult to identify with or stay informed about the diverse activities of a complex institution. It is perhaps human nature to relate to smaller entities and base one's sense of belonging on specific shared interests. Most large universities have designed their fund-raising programs accordingly, to recognize and capitalize on these focused interests of special constituencies.

In Chapter 19, Kathleen Kavanagh discusses programs designed to solicit support from an important constituency—parents. Chapter 20 by Jeffrey Gray and Chapter 21 by Robert Ashton discuss fund-raising programs for athletic programs and for professional schools within a university. Ashton's chapter discusses a number of problems that *can* occur in institutions that have both centralized and school-based programs. While school-based programs are relatively new in some universities and have been recently expanded in others, there are also a number of institutions that have combined central and school programs effectively for many years without many of the problems that Ashton cites. The role and relationships of school-based development officers and programs may reflect the broader culture and style of each specific institution.

Basic fund-raising principles and techniques are the same regardless of the constituency from which funds are to be raised or the program that is the focus of the gifts. But as these chapters discuss, special considerations influence the design of constituent fund-raising programs, and various models exist for relating these programs to the institution's other development programs.

Chapter 19

Raising Funds from Parents

Kathleen A. Kavanagh

The fundamental principles of educational fund raising—identifying prospects, developing their interest, involving them, and providing them with opportunities to support the institution's mission and goals—apply to parents of students and parents of alumni just as they apply to other individuals. The questions involved in parent fund raising concern not only how to secure philanthropic support, but also how much staff time and resources to devote to this special constituency.

A large research university or graduate school clearly has a different relationship with parents—if it has any relationship at all—than a small, private liberal arts college or an independent school. The university or graduate school might have a significant number of students who pay their own bills, or it might choose not to keep records of students' parents. Similarly, a community college whose student body includes a large proportion of adults might not find parents an important constituency. In contrast, an independent school will almost always have a parent population that is involved and interested in the day-to-day life of the school. The average college probably falls somewhere between these extremes, with different levels of parent interest, different ways of keeping information about parents, and different levels of programs for parents of students and parents of alumni.

The first questions to ask, then, when considering an institution's potential for fund raising from parents, are these:

- Is a parent fund-raising program the best use of the development program's time and resources?
- Can the institution expect an adequate return on the investment it will make?
- Does the necessary information exist—or can it be obtained—to undertake some kind of parent fund-raising program?

- If a program is in place, is it producing results commensurate with the institution's investment?

An institution must also consider the role of parent fund raising in the total context of parent programs. A case can be made that special events and communications directed at parents will create a stronger climate for philanthropy. Many institutions with broad-based parent fund-raising programs devote considerable time and resources to on- and off-campus parent gatherings, newsletters directed specifically to parents, and staffing for a formal parents organization. Other institutions simply include parents, or certain segments of their parent populations, in generic institutional programs.

In this chapter we will discuss two key opportunities for parent fund raising and some of the considerations in supporting those programs.

MAJOR GIFT PROGRAMS FOR PARENTS

Even if an institution elects to undertake no other kind of parent fund raising, it can at least consider the possibilities of a major gifts program for parents. The most cost-effective money to raise, major gifts do not require extensive volunteer structures, massive direct mail and phonathon programs, or contact with the majority of the parent population. Instead, major gift fund raising allows an institution to focus on the small percentage of parents who can make a significant financial difference to the institution.

Traditional fund-raising wisdom suggests that major gift fund raising must be built on a successful annual giving program. Institutions with well-developed parent programs can combine major gift fund raising with a traditional parents annual fund. But in today's climate of sophisticated major gift prospects, heightened competition from other deserving institutions, increasing demands for effective use of staff and budget, and limited time in which to develop parents as prospects, institutions that cannot commit to a full-fledged program of annual giving might well consider starting their parent fund raising with a major gifts program.

Identifying Prospects

There are a variety of ways to identify those parents who have the potential for giving significant support. Of course, these methods depend upon the institution's culture and commitment to parent fund raising. What will be relatively easy for one institution may be impossible for another.

In the best scenario, the development office has access to student information that includes data about parents' occupations and educational affiliations. This information may be in a computerized database to which the development office has access, or may be on forms completed in the application or registration process. In either case, it is important to scan this information each year and identify those parents who by occupation alone may appear to have potential for major gifts.

Reviewing this information can be a simple process in a small institution, where a development officer might check the list parent-by-parent. In a medium-sized program with a research staff, parent prospects might be identified by the research office and brought into whatever process is used for prospect review. A large institution with thousands of parents might use computers to scan database records for particular professions, zip codes, and other indicators of wealth.

But many institutions limit access to data on parents. Some prohibit sharing parent information with the development office as a matter of institutional policy. In these cases, formal and informal screenings may be necessary to identify major gift prospects. If parent information is not sufficient to include parents in the institution's ongoing prospect-screening program, the staff can include student names and addresses that may trigger a screener to recognize potential donors.

Involving Parent Prospects

Colleges and universities are at a distinct disadvantage in developing programs to interest and involve parents in preparation for soliciting gifts. Unlike an independent school that has as many as 13 years in which to nurture parent involvement and commitment, colleges and universities have at most four years for the crucial processes of identification, involvement, and solicitation. It makes sense that in general, parents' interest in an institution is at its highest during their children's student years, and particularly during the student's first year. If that interest and commitment is developed and nurtured, those parents may continue their support after commencement—which can coincide with an increase in discretionary income once tuition bills are paid in full.

In the realm of major gift fund raising, this short time frame requires that institutions have systems in place for moving quickly with parents who are prospects for significant gifts. The process for nominating members of the governing board must be able to accommodate parents identified during their first year of affiliation with the institution. Parents who have been noted as major gift "suspects" need immediate research so that they can be engaged appropriately early on in their parent years. Involvement might include, for example, requests to serve on special advisory committees; invitations to presidential-level events (such as the "weekend update/discussion" format used successfully by many institutions); or appointments with staff or faculty members who can discuss special programs that relate to the prospects' interests. The long-term cultivation strategies used with alumni are not always as successful with parent prospects unless the institution has done a good job of attracting parents' special interest early in their relationship with the institution.

Soliciting Major Gifts

Just like major gift fund raising from other constituencies, parent solicitations generally follow the "rule of rights": the right person asking the right prospect for the right amount, for the right program, at the right time. That means having a qualified prospect with the potential to make a major gift; sending a solicitor or team of solicitors to whom the prospect is likely to respond favorably; asking for an appropriate and specific amount; and asking for a gift to support a program or project that is of interest to the prospect. There isn't any better way to solicit any prospect, parent or otherwise.

Some undergraduate institutions and independent schools make a special effort to solicit major gifts from qualified parent prospects during their child's final year. They use the years prior to that year to identify and involve their best prospects and then ask for a significant major gift in honor of the child's graduation. Institutions could consider extending this program by soliciting those parents again in years when their children—now alumni—are celebrating major reunions; those parents' gifts could add to the class reunion gift total.

ANNUAL GIVING PROGRAMS FOR PARENTS

Traditional annual giving programs invite all members of a constituency to express support of the institution by making a gift, usually for current operating expenses. Annual giving provides an opportunity for parents to signal a vote of confidence in the institution and its programs. It is for that reason that many institutions consider rates of annual giving participation as important as total dollars raised.

Successful annual giving is staff- and volunteer-intensive. It requires focus on leadership prospects while still paying attention to the "masses." Institutions that engage in full-scale parent annual giving must be able to conduct mail and phone campaigns and should have parent volunteers who assist in the solicitation process.

What Parents Want

To secure that vote of confidence expressed by an annual gift, institutions should consider parents' relationships to their children's institutions. On the most basic level, it would appear that parents might want three things from an institution: a quality education for their children, accessibility and accountability from faculty and administrators, and reasons to be proud of the institution.

Guaranteeing that these are provided to every parent may be out of the development officer's hands. But if a broad-based fundraising program is to succeed, fund raisers must be aware of how the institution is meeting these needs and do their best to encourage an institutional commitment to parent relations. Annual giving from parents is about letting parents know that they are investing their tuition dollars well and that annual support will help maintain the value of their child's diploma long after he or she has graduated.

Annual giving appeals should focus on the sense of pride that parents have in their children's institution. You never hear a parent say, "Susan is going to go to XYZ College. It really isn't a very good school." On the contrary, parents start their relationship with us on a most positive note: It is parents' nature to believe that whatever institution was smart enough to accept their child must be a fine institution indeed.

Almost every school, college, and university can make the case that tuition dollars do not pay for the full costs of educating a student. Appeals to parents to help make up that difference with annual giving dollars should not imply that parents have an obligation to give—an obligation unlikely to generate support from parents who feel the impact of increasing tuition. Rather, appeals should offer them the opportunity to be part of a tradition of giving that has kept the institution strong. Many parents want some recognition that they are sacrificing to send their child to your institution; beating them over the head with "all that you pay still doesn't pay the bills" in unlikely to produce a philanthropic impulse. On the other hand, many parents don't know what their tuition dollars do and don't pay for. Annual giving appeals can help inform parents about the finances of education.

Soliciting Parent Annual Gifts

Just as the fundamentals of major gift solicitation apply to all constituencies, so do the basics of annual giving. Again, depending on the resources that the institution wants to invest and the information available about the parent constituency, an annual giving program can be as simple as a few direct mail appeals or as sophisticated as segmented appeals, intricate volunteer structures, and personal or telephone solicitations.

Institutions that want to invest in a full-scale annual giving program for parents should first evaluate their parent constituency and set realistic goals for participation and dollars to be raised. Like most annual giving programs, a successful parents fund will rely on leadership gifts. Many successful parents fund programs start with a volunteer structure composed of parents who commit to a leadership gift—say, $1,000—as part of their agreement to serve as solicitors. Those parents form the nucleus of the parents fund. They in turn contact, in person or by phone, all parents who have been rated as leadership prospects for the annual giving campaign.

Once the leadership phase of the effort is under way, staff can turn its attention to the general parent population, using direct mail, volunteer parent phoners, or paid callers. Many institutions, sensitive to issues of confidentiality, resist using student callers to solicit parents; many parents may prefer that their giving records not be seen by their children's classmates.

Institutions with highly developed parents funds pay particular attention to the calendar. Appeals may be inappropriate at some times (such as around dates when tuition bills are mailed) and more appropriate at others (say, after successful parent events or as commencement approaches).

The development staff should also recruit, train, and communicate well with a strong cadre of parent volunteers. As with any other constituency, parents respond best to personal solicitations, whether in person or by phone. Parent volunteers trained to articulate the institution's case for support and their own reasons for making gifts to the institution can be the most effective solicitors of other parents.

GRANDPARENTS

Several institutions have developed giving programs for grandparents. These programs can provide additional revenues to a parent giving program that has reached a plateau. In some cases—for instance, where a grandchild is the first in the family to attend college—grandparents may have particularly strong sentiments toward the institution and may be good prospects for support.

You can often obtain mailing information for grandparents from a registration form or other form that asks if the student would like institutional publications and information mailed to his or her grandparents. Those grandparents are then added to the general mailing list for publications, invitations, and fund appeals.

AFTER COMMENCEMENT

It is important not to neglect parents after graduation, if for no other reason than the fact that some of them will now enjoy a reduction of as much as $10,000 or $20,000 in their annual expenses. Maintaining ties to the institution may be important to some parents, particularly those who do not have other educational affiliations. Again, good research can identify those parents of alumni who might be likely prospects for ongoing philanthropy.

Participation by parents can be expected to drop after their children graduate. At the same time, many institutions have a strong core of parents of alumni who continue to support the university, college, or school. Parents of alumni should continue to receive annual giving solicitations until it becomes clear that their philanthropic interests are no longer directed toward their children's institution.

Chapter 20
Raising Funds for Athletics

Jeffrey W. Gray

"The truth is more athletic departments operate in the red than in the black."
—Dick Schultze, NCAA Executive Director

In 1990-1991, more than 1,800 colleges and universities competed in intercollegiate athletics. Most institutions support several different teams, with some having as many as 25 to 30 men's and women's varsity teams. The costs of operating these programs (including coaches' salaries, facilities, recruiting, equipment, travel, tutoring and counseling, publicity, and other costs) are substantial; some NCAA Division I institutions—such as Stanford, UCLA, and the University of Michigan—report annual operating budgets of more than $20 million for athletics alone. As program costs expand and inflation continues to rise, many athletic departments must find ways to increase income.

While private support of intercollegiate athletics has been a long-standing tradition for many colleges and universities, it has received greater emphasis in the last several years. The implementation of Title IX legislation in 1972 significantly increased the costs of women's intercollegiate athletics; the 1984 Supreme Court decision in *University of Georgia and University of Oklahoma vs. the NCAA* significantly reduced income from televising men's intercollegiate football. As ticket prices and sales reached their limits, and television and radio revenues dwindled, financially strapped athletic departments began to look beyond these traditional sources of income. Institutions of all sizes started to ask alumni, fans, and friends for increased financial support of intercollegiate athletics.

DETERMINING PRIORITIES

Whether you are beginning an intercollegiate athletics advancement effort or developing an existing program, a crucial first step is to determine your fund-raising priorities. What will you ask your constituency to support—scholarships, operations, facilities, endowment, or some combination? The fund-raising priorities of the department will be the cornerstone for your development effort. All subsequent issues—such as organization, staffing, and budgets—should flow from this decision.

The knowledgeable development officer will include the athletic department leaders and institutional academic leadership in the process of determining these priorities. While unanimity may not be possible, involving key people in this decision will lend credibility to the subsequent fund-raising efforts. If the institution's leadership, both athletic and academic, are part of the process, their sense of "ownership" will help further the program.

ORGANIZING THE PROGRAM

There is no best way to organize the development effort; rather, each institution's unique character will shape or dictate the organizational structure. Generally, most athletic development programs operate under one of these organizational models: as a function or division of the athletic department, as part of the institution's development operation, through a related foundation or booster organization, or through some combination or variation of these arrangements.

Fund Raising as a Function of the Athletic Department

This arrangement provides credibility and identification for donors and volunteers, who perceive that their support goes directly to athletics and is not diverted to some other program within the institution. And because intercollegiate athletics is such a high-profile endeavor, donors and volunteers enjoy the sense of "being on the inside" that often accompanies supporting a program so closely affiliated with the department.

Some institutions are adding experienced development personnel to their athletic department staff and providing the necessary support for a concentrated fund-raising program. The fact that the institution is willing to dedicate resources to the effort establishes the fund-raising program as an important component of intercollegiate athletics. This arrangement also enables development staff to interact daily with the coaches (some of your most powerful solicitors) and to involve the department in the development effort. As a long-term benefit, current student-athletes are exposed to the idea of giving for athletics, which may plant seeds for their future involvement as donors and volunteers.

A drawback to this type of organization is the extensive initial cost of a development program. Returns are minimal in the early years, and it may take several years for the program to generate substantial income. Financially strapped athletic departments may not have the patience to allow the advancement effort to develop.

Also, expecting existing personnel—such as athletic directors or coaches—to assume direction of the fund-raising effort is a sure path to problems. Staff members who take on fund raising as merely one of many responsibilities will not give it the time and effort necessary to achieve positive results. Successful fund raising is a full-time occupation, and you will need to hire one or more people devoted solely to that task.

Fund Raising as Part of the Institution's Development Operation

An institution that conducts athletic fund raising through the development office may be able to commit more resources and personnel to the effort than is possible if the athletic department does it independently. This arrangement may increase the prospective donor pool for athletics. A centralized system may also reduce conflicts with other institutional fund-raising activities— for example, by ensuring that top prospects do not receive unrelated solicitations for different causes at the same time.

At the same time, this arrangement can diminish the impact of the athletics appeal by making it only one of several appeals coming from the institution. And without direct responsibility or control, athletic department personnel may be less inclined to become involved in fund raising.

Fund Raising through a Related Foundation or Booster Organization

Separate foundations or booster organizations can often provide more flexibility than can institutions mired in administrative red tape. But this flexibility, and the entrepreneurial spirit that characterizes many of these operations, also has been the source of serious problems with the NCAA for a number of institutions. Control, accountability, and record-keeping are crucial with any such organization. The institution must insist on direct involvement or risk severe NCAA sanctions should problems arise.

Each of these approaches has positive and negative aspects. In determining which method or combination is appropriate for a particular institution, staff should analyze both the internal and external issues. The most successful athletic fund-raising programs are marked by their professional approach and ethical operations, regardless of the organizational structure.

ANNUAL GIVING

The most common annual appeal on behalf of intercollegiate athletics is for scholarship support. Donors understand the need for athletic scholarships and find it very appealing to provide the opportunity for a student-athlete to attend their favorite institution. Institutions have capitalized on this interest by establishing complicated donor structures and approaches.

Gift Clubs and Premiums

Traditionally, athletic fund raising has been characterized by a *quid pro quo* attitude on the part of the donor and the recipient institution. The institution establishes several gift clubs, or contribution levels. These typically range between $100 and $5,000 per year, though they can reach as low as $50 and as high as $25,000. Each level has a distinguishing name, such as Coaches Club, Varsity Giver, Diamondback, Bruin Bench, or the like. Donors receive benefits according to the size of their annual gift to the athletic program. These donor benefits often include items such as membership cards, decals, bumper stickers, newsletters, clothing, meals with coaches, campus or stadium parking, travel with the team to away games, or complimentary game tickets.

In the eyes of many athletic administrators, private donations are inexorably linked to such tangible premiums. In a recent survey of athletic fund raisers, most of those asked perceived the most significant benefit for donors to be well-located season tickets.[1] The Internal Revenue Service seems to share that view, as evidenced by rules limiting the tax deductibility of gifts tied to season tickets and other premiums.

Yet a 1985 study of donors at 16 NCAA Division I football schools contradicts that widely held notion. One hundred athletic boosters from each institution were asked to rate the importance of 19 possible motives for contributing to athletic programs. Interestingly, the motive that ranked highest was "personal enjoyment of viewing a school's athletic events"; ranked fifth was "the opportunity to obtain tickets," and "receiving specialty items" was ranked 18th.[2]

An obvious drawback to this form of inducement is the cost of these benefits—not just the "hard" expense of purchasing or manufacturing these items, but the "soft" costs of staff time to administer the program. The use of premiums can also help foster an attitude among donors of "What's in it for me?" rather than developing a loyal base of donors who wish to support and maintain the athletics program because they believe in the cause.

It should be the long-term objective of the athletic fund-raising program to sharply curtail the reliance on donor perquisites. By educating the constituency to the need for private support of intercollegiate athletics, an institution can free itself from the *quid pro quo* attitude and actually develop an attitude of philanthropy within its constituency that will eventually result in more and larger gifts.

Until that objective is achieved, athletic fund raising will remain tied to priority seat location for athletic contests. Some institutions have increased annual giving totals by as much as $500,000 or more by employing a priority seating system, in which people are required to make a contribution to the athletic program to purchase season tickets in the most desirable areas. Programs in which tickets are in great demand may link the number of priority-area tickets available to donors to the size of the gift. For example, donors of $250 may be allowed to purchase a maximum of four tickets in the preferred area; donors of $500 may purchase six preferred tickets; contributions of $1,000 may buy eight tickets; and so forth.

Many institutions have installed a point system for allocating season tickets. Such a system can provide an equitable method of determining seat locations. Donors receive a certain number of points based on their current annual gifts, cumulative giving totals, and successive years of membership. Other factors may include successive years as season ticket holder, major gifts, and recruitment of additional donors. A formula assigns a point value to each category and then adds the total points to determine a ranking for priority seating.

Volunteer Solicitation

A popular method of athletic fund raising is the *team concept* campaign, an intense annual fund campaign lasting a month or two. Volunteers are divided into solicitation teams consisting of a captain and 6 to 12 members. The teams compete individually and collectively for prizes based on the number of contributions obtained, with new gifts receiving greater point value than renewals. The campaign begins with a kickoff event, and weekly or semiweekly reporting sessions are held to recognize progress, announce team and individual standings, and generate enthusiasm among volunteers. Many of these campaigns rely on a community's business leaders. To maximize their involvement, the kickoff and reporting sessions are generally luncheon meetings.

A *regional representative program* extends the team theme to solicitations outside the local area. Volunteers, selected from areas with large numbers of alumni and prospective donors, are designated as regional representatives for the athletic annual fund. These representatives are expected to make their own contribution and then to personally solicit others in their region. The representatives can earn points toward prizes and awards by recruiting new and renewed donors. In contrast to the local campaign, which involves a large number of solicitations in a short period of time, regional representatives are expected to make three to five calls a month throughout the year.

Direct Mail

Direct mail has become an increasingly important component of sophisticated athletic annual giving programs. Direct mail can be used to acquire new donors. As with all direct mail, the response rate for an acquisition mailing is usually 1 percent to 3 percent. Other uses of direct mail are to renew existing donors or to upgrade the level of contribution. The response rate will be higher for renewals than it will be for either acquisition or upgrade because this donor base is proven.

Direct mail also provides an opportunity to involve former athletic standouts, who can sign the mail pieces. The name recognition value of a former student-athlete appeals to many alumni and friends. At the same time, this introduces the former student-athlete—one of our most reluctant constituencies—to the notion of "giving back."

Telephone Use

Like direct mail, telephone marketing can be used to recruit new donors and to renew current or lapsed donors. Another use is to thank donors for their contributions.

If you are contemplating a telephone program, you must determine who will do the calling. Some institutions hire telemarketing firms with off-site calling; others enlist students or student-athletes to call. Student callers, whether paid or volunteer, can provide a positive contact between the institution and its alumni and friends. For some donors, the opportunity to talk with a current student-athlete is the perfect incentive for renewing their support. At the same time, the activity educates student callers about the need for private support and cultivates their interest for future gifts of their own. A drawback to using students is that the fund-raising program is then subject to the vagaries of their schedules (study, work, or social).

A major factor in the success of any telephone marketing effort is attention to administrative detail. Prior to any calling, staff must do a thorough preparation including choosing a site, producing pre-call and post-call mailings, writing a script, recruiting and training the callers, and other tasks. After a night of calling, there must be immediate follow-up with letters and pledge reminders, a means for loading acquired information into the record system, and a method to deal with any complaints. Because of the need for intensive staffing, many institutions opt to hire telemarketing firms to handle all or part of the effort.

Special Events

One would be hard-pressed to find an athletic fund-raising program that does not sponsor at least a golf tournament annually. Auctions, raffles, bingo games, dinners, and receptions have become a very time-consuming portion of many athletic fund-raising programs. These types of events are extremely labor-intensive. Often, the dollars raised are relatively small when compared to the amount of time and energy required of staff and volunteers for a successful event.

Consider using these events as cultivation activities, rather than as major fund-raising vehicles. By making the involvement of prospective donors the primary purpose of the event, you will not be disappointed when your six months of planning and preparation result in minimal dollar returns. Once the event has become established and successful over a few years, do not allow the invitation list to become stagnant. Instead of inviting the same people year after year, consider asking your regular donors to participate by inviting and bringing new guests—preferably nondonors. Be prepared to follow up in less than a week with any new participants. Ask them to contribute to the program and to help identify additional prospects.

MAJOR GIFTS

A growing number of athletic programs are expanding their fund-raising efforts to obtain major gifts along with the annual operating support. These gifts typically go to establish future sources of funding, or endowments. With all endowments, the principal is invested and the interest earned is used to support a specific cause or program.

For example, an exciting gift opportunity for some major donors is to permanently endow an athletic scholarship. Other endowment opportunities might include coaches' salaries, academic support services, travel funds, facilities maintenance, sports medicine, or housing loans.

The amount needed is dictated by several factors including the cost of the program (for a scholarship, this would depend on tuition, room and board, and books); the rate of return on the institution's investments; and the attitude and resources of the constituency. Currently, the gift required to endow athletic scholarships ranges from as little as $50,000 in some state institutions to as much as $450,000 in some private universities. Allowing donors to make a multi-year pledge can make endowments a more attractive option.

Where do the prospects for these major gifts come from? Unlike many areas on campus, intercollegiate athletics has an established pool of prospective donors. Members of that pool have demonstrated their interest in the success of athletics and have proven their willingness to financially support it. First, look to your existing donors—those alumni and friends giving on an annual basis. Next, look to season ticket holders. Consider, also, former student-athletes, former coaches, and former student-managers, as well as parents of current and former players.

These major gifts should be solicited in a personal meeting. (Mail or telephone appeals for gifts of this magnitude not only tend to fail, but they may also alienate the prospective donor.) A crucial factor is to determine the best or most appropriate solicitors. This is done on a case-by-case basis. The development officer should ask, "Who will this prospective donor have the most difficulty saying 'no' to?" Do not overlook the athletic director or coaches as potential solicitors. Who better to represent the program, and explain the importance of private support, than the man or woman responsible?

CONCLUSION

Institutions are aware that in addition to the educational opportunities that accompany athletic competition, the visibility and enthusiasm associated with intercollegiate athletics are an important part of the institution's identity. There is an ever-increasing cost to maintain an athletic program that is representative of the institution's mission.

Today, alumni and friends of these institutions are being asked to shoulder more of the financial responsibility for such programs than ever before, and athletic fund-raising programs are growing accordingly. As these programs become increasingly professional, they will serve not only to enhance the financial health of the athletic program, but as vehicles for gaining new friends and donors for the entire institution.

NOTES

1. Survey of nearly 100 professionals participating in the 1991 meeting of the National Association of Athletic Fund Raisers in Atlanta, Georgia.

2. John E. Billing, Donnell Holt, and Joseph Smith, "Athletic Fund Raising: Exploring the Motives Behind Private Donations," research report prepared for the National Collegiate Athletic Association (Chapel Hill, North Carolina: University of North Carolina, December 1985).

Chapter 21

Fund Raising for Professional Schools within a University

Robert R. Ashton

Professional school development officers face a different—or perhaps additional—set of challenges than do general college or university development officers. The fundamental principles of fund raising do indeed apply equally to all constituencies. But the professional school setting involves some special considerations. These revolve around the relationship of alumni with the school, of the school with the university, and of the development staff with the school's administration.

ALUMNI AND THE PROFESSIONAL SCHOOL

Compared with the general alumni body, the alumni body of a professional school is homogeneous. A university development officer typically deals with many alumni who have only four-year degrees and, perhaps, some who have advanced degrees. A professional school development officer works with alumni who, by definition, all have achieved advanced degrees.

Even more important, these alumni have shared the professional school experience. Law school, business school, medical school, dental school all involve experiences very different from those of the undergraduate school and more or less different from one another. These experiences shape the later relationship of the alumni to the school, and that relationship forms the basis for all professional school development work.

For undergraduates, college typically marks a rite of passage from teenager to adult. Along with their classroom education, most undergraduates also experience their early love(s), their first independence, their first intellectual and physical freedom. Those heady days are suffused in our memories with a warm, golden light, especially as time softens the focus. The bonds we feel to those days, to the friends, the music and, yes, the college, are easily as emotional as rational. And those bonds link us forever, on that emotional level, to our undergraduate institutions.

Professional school students come to school at a different point in their life, with different responsibilities, needs, and expectations. They also come seeking something different than they sought from undergraduate school. They have already been through that transformational life experience. They have decided to return to school—often after some work experience—because they have chosen a career that requires additional training. They are not seeking emotional and intellectual growth; they are seeking credentials. Professional school students have told me, only half joking, that they would just as soon give the school the tuition money and collect their diplomas, skipping the painful and time-consuming hours in the classroom. Later, as alumni, they tend to look back on that experience more as a necessary stint of work than as a warm and growth-filled period.

Instead of enjoying the pleasures of dating and romance, professional school students are more likely to be juggling their studies with responsibilities to a spouse and even children. Rather than living in a dormitory or a sorority or fraternity house, professional school students typically live in an apartment or house off-campus, trying to meet monthly rent or mortgage payments, finding time between classes to cook meals and clean. It is more common for professional school students (especially law and business) than for undergraduates to work at a career as well as study, or even to earn their degree on a part-time basis while supporting themselves and perhaps a family. This leaves little time or energy for social interaction with fellow students, for non-essential study, for discussions with faculty outside the classroom.

When they finish school, professional school students frequently face ten years of monthly student-loan bills of $400 or $500 or more. They have also forgone several years of income and career advancement. Undergraduates leave commencement ready (one hopes) to begin; professional school graduates leave in order to continue.

In short, alumni of graduate professional schools usually have few warm fuzzies, the emotional ties to alma mater prevalent among undergraduate alumni. (A notable exception seems to be medical school, where classmates tend to form strong personal bonds.) Thus, in most cases, the most effective appeal for alumni support of graduate professional schools rarely lies in nostalgia or evocations of lost youth. The more sensible solicitation strategy is to encourage alumni to improve the value of the credential they "bought" years ago by helping to improve the present-day quality (and reputation) of their school.

THE SCHOOL AND THE UNIVERSITY

Like subsidiary divisions of large corporations, most graduate professional schools are stars in a larger constellation. True, a few schools of good repute stand alone, without the support and encumbrance of a mother university. And a few universities (Harvard is the most commonly cited example) advocate significant autonomy for their separate schools and colleges. For most, however, the Harvard notion of "each tub on its own bottom" is far from reality. Indeed, many professional school faculty, if they revealed their innermost beliefs about university governance, would complain that the university uses the professional school as a "cash cow," generating significant net income for the university. And, they would argue, the university doesn't put as much back into the school as the school gives to the university.

On the other hand, trying to maintain a consistent long-term strategy when various components are pulling in their own directions makes life tough for central management, too. A former president of the University of Vermont joked with me some years ago that his worst nightmare—one from which he awoke in a cold sweat—is that his university suddenly had *two* medical schools!

Tension between components and the central management is probably inevitable. For one thing, the goals of the school's management are not always congruent with those of the university's management. For another, the university management usually has responsibility for allocating resources, and each component usually believes it isn't getting all it deserves.

THE SCHOOL AND THE DEVELOPMENT OFFICE

For development officers, prospects are a crucial limited resource. It is in prospect assignment procedures and database management systems that a well-managed central university development office can shine. And it is over these systems that cooperation between component and central development offices is most apt to founder, to the detriment of both. Too often, the central and unit development offices will disagree over who has priority in approaching a top prospect and over who should make those decisions.

In addition, the professional school development officer is frequently pulled by two chains of command—one leading to the school's dean, the other to a university vice president or president. When both the school and the university agree on objectives, strategy, and tactics, this is not a problem. When there is disagreement, however, the development officer must spend much energy and time trying to work around that conflict, rather than generating resources for the school. All too frequently, conflicts between school and university management over other issues will also cloud their relationship in development matters, making an already complex job truly byzantine.

Universities and colleges were founded initially as loose affiliations of often peripatetic faculty. The administrative structure was developed by those faculties to provide the faculty members with necessary services. Today, the exercise of administrative authority is far more complex in higher education than in other organizations, since most faculties still wield at least tacit authority over some crucial aspects of administration. That may explain why so much of the business of higher education is carried on through committees, usually to no one's great satisfaction, if seldom to anyone's great distress.

Thus, to establish an effective structure for prospect management and assignment in a university with active professional school fund-raising offices, the best approach may be to form a committee. This group should be representative of each interested unit, with senior development officers as members. The committee can establish general guidelines, and specific cases of disagreement can be brought before the group for a determination. With each member secure that her or his unit's interests are protected, decisions can be made relatively quickly and with the least disruption. While such a system does little to mitigate inherent conflict among components and with the central management in general, it does provide the development professionals of the university—regardless of their affiliation—a collegial support unit and a simple way to resolve development-related conflicts outside the tangle of internecine politics.

Frequently, component advancement officers feel that university-wide advancement programs compete with, or even run counter to, their own. The vitally important backdrop of alumni programs, publications, and publicity that sets the stage for a successful development program is most susceptible to this conflict. While the professional school may be trying to send its alumni a particular strategic message about its programs, that message is obscured—sometimes even contradicted—by the myriad of other information sent by the university's central management.

The answer is *not* simply to stop the mailing of university-wide publications to professional school alumni. This may cut down on conflicting or confusing messages, but it also reduces the generally positive image of the academic setting in which the professional school is placed.

Rather, a well-run advancement operation brings together the advancement professionals of the components and the central management to set long-term goals and strategies that will support all of them, along with near-term tactics. This way, the various audiences will receive reinforcing messages from the university as a whole and from the components with which they may be affiliated. Within such an environment, the relationship of the school with the university, as well as the relationship of the alumni to the university and to the school, will be healthy and fruitful.

A LIMITED COMMITMENT

Perhaps the most pernicious problem for professional school development officers, however, is the frequent lack of understanding of, and commitment to, a full-scale development program on the part of the school's management. While professional school fund raising is a fast-growing field, most professional school development offices are expected to accomplish their task with far fewer resources—by any measure—than their colleagues in the university's central development office or at a small college. A small liberal arts college with 30,000 alumni is likely to have twice or three times the professional and clerical staff in the advancement areas as a professional school within a larger university, even though the professional school staff may even be working with more alumni. It is often assumed that the university's central advancement offices will provide support, minimizing the need for additional staff at the school level. But given the inherent tension between the school and the university—not to mention the myriad other demands on the central staff and the lack of authority on the part of the component development officer to direct the activities of the central staff—such expectations are often unrealistic.

The plain truth is that most professional school development officers have to do more with less than their colleagues in other settings. And it's not just personnel and operating resources that are reduced. So, all too often, is the understanding and commitment of the dean's office.

Many professional school deans have risen out of the ranks of senior faculty. Their experience in fund raising is limited. Most have participated only as occasional coordinators of "dog and pony shows" for visiting prospects or as part of a solicitation team for a major gift or grant. Many have little understanding of long-range strategy or the lengthy and detailed behind-the-scenes work in research and screening. This lack of understanding can lead to unreasonable expectations, to disinterest, or even to fear and avoidance of fund raising.

Deans of graduate professional schools have their hands full with the many duties of front-line academic leadership. If an army's success depends upon its officers on the field of combat, so a university's success must depend on the strength of its deans. These dedicated men and women must deal with all the disputes— from tenure to office space to promotion to allocation of secretarial support—that arise among the faculty; lead by example and suasion (for no academic leadership is accomplished by fiat or demand); fight for budget and other resources; ensure that admissions and placement operations are competitive; and stay current in applicable academic disciplines. The dean even catches complaints about the temperature in the office or flaking paint in the restrooms! Is there any wonder the dean sometimes seems less than completely focused on fund raising?

It is absolutely vital to the school's success that the chief advancement officer of a graduate professional school remain continually alert for opportunities to educate the school's leadership about fund-raising strategies and techniques. Information on staffing levels, organizational structures, salary levels, volunteer organization, and so forth at peer institutions can help educate the school's leadership. So can attendance at the workshops on development for deans sponsored by various academic accrediting organizations and by the Council for Advancement and Support of Education.

As a professional school development officer, you must remain firm about the need for appropriate levels of staff, budget, and support. To fail to establish those requirements up front is to program your office for failure. You should also set fixed times in the dean's schedule—at least once every other week—for a focused hour-long discussion of specific prospects as well as progress on specific programs. Finally, work with the dean's staff to set aside blocks of time—half a day a week is a good goal—for appointments the advancement staff will set with important prospects, donors, or others. Then make sure you fill those blocks of time, or release them to the dean's schedule far enough in advance that the dean can schedule other activities.

Advancement work in a professional school setting has many particular challenges—a different, less friendly, experience by alumni; possibly thorny relationships with the university's central staff; less attention and understanding than needed from the school's leadership. Yet such work, on the front lines of advancement in the university, is full of special rewards.

While operating in the enriched environment of a large university, the professional school fund raiser also has the opportunity—indeed, the requirement—to get close to faculty and students and to take an active role in the management of the school. In this setting, you can help to focus the school's mission, set long-range goals, directly support interesting and worthy academic programs, work daily with the very students who benefit from the philanthropy you help stimulate, and interact with some of the most brilliant researchers and teachers in the world. You help to send men and women off, each commencement, into careers that will make our society's future better than its past. There is no greater reward than that.

Part Eight

Organizing, Managing, and Supporting Development Programs

As development staffs and budgets have grown in recent years, so has concern with the cost-effectiveness of development programs and the need to manage resources for maximum impact. Issues of how to organize, manage, and provide support services to the development program have made up an ever-larger part of the professional literature and discussion in the past decade.

Many development offices today include dozens, even hundreds, of staff members with increasingly specialized skills and responsibilities. The cost of finding and training a development officer can be substantial. That individual's departure after only a brief time, whatever the reason, not only disrupts the fundraising program but also represents a terrible waste of resources. In Chapter 22, Karen Osborne discusses guidelines for selecting, training, and managing development staff to reduce turnover and ensure a more effective operation.

Perhaps no area of development has grown more in the past decade than that of donor research. Nearly every development office has at least one researcher, and large universities have substantial development research staffs. As the donor research function has grown in size, its role has grown as well. Researchers are now vital partners with front-line development officers in the design of fund-raising strategy. In today's competitive environment, this support function is essential to a successful development program. In Chapter 23, Eric Siegel describes the role, organization, and operation of an effective development research office.

As budgetary constraints increase, careful planning, budgeting, and management are likely to receive even greater emphasis. In Chapter 24, Richard Boardman looks at the costs of fund raising and reviews considerations in planning and budgeting for the development program. In Chapter 25, Gary Evans discusses models for the organization of development staff and functions.

The view of fund raising as an income-producing "investment" by the institution will not be taken on faith in the climate of the 1990s. We will need to demonstrate the effectiveness of our programs, the efficiency of our organizations, and the soundness of our management if we are to receive the confidence and support of our institutions in the years ahead.

Chapter 22

Hiring, Training, and Retaining Development Staff

Karen E. Osborne

Maud Jones has found a new position. With 30 days' notice and a handkerchief full of tears, she is leaving the college she has loved for the past four years.

Leslie, her supervisor, is sorry to see her go. She found Maud to be a dedicated, productive worker with a "can-do" attitude. Now Leslie will have to replace four years of needed experience and skills in the middle of the fund-raising year.

It happens. Good people leave good jobs for positions they perceive to be better ones. Try as we might, we cannot prevent turnover, especially in the highly competitive field of development. Right?

Wrong! Keeping good people is an essential and doable part of our jobs as managers. The most successful development programs result from establishing and cultivating long-term, mutually rewarding relationships with donors and volunteers. How can we achieve that when, as studies suggest, development officers stay in one position for an average of two years?

"The most valuable capital is human capital; the most powerful technology is people," asserts Martin Yate in *Keeping The Best,* a book directed to corporate managers.[1] If that is true for corporate America, it is doubly true for development, an endeavor that depends upon successful relationships built over time.

So what can we do to keep good employees like Maud? What could Leslie have done to prevent her departure? To find out why Maud chose to take a new job, Leslie asked her to participate in an exit interview before she left. Exit interviews conducted by objective parties can provide important clues to our success in creating an environment our employees find motivating and rewarding.

"Why have you decided to leave, Maud?" asked the interviewer, a human resources employee.

"I've been here a long time," Maud replied, shifting uncomfortably in her chair. "This offer is a promotion, more money, a chance to run my own program. I guess it is just time to go."

"There have been a number of openings in the department. Why didn't you apply for one of them?"

"I would have," Maud responded, now looking the interviewer straight in the eye. "Leslie felt I wasn't ready. They were looking for someone with management and budgetary experience, I guess. They hired someone from another college."

Changing the line of questioning, the interviewer asked, "Would you recommend our development department to a friend?"

"No," Maud said emphatically. "They seem to like outsiders, paying new hires better than they pay old ones who stay. Besides, it's a thankless job. We work long hours, have lots of pressure, and receive almost no appreciation."

Maud considered her remarks. "Don't get me wrong. I love the college and Leslie has always been good to me. I just think my new college has a better team spirit."

Maud's answers made Leslie look differently at a relationship she thought she had understood. After four years, why wasn't Maud ready for a promotion? Whose responsibility was that? And, if not Maud, why not someone else from within? Why did Maud feel unappreciated when Leslie thought so highly of Maud's work?

Perhaps most important was Maud's sense that her department lacked a team spirit. Building a strong team is a vital management task. It is also one of the most successful ways to create a motivating and rewarding environment. To build an outstanding work force that will produce, stay, and flourish, our first step is to hire the right people.

HIRING WELL

Leslie will have to replace Maud. Pressed for time and already working long hours trying to meet her fund-raising goals, she's afraid she'll have to settle for less than the best.

This is a familiar situation and an understandable attitude, but definitely the wrong conclusion. Leslie will be able to hire well if she first thinks through her needs. Although this takes time, it is time well spent. A Japanese business practitioner once described the difference between American management and Japanese management as a function of where we put our time. Americans, he explained, take a very short time to plan, a longer time to implement, and an equally long time to correct mistakes. Japanese, on the other hand, take a long time to plan, about the same amount of time to implement, and, therefore, need almost no time to correct mistakes.

DETERMINING YOUR NEEDS

Begin by writing a good job description. What do you need this person to do? What skills and abilities are required to carry out those responsibilities? Too often our job descriptions read like an advertisement, lacking the specificity needed to make good judgments. Are you looking for someone who writes letters and proposals well, travels well, has excellent verbal skills, can influence others, has asked for gifts successfully before? Write down the tasks and then the skills and abilities needed to accomplish those tasks.

Another preparatory step is thinking through the work style or personality type that will complement the others in your current work group. Understanding your style of behavior and leadership, and learning how to recognize others' styles, is a good approach to keeping the office balanced.[2] Often we hire people who are just like us—who work, act, and think like we do—because that is the style with which we are most comfortable. If we are extroverts, take risks, and thrive on change, we immediately associate those traits with productivity and look for them in our hires. Perhaps what we really need is a more cautious person who enjoys stability and will ask us tough questions—in other words, someone to balance our act.

Our penchant for hiring people like ourselves also carries over to decisions about race and ethnic background. We must be clear about needed skills, abilities, and style as well as aware of our natural inclination to discriminate. This point becomes even more significant as the work- and school-age population shifts, adding more minorities and more women to the hiring pool. Networking, developing existing minority and female staff, and seeking candidates from other sources will help bring about a stronger as well as more diverse work group.

What Makes a Good Fund Raiser?

Finding good employees is often difficult. Finding an individual with the skills, abilities, and characteristics needed to become an outstanding development officer deserves some special consideration.

For his book *Born to Raise,* Jerald Panas surveyed more than 2,700 professional fund raisers, interviewed 48 people he believes are outstanding fund raisers, and then came to some conclusions of his own. According to Panas, the top ten attributes, skills, and characteristics required for a fund raiser are:

- impeccable integrity,
- ability to listen well,
- ability to motivate,
- high energy,
- concern for people,
- high expectations,
- love of the work,
- perseverance,
- presence, and
- a quality of leadership.[3]

I would add several other characteristics to Panas' list.

First, good fund raisers have to be philanthropic themselves if they are to understand what motivates others to give and volunteer their time. I ask that question directly during interviews. It always surprises the candidate. I can usually tell from the response and the examples given whether or not the invariable "Yes, I am philanthropic" is true.

Another characteristic that made Panas' longer list of thirty attributes, but not the top ten, is innate intelligence. While the basic tenets of our profession are not difficult to understand, the ability to carry them out well requires a quick, bright mind. I describe to the candidate actual situations I've encountered over the years and ask how they might go about solving the many problems involved. This technique helps indicate whether they are good listeners as well as how bright they are.

Finally, I would add the ability to see the big picture—to have a clear vision and communicate it to others. An old, oft-told story has a great deal of relevance for our work.

A passerby stops at a construction site. He approaches a worker and asks, "What are you doing"? "I'm making cabinets," the young man replies, pointing to his craftsmanship. "I am responsible for all the woodwork." The passerby moves to the second worker and asks the same question. Looking up, she beams with pride. "I'm the electrician, putting in all the wiring." Not far from her is a large man perspiring heavily and stirring a huge vat of cement. Although it is obvious what he is doing, the passerby decides it would be polite to ask the same question he asked the others. The cement mixer's reply surprises him: "Me? Why, I'm building a cathedral."

Hiring cathedral builders is important for all work forces, but especially true for development officers. We must always remember that we are not simply working to close a gift or meet a goal; we're working to advance our institution and its educational mission.

Interviewing Candidates

Once you are clear about what you need, you must decide how widely you need to search to find a pool of qualified candidates or whether you have the talent in-house. If you are successfully building a team, you should have several internal candidates. Begin with them.

Few of us are good interviewers. We ought to be, since an essential skill in being a good development officer is the ability to listen well and discover the interests and motivations of our potential donors. The same skills are essential to skillful interviewing.

Earlier I mentioned several techniques for determining whether or not a candidate has certain skills. The key is asking open-ended questions, listening more than speaking and paying close attention to body language. Taking the time to read one or two books on the interview process is another good preparatory step that will save time and disappointment in the long run.[4]

ORIENTATION AND TRAINING

Jeff had just joined the development office. Every time I walked by his office, his head was bent over his desk, and he was either diligently writing or absorbed in reading. Because a good development officer spends most of the time speaking on the phone or traveling, I was naturally concerned. Jeff didn't report directly to me, so I wanted to be careful how I handled my inquiry.

"Jeff, let's have lunch," I said brightly. Startled and nervous, he agreed, and we set off. (The fact that it was only 11:30 in the morning might have added to his discomfort.)

After chitchat about his family's move to the area and the high cost of housing, I slid gently into the subject at hand. "How would you rate your orientation and training program?" I asked. "Has it been helpful? Do you understand what is expected of you and how to accomplish your tasks?"

Well, it turned out that he had met lots of people and read lots of articles and books. But he was afraid that figuring out what he was supposed to do and how he was supposed to do it were part of a test—a test he was failing miserably.

Everyone—no matter how seasoned or how high or low in the organization—needs a well planned, well thought-out orientation and training program, with clear expectations and direction. Understanding what is expected should *not* be part of a test.

Structuring a Training Program

First impressions are lasting. A personal note or a phone call before the arrival date is a great way to make a new employee feel really welcome. I make sure that on the desk are his or her name plate and business cards ready for the first day on the job. Basic tools—a computer, paper, and pens—are all there waiting. A "welcome to the office" plant or bouquet is a nice touch as well.

I schedule lunch dates for new employees during the first and second weeks. I ask friendly, outgoing coworkers to show the new member of the team around and introduce him or her to the others in the building as well as the others in our unit. I also include in the welcome package a list of individuals I'd like the new person to meet over time and a list of useful books to read.

Formal training starts with the big picture: Class number one is a history of the institution and a campus tour. From the history I move to the present, giving each employee an overview of the school's organization and mission and the organization and mission of the unit to which the new employee will report. Only then do I begin to explain office goals and objectives and their individual responsibilities for helping achieve these goals. Now they have some context as they begin to learn the nuts and bolts of the job.

Another important topic is the chief development officer's philosophy of management and development. A one-hour discussion about my philosophy is a required subject and prerequisite for moving on to the other phases of training.

Problems like Jeff's—not being clear about what he is supposed to do or how he is to get it accomplished—are not always a function of a poor training program. Sometimes the problem is a manager who is unclear about his or her own goals, objectives, and tasks, or who is unable to communicate. A good check point is to have the next level of supervision review all training programs. This helps ensure everyone is on track.

Taking Your Act on the Road

Development is a people-to-people enterprise. Key to a new development officer's training are visits to donors and volunteers with a supervisor and perhaps a peer or two. During the first visits, the experienced person takes the primary role. In subsequent visits, the new employee plans the meeting and is allowed to make his or her own mistakes.

I remember my very first visits as a development officer. An experienced staff member took me on a stewardship visit to a prestigious foundation. I was amazed at the amount of paper she carried. She had spoken to professors and the president about the project the foundation had funded. To answer a question from the program officer, she would whip out just the right piece of paper and quote the appropriate person. The visit went well. Her style worked for her.

My second visit was a solicitation call with my supervisor. He carried no paper. I was awed by his memory for facts and his ability to meander through a conversation, never losing track of the key points he had intended to make. I was allowed to make the ask and, in fact, eventually got the gift.

Both experiences were important and provided excellent lessons for me. I saw both ends of the spectrum in style as well as purpose. Choosing a variety of styles and types of visits on which to send the trainee strengthens the training experience.

I do have a caution to offer, however. After hiring three new development officers in a short period of time, I decided to ask them about the effectiveness of our program. Jeff's responses you already know. Donna offered another perspective. A mature, experienced manager, new to development, she had trained many employees herself.

"It was overwhelming," she said. "I met too many new people at once, and learned too much about too many different jobs before I understood mine. And I spent entirely too little time with you, my boss. If I were you, I'd spread the training out over a longer period of time and concentrate on the people and things I have to know before branching out."

Since that discussion, I have altered my training programs. I let employees meet new people at their own pace, give them lots of time with me, and, after three months or so on the job, revisit some of the earlier discussions. It seems to be working better, but I probably need to ask again.

CREATING A MOTIVATING ENVIRONMENT

Remember Maud and Leslie? Maud felt unpromotable and unappreciated. Outsiders, according to her, were valued more highly than insiders. If Leslie had understood some of the principles involved in motivation, the scene that opened this chapter would have been very different.

Leslie needed to find Maud's strengths, to build upon them, and to reward the results. This key idea can be summed up in the phrase, "Catch them doing something right." As parents we praise our children enthusiastically when they do well, even by accident. We glow when we are successful ourselves, and we often find face-saving excuses when we are not. Yet somehow, we forget this simple, basic need for recognition. We structure our systems to punish errors and take accomplishment for granted.

Management analysts Thomas Peters and Robert Waterman, in *In Search of Excellence,* recommend that we design systems that reward positive behavior rather than punish negative behavior. This allows us to use individuals' strengths to our advantage.[5]

Peter Drucker goes even further. In *Managing the Nonprofit Organization,* he notes that most of us employ average individuals to perform at extraordinary levels of excellence. Identifying each individual's strengths and building on those, by developing new skills and enhancing existing ones, is one of the best ways to create a powerful organization.[6]

Encouraging Motivation

One of the most painful lessons I had to learn (and I tend to learn all my lasting lessons painfully) was that I cannot motivate anyone on my own. People are self-motivated. They are driven, if at all, by their own agendas and needs. The key is to create an environment that they find personally motivating and rewarding, and provide, with that environment, clear and high expectations.

I learned this when, as a manager of a development office, I was besieged with complaints about the quality of the space in which the staff had to work. While working on a long-term solution, I decided it would be a wonderful gesture to have all the carpets cleaned, organize a volunteer clean-up crew, and then decorate the existing spaces with beautiful plants.

The plants gathered dust, shriveled, and died. Not only did they die, disagreements broke out among the staff about who was responsible for the care of the plants. Plants were shoved out of offices and into the halls. I felt unappreciated and annoyed. After all, I was trying to make them feel good and instead everyone felt bad.

Discouraged but determined, I called the entire staff together. I resisted the urge to complain about their lack of gratitude and instead broke them up into small groups of four or five. "What nonsalary things," I asked, "do you currently get from your job that make you feel rewarded for your work?"

The answers were wonderful: "The ability to travel and stay in nice places." "Meeting interesting people we might not have met." "Thank-you notes from my supervisor." "The autonomy I am given." "The level of responsibility I am given." "The ability to have an impact on how things are done in the office and at the college." "The conferences and classes we are able to take."

Then I asked them, "What nonsalary things would you like to have that you currently don't have, that would make you feel rewarded?" I recommended that they start with things they could do for themselves, since those things could happen easily. Then they should suggest things I had control over, then those controlled by my supervisor. I reminded them that the higher up the organizational ladder the control resided, the more difficult it would be to get.

Again, the response was wonderful. Some suggested getting a sign to indicate where the development office was. Some wanted a new refrigerator for the lounge area. Others asked for the ability to come in late on Monday mornings or go home early some night after reunion or another major weekend. Still others wanted more opportunities to work with the vice president and president.

It was so easy, and it cost no more than those ill-fated plants.

Investing in Individuals

Building on strengths and rewarding often and well are only part of the story. During Maud's exit interview she was asked why she had not applied for some of the promotion opportunities in the development office. She had replied, "Leslie felt I wasn't ready."

Leslie and Maud missed an important aspect of creating a motivating environment. My staff said it clearly when I asked them about the things they received that made them feel rewarded: autonomy, responsibility, impact, opportunities for training.

All of these things are tools in the development of people. Helping your staff learn new skills, especially those skills needed for a higher-level job, is essential. We cannot promote everyone, but when the opportunity arises, someone should be ready. When we can't promote, we can expand or enhance responsibilities. Investing in our staff members will be rewarded tenfold. Sometimes we will be disappointed. Sometimes we train people to see them go and achieve for someone else, somewhere else. But more often than not, we win.

EVALUATING PERFORMANCE

The room is filled with noises and laughter. Occasionally a voice raises above the steady murmur and one can catch a phrase or two as small groups discuss the topic at hand—determining criteria for performance evaluations.

" 'Communication' and 'interpersonal' are too much the same."

"Going the extra mile."

"How much more time do we have?"

The staff is meeting to identify those characteristics essential to getting an "A." Every time I do this, no matter where or what the mix of people, the final list comes out pretty much the same. Nevertheless, I start from scratch with each new group or every time the old group has changed substantially enough to warrant a revisit.

"Judgment" and "decision-making" always get on the list. As a member of the discussion groups, I put them there myself. Basic competence in the needed technical skills, communication skills, the ability to work and play well with others (better known as interpersonal skills), organizational skills, and the ability to set and understand priorities, are always on the list as well. Management and supervisory skills, for those who have such responsibilities, usually have a long list of qualifying attributes such as: ability to plan, lead, motivate, inspire, evaluate, have a vision, delegate, coach, direct, and influence others.

The evaluations themselves take time. On the average, they take one to three hours to think through and write, per employee. The employee goes through this as well, writing a self-evaluation and sharing it with you prior to the evaluation meeting. Evaluation discussions should also take time. The discussion should center on progress, results, strengths, plans for growth and development, and achievements.

No matter what the rules are at the institution in which I work, I require two evaluations per year. One is for course corrections, and one is the formal review that goes to the human resources office. At the end of each evaluation discussion, employees know exactly what it will take to get an "A" next time, whether or not they received an "A" this time.

Dealing with Mistakes

Sometimes, no matter how carefully you plan, no matter how well you interview or how clearly you spell out the expectations, you and the new hire make a mistake. The skills he has are not the ones you need, and he's not willing or able to learn. It's not a match. She isn't having fun and never will. The pace is wrong.

Sometimes you have to let people go. Before you do, document behavior, discuss a plan with a short time frame for immediate improvement, and keep the human resource office and your supervisor informed and involved.

But when you are sure, do it. Carrying dead weight for any length of time demoralizes others, jeopardizes your program, and hurts your credibility. Peter Drucker states it clearly, "If they try, they deserve another chance. If they don't try, make sure they leave."[7]

BACK TO THE BEGINNING

So, what happened to Maud? What did Leslie do or not do that could have left them both winners? Here is a short list of suggestions to add to the do's and don'ts already discussed.

- Listen to your employees.
- Develop natural successors.

- Provide frequent informal feedback on progress against goals and expectations.
- Keep listening to your employees.
- Demonstrate yourself the behavior you seek.
- Achieve yourself the results you hope they will achieve.
- Share the blame and give away the glory.
- Delegate responsibility and authority while remaining ultimately responsible.
- Have and share a vision and a philosophy.
- Continue to listen to your employees.
- And remember to build cathedrals!

NOTES

1. Martin J. Yate, *Keeping The Best: And Other Thoughts on Building a Super Competitive Workforce* (Holbrook, Massachusetts: Bob Adams, 1991).

2. One of the more widely used instruments for learning about personal style is the Myers-Briggs Type Indicator, a brief test that helps you profile personality type.

3. Jerold Panas, *Born to Raise: What Makes a Great Fundraiser: What Makes a Fundraiser Great* (Chicago: Pluribus Press, 1988), 212.

4. One of my favorites is Martin Yate's *Hiring the Best: A Manager's Guide to Effective Interviewing* (Boston: Bob Adams, 1987).

5. Thomas J. Peters and Robert H. Waterman, Jr., *In Search of Excellence: Lessons from America's Best-run Companies* (New York: Harper & Row, 1982).

6. Peter F. Drucker, *Managing the Nonprofit Organization: Practices and Principles* (New York: HarperCollins, 1990), 147.

7. Ibid., 150.

Chapter 23

Operating a Donor Research Office

Eric Siegel

To many people, the term "donor research" conjures up an image of clerks laboriously copying biographical information out of reference books and alumni files because the development office thought it would be a good idea to know something about prospective donors. This may have been true in the development office of the 1970s. However, as fund-raising campaigns have become more demanding and complex, and fund-raising techniques more sophisticated, the donor research process has evolved as well.

Donor research at most educational institutions has progressed far beyond the simple task of compiling information from printed sources. It is now a multifaceted process of information retrieval, analysis, maintenance, and dissemination that forms the foundation for identifying, cultivating, and soliciting major gift prospects.

WHAT IS DONOR RESEARCH?

The definition of donor research, and the responsibilities of the donor researcher, vary with the fund-raising operation itself. Depending on the size and scope of development activity, donor researchers frequently double as proposal writers, gift processors, administrative assistants, or front-line development officers. Fortunately, most educational institutions, especially those conducting major campaigns, now realize that donor research is an essential component of development and, as such, requires full-time staff.

Even with this understanding, the meaning of donor research can vary. Many research offices still function entirely reactively. Development officers unearth new prospects or reactivate old ones and ask the research office for information on these prospects. The researcher's role begins and ends with this task.

Although this will always be a crucial element of the researcher's job, progressive institutions realize there is much more to donor research. Specifically, there is proactive research, in which individual researchers and especially the director of research play a key role. Proactive research includes identifying individuals who appear to have the capacity for significant giving (called "suspects"), screening these suspects to determine who among them may be bona fide "prospects" for major gifts, and then classifying them according to potential giving level.[1] Prospect "tracking," the systematic monitoring of steps in the cultivation of a prospect, is also a part of the prospect information continuum, and as such is also a logical duty of the research office.

RESEARCH RESPONSIBILITIES

All these tasks—suspect identification, prospect screening, information development, prospect classification, and prospect tracking and management—are part of a collaborative effort between front-line development officers and the research office. Let's examine each of these steps in more detail.

- *Suspect identification.* The research staff should play a pivotal role in discovering suspects, both within and beyond an institution's identified constituency. Suspect names come from many sources, but the research office can contribute significantly by routinely perusing major newspapers and magazines. However, merely collecting information is not enough. The research office must develop procedures for maintaining data and tracking suspects, and research staff must routinely inform key development officers of potential prospects.

  Electronic demographic screening has greatly enhanced the suspect identification process. Many fundraising consultants now offer services for ranking and analyzing an institution's constituency based not only on demographic data but also life styles, consumer habits, and prior giving history. It is essential to remember, however, that demographic screening can only predict people's giving capacity; until they are examined individually, they remain suspects.

- *Prospect screening.* As suspects are identified, their names go to volunteer and staff screening committees who try to separate those who have major gift capacity from those who do not. The research office's role in the screening process can include preparing suspect lists, supervising screening sessions, tabulating accumulated data, and, more importantly, providing preliminary research on suspects for whom the screening process is inconclusive.

- *Information development.* Screening produces rosters of major donor prospects. Substantial research is then necessary before development officers can decide how to cultivate and solicit these people. Gathering this information is the research staff's primary responsibility. As researchers develop comprehensive biographical portraits of major gift prospects, the emphasis must be on assessing a prospect's net worth or capacity to give, philanthropic interests, relationships with people affiliated with the institution, and attitudes toward the institution.

  However, even the most sophisticated and well-equipped research staff cannot always accurately assess all prospects. The development officer can help by providing contact reports detailing information from personal visits with prospects and volunteers. This information often provides the hints researchers need to transform sketchy data into a comprehensive overview of a prospect's potential.

- *Prospect classification.* Thorough donor research provides the criteria necessary for classifying prospects. Using accumulated data and input from staff and volunteers, research staff can rate major gift prospects according to their financial capacity, interests, and readiness to give. This classification information is then incorporated into a prospect tracking and management system that routinely charts and assesses progress regarding each prospect.

- *Prospect tracking and management.* The research staff can be enormously helpful in rating and designing strategy and should take the lead in devising a workable tracking/management system. Additionally, even when the bulk of research is done, the research staff should be continually aware of new information that may affect a prospect's capacity or willingness to give.

This progression through the major gifts process, from identification to solicitation, is cyclical. Even as the solicitation of top
prospects comes to closure, other prospects are being classified,
researched, screened, and identified. Major gift donor pools must
continually grow. Routine identification of new prospects fuels the
growth of development programs for years to come.

THE RESEARCH OFFICE AND THE ORGANIZATION

The question of where the research office fits in the
organization's reporting structure bedevils advancement operations. At some institutions, research reports directly to the development director or the director of major gifts. At other, larger
institutions, research reports to a director of development operations or the head of administrative and financial services.

Reporting relationships notwithstanding, the primary emphasis of a donor research program should be on major gifts.
Contemporary educational fund raising, especially in the context
of large, multi-year campaigns, places an enormous burden on the
research staff. There are more than enough major donor prospects
requiring thorough research, and the research office can ill afford
to be bogged down preparing profiles on potential alumni award
recipients, honorary degree nominees, annual fund donors, and
the like. Yet this often occurs. Since many of these special projects
are high-volume and seasonal, large backlogs of pending major
donor research can develop. Thus, advancement leaders must ask
themselves these questions:

- What is the most cost-effective use of the research staff's
  time?
- What advancement priorities are best served by the research office?

More important than the research office's position in the
organizational hierarchy are issues of communication and access.
When the research department does not report directly to the
director of development, and even more so when it reports to a
separate service department, there is significant potential for
isolation. In the worst cases, the research office cranks out
voluminous amounts of major prospect profiles only to see them
disappear into the major gifts office. Research staff receive no
feedback on how the information is used or whether their work is

truly instrumental in major gift cultivation. They feel no sense of involvement in the development process.

Donor research must be regarded as an integral part, rather than an adjunct, of the development process. The research director and staff are in fact development officers who possess considerable knowledge of an institution's prospect base, even though they are not involved in daily contact with donors. Indeed, donor researchers, along with the development director and major gifts director, probably have the broadest knowledge of an institution's major gift potential and should be consulted every step of the way toward a major solicitation. Regular reliance on research expertise will enable the development office to maximize its major gift opportunities.

Regardless of reporting structure, the research staff should attend all meetings where major gift prospects are discussed and should be prepared to add new information to enhance cultivation and solicitation. The research director should be in routine contact with all development personnel with major gift portfolios. By emphasizing interaction between research and senior development personnel, an institution will be better able to take advantage of the knowledge and skills of donor researchers and will be able to devote less time to organizational issues.

STAFFING AND TRAINING

Donor research is a labor-intensive effort, particularly when an institution is launching a major campaign. Research will be conducted on many more prospects than the relative few who will actually become major donors. A well-designed screening program, however, will eliminate many prospects before research becomes too heavily involved in the process. Development planning, and especially campaign planning, must take into account how many major donors will be needed to ensure a program's success, how many prospects will be needed to guarantee the desired number of major donors, and how many researchers will be needed to provide adequate financial and biographical data on all of the identified prospects. One must also factor into this equation what responsibilities other than major donor identification and research are assigned to the research office.

There is no rule of thumb governing the size of the research staff. Some commonly repeated formulas are one full-time researcher for every $10 million of a campaign goal, one for every $10 million raised annually, or one for every four development officers with major gift responsibilities. These formulas are rarely put into effect. The ratio of research staff to major gifts officers is rarely 1:4; more often, it is 1:8, or worse. Unfortunately, at most institutions, development planning rarely anticipates the vast quantities of research requests generated by a large major gifts operation. To avoid creating a large backlog, the research office frequently has to cut back services or produce less-thorough research. Such a situation can also preclude proactive research as the staff struggles to keep pace with research requests.

Even if an ideal ratio is unattainable because of budgetary constraints or other factors, a commitment to a full-time professional research staff is essential. Institutions that rely heavily on students to do their donor research run the risk of high turnover rate and lack of employee loyalty.

A commitment to full-time employees also necessitates a commitment to providing salaries that will attract and retain skilled researchers. The days when successful advancement offices could get by paying researchers an administrative assistant's salary are over. In the increasingly complex world of information, it takes a trained professional to sift through the myriad of printed resources and online databases that have become the working tools of the donor research office. Competitive salaries will greatly reduce turnover—an important factor in developing staff loyalty and continuity—and boost recruitment potential, ensuring a choice among qualified candidates. The person assigned the responsibility of overseeing the identification and research of major donor prospects should be accorded the same status and salary as a senior development officer.

Researchers, like their development counterparts, come from a wide variety of educational and professional backgrounds. The best researchers, however, share some common traits. Most are well read and have a tremendous amount of curiosity about the world around them. They are thorough and highly detail-oriented. They are persistent; if information exists on a prospect, they will find it. Most have done extensive research in the past and, even if they have never worked in libraries, are not bewildered by the vast array of information available in a major academic or public library.

When hiring a new researcher, it is best to look for people with these traits and, whenever possible, to seek those with extensive, if not professional, library experience. An applicant with professional library and information science credentials is already well versed in information storage and retrieval and will be much easier to train in the intricacies of donor research. Writing skills are also important, but the ability to retrieve, analyze, synthesize, and disseminate information quickly is the chief hallmark of a good donor researcher.

Hiring the right person makes training that much easier. A new researcher with the requisite information skills needs only to be introduced to the fund-raising environment: the alumni/donor database and record systems, the confidential nature of development work, and some of the specialized resources used in donor research. If a new researcher requires little or no training in research resources and methodologies, the training period can be as short as one month and certainly no more than three.

Training a director of research is another matter entirely. Assuming there are no internal candidates, emphasis should be placed on hiring an external candidate with donor research experience. The candidate must be a self-starter, because there will rarely be anyone in-house with sufficient donor research background to be of much assistance to the new director. If none of the candidates possess adequate donor research experience, it is advisable to opt for information experience over development experience. The transition will be easier for someone with professional information skills even if experience in a development setting is lacking.

RESEARCH RESOURCES

Developing a professional donor research office requires not only a serious staffing commitment but also a commitment to provide the staff with the resources needed to do the job. Primarily, this means devoting significant funds toward building a donor research library and providing access to (and training for) computerized databases. The size and scope of a research library and online database access will vary greatly depending on an institution's major donor constituency. Those institutions with national or international constituencies will require different publications and access to different databases than an institution with a regional or local base of support.

Other factors are the relative proximity of the research office to an institution's library, the library's collection development policy, and the nature of the working relationship between the research office and development officers. If the research office is located near the campus library, the need for a comprehensive in-house library may be lessened; still, the most efficient and cost-effective research operations are self-sufficient ones where a minimum amount of staff time is lost to travel. Additionally, the libraries at many institutions, even some fairly large universities, do not satisfy some basic needs of donor research. This is especially true of institutions not offering a business curriculum.

One must also consider the development-research relationship. Is there a frequent demand for immediate information? Is the research office in constant telephone contact with field officers? If so, the need for comprehensive internal resources will be greater. An advancement office must be willing to budget at least $5,000 annually for a bare-bones reference book collection and for journal subscriptions. Ten thousand dollars annually will buy an adequate library, but it takes about $20,000 per year for a truly state-of-the-art library.

Budgeting for online database searching depends greatly on how many services a research office selects. An annual budget of $12,000 should cover thorough database searching on all major donor prospects; high-volume operations or those that lack printed resources will probably require more.

If one is forced to choose between online and printed resources, the emphasis should be on building at least a core reference library while developing online capability. It is important to remember that a library is a resource for the entire advancement staff, while database searching is something that can only be done by a few skilled practitioners. Finally, many key databases reach back only a few years; the active careers of many major donor prospects require older references. For now, books are still needed to supplement database information.

Essential References

This chapter will not attempt to provide a detailed bibliography of the books routinely used by donor researchers. But some of the resources that should be part of every donor research library deserve note here.

The Bibliography and Genealogy Master Index is an essential starting point for all research on individuals. This index covers most major biographical reference materials starting with the early 1970s and will quickly tell the researcher if information on a particular prospect is readily accessible. The index is expensive—more than $2,000 for three multi-volume cumulations. (Research offices subscribing to the DIALOG online database system can search a more comprehensive Biography Master Index database for as little as $3 per name.)

Essential biographical reference tools include the Marquis Who's Who series, particularly *Who's Who in America, Who's Who in Finance and Industry,* and the regional volumes that most closely match an institution's major donor constituency. Marquis Who's Who also publishes professional volumes covering advertising, entertainment, law, and other fields, some of which may be useful depending on the constituency in question. Other basic biographical resources are the *Directory of Medical Specialists, Martindale-Hubbell Law Directory, Standard and Poor's Register,* and Dun & Bradstreet's *Reference Book of Corporate Managements.*

For researching corporations, *Standard and Poor's Register* and Dun & Bradstreet's *Million Dollar Directory* are excellent resources with national orientations. Corporate directories are available for most regions and large urban centers around the country. *The Directory of Corporate Affiliations* provides valuable corporate subsidiary information. The series of Moody's manuals, although expensive, are essential resources for corporate histories and merger/acquisition activity.

Essential foundation reference materials include publications of the Foundation Center and Taft Group. A number of regional foundation publications are available as well. The Foundation Center also offers an Associates program for a nominal cost, offering participating institutions telephone access for detailed foundation information and other services.

Online Databases

The most revolutionary trend in donor research in the past decade has been the increasing reliance on online database searching. Armed with a computer, a modem, and specialized software, the researcher can now access in minutes information that used to take hours or days to accumulate using printed indexes and reference materials. Many databases contain information that is inaccessible, or difficult to locate, in print. Thus database searching not only makes research more efficient, it also provides the researcher with a greater abundance of resources.

Once perceived as being inordinately expensive, database searching is now considered the most efficient, cost-effective way of conducting donor research. Many of the available databases are expensive to use, especially if researchers do not have proper and thorough training. Nevertheless, the time saved by having relatively complete prospect information at one's fingertips far outweighs the costs involved.

Many databases simply provide citations to other reference works. More, however, offer "full-text" options, which allows the researcher to examine the complete reference on the computer. This eliminates the labor-intensive process of rummaging through library stacks, finding an operating photocopier, and searching through endless reels of microfilm and microfiche cards. However, full-text searching is significantly more expensive than pulling up a bibliographic citation. So, one must weigh the cost and time of taking citations to the library versus searching databases using the full-text option.

Researchers generally do much of their online searching through vendors who provide access to many different databases. Perhaps the most useful of these services is DIALOG, which offers access to hundreds of databases, about fifty of which are useful for donor research. These cover newspaper and magazine articles, press releases, corporate reports, foundation grant information, biographical directories, and more; some indexes reach as far back as the 1970s.

DIALOG charges a minimal annual fee; subscribers then pay for actual online time and print charges, which vary from database to database. DIALOG, however, is not a particularly user-friendly system, and users should receive training from DIALOG as well as from an experienced researcher. Several cost-reducing tricks and shortcuts can be learned only from someone with considerable donor research experience.

The list of available databases and services is immense, and growing far too rapidly to cover fully here. Examples of other useful databases are DataTimes and Vu-Text, both of which offer a broad spectrum of national newspaper coverage, a must for advancement offices with dispersed constituencies or for institutions in areas not covered by the major newspapers indexed in DIALOG. The Invest/Net system, another favorite of researchers, provides up-to-date Securities and Exchange Commission stock transaction information. Some databases are of regional use; for instance, Californians or those with large California constituencies can subscribe to online real property and tax assessors information through DataQuick or Damar. This enables a researcher to retrieve a list of properties owned by a prospect in a matter of minutes.

Other Sources

In conducting donor research, one must also consider non-published, public information sources. Courthouse information such as probate files, divorce settlements, and civil actions offer the researcher important financial information on major donor prospects that is only rarely available in print. These resources should be used judiciously—only when a prospect is considered capable of a significant gift and previous research has failed to back up this perception with hard data. The overall research budget should allow for occasional travel to county courthouses.

Another important resource is the interview—either with prospects themselves or with volunteers who know a prospect well. Interviewing should be the responsibility of field officers, who should file contact reports after meeting with volunteers and prospects. However, it is advisable to recruit a few well-placed volunteers on whom researchers, or at least the director of research, can rely for additional prospect information.

RESEARCH PRIORITIES

Even with sophisticated databases and a current reference library, it is not always possible to find substantial information on all prospects. Even finding nothing takes time—about three or four hours of thorough searching. Conversely, information on some prospects is so plentiful that a researcher must be trained to recognize the point at which research becomes redundant. The researcher must keep in mind the essentials of donor research (net worth, philanthropic tendencies, connections with and attitudes toward the institution) in deciding when to press on or when to quit.

Still, the volume of research requests generated by a large development operation can overwhelm even a sizable research staff. Guidelines enabling development officers to best use researchers' skills and knowledge are essential. A simple and perhaps obvious notion is that not all prospects require the same amount of research. To avoid spending as much time on a $1,000 prospect as on a $100,000 prospect, one must introduce the concept of levels or tiers of research. First, the development office must define what it means by a major gift, a leadership gift, a special gift, and so on. It must also establish a bottom-line figure for prospects for whom any research will be done. These figures will vary considerably from one institution to another, but once established, they help bring a coherent structure to the research process.

Other factors involved in developing a tiered research system include request deadlines, prospect status and rating, and prior research. Urgent requests cannot be given in-depth treatment. Prospects further along in the cultivation process and with higher capacity ratings will warrant more substantial research. In-depth research should only be conducted on prospects with significant major gift capacity; the most difficult and sensitive channels (such as courthouse documents) should be requested only if lower-tiered research yields unsatisfactory results. Tiers, however, should not have rigid boundaries. A researcher assigned to a prospect should keep in close contact with the requesting development officer, suggesting that some projects be curtailed if the prospect seems unpromising or expanding the research if a prospect turns out to have greater resources than previously assumed.

Another integral part of the donor research process is the maintenance of an accessible central file system. The rapid growth of database searching technology has caused some researchers to question the need for maintaining paper files at all. They argue that all pertinent research information can be stored on a computer and that additional information can be pulled up during a simple database search. This, however, deprives the institution of a valuable archival resource, a complete history of an institution's relationship with its donors. From the researcher's point of view, files with years of accumulated newspaper and magazine clippings may pose space and storage problems, but they significantly reduce the number of unnecessary research requests. If development officers have access to extensive donor and prospect files, some prospects may require little or no additional research. If there is a future for the paperless office, it will come not from eliminating aspects of a vital institutional resource, but rather from image processing systems capable of storing large quantities of file materials.

Collecting prospect information for central files and breaking down the research workload into tiers greatly improves the efficiency of the research operation. But there are still times when even a large research staff faces conflicting priorities. One solution is to involve the director of development or the director of major gifts in setting priorities for research. When requesting research, development officers should be asked to indicate not only a level of research, but also whether the request is of high, medium, or low priority. The director of development can then be asked to approve all high-priority requests, as well requests for in-depth research, in light of overall institutional priorities. When conflicts or competing deadlines arise, the director of research can consult with the development director to determine an appropriate course of action.

ETHICS AND CONFIDENTIALITY

In the summer of 1988, donor research became a hot news item. The nation's press suddenly "discovered" research and began to call into question some of the profession's practices.[2] Since then, the ethics of contemporary fund raising, and donor research in particular, have dominated much of the discussion at professional conferences and workshops. The concerns expressed both by the press and by researchers themselves revolve around the lengths to which one will go to collect prospect information and the idea that philanthropy is a noble calling and therefore does not merit prying into the lives of potential donors.

Reporters looking for a good story are capable of exaggerating certain aspects of donor research; the idea of a "nonprofit CIA" is certainly more glamorous than that of researchers sitting at a computer terminal or browsing through library stacks. Still, donor researchers are at times overly aggressive in their pursuit of information, and data maintained in donor files may sometimes portray prospects in an unflattering light. Researchers and development professionals must learn how to police themselves. In the ever-increasing competition for philanthropic dollars, the tendency to over-research must be avoided. Bobbie Strand writes:

> Respect is at the heart of [donor research]. Information that could damage a prospect's reputation or cause embarrassment to him or her should not be recorded or shared indiscreetly. . . . Security for any personal information should be assured. . . . Respect for the institution and its needs and respect for possible donors will enable the researcher to produce information and suggest strategy to meet those needs with integrity and pride.[3]

Donor researchers are very much caught up in the information explosion and the technological innovations that have made that explosion possible. Prospect data will become even more plentiful and accessible. Providing the essential information to fuel the development process is an enormous responsibility, one that must be undertaken with a clear understanding of an institution's mission and a respect for the privacy of donor prospects.

NOTES

1. Emily P. Henderson, "A Prospectus for Prospect Research," in *Prospect Research: A How-to Guide*, eds. Bobbie J. Strand and Susan Hunt (Washington, D.C.: Council for Advancement and Support of Education, 1986), 5-18.

2. Anne Lowrey Bailey, "Today's Fund-raising Detectives Hunt 'Suspects' Who Have Big Money to Give," *Chronicle of Higher Education*, June 22, 1988, A1ff; Connie Leslie, "Prospecting for Alumni Gold," *Newsweek*, Sept. 5, 1988, 66-67; Stephen Davis, "Universities Strike Gold with an Academic Shake-Down," *The Sunday Times* (London), December 11, 1988.

3. Strand and Hunt, *Prospect Research*, i-ii.

Chapter 24

Measuring Fund-raising Costs and Results

Richard B. Boardman

One of the "10 basic laws or principles" of fund raising Harold J. Seymour laid out in the 1950s was this: "You can't raise money without spending money; within reasonable limits the return is likely to be commensurate with the investment."[1] In his classic text, *Designs for Fund Raising,* Seymour goes on to list "parsimony" as one of fund raising's seven deadliest sins. In the world of philanthropy, that word surely catches your attention.

Now, some forty years later, everyone agrees that if you want to raise money you have to spend it—or, rather, to "invest" it. The issue today is how much of an investment successful fund raising requires. To address that, development officers must answer three broad questions: What is the gift potential of my institution? How much should I invest to realize that potential? How do I evaluate my results?

The question of gift potential is the most elusive and difficult to predict. Institutions differ in important ways from one another, and comparisons are difficult, if not impossible, to make. Each institution changes over time. Expectations about gift income also vary and often reflect institutional need rather than reality. (The questions in table 1 suggest some of the factors that influence the complex question of gift potential.)

The question of how much to invest is easier to approach. Pressures to control costs—from the president, governing boards, and budget committees—are increasingly intense, and directors of development now receive explicit guidelines for setting their budget requests more often than in the past. Fortunately, standards exist today that help development directors be more precise about expectations than they could be years ago.

Table 1. Factors Contributing to Institutional Potential

1. Is the institution private, with a long tradition of charging top dollar for tuition and fees, thus ensuring that the great majority of students will come from wealthy successful families and will, because of example or inheritance, become wealthy and successful themselves?
2. Is it old and prestigious and thus able to provide prestige to those who support it?
3. Although private, does it behave like a public university, solving the problems of the region and contributing to the ability of businesses to make a profit?
4. Does it have professional degree programs and thus alumni of schools of medicine, engineering, business, and law?
5. Has it been and is it today large, with hundreds of thousands of mature alumni from whom to draw financial support?
6. Is it located in a major metropolitan area that is healthy and expanding?
7. Has it been and is it today a wealthy university that has been able to take the long-term view and invest whatever is needed to support and expand an aggressive development program?
8. Do most of its alumni live within or near the city in which the institution is located?
9. Are many of its alumni active and well connected, and can they bring influence to bear on philanthropists, foundation heads, and corporate executives?
10. Does the president of the college or university have a sincere interest in people, and does he or she take the time to cultivate their support of the institution?
11. Is the president good at soliciting major gifts, and does he or she take the time to do it?
12. Does the board of trustees take an active interest in fund raising, and is there a cadre of dedicated, dependable, and effective fund raisers among them?
13. Is the advancement staff highly competent, properly rewarded, and loyal; is turnover held to a modest level?
14. Does the institution do everything it chooses to do very well, meriting the support of alumni, other individuals, businesses, and foundations?
15. Has it had a strong alumni program through the years, and is its alumni leadership actively supportive of the development program?
16. Does it have a good public relations program that maintains the sympathy and support of all its constituencies?
17. Does it have a good record-keeping system, and does it do good research on its major prospects?

Questions from *Expenditures in Fund Raising, Alumni Relations, and other Constituent (Public) Relations,* a 1990 joint study by the Council for Advancement and Support of Education and the National Association of College and University Business Officers.

Evaluation of results is tricky. Numbers are easy to come by, but their interpretation is more elusive. But fund-raising professionals are developing new methods to measure return on investment and to make other meaningful comparisons. Presidents and board members always want to know how their institutions compare to others, and development operations now have access to information that will both explain their actions and show why alternative courses of action will or will not work.

THREE VIEWS OF INVESTING IN DEVELOPMENT

Consensus on development budget decisions is important. But it may not be easy to reach, partly because each of the parties involved tends to see development—and its costs—differently. Development managers must understand the natural prejudices and biases that each of these people brings to the discussion of investing in development.

The typical development officer is quick, and correct, to say, "Give me $50,000 for a new staff member and program support, and that person will raise $150,000." The fund raiser recognizes that successful fund raising involves developing strong and personal relationships with prospects, and that this takes time. In turn, he or she encourages the institution to invest adequately and early—for example, by increasing staff in the planning phase of a campaign rather than waiting for its announcement. The fund raiser will try to convince superiors to evaluate results according to the institution's fund-raising potential and long-term return on investment.

The president, in contrast, feels institutional needs dramatically and wants to set goals that relieve immediate financial pressure. The president sees that a $50,000 increase in annual giving now will solve current problems better than a $1 million pledge paid over five to seven years. He or she will ask if gifts to capital or special programs will free other monies that can then be used for unrestricted purposes. The president will feel the need to put pressure on all departments to be efficient. From this point of view, the often-raised question is, and should be, how much will it cost to take in a particular gift?

The president will also be concerned about how much of his or her own time must be spent on public relations, alumni affairs, and development. In the end, the president will realize that much of the time he or she spends in cultivating major gifts may benefit not the current administration, but those that follow.

The business manager, always interested in controlling costs, might not understand the subtleties of development. This officer's view of expenses tends naturally to be quantitative rather than qualitative. For this reason, the business manager may not see the sense in the way a fund raiser does business. Fund raisers don't help improve this perception; traditionally, development officers have been stronger in strengthening relationships externally than in building alliances internally.

Before development officers can institute an effective program outside the institution, they must make sure that others within the institution understand and accept fund raising's essential processes of involvement, education, and solicitation.

RESEARCH ON COSTS AND EVALUATION

No reliable data exist on fund-raising costs over the years. Still, as one looks at how the world of philanthropy has grown in size and complexity, it is obvious that costs have risen considerably. A good guess is that costs as a percentage of cash returns have probably doubled in the last twenty-five years. Take something as simple as telephones: In 1970, Brown University's three-year, $30 million capital drive required only four telephone lines for capital, annual, and planned giving. Life was easier then.

If you read everything that has been written about fund raising over the last thirty-five years, you won't find much on costs and evaluation. The subject has not been studied with the kind of care required for decisions today because, until recently, there was no real pressure to do so. A survey of books, articles, and publications of the Council for Advancement and Support of Education (CASE) turns up a lot of good advice but few hard facts.

John W. Leslie's *Focus on Understanding and Support: A Study in College Management,* published in 1969, was the first comprehensive survey on the status of development in general and went a long way to improve awareness, trust, and understanding of the subject.[2] The study identified "yardsticks" for measuring fund-raising effectiveness, many of which are in use today.

In 1976, the Consortium on Financing Higher Education produced a report for its member institutions titled "A Comparative Study of Development and University Relations at Twenty-Five Colleges and Universities." This study, which focused on advancement, organizational structure, analysis of gifts, and capital campaign profiles, added a great deal to our understanding and offered useful benchmarks.[3]

But perhaps the most useful study on the subject is one completed recently by CASE and the National Association of College and University Business Officers (NACUBO). In 1986, these two organizations undertook a joint study of expenditures in fund raising, alumni relations, and other constituent relations at 51 institutions of higher education nationwide. Survey participants represented every institutional type: public, private, community college, and more. Warren Heeman, vice president for development and alumni relations at the University of Chicago, guided the project, enlisting the help of an advisory committee of development professionals and business managers.

The study succeeded in defining advancement costs in the standardized terms all institutions use today to report gift results. The researchers collected data on three years of fund-raising costs and compared that information to the gift reports the institutions made each year to the Council for Aid to Education (CFAE). The study confirmed the conventional wisdom that total fund-raising costs usually run about 15 percent of the total amount raised. But the study authors went on to say that this "does not mean that a good fund-raising program is by definition one that costs less to operate." The report cautions that "fund-raising efficiency should not be confused with fund-raising effectiveness."[4]

In addition to producing valuable data, the CASE/NACUBO study also established a means for institutions to evaluate their own fund-raising costs. Now, any institution can organize its development, alumni, and other constituent cost accounting; complete the forms published with the study; use readily available CFAE data to compare itself to other institutions; and generate institutional data to compare with the larger sample in the study itself. In many ways the standards and definitions produced by the study are as important as its findings; these methods will permit researchers to track any significant changes in the future.

LESSONS FROM THE STUDY

Development officers can learn much from the findings of the CASE/NACUBO study, some of which appear in table 2. Useful conclusions and recommendations include the following:

- *On average, fund-raising costs run about 16 cents on the dollar.* Although the study confirmed that direct development costs for annual, capital, and planned giving amount to about 16 percent of gifts, the range was huge. Even the middle 50 percent of those surveyed showed a range of 8 to 16 percent. Many reasons contribute to this variation. Typically, colleges and universities with established long-range development programs tended to fall at the lower end of the cost range, while institutions newer to development or just starting programs—and thus making significant investments for donor acquisition—were in the upper ranges.
- *Measure results in terms of return on investment.* When every dollar spent produces an annual return of $5, $8, or even $25, that is a better return than if you had bought IBM in the early 1950s or the Magellan Fund in the late 1970s. Viewing development expenditures as a return on investment can be considered a bit misleading, but such a view does help remind institutional officials that development expenditures are not simply administrative expenses, but rather investments in one of the few revenue centers at a college or university.
- *Be sure to differentiate between the costs of development, alumni relations, and other constituent relations.* The study points out the complementary nature of alumni and other constituent relations and recognizes their importance to development. Too often, however, boards of trustees and institutional leaders add up the cost of all "advancement activities" as part of fund raising. Nothing could be more misleading. The cost of complementary programs varies according to their size and function. For example, the public relations department of a state university might be considerably larger than one at a long-established private college, and it might spend more time on creating and maintaining good relations with the state legislature than on fund raising from private sources.

Table 2. Selected Findings from the CASE/NACUBO Study

EXPENDITURE	MEAN	MEDIAN	MIDDLE 50% OF INSTITUTIONS
Amount spent on fund raising per gift dollar raised	16 cents	11 cents	8 cents - 16 cents
Gift dollars raised for current operations (excluding gifts for capital purposes) as a percentage of total educational and general (E&G) budget	10.23%	8.01%	3.51% - 12.68%
Amount spent on fund raising as a percentage of total E&G budget	2.21%	1.94%	1.21% - 2.84%
Amount spent on total institutional advancement as a percentage of total E&G budget	4.02%	3.80%	2.01 - 5.23%
Amount spent on fund raising			
• per student enrolled	$258	$203	$67 - $379
• per alumnus of record	$35	$30	$20 - $47
Amount spent on total fund raising, alumni relations, and other constituent relations			
• per student enrolled	$473	$445	$131 - $706
• per alumnus of record	$66	$56	$35 - $91
Amount raised			
• per student enrolled	$3,096	$2,722	$310 - $4,947
• per alumnus of record	$389	$277	$111 - $555
Average amount raised per fund-raising professional staff member	$983,113	$738,502	$557,722 - $1,145,912

Data from *Expenditures in Fund Raising, Alumni Relations, and Other Constituent (Public) Relations*, a 1990 joint study by the Council for Advancement and Support of Education and the National Association of College and University Business Officers.

Institutions need to keep in mind the balance of investment they make to the various areas of advancement. In general terms, the study found that with established programs, about 60 percent of total advancement spending went to fund raising and the balance to alumni and other constituent relations. But, again, results ranged widely.

- *Annual giving programs should seek to provide an increasing proportion of the annual operations budget.* On average, annual giving programs in the study provided about 10 percent of the institutions' annual operating budgets. That proportion ranged from 3.5 percent to 12 percent for the middle 50 percent of institutions. Institutions in the lower end included those just starting out, those with large endowments, or those that rely significantly on government support. Over time, an effective development program should see a moderate increase in the percent of the annual budget provided by gift income.

- *Keep track of expenditures and dollars raised per student and per alumnus.* Looking at fund-raising costs and dollars raised on a per-student or per-alumnus basis helps define some of the issues in human terms. To see figures broken down by individuals strengthens accountability. You can also compare the cost of maintaining an alumnus on your record, for example, with average giving per alumnus.

- *Measure dollars raised per staff member to help individual goal setting.* More and more development operations are establishing individual goals for their professional staff members. The study provides some benchmarks. On average, each full-time professional staff member raised more than $900,000 per year. Variation among institutions, however, was broad; the range among the middle 50 percent of institutions was about $550,000 to $1,100,000. Such measures, and the accountability they imply, help ensure that professional staff members are spending an appropriate amount of time on cultivation and solicitation. Further, individual goal setting works to hold down the natural tendency to increase support service areas not directly involved in the fund-raising task. Finally, particularly in larger offices, it gives individual staff members a sense of exactly what they have accomplished, which is important to personal satisfaction, professional growth, and longevity in the job.

- *Monitor line-item development expenditures.* Development managers should be aware of the balance of their expenditures within their budget, and the study provides some good benchmarks. On average, just under two-thirds of total expenditures for fund raising went for personnel, with the balance going for support services, supplies, travel, communications, etc.

DETERMINING HOW MUCH TO INVEST

Each institution has to determine its own level of reasonable expenditure based on its own development routines and history. For some, costs might be as low as 8 to 10 percent. Other institutions could well justify expenditures of more than 30 percent to establish a program. In the end, you must look at the net return on the total investment in fund raising, and not just focus on a low cost or "efficiency" rate.

The first step to establishing reasonable levels of expenditure is to develop a means to measure costs. College and university officials should insist on standard definitions of cost that allow comparisons with other institutions, while at the same time recognizing that institutions vary widely. The standards established by the CASE/NACUBO project allowed individual institutions to compare costs intelligently for the first time.

To set a meaningful fund-raising goal, chart growth over an extended period of time—from five to ten years. You can then determine a growth pattern and set goals. Further, you can compare your institution with other similar institutions or national averages using CFAE data. Your resulting development projections should be part of the long-range planning process of the institution.

Evaluation that measures dollars raised can be straightforward. But successful fund raising involves many other factors. Ideally, the development office persuades administrators, presidents, governing boards, and volunteers to participate in the fundraising process. That process, which begins with defining needs and presenting them to prospective donors, does not always provide immediate bottom-line results, and it is not always personally satisfying. Therefore, the development staff should be judged not only on dollars raised, or even on its ability to implement the best fund-raising strategies and techniques, but also on its ability to manage a process involving a variety of important individuals who would rather be doing something else.

NOTES

1. Harold J. Seymour, *Miscellaneous Memoranda* (New York: American Association of Fund-Raising Counsel, 1960), 5.

2. John W. Leslie, *Focus on Understanding and Support: A Study in College Management* (Washington, D.C.: American College Public Relations Association, 1969).

3. "A Comparative Study of Development and University Relations at Twenty-Five Colleges and Universities," (Hanover, New Hampshire: Consortium on Financing Higher Education, 1976).

4. Council for Advancement and Support of Education and National Association of College and University Business Officers, *Expenditures in Fund Raising, Alumni Relations, and other Constituent (Public) Relations* (Washington, D.C.: Council for Advancement and Support of Education, 1990).

Chapter 25

Organizing the Development Program

Gary A. Evans

Is there an ideal organizational structure for a university or college development program? In an ideal world, probably so. Is there a college or university where this ideal organizational structure exists? In the real world, probably not.

Organizing a development office is akin to designing a house. There is no right or wrong floor plan, but there are certain basics common to all—a kitchen, bedrooms, one or more baths, some living and recreational space. How these components fit, flow, and relate is a matter of size, budget, and personal preference.

This analogy has its limitations, of course. While some people may both design and build a house, very few development officers ever have the opportunity to build a development organization from the ground up. Most development officers work in an existing organization that is not the result of some grand design, but rather of an interesting mixture of the institution's history and tradition, the abilities and personalities of the people involved, budgetary limitations, and a healthy dose of the chief development officer's ideas on how things should work. Because the times, the people, the resources, and the circumstances change, the organizational structure constantly evolves to reflect these changes.

Because we live and work in the real world and not in a theoretical one, there is little value in proposing an ideal development organizational structure. But there is merit in identifying the necessary elements—the kitchen, bathroom, and bedroom, if you will—that must function together for the development office to achieve its goals.

BASIC PURPOSES

In its most basic terms, the purpose of the development office is to raise money for the needs of the institution. Once these needs are identified through an institutional planning process, the development office's role is rather straightforward.

First, it must identify persons and organizations capable of giving support. These potential donors are usually drawn from lists of alumni, friends, parents, past donors, corporations, foundations, and community organizations. After identifying potential donors, the development office must engage them with the institution so they will understand the needs and want to help meet them. Engagement begins by sharing information through newsletters, invitations to special functions, planning reports, and similar activities. Engagement gradually leads to involvement through participation on committees, advisory councils, or governing boards, or as active volunteers in the fund-raising program.

Following engagement, the development office must initiate a request for gift support. Such requests may be part of the annual fund drive, a capital campaign, or special appeals, and may be handled personally, by phone, or by mail. When a gift is received, the development office must then appropriately record and acknowledge it. And finally, the office must ensure responsible recognition and stewardship through donor clubs, special letters to individuals, public reports, and other such methods.

Therefore, a development office must be organized to accomplish these five basic functions: prospect identification; engagement (cultivation and involvement); solicitation; receiving and recording; and stewardship. As long as these five core areas of development are handled responsibly, the office's organization can take any of a variety of configurations.

ORGANIZATIONAL MODELS

Figure 1 shows the simplest way of arranging these five core areas to form the development office. This diagram does not suggest who reports to whom; nor does it suggest whether any of these functions is or should be an extension of another.

The arrangement of the functions actually will depend in large measure on the size of the institution and its development budget, on the talents and skills of the individuals involved, and quite often on a pragmatic accommodation to personalities—who will work together and who will not. At a small institution with limited staff, several of these core areas of activity may be

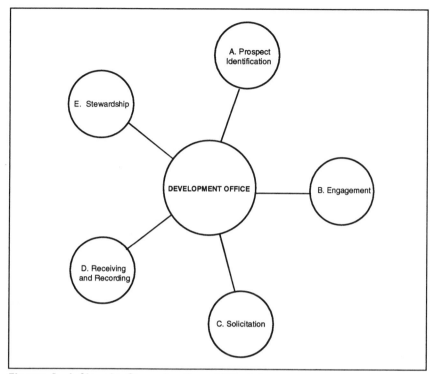

Figure 1. A Simple Organizational Model

clustered and assigned to a single individual or to a small group with similar interests and skills.

For instance, in a small office the person or people responsible for prospect identification may also handle gift receiving and recording, because both tasks require many of the same skills—attentiveness to detail, curiosity, orderliness, facility with numbers, and accuracy. Similarly, the people working directly with donors are likely to carry out the full range of prospect contact, including both cultivation and solicitation. This same staff might also be responsible for stewardship, since the interpersonal skills involved in donor contact also play a role in stewardship, and stewardship often serves as part of the cultivation process for subsequent giving.

Figure 2 shows how this clustering of core activities might work in a small development office.

In a large development office with more staff and more budget, the five core activities will frequently have subsets, making possible specializations and refinements. Each of these

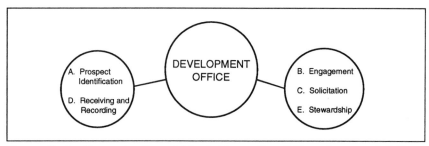

Figure 2. An Organizational Model for a Small Development Office

subsets has its own staff and activities. The variety of possible organizational structures increases with the size of staff and complexity of the program. That is, the more sub-functions an institution develops, the more ways there are to arrange them.

Figure 3 gives an example of some of the sub-functions that may emanate from the core areas.

ORGANIZATION CHARTS

The previous illustrations are not organization charts—that is, they do not indicate lines of authority among staff members. They simply illustrate some of the many activities of a development office and show how those activities help accomplish the five core responsibilities of a comprehensive development program. Some of these activities are closely related in purpose, and it would appear, therefore, that they should be closely related in the organizational structure. However, when it comes to creating an organization chart, personal preference and individual talents may be more important than inherent logic.

For instance, some development officers find it appropriate to have each solicitation activity (annual fund, major gifts, planned gifts, corporate and foundation relations) assume responsibility for stewardship of gifts generated through those programs. Other development officers believe that stewardship should be centralized and performed as the final step in the process of receiving, recording, and acknowledging gifts.

Similarly, in some development offices reunion solicitation is a responsibility of the annual fund, because the class structure used for solicitation is a basic component of the annual fund program and because reunion solicitation emphasizes large unrestricted gifts. In other offices—where reunion classes target their giving toward special capital projects or where the reunion effort

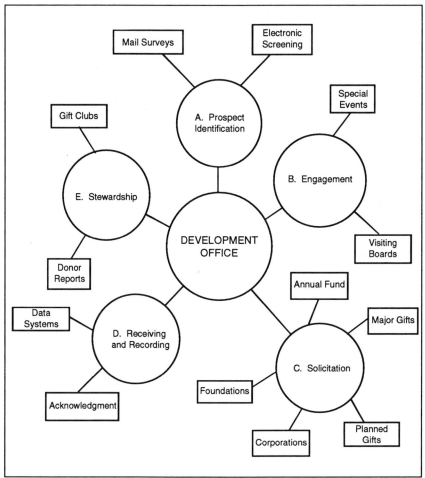

Figure 3. An Organizational Model for a Large Development Office

is a strategic part of a larger capital campaign—reunion campaigns are part of a major gift program.

Figure 4 is a basic organization chart for a medium-sized development office. The chart simply shows the relationships of key departments; it does not indicate who has responsibility for specific activities and programs. A list of typical programs and activities appears below the diagram, with an indication of where different development offices might place those activities within their organizations.

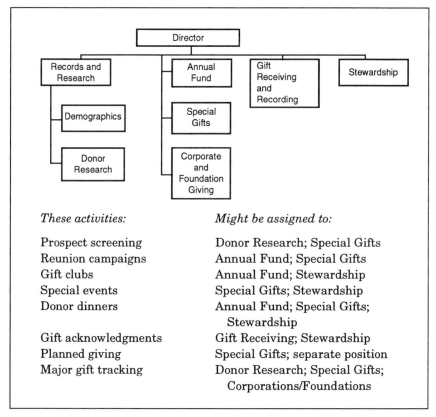

Figure 4. A Basic Organization Chart

CENTRALIZED AND DECENTRALIZED ARRANGEMENTS

Perhaps the challenge of organizing the development office is most acute in large institutions, where there exists the debate over centralized or decentralized operations. In a *centralized* program, all development officers and programs are organized under a central development office. In a *decentralized* program, development efforts are divided by units—schools, colleges, or other programs within the university—with development officers reporting to the deans or program directors of the units they serve.

Most senior development officers prefer the centralized approach, which gives them direct managerial responsibility for all development functions. However, the discussion over centralized versus decentralized organization should not revolve around the question of who is in charge. Regardless of the lines of authority, any decision about centralization or decentralization should take into account the following issues.

- *Commitment to the unit.* If a development officer is to represent a school or program, he or she must know that program well. Too often, development officers who work in a central office but are assigned to serve particular units on campus see those assignments as temporary; they may serve a school or program for a year or two and then be reassigned to another unit. Consequently, they may not be as immersed in the unit's activities as are development officers in a decentralized arrangement, who are permanently part of the unit's administrative structure and who report directly to a dean or a program director. These officers are often closer to and more knowledgeable about the units they serve. Senior development officers managing a centralized program would do well to ensure that officers serving campus units are fully informed about those units and serve them over a sufficient period of time to develop and demonstrate strong commitment.
- *Goals and planning.* In a decentralized setting, the quality of goal setting and planning may vary greatly among various units. A centralized development program usually provides a better means for establishing unit goals and plans that are coordinated and complementary. The chief development officer in a decentralized arrangement must make a special effort to help improve fund raising, planning, and implementation in units for which he or she has no direct authority.
- *Evaluation and compensation.* Whether an institution is centralized or decentralized, it is important that the unit head (dean or program director) and the chief development officer meet regularly to evaluate the development officers serving these units. In a decentralized system, the unit director needs the input of the chief development officer in order to judge whether the unit officer is both doing the right things and doing things right. Unit heads, whose expertise may be law, business, library science, or medicine, are not ideally equipped to judge the professional competence of their development officers. Conversely, in a centralized program, the chief development officer needs the input

from unit heads to know whether the staff members assigned to units are serving the faculty, deans, and directors to their satisfaction. Whatever the arrangement, if unit directors and their development officers are not working well together, successful results are unlikely.

It is also wise, in both centralized and decentralized systems, to set salary guidelines that are equitable to all parties. Otherwise, units and the central development office may compete for staff and may seek to "buy" staff away from one another. This competition leads to an erosion of morale and unsatisfactory fund-raising results.

- *Training and career development.* In a decentralized system, where little communication exists between unit development officers and the central office, it is very difficult for unit people to acquire good training and career enrichment. A development officer working alone in an academic unit may have good relations with the faculty and the dean, but that officer has little peer support. Without peer contact and internal training, decentralization can mean isolation of development officers and less productive performance. It is highly important, in both centralized and decentralized systems, for the central development office to offer a forum for interaction among all development staff and to provide training programs that lead to career enrichment for all development officers.

- *Major gift management.* Perhaps the most important activity requiring constant attention in both types of organizational structures is major gift management. If units in a decentralized system perceive themselves as "owning" prospects who have supported them, or if the central development office thinks of all prospects as "belonging" to them, to be shared with units only by benevolent dictatorship, then problems will arise. Decentralized development units must realize that prospects have multiple interests and much of their interest in a unit derives from a greater interest in the university at large. Conversely, central development staff must understand that a prospect will find it easier to become interested in and attached to a unit with a mission close to the prospect's beliefs and values. Competition for prospects in both systems is harmful to all parties and detrimental to the whole.

Arguments can be made for the merits of both centralized and decentralized organizational structures. Whichever the choice, it is important that all parties cultivate and practice cooperation, coordination, communication, and goodwill.

It appears that the ever-expanding demand for funds has created a centrifugal force that is always pushing even the most centralized of programs toward some level of decentralization. Once deans or program directors experience some personal fundraising success, it is likely that they will never again be fully content to have all fund raising managed from some distant university office with which they have little involvement and even less influence. For each unit's success to continue to the benefit of all parties, the good senior development officer must be responsive and reasonable.

GUIDING POINTS

Although there is no perfect organization plan, several common issues emerge. The chief development officer should keep these ideas in mind when organizing and reorganizing the development program.

First, making assignments according to individual strengths is preferable to making assignments according to job descriptions. Some staff members are strong at managing processes, events, and systems. Others are best at cultivating donors and asking for a gift. It is a mistake to assign a responsibility to an individual simply because that responsibility seems to belong under the individual's job description. If a director of annual giving excels at working with volunteers and soliciting lead gifts, but is weak at managing the logistics of annual fund gift clubs, then the responsibility for those gift clubs should be assigned to someone whose skills are better suited to the responsibility.

Second, whenever there is a change in personnel, through the departure or addition of staff, it is time to reassess the organization chart. The chief development officer should ask: Are we now operating as effectively as we should? Am I using the strengths of my people to best advantage? What skills do we need to complement those of existing staff, and should I do any reorganization in order to introduce those skills when hiring a new person? The office should not be reorganized just for the sake of reorganization. Nor should the existing organization be considered inviolate if a modification will strengthen performance when a new person is brought into the office.

Reorganization can be disruptive, or it can be invigorating. If the reorganization is perceived merely as an exercise of the director's authority, it will accomplish little. However, if it is understood that reorganization is occurring in order to take fuller advantage of individual strengths and lead to opportunities for growth, it can be exciting and enriching.

Third, in a large office with several levels of supervision, the chief development officer should give careful attention to each supervisor's span of control. Traditional management theory suggests that no more than five people should report directly to any one supervisor. Practice demonstrates that the number can be greater if each employee is doing comparable work. For instance, the head of prospect research can supervise more than five researchers, and the head of gift processing can supervise more than five data entry clerks. However, if a supervisor is managing people who are all doing very different functions, then the span of supervision should not be excessive.

Fourth, good communication within the development office is vital to success. Often those working with volunteers in annual giving will learn information about top prospects that will be important to major gift solicitation. Staff members working on special events will learn much about the preferences and person-alities of individuals; this can help other staff members who are planning cultivation and solicitation strategies. But if the annual fund staff talk only with one another, or if prospect researchers talk only with the major gift staff, much is lost. Consequently, the chief development officer must periodically ask, "Is our organiza-tional structure helping or hindering internal communication?" An organization that is highly vertical in its structure—that is, with communication occurring only among people doing like activities—will not have the cross-fertilization it needs to gener-ate creative thinking and new ideas.

Correcting this problem does not necessarily require reorga-nizing the office. Instead, the chief development officer can en-courage communication through the use of internal task forces made up of people from different program functions who face common challenges. For example, a task force comprising repre-sentatives from research, major gifts, annual fund, and special events addressing the question "How can we better use our special events to learn more about our donors?" will encourage cross-office communication that will not only help answer this question but will lead to continued communication on subsequent issues.

Finally, if an important activity or program is not being done satisfactorily—or not being done at all—the chief development officer must assess why. More often than not the answer will be lack of training, the absence of clear goals, or a misunderstanding about assignments. Reorganization is not necessary to correct these deficiencies. In fact, reorganization may have no effect at all if the real issues are not addressed.

A development officer at any institution—large or small, public or private—can build an effective, efficient development program using any one of numerous organizational configurations. The key is to make certain that all necessary, important, and appropriate activities are receiving the staff attention they deserve. If job assignments match individual strengths, then good performance will usually result. Of secondary importance is the precise pattern of the elements in the organizational structure.

The test for any development office is not whether its organization chart conforms to a theoretical ideal, but whether it functions successfully. If it does, the organization is right. If the development office is not achieving its objectives, the chief development officer must determine why. Rearranging the boxes and squares on the organization chart is only one of many solutions to consider.

Part Nine

Development and Other Fields

Development is part of the broader concept and function of institutional advancement, and the coordination of various advancement specialties is essential to the institution's overall success. These specialties both support one another and depend upon one another.

Each of these areas plays an important role in accomplishing the institution's goals. But since this book focuses on educational fund raising, our particular interest in other advancement specialties is their impact on development. In Chapter 26, Roger Williams discusses the role of public relations in fund raising, and in Chapter 27, Charles Webb looks at the role of alumni relations programs and alumni associations.

For reasons of space, this book does not offer detailed discussion of the student recruitment or government relations functions. Both of these areas may be considered parts of institutional advancement, and both influence fund-raising efforts. For example, alumni are often involved in student recruitment, and recruitment programs certainly influence parents' attitudes toward the college or university. These programs therefore are bound to have an effect on giving by both constituencies. Government relations becomes particularly important at public institutions, which depend on various levels of government for substantial amounts of support.

In the last chapter of this section, James Asp describes the relationship between development and sponsored research. This is a question of particular relevance to universities that receive grants from corporations and foundations for specific educational or research programs. In smaller colleges, the development office typically handles grants for sponsored programs as well as outright gifts. Larger universities that receive substantial corporate and foundation support often divide responsibilities for gifts and grants between the development office and an office of sponsored research. That office might report administratively to the business officer, the chief academic officer, or a vice president for research.

In most cases, the distinction as to what goes where is clear. A grant for a specific research project is not a "gift" for institutional purposes, and it should be handled by the sponsored research office. But other grants are not quite so simple to categorize. As corporate and foundation giving has become increasingly focused in recent years, the line between what is within the proper purview of development and what is more properly administered by the sponsored research office has become somewhat blurred. Sorting out the distinctions between development and sponsored research is essential to maintaining good working relationships between these two offices, avoiding faculty confusion and frustration, and assuring coordinated, professional treatment of corporate and foundation sources.

Chapter 26

The Role of Public Relations in Fund Raising

Roger L. Williams

Major campaigns, launched for purposes well beyond capital projects, became a staple of educational fund raising in the 1980s. As an expanding economy offered the opportunity for philanthropic growth, colleges and universities rushed to orient themselves to the world beyond their gates—to great financial benefit. But these ambitious ventures would not have enjoyed such success without an unprecedented degree of cooperation among institutional advancement functions.

Indeed, one of the chief by-products of campaign proliferation is often overlooked: Development and public relations officers have come to work together as never before, much to the benefit of their institutions. Of course, development professionals need not wait for a campaign to establish links with their public relations counterparts. But a campaign typically provides the impetus for such a connection. And, once established, the relationship can—and should—last long after the campaign is over.

For example, in an informal survey in 1989 of a dozen universities engaged in capital campaigns, I found that all had devised formal public relations plans to support these ventures. In addition, the development officers at these institutions said they were impressed and pleased with the performance of their in-house campaign communications and public relations professionals.[1] It appears that development officers like these are relying more and more on their in-house colleagues for public relations support.

An early example of the heightened role of public relations in support of educational fund raising was the University of Notre Dame's campaign in the 1970s. Public relations played a crucial part in the campaign's planning. Before the campaign was launched, the public relations staff developed a 24-page campaign prospectus and an internal campaign handbook.

The public relations staff also initiated the Notre Dame "fly-in" program to cultivate major gift prospects. "On 20 weekends over 15 months—before we announced the campaign—we brought these couples, five or six at a time, to the campus," James E. Murphy, then associate vice president for public relations and development, explained in a 1979 article. "We sent private planes to pick them up. From Friday evening to Sunday morning they were the personal guests of the president."

The weekend included a get-acquainted dinner with then-President Theodore Hesburgh, presentations on the university and the campaign, an overview of the university's academic programs, site visits to university centers or institutes of special interest, a private mass celebrated by Father Hesburgh, and an intimate dinner atop the university library. Before leaving, the guests were told a university representative would soon call on them to discuss their campaign commitment. The eventual commitments of the 125 couples involved averaged $600,000.

Public relations continued to make other spectacular contributions to Notre Dame's campaign. Events included the campaign inaugural for 400 guests, which included a 25-year anniversary celebration of President Hesburgh's tenure, and a commencement visit by President Jimmy Carter that captured national attention.[2]

WHAT PUBLIC RELATIONS CAN DO

Public relations can contribute to educational fund raising on three levels:

1. *Contextual*—creating visibility for the institution and enhancing its reputation with a variety of constituencies so that fund raising can succeed;
2. *Strategic*—helping to resolve the "what" and "why" issues of educational fund raising (that is, "what are we going to do" and "why are we going to do it?"); and
3. *Tactical*—determining how to fulfill goals and objectives with specific events and activities.

An effective public relations plan will tie the strategic and tactical components together.

Before these contributions can become real, however, public relations professionals need to work with development leadership to secure the resources necessary for the communications operation. In the survey mentioned above, most of the institutions strengthened their public relations considerably as they launched their campaigns. They added new positions and reconfigured reporting relationships—not only to provide support for the campaign, but also to increase general visibility for the institution.

Institutional leaders must also address the larger question of formally integrating the three fundamental advancement functions: development, public relations, and alumni affairs. In a 1991 article, G. David Gearhart and Michael Bezilla wrote that a united structure under one senior administrative officer provides benefits not only in executing a campaign but in preparing for it as well.[3] Because of the need to coordinate all aspects of a campaign, a unified structure may be more important in a campaign situation than it might be in "normal" times.

CONTEXTUAL ISSUES

Public relations' most valuable contribution to the educational fund-raising process is to help create the wide context for success. This is accomplished through activities that define, sharpen, and market the institution's identity; strengthen the institution's reputation and relationships generally and among key audiences; and heighten the institution's visibility in key geographic regions.

Public relations officials should keep development leadership informed about the public relations plan for the institution or the context of goals and objectives within which public relations operates. Our public relations plan at Pennsylvania State University, for example, focuses on six strategic objectives that support larger university goals, including fund raising: (1) to gain high visibility in statewide and national media for the university's academic accomplishments; (2) to support educational fund raising; (3) to support the institution's agenda for multicultural diversity; (4) to support student recruitment; (5) to sustain institutional identity through a comprehensive graphics program; and (6) to lend public relations assistance, as needed, to the university's twenty-two campuses, ten colleges, and other units.

Aside from ongoing activities on behalf of larger institutional goals, public relations professionals can help by conducting opinion polls to assess the strengths and weaknesses of the institution's reputation. With that information, they can then devise communications strategies to market the institution as they wish the public to see it and to influence the public's behavior toward it.

This shaping of institutional identity and reputation is of extreme importance to fund raising. Study after study has shown that the single most important variable in fund-raising success is institutional prestige—in fact, in a 1986 study, we found that prestige far overrode the institution's status as public or private.[4] A prime example is the significant fund-raising success public colleges and universities have enjoyed in the 1980s. As the academic prestige of these institutions has increased, so has their ability to raise funds from the private sector (particularly the corporate sector).

"Obviously, donor recognition and publicity are very important," Susan Bonnett, assistant vice president for university relations at the University of Miami, told me during my 1989 survey. "But even more important is the activity that heightens overall awareness of the university in the donor community. People need to know it's a good institution, one they can be proud of. When they're approached for a contribution, it's not out of the clear blue sky. Your real emphasis should be on building a general climate of support for the institution in the community."

Toward that end, many colleges and universities strengthen their public relations staffs well before launching campaigns. For example, before starting its $350 million campaign, which ultimately raised $470 million, Ohio State University added six new communications professionals to raise the university's profile.

PRELIMINARY STRATEGIC CONSIDERATIONS

In order for public relations to contribute directly to the fund-raising process, development must have easy access to public relations expertise. To increase this access, some institutions establish additional channels through which fund raisers can draw on the public relations function. One popular arrangement is to establish a special unit for development communications; another possibility is to form an advisory council.

Development communications units. In my informal poll, I found that about two-thirds of the universities I looked at had established a unit dedicated to "development communications" to assist with their campaigns. A development communications unit offers a twofold advantage: It provides an exclusive focus on fund-raising communications, and it also precludes an "overload" situation that can overwhelm the public relations staff. An overload can impair communications support for development and dilute the effectiveness of institutional communications overall.

The chief obstruction to establishing a dedicated unit is cost. "The problem is that universities are reluctant to build up staff for a limited activity because it's hard to reduce staff afterwards," noted Don Edwards, vice president for public affairs and development at Rutgers, the State University of New Jersey, which mounted a major campaign without such a unit. "For the most part, the Campaign for Rutgers has become an overload project, and that's not the way to do it," Edwards said.

At the other end of the spectrum is the University of Pennsylvania, which established an eight-person development communications unit as it launched its $1 billion campaign in 1989. Penn's development communications unit includes specialists in media relations, special events, video, photography, and publications. In fact, Penn retrofitted its campus information center as the headquarters for campaign communications.

Reporting arrangements vary widely. At some institutions, members of the development communications unit report to the development office; at others, to public relations. In all cases I found, however, the unit's media relations activities are funneled through the existing news bureau or public information department.

Campaign communications councils. College and universities often hire external fund-raising counsel to help plan and execute their campaigns. Rarely, however, do they retain a professional public relations firm in a similar capacity to provide continual campaign public relations and communications, although public relations firms are often hired on a task-specific basis—for example, to mount a gala or to produce the case statement.

Many colleges and universities have turned instead to another resource for outside advice on the public relations aspect of educational fund raising: a council composed of alumni who have distinguished themselves as journalists, editors and writers, advertising and marketing executives, and public relations professionals.

Wittenberg University's director of public relations, Donald R. Perkins, is a strong advocate for such a council. Perkins formed a communications advisory committee during Wittenberg's $16.7 million campaign, which ultimately raised $20 million. Perkins's committee members helped open doors for media visits in key markets and even accompanied him on those trips. They advised him on the worthiness of campaign story ideas and offered advice on his master public relations plan, the campaign slide show, and campaign publications.

"Pittsburgh was one of our areas for fund raising," Perkins explained in a 1985 presentation. "A member of our board of directors is a high-placed official with Alcoa, whom I asked to be on my advisory committee. He arranged for me to have one of his top public relations officials visit Pittsburgh media with me. Between us, we decided that we could market our president as a manager of higher education and as a spokesman for the need for cooperation between campus and big business. The result was a half-page story in the Pittsburgh Press with Wittenberg in the subhead and a photo of our president."[5]

As effective as a council can be, there seems to be an inverse correlation between institutional size and the proclivity for forming such a group. Smaller institutions tend to use them more than larger universities. "If you have the in-house talent and the kind of institutional clout that attracts national attention, there's not much need for an alumni communications council," said Malcolm Baroway, executive director of university communications at Ohio State University.

STRATEGIC ISSUES

Given reasonable communications between the development and public relations functions, public relations can contribute to the fund-raising process in additional strategic areas.

The Case Statement

One key task that should significantly involve public relations is the creation of a case statement—whether for a large major gifts campaign, for a smaller focused campaign, or for the institution's educational fund-raising programs in general.

The case statement has been described as "the single most important document of a capital campaign"[6] and "the communications backbone of any capital campaign."[7] Indeed, it is all that and more. The case statement is the basic argument for philanthropic support of an institution. It also functions as the rhetorical primer and the "copy platform" for all campaign communications. Campaign speeches, publications, videos, and news stories should borrow heavily from the case statement. The case statement positions both the institution and the campaign by describing institutional goals and aspirations (ends) as well as strengths; specific institutional needs (barriers which must be surmounted in order to achieve the ends); and the specifics and "spirit" of the campaign (the means for achieving the ends).

One of the major considerations in writing the case is whether to employ outside experts or to do it in-house. The advantage of outsiders is the fresh perspective they provide as well as the considerable skill they can bring to the task. But going out-of-house does not mean less work for the in-house staff. Many hours and much energy will go into acquainting the outsider with your institution.

The chief arguments for staying in-house are that it costs less and that in-house staff are already familiar with the institution. If you do stay in-house, the key is to encourage your public relations writers to somehow "step outside" the institution and view it with a fresh, unbiased perspective. It helps if they can look at the institution critically, adopting a "show me" skepticism, to ensure that the case is not polluted with vague generalizations and unsubstantiated claims.

This chapter cannot describe how to write a case statement—a separate literature already exists on that subject. It is worth noting, however, that as communications become more carefully targeted to smaller audiences, the idea of a single case statement may become obsolete, to be replaced by a series of case statements designed to appeal to the differing needs, values, attitudes, and lifestyles of target audiences. In addition, video case statements are growing in popularity, not so much as a replacement of the printed case statement but as a supplement to it.

The Public Relations Plan to Support Fund Raising

The heart and soul of communications support for educational fund raising—particularly a major gifts campaign—lie in the public relations plan, which combines strategy and tactics. Do not mistake the plan for holy writ, however; it will be subjected to revisions, additions, deletions, and improvisation over time. All good plans encourage continual correction.

The art and science of educational fund raising is a variant of the marketing process, and the public relations plan should also reflect a strong marketing orientation. Fund raising requires the identification of "suspects" and then "prospects." This calls for extensive market research. After identification and ranking of the prospects (the target market), the cultivation (sales) process begins, culminating in a successful solicitation. A public relations plan to support educational fund raising must harmonize with this process.

One of the best examples of a public relations plan for a campaign is that devised by Wittenberg's Donald Perkins. His plan consists of six elements:

- *statement of mission,* "to increase awareness, understanding, and support for the institution and the campaign."
- *statement of priorities,* reflecting the timetable for solicitation and the geographic areas in which campaign activity will take place.
- *target audiences,* noting the division of prospects into particular giving levels as determined by the development leadership. For example, prospects over $100,000 will require and respond to different communications tactics than will those whose giving will fall below $10,000.
- *campaign themes,* reflecting general positioning themes of the university as well as institutional strengths. These themes should be repeated in all public relations materials.
- *methods,* including the tactics for getting the themes and messages to the right audiences.
- *evaluation,* meaning measurement of the public relations plan's results.[8]

Public relations plans for campaigns are tied to the campaign chronology and sequence of events. They should never devolve into mere publicity plans, in which "activity" is undertaken for its own sake. An effective public relations plan will also view a campaign not just as a noble cause that deserves communications support, but as a "communications event" in and of itself—a vehicle for carrying important institutional messages to key audiences, or for changing the way in which the institution is perceived and supported.

Whether for a specific campaign or general fund raising, plans should support a variety of goals and objectives, the more pointed the better. Thus, in addition to promoting overarching goals such as awareness, understanding, and support, a public relations plan might, for example, also seek to:

- reposition the institution and build a new identity, for example, as "one of the foremost liberal arts colleges in the nation," or "the best private research university in the southeastern United States."
- provide a high level of visibility for volunteer leadership among key audiences—for example, the alumni body.
- clarify a relationship the institution has with state government, or with a religious denomination, or with the community in which it is located.
- demonstrate to the faculty and staff a determination to move the institution to greater heights or to reach new levels of effectiveness.

TACTICAL ISSUES

Given specific goals and a well-defined plan for supporting fund raising, public relations staff can then proceed to plan and carry out specific activities to accomplish those goals. Some typical examples follow.

News Media Visibility

Fund raising activity—especially during a campaign—produces many unique and newsworthy events. Pursued aggressively and handled wisely, these events can result not just in heightened visibility, but also in golden opportunities to help reposition the institution.

Gift stories carry many creative possibilities. News about gifts for minority scholarships, for educational partnerships, for novel ways of improving undergraduate education, and for special research programs (especially in the medical and health fields) are among those that carry strong potential for high media visibility.

For example, the University of Pittsburgh built on a $1.4 million gift from Westinghouse that dealt with creating new methods of educating engineers. "The topic was especially newsworthy, so we pursued the story in different ways over a period of months, and it worked well," said Mary Ann Aug, assistant vice president for university relations at Pitt. First, Aug and her staff gave daily newspapers the straight news of the gift. Then they placed it as a business feature in regional business periodicals. From there, the technology writer on a Pittsburgh daily used it as a technology-education feature. In short, the story took on a life of its own.

Consider what you can persuade major gift donors to say about the institution in the press release or at the press conference. As an independent third party, a donor has enormous credibility. When Penn State received a $10 million gift to endow eight faculty chairs in its College of Science, we asked the donor to make certain statements to help position the academic unit. He did so, saying the college was "on the verge of moving into the ranks of the nation's very best. We believe our gift will provide the means for Penn State's College of Science to make these moves a reality." Both United Press International and the Associated Press picked up the story, which was carried widely around the state.

Campaign progress reports provide other news possibilities. The point to remember here is not to talk about the campaign as an end, but as a means to an end—to strengthen the institution and its capacity to serve society.

Publications and Periodicals

The alumni magazine should accord a measure of visibility to educational fund raising. Many alumni magazine editors are fiercely independent, and some are quite resistant to development stories. While the editorial judgment of alumni magazine editors deserves respect, most will also agree that their publications should work within a framework of institutional goals and objectives, and that there are clever ways to handle important development stories without making them appear as such.[9]

For some target audiences, the best vehicle is a separate fund-raising publication. As Ann Waldron, editor of Princeton

University's campaign bulletin, wrote, "A newsletter is as necessary to a fund-raising campaign as matches are to fire building."[10]
A campaign newsletter keeps key people interested in the campaign. It can also relate fund raising to academic achievement in
ways that might not be convenient or appropriate in regular
communication channels. And it can establish links between
donors and the programs they support, reinforcing overall campaign objectives.

Special Events

Although special events offices exist on many campuses,
campaign events should also engage the expertise of the public
relations staff. Indeed, such occasions should be viewed not just as
"cultivation events," but as "communications events," because
they communicate in an extraordinarily powerful way.

The key to staging a successful event, such as a campaign
kickoff, are "planning and panache," wrote Heather Ricker Gilbert, a special events consultant. In a 1989 article, she advised
that you:

- Know your purpose: Why are we having this event?
- Understand your audience and situation: Is a black tie gala
  appropriate for the culture of your institution?
- Promote a theme that plays up what is special about your
  institution and its aspirations.
- Create clear and compelling invitations, and mail them at
  least eight weeks before the event.
- Consider the aesthetics—the food, flowers, decor.
- Analyze the program: What's the best way to showcase key
  volunteers? Do you need a celebrity or will a famous alumnus make a better emcee?
- Rehearse and prepare: Assume nothing, practice everything
  possible on site—musicians, sound, lighting, etc.[11]

Events don't have to be limited to campus. Potsdam College
tied the kickoff for its centennial campaign to the 100th anniversary of the Statue of Liberty. On July 3, 1986, the 200-member
college chorus performed at the Liberty Island celebration in front
of President Reagan and millions of television viewers. Indiana
University created an ad hoc television network for its campaign
gala, spending $105,000 to broadcast the event via satellite to
some 35,000 alumni and friends at 46 sites across the nation.[12]

And to energize campaign leaders nationwide, the University of Illinois Foundation staged a 1984 teleconference, "Reaching Across America," that linked volunteers at concurrent meetings in 19 cities.[13]

Special events can inject excitement, spark enthusiasm, and generate momentum in a way that nothing else can approximate. They can introduce, recognize, thank, and motivate volunteers and major donors; communicate key messages about your institution; and dispel myths and misinformation. They exhilarate participants far more than most football games can, and they can be designed as creatively as the imagination will allow.

Video

The use of video in fund raising is gathering a head of steam, and, as a communications specialty, should fall within the purview of the public relations staff.

"The future of institutional advancement lies with increasingly sophisticated use of electronic systems (computer technology and database management) to integrate direct mail, telemarketing, and personal solicitations," wrote Robert Roehr. "Video will come to play a larger role in that mix, to some degree replacing but more often supplementing both print and people."[14]

In fact, the videocassette has become part and parcel of daily life. A Merrill Lynch study, VIDEO 1995, predicted that by the mid-1990s, over 85 percent of American homes will have videocassette recorders and that Americans will be renting, for home viewing, more than four billion videocassettes each year.[15] Small wonder that many development officers carry the latest overview video and their own display equipment for visits with prospects.

But in the midst of what would seem to be a budding video mania, experts caution that such productions need to be carefully thought out, targeted to certain markets, and produced with the right set of expectations. In addition, keep in mind that video works much better in the realm of emotion than that of cognition. Video can enthuse, arouse, stir passions and elicit warm feelings, but it is not the best tool for conveying facts and information; print works better for that purpose.

Basic marketing principles need to prevail when crafting a video. It should be targeted to the specific interests and attention spans of the intended viewers. And, despite those impressive projections for home videocassette use, videocassette ownership is lower in households where the head is more than 50 years old. This will change, of course, as the lead cohort of the Baby Boom reaches the half-century mark in 1996.

A PLACE FOR PUBLIC RELATIONS

People outside public relations often view the profession as little more than publicity work and news release and article writing. Fortunately, the development leg of the institutional advancement triad has come to recognize the strategic value of public relations in the context of educational fund raising.

"The most valuable contribution our communications people made was to help us develop a strategic plan for the campaign," Roy Muir, the former director of combined campaigns for the University of Michigan, told me in my 1989 survey. "Their work went beyond creating themes. It helped us think through what our market is and the ways in which we can best reach it. As we look toward a new campaign for the 1990s, communication marketing will be a very significant part of it."

In today's climate of intensifying competition for resources, however, educational fund raisers cannot afford to wait for the next campaign to harness the contributions that public relations and marketing communications have to offer. The need for communications support is continuous. In the absence of a major gifts campaign, public relations expertise can help to sharpen baseline programs in annual giving, planned giving, corporate and foundation relations, and the other components of educational fund raising. Most important, public relations support can be vital to maintaining the levels of private gift support created by the previous campaign—and to building support inside and outside the institution in preparation for the next comprehensive campaign.

NOTES

1. Roger L. Williams, "They Work Hard for the Money: An Informal Poll Reveals that PR Officers Play a Major Role in Supporting Capital Campaigns," *CASE Currents*, June 1989, 36-41. Unless otherwise indicated, quotes and case studies used in this chapter come from this *CASE Currents* article.

2. Murphy, James E., "The Campaign Needs PR," *CASE Currents*, March 1979, 44-45.

3. G. David Gearhart and Michael Bezilla, "Fund-raising Success Takes Teamwork," *Fund Raising Management*, March 1991, 42-46.

4. Roger L. Williams and Robert M. Hendrickson, "In Fund Raising, Prestige Means More Than Public or Private," *AGB Reports*, November/December 1986, 20-23.

5. Donald R. Perkins, "Public Relations Support for the Capital Campaign" (presentation at the Conference on Capital Fund Raising, sponsored by the Council for Advancement and Support of Education, Nashville, Tennessee, April 1985).

6. Richard Chamberlain, "The Campaign Case Statement," in *The Successful Capital Campaign: From Planning to Victory Celebration*, ed. H. Gerald Quigg (Washington, D.C.: Council for Advancement and Support of Education, 1986), 87.

7. Roland King, "Stating Your Case: The Art, the Science, and the Future of the Quintessential Campaign Document," *CASE Currents*, June 1989, 46.

8. Donald R. Perkins, "Public Relations Support for the Capital Campaign," in *The Successful Capital Campaign*, ed. Quigg, 167-176.

9. Robert J. Bliwise, "Detente with Development: Editors Can Give Fund Raisers the Support They Seek by Listening, Defending, and Innovating," *CASE Currents*, November/December 1988, 48-52.

10. Ann Waldron, "News You Can Use: Publishing a Campaign Newsletter," *CASE Currents*, May 1985, 34.

11. Heather Ricker Gilbert, "The Winning Combination: When You Put Together Planning and Panache, It Adds Up to a Successful Campaign Special Event," *CASE Currents*, June 1989, 42-44.

12. Caryl Levine and John F. Marshall, "Start Your Campaign with Style: PR and Development Officers Tell How They Kicked Off Their Capital Campaigns," *CASE Currents*, April 1988, 38-44.

13. Jim Gobberdiel, "Live, by Satellite: How the University of Illinois Used a Space-Age Campaign Tool to Help a Capital Campaign Take Off," *CASE Currents*, June 1985, 38-40.

14. Robert J. Roehr, ed., *Electronic Advancement Fund Raising* (Washington, D.C.: Council for Advancement and Support of Education, 1990), i.

15. J. Arthur Stuber, "The Electronic Environment," in *Electronic Advancement Fund Raising*, ed. Roehr, 2-3.

Chapter 27

The Role of Alumni Affairs in Fund Raising

Charles H. Webb

On many campuses, the relationship between the alumni office and the development office seems precarious, like that of two nations at odds over a border. Programs often seem to be in competition, if not outright conflict. Yet the two roles can actually serve and enhance each other, much like the offensive and defensive units of a football team. Just as each is needed to secure a victory on the gridiron, both alumni and development must cooperate to achieve overall institutional goals.

In most cases today, the alumni office exists for two reasons—to provide diverse and quality programming for alumni, and to provide opportunities for alumni to engage in a lifetime of service, including financial support, to their alma mater.

Like its parent institution, the alumni office—whether an institution-run function or an independent association—serves a multiple purpose and accommodates multiple interests. This many-faceted mission derives from the diversity of talents and interests of its constituents. Alumni become donors, assist in student recruitment, help promote legislative programs, give advice, sit on governing boards, serve as guest lecturers and adjunct professors, and act as the institution's best advocates.

The alumni office is crucial because a college or university has no greater resource than its alumni. Higher education institutions cannot buy the support the alumni can provide. When that support is forthcoming, it represents a tremendous source not only of economic power but also of intellectual advocacy. In this sense, one major function of the alumni office is to harness the institution's alumni resources in support of the basic mission of the institution. To be most effective, alumni program goals must be in concert with the institution's goals and mission.

The goals of the development office, however clear and established, must remain consistent with the same institutional goals that the alumni office supports. The reason for raising external funds relates directly to the advancement of the institution. Therefore, both development and alumni goals are, at the very least, compatible in their support of the institutional mission.

ALUMNI INVOLVEMENT AND GIVING

I once heard a colleague say that if the alumni office went out of business, it would have to be re-invented by the development office. This is a truth most professionals know—that involvement of alumni in their alma mater generates interest, and that interest often translates into the giving of time and money. Alumni who are interested, concerned, and involved not only are a good source of substantial dollars, but they also can be instrumental in securing dollars from corporations, foundations, friends of the institution, and other sources.

Studies confirm that the degree to which alumni are involved with college or university activities directly correlates with the level of their financial support to the institution. For example, in 1989 the Massachusetts Institute of Technology Alumni Association published a study that measured this relationship. Their findings were stunning: Regardless of graduating class, department, or current geographic location, alumni who were "involved in MIT alumni activities" gave "much more frequently than their uninvolved peers." Overall, involved alumni gave more frequently than uninvolved alumni by a ratio of more than 3 to 1. That held true at each of the three giving levels examined: four-year giving totals in excess of $500, $1,250, and $5,000. Interestingly, the study found that merely attending class reunions or centennial activities was as significant a factor as actual volunteer activity—if not more so.

Although the study did not determine whether alumni involvement caused superior fund support or vice versa, it concluded that the issue was moot: "To the extent that alumni activities—reunions, club events, departmental events—serve as gathering points for our very best supporters, they serve as the best possible means of cultivating those who are not contributing to the alumni fund or who are contributing at a nominal level. By supporting a broad spectrum of high-quality alumni activities, we are providing an atmosphere . . . where the norm is to support the alumni fund in a significant way. There could hardly be a more effective way to enhance the overall quality of alumni fund support." At the same time, the study added, universities do well to provide their best supporters with high-quality alumni activities to reinforce their commitment. In other words, it doesn't really matter which came first, the chicken or the egg. What matters is to "recognize that the chickens are laying eggs and the eggs are turning into chickens . . . in our own backyard!"[1]

The findings of the MIT study are consistent with an earlier study conducted by the Ohio State University Alumni Association in 1983, which compared gifts made by members of the alumni association and by alumni nonmembers. The study found that, of some 134,000 alumni in Ohio, one out of five contributed to the development fund in 1982. Two-thirds of the donors were association members, and their gifts accounted for 90 percent of the $5 million received that year from Ohio alumni. Of a total alumni pool of 231,680 worldwide, nearly 36,000 alumni (15.5 percent) made contributions. Again, slightly more than two-thirds of the donors were association members, giving 85 percent of the $6.2 million received from alumni.

In Ohio, 57,363 alumni (42.7 percent of in-state alumni) belonged to the association. Of those, 30.9 percent were donors. Worldwide, the association counted 84,679 members (36.5 percent of the total); 28.4 percent of them were donors. By comparison, only 6.5 percent of Ohio nonmembers and 5.1 percent of nonmembers worldwide gave that year. Paralleling the MIT study, the Ohio researchers concluded, "Association membership coupled with participation in alumni activities produced the most faithful and generous donors."

The study also evaluated contributions made by alumni members according to their involvement in alumni activities. In 1982, more than half of alumni who participated in alumni tours were donors. Of the 1,200 alumnae who had attended Women's Day activities, 45.2 percent were donors. In both cases, donors who were also association members gave about three times as much as nonmember donors.

Not surprisingly, the greatest participation came from association members who formerly served on either the Alumni Advisory Council—a body composed of alumni representatives of Ohio State's various branches—or on the association's governing board. In 1982, 74 percent of former Advisory Council members were donors, with an average gift of almost $1,350. Nearly 71 percent of former board members contributed an average gift of $671.

For Dan L. Heinlen, director of alumni affairs for the Ohio State University Alumni Association, these statistics had clear implications. "It is vitally important to the future of our university that these and similar involvement activities be continued and, where possible, expanded," he wrote. "The time and resources that have been invested over the years to keep alumni in touch with and actively interested in their alma mater produce tremendous dividends, both in terms of loyalty and funds contributed."[2]

It must be noted that following this study, the Ohio State University development office aggressively and systematically contacted its alumni through phonathons as part of its $460 million campaign. As a result, the difference in giving between alumni association members and nonmembers has been reduced dramatically.

A third study worth noting was conducted in 1985 by the University of North Carolina at Chapel Hill. That year, S. Philip Harris, president of the University of North Carolina's General Alumni Association and also acting director of development, reported to the board of trustees:

> The association's expanding membership efforts in recent years, which have seen membership move from 28,000 to 37,000 in just two years, have been essential in building the base for strong development efforts. Over 90 percent of all donors are General Alumni Association members. Those who are members of the General Alumni Association make gifts to the university that are three to four times greater than gifts from those who are not members. Thus, by continuing to increase our membership, the association provides the needed base from which to build an ever-expanding donor pool. . . .
>
> In short, this "friend raising" by the General Alumni Association . . . is essential to a successful development effort. It can be argued that the basic identification and cultivation of donors is in large measure done by the General Alumni Association through its records, publications, chapter meetings, reunions, programs, seminars, tours, and other activities. Furthermore, the officers and directors of the association who participate in our quarterly board meetings . . . have became some of the strongest leaders in the university's overall development efforts.[3]

ALUMNI PROGRAMS AND DEVELOPMENT

These three studies, and many others conducted across the country, provide incontrovertible evidence that alumni involvement in meaningful alumni activities correlates directly with the size and frequency of gifts. Clearly, an institution of higher education cannot reach its fullest potential without actively engaging its alumni.

Offering a wide range of opportunities for alumni service not only involves alumni but also creates a more conducive climate for financial gifts from these individuals. The following types of alumni programming have proven effective in achieving both goals—that is, in providing alumni with opportunities to serve their alma mater, and in creating a positive climate that enhances their participation in fund raising.[4]

This list is not all-inclusive, but it does show different ways alumni programming can reinforce the development program. Some of these programs place alumni in contact with students and campus life, providing obvious reasons for giving; some provide opportunities for alumni to return to campus for positive experiences. Keep in mind, however, that merely having a program is not enough; to be effective, it must be well-executed.

- Alumni involvement in student recruitment.
- Student career assistance, including on-campus lectures by alumni or off-campus visits to alumni on the job.
- Student-alumni programming to acquaint current students—future alumni—with the alumni and development programs.
- Homecoming, Alumni Day, and other special events that bring alumni back to campus.
- Class reunions. Many reunion programs are tied to a class gift program and hence directly support development efforts.
- Awards recognizing alumni achievements and service.
- Minority alumni programs.
- Young alumni programs. Young graduates pose a special challenge to both fund raising and alumni associations; alumni programs geared specifically to young alumni's needs and interests can stimulate their involvement and, in turn, their giving participation.
- Senior alumni programs. With more time and more discretionary income, alumni over age 55 become an increasingly important market for alumni and development programming.

- Constituent alumni associations—special-interest groups affiliated with an academic program on campus.
- Regional alumni clubs, which offer programs for alumni in a geographic area. Clubs also provide an existing network from which to launch a capital campaign regionally.
- Alumni magazines, tabloids, newsletters, or other publications. These serve as excellent vehicles to educate alumni about fund raising through news about campaigns, articles on major gifts and givers, and honor rolls or donor club listings.
- Alumni family camps.
- Alumni lifelong education, including classes as well as travel programs.
- Alumni community service programs, such as literacy programs, assistance with food banks, senior citizen programs, or other projects. Many of these programs have high visibility and open new markets for development.
- Alumni legislative programs—advocacy programs designed to influence legislation that would enhance philanthropic giving to institutions.
- Outreach programs to re-establish relationships with alumni who have not maintained connections with the institution. This function also expands the prospect pool for development.

INVOLVING ALUMNI IN DEVELOPMENT

The alumni activities on the above list benefit development indirectly by helping create an environment that encourages alumni to give. However, alumni can help with fund raising directly as well.

I remember hearing a president of a major university observe that he knew of no successful development office that did not make significant use of its alumni in securing gifts. Such a statement underscores how important alumni are to the success of the development program.

Here are some ways alumni are directly involved with development efforts:

- Alumni are donors.
- Alumni help to secure gifts from other alumni and nonalumni friends.

- Alumni serve on development boards and on the institution's governing board.
- Alumni are instrumental in securing major corporate gifts.
- Alumni are instrumental in securing major foundation gifts.
- Alumni are the key component of a capital campaign.
- Alumni assist with capital campaign feasibility studies.
- Alumni serve as volunteers for phonathons.
- Alumni contribute their professional services.
- Alumni organize special events for fund raising.
- Alumni serve as professional consultants for clients interested in making planned gifts.
- Alumni are essential to the success of the major donor clubs.
- Alumni assist in local business community solicitations.

LINKING THE ALUMNI AND DEVELOPMENT OFFICES

Above all, the alumni and development staffs should work together closely. The development program should make a point of actively involving alumni professionals who have been with the institution a long time and have developed strong relationships with graduates. Alumni staff, who are in contact with alumni daily, can open doors to potential alumni donors, provide background information, and help rate donor potential. Alumni professionals should be visible at development activities, and development professionals should be visible at alumni activities. This mutual support reinforces the close ties between the two functions.

Some development offices invest in their alumni offices: They provide annual funding based upon their belief in the long-term approach and the benefits of an effective alumni operation. This is a true test of shared vision.

When one takes a close look at the development and alumni offices, it is clear that they carry out similar steps in dealing with their constituents, whether alumni or nonalumni friends. Both alumni and development offices carry out identification, research, and cultivation. Only the last step of the fund-raising process—solicitation—is unique to development.

To minimize duplication of efforts, it is essential to eradicate territorial space. Some would even argue that both groups occupy essentially the same territory. Gary Ransdell, vice president for institutional advancement at Clemson University, takes this view, but he also draws a fine distinction.

"Everyone is in the alumni relations business and everyone is a fund raiser—some just have more specific and pragmatic duties and different accountability channels," he argues. "Everyone should be conscious of everyone else's role and work to enhance it. However, the alumni relations professional's role is more broad and altruistic. The development professional's role is more narrow and statistically driven. And while we all can be fund raisers, *only* the development staff should be the fund collectors. The alumni relations officer is being counterproductive if he or she gets into the gift collection business and the development officer is counterproductive if he or she gets into the programming/event/publication business."[5]

It seems clear that both alumni and development, like the offensive and defensive units in football, are partners dedicated to a common purpose. As someone who has worked in both areas, I strongly believe in this idea. Each area is important in its own right, but when each works to enhance and reinforce the other, the institution as a whole benefits even more.

Good alumni relations is a responsibility of the institution whether or not a dime is ever raised. The development program fulfills a basic institutional need. But the development program can never reach its potential without an effective alumni program.

NOTES

1. Jeffrey R. Solof, "Measuring the Impact of Alumni Activities on the Quality of Alumni Fund Support" (Cambridge, Massachusetts: Working Group of Alumni Activities Measurements, Massachusetts Institute of Technology: 1989).

2. "Alumni Activities Aid Development," *News of Fund Raising Developments at the Ohio State University*, December 1983, 6.

3. S. Philip Harris, remarks to the trustees of the University of North Carolina at Chapel Hill, June 28, 1985.

4. Stephen L. Barrett, "Basic Alumni Programming," in *A Handbook of Institutional Advancement*, 2nd ed., ed. A. Westley Rowland (San Francisco: Jossey-Bass, 1986), 416-425.

5. Gary A. Ransdell, "Alumni and Development: The Solid Gold Partnership?" (presentation at the District III Conference of the Council for Advancement and Support of Education, Nashville, Tennessee, February 14, 1989).

Chapter 28

Development and Sponsored Research

James W. Asp II

Little has been written about the relationship between the development office and the sponsored research office in the research university. Yet university development officers often face questions, and occasionally disputes, concerning which office should handle a particular grant.

An informal survey and my conversations with development officers over the years suggest that each university adapts to this situation in its own way. Even nomenclature varies from institution to institution. While the name "development office" appears to be universal, the terms "sponsored research," "sponsored programs," "sponsored projects," and "grants and contracts" have different meanings at different universities. For purposes of clarity, I will use the term "sponsored research" to refer to the entire array of grant and contract solicitation, reporting, and accounting conducted outside of the development office.

In general, the two offices work from opposite perspectives and with different goals in mind. The development office's goal is proactive: The development officer engages in activities that will raise funds for the institution. The sponsored research office tends to be reactive: The faculty generally takes the initiative in identifying funding needs and opportunities. Sponsored research's role is often limited to approving the approach to the prospect and ensuring that the terms of the grant or contract can be, and are, fulfilled. Sponsored research personnel tend to view reporting requirements as the final step in completing a grant, while the development officer looks at the report as the first step in soliciting the next grant.

In the past, the two offices had little need to communicate, as their functions were fairly discrete. In recent years, however, development and sponsored research each have encroached upon what was once considered the other's territory. The boundary between grants properly handled by the sponsored research office and grants that come under the development office's purview has become less distinct.

At least three reasons account for these changes:

1. *Corporate and foundation grants have become increasingly focused and restricted.* Foundations in particular have been under pressure from the Internal Revenue Service to demonstrate that they are making awards in accordance with their mission and charter. Documenting this in detail is an onerous task. The IRS has permitted grantmakers to shift some of this accountability to the recipient institutions. The result has been narrower, more targeted funding of institutional programs, combined with broader, more comprehensive reporting requirements placed on the institution.

2. *Corporations and higher education institutions are placing more and more emphasis on "partnerships."* In many cases, the term "partnership" is used loosely and does not indicate a meaningful shift in the traditional campus/corporate relationship. In other situations, however, corporations and universities have formed a different kind of relationship to further the goals they share. At times, some of these goals have stretched the traditional understanding of philanthropy and have resulted in tangible benefits for the corporate donor. For example, corporations may become involved in structuring curricula[1] or may cooperate closely with universities in choosing areas for basic research.[2]

3. *As federal funding in many program areas has declined, faculty members have turned more toward the private arena for program support.* Therefore, the sponsored research office, responding to faculty requests, may now be pursuing foundations once exclusively "assigned" to the development office.

For these reasons, the development and sponsored research offices must work in concert, despite their differences in purpose. Representatives of both offices must determine where their interests coincide and collide. And they should work out how best to use the coincidences while attempting to avoid the collisions. The work of the development and sponsored research offices generally intersects at three points: grant solicitation; grant accounting and administration (including reporting grant activity and expenditures to the donor); and external public reporting of grant income.

GRANT SOLICITATION

Determining who should approach a potential funder is a well-established practice in many development offices. Most universities already have in place a system to routinely "clear" prospects to a specific staff member or volunteer. Once a prospect is assigned, that prospect is considered off-limits to other staff and volunteers. Usually this assignment covers a specific time period, during which the staff member or volunteer may proceed with cultivation and solicitation. At the end of this time period, the prospect is "released" and is available for reassignment. Typically, the staff member or volunteer can retain the assignment by demonstrating that the process of cultivation or solicitation is under way.

This practice works as well between the development and sponsored research offices as it does within the development office. It is a relatively easy matter to include faculty members, working through sponsored research, in an existing prospect clearance/ protection system, assuming all parties agree in principle. In some cases, a prospect may be assigned simultaneously to representatives of both offices. In any event, it is necessary that the offices agree who ultimately makes the assignment decision. Both offices must abide by this decision, or the system will disintegrate.

The clearance procedure should be as simple as possible. Faculty members often consider these requirements as irritating bureaucratic obstacles that prevent them from completing other legitimate work. If development and sponsored research do not work together, securing approval for solicitation may be viewed on campus as a cumbersome, overly restrictive, and unnecessary hurdle.

GRANT ACCOUNTING AND ADMINISTRATION

Generally (though not always) the office that solicits the grant should administer it as well. Still, because some support falls into a "gray area" between the two jurisdictions, staff from both offices should discuss, on an ongoing basis, both theoretical issues and practical matters of grant accounting and administration.

From a purely theoretical standpoint, the determination of which office administers a particular grant is fairly simple. The Management Reporting Standards issued jointly by the Council for Advancement and Support of Education (CASE) and the National Association of College and University Business Officers (NACUBO) state that "a private grant, like a gift, is bestowed voluntarily and without expectation of any tangible compensation; it is donative in nature."[3] Because *donative intent* is the central issue, the decision as to which office handles a grant does *not* depend on the nature of the program being funded. Rather, the determining factor is the source of the funding and the intent of the funder.

Ascertaining donative intent may require a bit of mind-reading on the part of the university administrator. In some cases, the specific source of funding provides clues. For example, a check from a corporation's Office of Community Responsibility probably indicates donative intent. If, on the other hand, the funding comes from the company's research and development budget, it is more likely considered a cost of doing business rather than a charitable contribution.

Another, internal, factor may help the administrator determine donative intent: Would the faculty member conduct the research or run the program if the funder did not provide the means? Would the faculty member or department seek alternative support if these particular funds were not forthcoming? Or is the research or program being undertaken only because the money was available? Honest answers to these questions may be difficult to come by, but this approach may provide some indication of intent.

Despite these difficulties, donative intent provides the primary basis on which to distinguish gifts, grants, and contracts. This differentiation in turn helps determine which office should serve as administrator.

Gifts should always be routed through the development office. The donor expects nothing in return except a thank-you letter and perhaps other small tokens of appreciation or recognition. Support from individuals virtually always falls into this category, and individual donors should therefore be handled by the development office.

Contracts must be administered by sponsored research. Contracts are usually negotiated, are often legally enforceable, and always stipulate tangible—often proprietary—returns for the funder in goods or services to be delivered within a particular period of time. Contracts frequently require specific line-by-line reporting of expenditures, time and effort reports, and other terms of compliance. Because government agencies virtually always set such contractual requirements, public support is always under the purview of sponsored research.

It is not unusual for a particular program to receive both gifts and contract support. The source of these funds may even be identical. For this reason, the institution must determine the funder's intent when the check arrives.

For example, the Intergovernmental Health Policy Project at George Washington University routinely monitors all legislation concerning AIDS policy at the local, state, and federal levels. This information is available to the community through regularly published reports and press releases; in addition, interested parties may request particular data compiled according to specified criteria. A corporation may enter into a contractual agreement to secure specific data; such a contract must be handled by sponsored research. At the same time, another division of the same corporation may provide general support for the project in the belief that the program benefits the community. Because the company will receive nothing tangible in return, the check should be viewed as a gift and deposited through the development office.

Using these observations as guidelines, we can easily see what sort of outside support may raise questions of jurisdiction. Gifts are always the responsibility of development, while contracts always fall under sponsored research. Sponsored research administers government support, while development seeks and manages virtually all support from individuals (as well as most capital and endowed funds, for that matter). Therefore, the institutional income that exists in the "gray area" is grant support to current operating funds, given by corporations, foundations, and other organizations.

Although this is a relatively small part of overall support, the area of uncertainty is growing. As noted earlier, development officers are finding that foundation and corporate grants are carrying more stringent stipulations. Often, the funder requires the development officer to agree, in writing, to a higher level of accountability than in the past.

From the theoretical perspective, this should not make a difference in the administration of the funds, as long as the grant remains within the confines of donative intent. The grantmaker will not gain anything tangible from an insistence on detailed reporting. Rather, the organization's officers are merely ensuring that the institution is carrying out its part of the agreement.

The practical issues, however, are varied and confusing. Sponsored research offices are typically designed to handle complex tracking of budget expenditures, staff and faculty time, and similar matters. Development officers, however, may feel uncomfortable signing an agreement calling for increased reporting. In practice, how much accounting and reporting responsibility can the development office assume?

The development and sponsored research offices must come to some agreement on what level of reporting is beyond the capacity of the development office. This will vary among institutions depending upon the size and expertise of the development staff. However, there are some tasks that few development offices can reasonably be expected to complete. These include:

- Ensuring compliance with certain university or government policies—for example, on the use of experimental animals or on the use of human subjects in research.
- Maintaining time and effort reports for faculty and staff.
- Accounting for detailed line-by-line budget expenditures, particularly if the budget has been approved in advance and requires the funder's permission to modify.
- Assuming costs of a project that will be reimbursed by the funding agency upon presentation of invoices.
- Committing the institution to additional costs (such as facility remodeling or extensive use of computer time) or special conditions (such as handling radioactive materials) necessary to the research.

These conditions, and others that the development office cannot fulfill, should be determined by the two offices' representatives and included in the agreement between development and sponsored research. Whether or not the agreement is a written document depends upon the relationship between the two offices and their level of trust in each other. However, without such an agreement, written or informal, there is a risk that the development office will accept gifts it cannot administer. Alternatively, if the development office attempts to manage too much, it may need to hire staff to respond to these requirements, and thereby substantially duplicate the capabilities of the sponsored research office. Few institutions can afford this inefficiency.

In the past, many institutions have simply settled on a broad policy: Sponsored research must manage any grant that requires reporting. This rule is a relic from the days when development officers were thought to lack sophistication in internal management. However, the development office can appropriately undertake many reporting requirements. Both offices need to accept the fact that the development office should be responsible for significant reporting to donors. This is essential for good stewardship and should be considered a regular part of the development officer's job.

As is often noted, good stewardship is the first step in resoliciting the donor. Therefore, it is imperative that the development officer accept this responsibility and continue to foster the institution's relationship with the funder. Reporting should certainly include a narrative on how the institution spent the grant, how it met the terms of the proposal, and what tangible benefits resulted (for the institution, not the funder). The development office should also be able to provide simple budget figures and general reports on how faculty and staff spent their time.

A second practical consideration—one receiving considerable attention today—is the issue of indirect costs. Frequently, questions of whether sponsored research or development is the appropriate conduit for funding do not reflect either the theoretical or practical concerns discussed above; the real issue is the reluctance of the grant administrator or the granting agency to pay institutional overhead.

This is a timely subject. As I write this in the fall of 1991, the federal government has just instituted a cap on the percentage of federal reimbursements for indirect research costs. In response, academic administrators have begun to monitor indirect costs much more closely. It is likely that funders will also view high overhead charges with increasing skepticism.

This trend has led to legitimate concerns that heightened accountability will lead to a real increase in costs borne by the institution. For example, one foundation has recently begun requiring outside audits of grants it awards, while at the same time insisting the grants be processed through the development office without the assessment of indirect costs. Who should pay for such audits? Many foundations will not do so. Therefore the universities will have to assume these costs.

EXTERNAL REPORTING

Finally, there is the practical matter of the institution's external reporting of support received. The sponsored research and development offices must have a clear understanding of who is allowed to count which grants in published figures.

Some grants may legitimately be included by both offices in their external reports. For example, the CASE/NACUBO guidelines state that private grants handled by sponsored research should be included in the development office's Survey of Voluntary Support. Contracts, however, are specifically excluded.[4] In the same way, sponsored research may also include in its totals some research-grant money deposited through the development office. These are fairly standard practices at most universities.

However, it is important to monitor such overlaps closely. We risk losing credibility if we are too casual in appropriating each other's numbers. Institutions should widely circulate—and strictly enforce—exact guidelines to ensure reliable published results. It does not serve us well as individuals or as a profession to publicize big numbers that are largely paper transactions.

POINTS TO RESOLVE

To prevent confusion in soliciting, administering, and reporting grants, the two offices should review their own and each other's policies. The discussion should address at least the following issues:

- What mechanisms should the offices adopt to keep each other informed of grant activity? What ongoing reports should the offices share?
- How can the two offices work together to prevent overlap in prospect clearance?
- Who should provide reports on the grants, and how? When is good stewardship adequate, and when is more detailed accounting necessary?
- Who should pay for the additional costs resulting from increased expectations of accountability?

- What grants are appropriately counted by both offices in their totals? How do we ensure credibility in our public reports?
- What funders, or categories of funders, require particular attention by representatives of both offices?
- When a grant does not fit into the generally accepted guidelines, what mechanism is there for a case-by-case review? When there are disputes between the offices, what mechanism is available to resolve the disagreement?

Each institution will have its own perspective on these issues, depending upon its mission, history, and organization. In all cases, however, sponsored research and development must work together to create a clear policy statement and associated procedures. Although mid-level managers will carry out those procedures, the overall policy and direction must originate at the highest level of the university's administration.

As our practices undergo ever-increasing scrutiny, universities are being held to higher standards than in the past. In most cases, we have already attained these high standards. Now, however, it is important that we articulate these standards clearly and follow them rigorously.

NOTES

1. Anne S. Alexander, "Understanding the Philanthropic Partnership: Corporations Don't Give Just to Support a University; They Give so the University Can Further Philanthropic Goals," *CASE Currents*, March 1988, 14.

2. Melinda J. Burdette, "Choose Your Partnership: A Sampling of Campus-Corporate Pairings," *CASE Currents*, March 1988, 22.

3. Council for Advancement and Support of Education and National Association of College and University Business Officers, *Management Reporting Standards for Educational Institutions: Fund Raising and Related Activities* (Washington, D.C.: Council for Advancement and Support of Education, 1982), 4.

4. Ibid.

Part Ten
Special Considerations for Institutions

Once an activity principally of private institutions, organized fund raising now exists at nearly all of the nation's colleges, universities, and independent schools—large and small, private and public. While basic fund-raising principles are the same in every setting, the unique characteristics and circumstances of these diverse institutions do present special considerations for the organization and implementation of fund-raising programs.

The three chapters in this section discuss fund raising in three particular types of institutions—public colleges and universities that have institutionally related foundations, independent primary and secondary schools, and community colleges.

The growth of fund-raising programs at public colleges and universities was a hallmark of higher education in the 1980s. With the exception of state universities in the Midwest, which have a long tradition of support from private sources, public institutions were relatively new to fund raising in the past decade. For many public colleges and universities, the independent, institutionally related foundation is essential to raising and managing private gifts. In Chapter 29, Royster Hedgepeth describes the benefits of such foundations, various models for their organization, and considerations in making them effective fund-raising vehicles for their host institutions.

Some of the oldest educational institutions in the country are independent schools. But aggressive and professionally managed development programs have only recently emerged at many of them. Again, while the principles of fund raising remain the same in the school setting, the independent school's program and constituency raise unique considerations. James Theisen discusses these factors in Chapter 30.

Community colleges have been the fastest growing segment of higher education over the past thirty years. But only in recent years have these institutions begun to mount serious efforts to secure private support. The community college's unique character offers both problems and advantages for development officers. In Chapter 31, Nanette Smith discusses how the community college's special mission and constituency shape its fund-raising programs.

Chapter 29

The Institutionally Related Foundation

Royster C. Hedgepeth

The quest for private support by public universities is essentially a phenomenon of the 1980s. To be sure, there have been some notable post-World War II exceptions, such as the University of Michigan and the Kansas Endowment Association. But in general, the widespread, concerted pursuit of private funds by public universities is a relatively new element in American philanthropy.

Two driving forces are behind this phenomenon. The first is heightened competition for shrinking resources. State funding for public universities has rarely increased as rapidly as institutional needs; in many cases, state support has provided a steadily shrinking percentage of the total operating budget. At the same time, federal support has become a particularly scarce resource, requiring greater and greater sophistication and effort to attract. Diminishing state and federal support, coupled with restricted ability to generate revenue from tuition increases, has forced public universities to look to nontraditional sources of support.

As public universities began to compete for private support in the early 1980s, they found they could be extremely successful. The early success of a small number of what were, at the time, very large public university campaigns was the second force driving the dramatic increase in private fund-raising efforts. Announcements of $100 million campaign efforts in the late 1970s and early 1980s were greeted with skepticism. As one success quickly followed another, skepticism quickly changed to a rush to get on the campaign bandwagon. Public universities realized they had found a potential source of economic growth and rushed to take advantage of it.

During the 1980s, the growth of support of public universities has been more dramatic than any other sector of philanthropy (see table 1). In turn, the structures and practices through which public universities raise money have drawn increased attention. The focus for much of this attention has been the institutionally related foundation.

Table 1. Growth of Philanthropic Support, 1980–1989

	Total Support (in billions)		Increase
	1980	*1989*	
Religion	$22.23	$54.32	244%
Education	$ 4.96	$10.69	216%
Health	$ 5.34	$10.04	188%
Human Services	$ 4.91	$11.39	232%
Arts/Culture	$ 3.15	$ 7.49	238%
Public Benefit	$ 1.46	$ 3.62	250%
TOTAL	$42.05	$97.55	231%
80 public doctoral universities	$0.72	$ 1.94	268%

Sources: *Giving USA 1989* (New York: AAFRC Trust, 1990) and *Voluntary Support of Education 1979–1980* and *1988–1989* (New York: Council for Aid to Education).

INSTITUTIONALLY RELATED FOUNDATIONS

Public universities began establishing institutionally related foundations for quite practical reasons. Some of the early foundations were created to buy property important to the institution that would not be on the market long enough to acquire through the state appropriations process. Others were set up to preserve an arms-length relationship between state treasuries and private gifts—particularly endowment gifts.

Those roles have changed dramatically. In many cases the institutionally related foundation has become analogous to the private university's development office. Foundations are now managing large, rapidly expanding endowments, running large campaigns, and engaging in comprehensive programs involving large staffs and multi-million dollar budgets.

There is no requirement that a public university have a foundation as part of its fund-raising operation. Some universities do not—for example, the University of Michigan, the University of Tennessee, and the University of Missouri. But most public universities do use some form of foundation in their fund-raising program.

Gary Ransdell, vice president for institutional advancement at Clemson University, has identified several basic advantages of using an institutionally related foundation. A foundation can operate in an environment that is politically neutral and operationally flexible compared to the university itself, allowing it to respond more quickly and efficiently. It can provide a public-private partnership to raise money that is separate from, but supportive of, basic state resources, and can allocate funds for urgent needs that cannot be met with public appropriations. It can manage donated funds and distribute their earnings according to guidelines monitored and authorized by its independent governing board, and it can invest assets more flexibly and expediently than the state system would permit the institution itself to do.

A private foundation can also more easily maintain donor confidentiality and ensure that gifts are handled in congruence with the donor's intent. And it can involve interested volunteers more effectively in the fund-raising effort and create in them the sense of pride, accomplishment, and ownership essential to fund-raising success.[1]

FOUNDATION STRUCTURE

The principles and practices of sound fund raising do not change when fund raising occurs in a public university or under the auspices of an institutionally related foundation. Good basics are good basics. The degree to which the foundation's advantages are exploited and the level to which the institution depends on the foundation reflect the foundation's organizational structure.

The public university is an entrepreneurial, decentralized place. While authority usually flows in a hierarchical manner, power is often distributed to colleges, departments, or centers. As fund raising developed in the public university, the structure of the foundation was determined primarily by the history of the institution and the way in which fund-raising budgets were funded.

To examine a foundation's role, we must look at its *range* (the number of development-related functions for which the foundation is responsible), its *scope* (the extent to which the foundation serves the university's component elements), and its *integration* (the degree to which the foundation is governed by the institution's priorities).

Range

In terms of range of activities, institutionally related foundations may be viewed on a continuum. At one extreme, the foundation may function as a bank—receiving and managing funds, but having no active role in actually raising money. Such a foundation has the advantages of keeping costs to a minimum and simplifying the task of gift management and fund transfer. In such cases, the foundation usually operates in tandem with a central development office that reports to the university president and is funded with institutional funds. The development office is more likely to be integrated into the senior management structure of the institution and involved in institutional decision-making.

While integration into university operations may be more effective in this situation, the fund-raising operation may lose a vital margin of autonomy in maintaining the separateness and flexibility of private gifts that is important to donor and recipient alike. Separateness and flexibility are also important in developing volunteer leadership. The public university development office must organize volunteers—advocates of institutional support—in relation to the institutional governing board rather than allowing them to function as an independent body focused on fund raising and fund management.

On the other end of this continuum are the foundations that function as comprehensive fund-raising and fund-management agencies for institutions that do not have separate development offices. These comprehensive foundations have the advantage of being able to consolidate the total fund-raising program and recognize significant economies of scale from limited budgets. In addition, comprehensive foundations can develop a quicker readiness for major campaign fund raising and enlist, develop, and motivate volunteer leadership that is focused intensely on fund raising.

While the comprehensive foundation offers exceptional benefits, it poses substantial risks as well. The comprehensive foundation may develop a level of autonomy that is counterproductive to the effective use of private gifts in support of the university's mission. The comprehensive foundation may come to act as a charitable foundation, seeking and awarding grants. In this case, the institution's leadership assumes the role of supplicant and does not have sufficient say in merging foundation actions with institutional goals and opportunities.

The comprehensive foundation may also be estranged from the academic leaders and students it serves. The university community often misunderstands development. As Robert Payton, director of the Center on Philanthropy in Indianapolis, says, "Advancement brings the values of the marketplace onto the campus. . . . Many faculty members applaud the ends but scorn the means of persuasion."[2]

Such misunderstanding of the structure and function of fund raising may lead to animosity, distrust, and lack of communication. When these occur, the comprehensive foundation may have difficulty fulfilling its purpose for the institution.

Scope

Another factor that defines the institutionally related foundation's role is the scope of its service to the institution. Most public universities have one foundation that serves the needs of the component elements of the institution. In this situation, management of the foundation is simple and accountability is clear.

Foundations that serve the broad scope of the institution have a great capacity to realize economies of scale in direct mail, telephone marketing, donor reports, database management, and other activities directed toward building and upgrading the donor base. They can also provide a highly consistent level of quality assurance, performance assessment, and coordination. This consistency and coordination is especially important for the effective management of major gift prospects.

Foundations that serve the entire university may be criticized for not understanding the special, specific needs of the institution's component parts. With so many voices competing for attention, the foundation may try to please everyone and end up pleasing no one. The broad-scope foundation is regularly forced to balance its ability to deliver efficient, effective service on behalf of the institution with the reality that the most effective fund raising occurs at the college or constituent level, where fund-raising readiness and potential may vary widely.

In contrast, some universities have multiple foundations, each with its own independent board, serving the needs of specialized components of the institution. These more narrowly defined foundations have the advantage of knowing the particular needs and opportunities of the components they serve.

The more narrowly defined foundations are able to build on college loyalties and attract both volunteers and donors more quickly because the smaller components are easier to "get one's arms around" than the more diffuse university. These foundations are also able to capitalize on the rich variety and unique strengths of the various components.

However, it is difficult to maximize budgeted resources in the multiple foundation setting. Systems for broad-based solicitation, gift management, and database development are often redundant and inconsistent. Efforts to attract major gifts and enlist top volunteers may be competitive at best and work at cross-purposes at worst.

At institutions in which provincial interests are formalized to the degree of creating multiple foundations, it is often difficult to develop the strength of an institutional presence in fund raising. Just as the university is greater than the sum of its parts, the strength of fund raising at the institutional level is greater than that achieved by adding the potential of the component parts.

The longer a donor is associated with an institution and the larger the donor's giving becomes, the more likely he or she will want to serve the larger needs of the institution. Even when support goes to a college, department, or special program, there is a need to serve the larger values of the institution.

Integration

Some institutionally related foundations, while functioning to serve the university, exist wholly outside the institution. In such cases, the foundation serves as a grantmaking entity for the university.

While entirely separate foundations maintain a high level of autonomy, they often have difficulty influencing or enhancing the institution's strategic agenda. They also have difficulty cultivating the internal relationships that create a sense of urgency and importance for donors.

Other foundations are well integrated into the institutional milieu from both an administrative and strategic perspective. The university's strategic agenda is the driving force behind their efforts. These foundations must maintain enough autonomy to protect donors' interests, while making sure their separate role supports the university's mission.

An Ideal Model?

There is no single "best" model for an institutionally related foundation. Foundation structure, function, and effectiveness depend far more on the dynamics of the university than on precise rules of fund raising. Each institution has to look at its particular situation and define how a foundation best enhances its development efforts.

Three guidelines provide a framework in which to organize and evaluate the foundation's functions.

1. The foundation should base its case for support thoroughly on the university's strategic agenda and clearly support the institution's mission.
2. The foundation should provide a frame of reference that keeps university leaders, development staff, and volunteers focused on fund raising.
3. The foundation should maintain the integrity of the philanthropic process by validating donors' rights and ensuring effective stewardship for gift funds.

Within these guidelines, such factors as institutional history, methods of funding development, and the role of private support in the university will determine the foundation's functions, the scope of its activities, and the degree to which it is integrated into the life of the institution.

FUNCTIONS OF THE FOUNDATION

The institutionally related foundation exists to raise and manage private funds and to enlist and nurture volunteers in support of the institution's mission. To fulfill this mission, the foundation must deal effectively with setting priorities for private support. It must then work to raise money effectively by supervising access to prospects, managing volunteers, supporting donors' rights, and providing sufficient funding for the development effort.

Setting Fund-raising Priorities

The role of the institutionally related foundation in setting fund-raising priorities is a crucial consideration for the practice of fund raising in the public university. While most fund-raising operations can raise money for virtually anything, they cannot raise money for everything, and the causes for which they can raise money are not always of equal financial potential. Fund raising introduces the question, "Of those things for which you can raise money, which have priority?"

Setting priorities can be particularly delicate in the public university setting. The public university's philosophy generally includes an egalitarian perspective: The belief that education should be available to everyone translates into an operational belief that everyone is equally important. Any decisions about fund-raising priorities will invariably leave out important needs and opportunities. The need to focus on a limited set of goals runs counter to the philosophy that everyone is more or less equal.

The foundation that has a comprehensive role and is well integrated into the university's development efforts should make certain that the university's academic leadership determines academic priorities and the priorities for which private support will be sought. While the foundation should not be the arbiter of fund-raising priorities, it should play the primary role in answering questions of feasibility and in assessing the relative potential of competing fund-raising needs and opportunities. The effective foundation will see not only that the academic leadership makes sound decisions but also that the broader university community knows of those decisions.

In a time of scarce resources, the foundation is also responsible for asking the right questions about the relationship between fund-raising priorities and the institution's strategic agenda. The oft-used phrase "vital margin of excellence" is appropriate in this regard. The foundation must constantly ask, "Will success with this priority contribute to the institution's margin of excellence?"

For the foundation serving a particular component of the university and for the independent foundation, the question of priorities and institutional gain are vital. The foundation's need for autonomy and organizational independence should not diminish the reality that the foundation exists to support and enhance the institution's mission. Maintenance of private support as a separate entity is valuable only to the extent to which it fulfills its primary function.

In the decentralized, entrepreneurial environment of the public university, support of institutional priorities is a difficult issue indeed. The foundation agenda should operate in conjunction with the institution's strategic agenda, not in competition with it. The effective foundation must take pains to see that its efforts, regardless of its structure, do not dampen institutional prerogatives or hamper the development of the institutional case for support that is the essential backdrop for large-scale fund raising.

Managing Prospects

The public university provides many gift opportunities for donors. There are also many potential recipients who may claim special interest in any given prospect. The comprehensive foundation must recognize that most donors relate to the college or department from which they graduated, or to some special interest they have developed in their life. The component foundation, on the other hand, must recognize that as donors mature, they become more concerned about the welfare of the larger institution and the impact their philanthropy has on the institutional agenda.

Once again, the foundation is responsible for seeing that the institution's best interests are served. The effective foundation will:

1. Assign prospects to staff members. The foundation must make certain that the prospect assignment process is rational, involves the appropriate university participants, and establishes responsibility for solicitation.
2. Make sure that staff move promptly to put the university in the forefront of prospects' awareness. The foundation must establish a formal method for ensuring that staff members cultivate and evaluate their assigned prospects effectively to prepare for responsible solicitation.
3. Maintain an openness to change as the foundation gains understanding of the donor. Foundation managers must be sensitive to the prospective donor and willing to change assignments when new information of the donor indicates a different approach is in order.

Managing Volunteers

Volunteer advocacy is essential to sustained success in large-scale fund raising; volunteer time is the most important resource the development effort has. Volunteers are also central to development on the college, departmental, and program levels through a wide variety of advisory groups.

Successful volunteer development follows a pattern similar to that for cultivating major donors. The foundation must ensure that professional staff and key academic leaders understand this process and are consistent and thoughtful in the "care and feeding" of volunteers. One often-heard lament from volunteers is that institutional efforts are not well coordinated; in short, they ask, "Don't you folks ever talk to one another?" Volunteers do not understand the peculiar politics that drive the public university and are not sympathetic to explanations about why things work— or don't work—the way they do.

Volunteers may serve a variety of roles, either simultaneously or sequentially, and foundation staff must recognize and coordinate those efforts. The foundation must also provide a clear focus on institutional strategy and mission so that volunteers gain a real sense of the value and impact of their service. In institutions with multiple foundations, it is important for the various foundations to develop the trust and communication that fosters an effective collaborative effort.

Finally, it is important for the foundation to see that volunteers are evaluated, promoted when appropriate, and rewarded for their efforts. All volunteers have the right to feel good about their service, and the foundation is responsible for seeing that they do.

Supporting Donors' Rights

Every gift to education is a donor's statement of his or her belief in the value of education. The foundation is responsible for letting donors know that their gifts made a difference and what that difference means. Regardless of the foundation's structure, the foundation must make sure that the donor never disappears as the focus of the philanthropic equation.

All donors have the right to expect that when they are asked for a gift, the request reflects clearly defined institutional priorities. Donors also have the right to expect that their gifts are used as they intended. The foundation is responsible for safeguarding the rights of donors and ensuring an appropriate level of accountability.

Clearly defined fund-raising priorities that both support the university's strategic agenda and match a donor's interest will yield private support that makes a difference in the life of an institution. Well-executed stewardship then becomes the basis for new cultivation and solicitation.

Funding the Development Effort

The character and structure of many public universities' development organizations reflect in no small way the means by which development has been funded. Some institutions devote a major portion of their time to raising unrestricted gifts and then allocate a proportion of those gifts to pay the operational costs of the fund-raising effort. Some universities are able to fund development operations as line items in their budgets. The creation of a stable, predictable method of paying the cost of fund raising for an extended period of time is an essential consideration for the public university.

A 1989 study of twenty-six public universities showed that all depended on multiple sources for supporting the fund-raising operation. The study also pointed out that failure to develop a stable funding model creates an inordinate drain on senior management time—time that should be devoted to raising funds, especially big gifts.[3]

The institutionally related foundation is responsible for seeing that the institution's leadership develops the sense of ownership necessary to ensure stable and sufficient support for fund raising. It is also responsible for clear reporting of fund-raising expenditures and for clear accounting of both funds raised and value added through private support.

THE FOUNDATION BOARD OF DIRECTORS

An independent board of directors is at the heart of every successful institutionally related foundation. In the past, these boards were often socially oriented, with few members selected for their fund-raising abilities. In today's highly competitive environment, that has changed. The foundation board's effectiveness depends on the clear definition of its roles, the quality of its advocacy, the soundness of its fiduciary responsibility, and the degree to which it relates effectively to the university's own governing board.

Role Definition

The adage that the board member should provide wealth, wisdom, or work—preferably at least two of the three—is still true. The primary determinants of effective board membership are how well the board member can cultivate support, solicit support, enlist volunteers, and build bridges to other prospective donors. For the contemporary board member the responsibility goes further. The board member is responsible for exercising sufficient managerial oversight to ensure the foundation's effective functioning. In addition, the board member is responsible for maintaining the level of external credibility necessary to raise money.

For the foundation board member, this means making sure institutional fund-raising priorities are well defined and that the institution is well-served by the successful attainment of those goals. The contemporary board member also should assume responsibility for evaluating the clarity of communications between university and foundation and establishing procedures for reporting results. Finally, the board is responsible for evaluating the performance of executive staff.

Advocacy

Every university needs advocates—volunteers who are willing to act repeatedly for the good of the institution. The foundation must make certain that the university's volunteers understand and believe in the institution's mission, strategic agenda, and fund-raising priorities.

While advocacy is important, well-informed advocacy is crucial to effective fund raising. The foundation board should take the lead in making certain institutional advocacy is accurate, conveys an appropriate urgency, and creates a compelling need for support.

The foundation board's responsibility for advocacy goes beyond institutional advocacy. The 1980s were years of diminishing confidence in higher education institutions in the United States. The foundation board should also strive to renew public credibility in the role and mission of higher education and to validate the central importance of the philanthropic enterprise.

The 1990s have begun with a disconcerting barrage of federal and state regulation of nonprofit organizations. The current legislative and regulatory direction seems to say, "Philanthropy and voluntary action are no longer valued in American society." The foundation board needs to take a strong position that the private investment of time, talent, and treasure for the benefit of social values is essential to a strong, free society.

Fiduciary Responsibility

A private gift initiates a relationship of trust. The foundation board is responsible for seeing that this trust is fulfilled. The board should make sure the foundation maintains a program of donor relations and accountability emphasizing the proper use of gifts and timely reporting to engage the donor and the institution.

The foundation board's fiduciary responsibilities also extend to the prudent management of assets donated to it. In the case of endowments, this means investing the assets in a way that ensures protection from inflation while providing a reasonable, predictable stream of spendable income to the institution. Trusteeship of life income gifts may involve a deeper level of stewardship, reflecting the personality of the donors, the timing of the gift, payout of the trust, and so on. In all cases, the foundation board should be aware of and work within appropriate state and local institutional and trust laws, designed to protect both the donor's and the institution's interests.

Relationship with the Institutional Governing Board

The value of an institutionally related foundation is its capacity to establish an unambiguous focus on private support. The foundation board's role is to make sure that private support efforts in turn support institutional needs and opportunities. The foundation and its board do not take the place of the university's governing board, which is usually elected in a general election or appointed by the governor.

The foundation board exists to support the institution and its chief executive. As the pressure for private support intensifies, the foundation board should work to develop an ever more articulate relationship with the university's governing board to ensure the mutual strength of their efforts.

THE FUTURE OF INSTITUTIONALLY RELATED FOUNDATIONS

Institutionally related foundations provide an important degree of autonomy and flexibility for fund raising in the public university. Their structure and function vary widely, depending on institutional history, demand for increased fund raising, and sources through which development operations are funded.

The standards by which foundations are maintained and evaluated have changed over the years. No longer are foundations institutional cookie jars to be manipulated by their boards or their institution's leaders. Today they are important components in the process of private support for public universities.

The foundation and its volunteer board play an important role in fulfilling the university's vision, in increasing and validating the level of private support, and in developing donors and volunteers. In effect, the foundation provides services similar to parallel organizations or offices in private institutions. The public university setting adds special needs, opportunities, and considerations affecting how the foundation carries out these functions.

While the structure of institutionally related foundations will change as fund raising for public universities grows and matures, such foundations will have an important role in the future of American higher education and the public university's capacity for enhancing the quality of life for all people.

NOTES

1. Gary A. Ransdell (presentation at a seminar on Establishing and Developing an Effective Public University Foundation, sponsored by the Association of Governing Boards, Denver, Colorado, Nov. 8, 1991); and Gary A. Ransdell, "The Foundation of Our Foundations, *AGB Reports,* July/August 1991, 30-31.

2. Robert L. Payton (speech made at the Annual Assembly of the Council for Advancement and Support of Education, Toronto, July 12, 1982).

3. Royster C. Hedgepeth (presentation at the District VII Conference of the Council for Advancement and Support of Education, Monterey, California, 1988).

Chapter 30

Raising Funds for Independent Schools

James M. Theisen

Thirty years ago, independent school fund raising was the province of a network of volunteers, mainly parents who gave their time each week to help organize auctions, plan dinners, and put out the school newsletter. The resident staff person was usually a part-time development director, part-time admissions interviewer, and anything else the school needed—a true generalist.

When inflation skyrocketed to double digits in the 1970s, and salaries rose slower than the cost-of-living index, trustees and heads realized resources and personnel needed more specific focus. Capital campaigns appeared as the long-term solution to school financial needs, and volunteers who gave their time freely in the 1960s joined the ranks of paid staff members in the 1970s. Many successful development officers today trace their beginnings to this volunteer background.

In the 1980s, independent school fund raising began to mirror the college and university models—large staffs made up of highly focused specialists. A college hires a development officer to handle one or two functions. This direction, proven effective at colleges, remains a luxury at most independent schools, but with growing financial needs, there is a movement toward it. Still, the typical school development officer—unlike his or her counterparts at colleges and universities—embraces almost every aspect of school life, from working with the trustees to writing the parent newsletter. The development officer who is a generalist brings a special perspective that should be preserved. Overspecialization leads to a myopic view of the development process.

WHAT MAKES SCHOOLS DIFFERENT

The job of the school development officer is free of the complexities that fund raisers in colleges and universities often face. Issues requiring decisions, for example, can be resolved quickly. Because the development officer interacts frequently with the school head, the business manager, admissions officers, trustees, and faculty, he or she can communicate more knowledgeably with the school's off-campus constituency. In most schools, all fund-raising activities originate with the development office: Few schools deal with separate "friends" groups that solicit special interest groups, and rarely does a school development officer have to coordinate individual faculty requests concerning particular projects.

The school development office strives to meet common goals of faculty and administration. The focus is on the whole, not on individual areas or departments. The development officer is a member of the school's management team, aware of broad concerns and the pressing needs of the school.

Most school development officers today, as in the past, have some responsibilities beyond their office duties—student adviser, chaperon, sponsor for the school newspaper, or member of a faculty committee. This is a perfect way for a development officer to become acquainted with the future constituency! The students gain an appreciation for how alumni and parents contribute to the financial strength of the school and how their help has enriched and broadened the educational programs. In turn, the development officer has a personal and active link to the school's future donors.

SUPPORT FOR DAY AND BOARDING SCHOOLS

All these points apply to both day and boarding schools. Still, these two types of schools differ in important ways in the kind of support they attract. At day schools, the vast majority of all capital and annual gifts come from parents. Day schools are in a good position to evaluate the true financial potential of parents living in their community. These parents chose a private school education because they want to give their children the best. They see and measure their children's progress daily. Children return home each afternoon to report on their activities and indirectly convey the school's needs. This closeness provides parents an opportunity to respond to the school's programs with both their time and financial resources.

While parents account for most of the revenue at a day school, most gifts to a boarding school come from alumni—perhaps 80 percent, paralleling support for residential colleges. For many alumni, the boarding school was their first experience away from home. The school acts *in loco parentis*, and thus the student develops strong bonds with the faculty and staff. Since many boarding schools have a long history, alumni associations are often well-developed and serve to link the school with graduates. Parents visit the campus less frequently and are less involved. Today, some boarding schools realize the important role parents play in their fund-raising efforts.

KEY PLAYERS

All successful organizations are managed from the top. The success of the school development effort depends on the vision and leadership of trustees and the school head in concert with the development officer. The trustees, working with the head, set the direction and tone of the school and all its programs.

Trustees are the stewards of the school's resources—people, plant, and financial assets—and should play a central role in school fund-raising efforts. Years ago, board members were selected because of their prominence in the community or through an "old boy" network. Today, independent schools emulate their colleagues in higher education and select trustees to represent the diversity of the school and the specific needs of the institution. Lawyers, architects, engineers, managers, educators, financial investors, and medical professionals serve on boards to guide the institution in dealing with today's complex issues. At boarding schools, most trustees come from the ranks of alumni, whereas parents make up the majority of trustees at day schools.

A well-managed institution has a good working partnership between the board and the head. The head is the educational leader, and his or her office becomes "command central." All academic, student, faculty, staff, and legal issues facing the school are channeled through this office. The board focuses its attention on policy issues, providing the head with the necessary tools to lead.

The head must also be the leading fund raiser. He or she cannot share this task with a host of other administrators, like a college president who can draw upon deans or department chairs.

Donors want to talk to the head when they make a major investment in the school. Substitutes do not work. This places a great burden on any head when weighed against the other demands of the job.

Heads of day schools concentrate their fund-raising efforts on those who live near the school. They never have to go far to meet their donors. The boarding school head, however, leaves the campus for days or weeks to visit and solicit a national constituency. As with day schools, the boarding school constituency wants to hear first-hand from the head.

ANNUAL FUND PROGRAMS

Every good development effort starts with a well-planned and carefully managed annual fund campaign. Major gifts, capital campaigns, and planned gifts rest on this all-important fund-raising platform. The level of sophistication varies with different schools, but the principles remain the same. The annual fund provides dependable yearly support, a known donor base, and the training ground for staff to learn how to work with volunteers on a specific task in a defined period of time. Eventually, this can be the starting point for capital campaign programs.

Annual fund programs include alumni, parents, past parents, grandparents, and friends, but the degree of support from each depends on the type of school—day or boarding. This distinction will direct resource allocation, staff time, and volunteer efforts.

In day school annual fund programs, parents contribute the majority of volunteer support and provide most of the yearly revenues. Solicitation teams are often organized by children's classes. Parents can assess one another's potential and can rely on friendships or business associations to motivate giving.

In recent years, schools have recognized the role grandparents play in their grandchild's educational experience. As people retire earlier, more and more grandparents have time to spend on the things that interest them. Studies show the wealthiest members of our society are not the young, two-income families, but people over 50. Many of these grandparents are demonstrating their willingness to invest in their grandchildren's future. As economic pressures on young families compel them to seek financial assistance, grandparents are increasingly helping with tuition payments at all educational levels. Today, "grandparent days" are built into the school academic calendar.

Parents of former students—called "past parents"—also may prove to be good prospects. As children progress from one educational level to the next, parental support shifts to the next school. However, many past parents look back and appreciate the educational foundation the independent school gave their child. The school's physical presence in their community serves as a constant reminder long after the child graduates and college tuition bills are paid. A grateful parent may not be ready to support the school immediately after graduation, but may express appreciation years after college or graduate school. Don't remove their names from your lists too soon!

As noted earlier, boarding schools receive most of their annual fund support from alumni. Many schools base their annual fund programs on a class system—classmates soliciting classmates. The five-year reunion cycle presents opportunities to raise larger-than-usual gifts, both for the annual fund and special projects. Reunions are the rallying point: They serve to reintroduce alumni to their alma mater and to articulate the school's most pressing needs.

Parents and grandparents play a smaller role in boarding school fund raising, but they cannot be ignored. While they provide less support than alumni, most annual fund campaigns would fall short without all forms of parental participation. No institution can afford to exclude potential donors. As competition for charitable dollars increases, parents play a much greater role in fund raising.

In all campaigns, various approaches are used to solicit gifts: letters, telephones (via phonathons), and—the most effective method—personal visits. Knowing that face-to-face solicitation is not possible in all cases, schools are turning to techniques of market segmentation—dividing the constituency into similar groups and targeting each with a specific appeal and combination of approaches. As schools shift to larger and more specialized staffs, market segmentation and other sophisticated fund-raising methods will become more common.

Many schools are emulating colleges by structuring their class and reunion campaigns using capital campaign techniques—advance planning (in some cases two years in advance), feasibility studies, and prospect screening. If schools compete in the broad fund-raising arena, they must employ these techniques. This approach will become the standard in the decade ahead.

CAPITAL CAMPAIGNS

Twenty years ago, educational institutions suspended their annual funds during capital campaigns. Eventually, institutions realized they had closed the door to an important volunteer network and donor base. Since not every person would contribute to the capital campaign, donors fell out of the habit of supporting the institution and shifted their loyalties elsewhere. Rebuilding annual support took precious time and cost significant revenues. Today, most schools either integrate the annual fund with the campaign or continue to run the annual fund drive separately.

A campaign cannot be successful if run by the staff alone; the board, administration, and volunteers must be committed and work as a team. The school must have a clear image of itself, and the campaign must be based on legitimate institutional planning, long-term goals, and an adequate budget and staff.

The board's role is crucial. It has long been true that the board should contribute about 25 percent of the announced campaign goal. Trustees must step forward before the campaign is publicly announced and pledge their support. Momentum comes from the announcement that "100 percent of the board gave!"

Campaigns run between three to five years, and schools must be flexible to accept not only cash gifts but also planned (or "deferred") gifts—trusts, bequests, and similar gift arrangements. Campaigns do not always match a donor's giving cycle, and one cannot afford to turn down a gift. The campaign leadership must try to project what percentage of gifts will come from cash and what will be in the form of planned gifts. If the role of planned gifts continues to grow—and there is no reason to think otherwise—schools must plan how these gifts will affect campaign totals and cash objectives.

Because school development staffs tend to be small and to have limited campaign experience, many schools hire consultants to direct capital campaigns. Outside counsel provides experience and serves as an objective barometer for the campaign's progress. The search for a consultant should begin as soon as a campaign is seriously considered. Choose a consultant who has a proven track record and experience at similar institutions.

SPECIAL EVENTS

Auctions, dinners, and carnivals are popular fund-raising events. For some schools, special events yield hundreds of thousands of dollars each year.

These events take an inordinate amount of staff and volunteer time. However, they serve the important function of bringing people together for a common purpose. This allows trustees, administrators, and volunteer leaders to meet their constituents and to further the school's cause.

An event is worth repeating only if it proves to be a money raiser and a popular rallying event in the school's academic year. Determine the time and effort needed to run it and the dollars it will raise; then compare that to the results expected from channeling the same resources into personal solicitations of the top 100 donors.

FOUNDATION AND CORPORATION PROGRAMS

Anyone who has worked in an independent school will have heard a well-meaning parent or graduate say, "I think you are missing the boat. There are real opportunities to raise dollars for this program from foundations and corporations. My college just received a grant for the same kind of program. Not only would it answer our needs, but it would also take the burden off the parents who are already paying a sizable tuition."

True, colleges and universities receive large support from corporations and foundations; also true, the independent school community receives very little. There are opportunities we must not miss, but for any school to place too much emphasis on these programs at the expense of parents or alumni is a risk.

Most foundation support at the school level comes when a parent or graduate has a special relationship with the foundation. Yes, some foundations independently support elementary and secondary education for specific programs, but they are few in number. Foundation grants will rarely, if ever, be the financial backbone of a school's fund-raising program. Consider the time invested against the return. Spend time cultivating alumni or parents who will do more over time than an occasional foundation gift.

Corporations support independent schools primarily through matching gifts to the annual fund program. Today, nearly 500 corporations match gifts to independent schools. Outright corporate gifts to schools usually occur when there is a community partnership or a direct benefit to the corporation. For example, a local computer software company might make a gift-in-kind of software to a school because many of the employees' children attend. Many times, corporations that support colleges and universities hope to attract future employees or benefit from research in which an institution is engaged; schools can offer no such direct benefits. Corporate and foundation grants have a place within the independent school development effort, but they are not the panacea some might imagine them to be.

PLANNED GIVING

Bequests, trusts, and life income arrangements are becoming more than occasional ripples in the well. As more individuals consider larger gifts, planned giving must be part of the development effort.

The planned giving campaign does not have to be highly sophisticated or expensive. Some donors will already be familiar with these methods, as other nonprofits promote planned giving as a giving option. You need simply tell donors that these gifts are welcome. You can include bequest reminders in alumni and parent newsletters and suggest to board members and key volunteers to remember schools in their estate planning. An outside consultant can help with specific questions, so the school need not invest in a full-time, trained planned giving director. However, someone on the staff should have a broad understanding of the different vehicles.

The planned giving program's cost-effectiveness cannot and should not be measured in immediate terms. The school should evaluate the program each year, but measure the investment versus financial payback on at least a five-year basis. Many schools invest time and energy in donor cultivation only to reap the benefits ten, twenty, or thirty years later. The real question is, How long can you afford to wait before you start a planned giving program, even on a modest scale?

RECOGNIZING DONORS

People like to be thanked. It is important that schools pay strict attention to this basic human need. Dinners, plaques, letters, and invitations to special events show donors we care. Recognition, along with careful stewardship, leads to future gifts.

Schools can frequently show their appreciation in a more personal way than larger organizations. Day schools, in particular, can honor donors and volunteers with events and public recognition because these people are physically close to the school. Boarding schools have a greater challenge to thank and recognize donors who live at great distances.

THE FUTURE OF SCHOOL FUND RAISING

What challenges face schools in the coming decade? Some financial analysts predict endowments will cease to grow at double-digit rates. Tuitions cannot continue to rise at their present pace, or institutions will price themselves out of the market. Therefore, successful fund raising will become more vital to the financial integrity of schools.

With limited budgets, the development officer must review how resources will be allocated and weigh programs on a cost-revenue basis. Questions like, "Can we afford to continue this event or program?" and "Are we receiving a maximum return on the dollars spent?" will merit careful consideration. "Nice-to-have" programs will be eliminated.

Schools must also do a better job of stewardship—of maintaining a close, ongoing relationship with donors. Individuals who have given in the past will be even more important in future funding. Individual cultivation will consume more time. Recognizing, thanking, and showing donors consistent appreciation will be imperative.

More donors will consider planned gifts to meet, first, their own financial needs and, second, the institution's needs. While many of these gifts will not mature for ten years or more, schools cannot sit idle and let other nonprofits reap the benefits. Planned giving programs must be on every development officer's menu.

Reports of mega-campaigns at colleges and universities fill fund-raising journals. Donor's sights are being raised, and the effects will certainly filter down to independent schools. Schools must not be afraid to take advantage of the current fund-raising climate and ask for larger gifts.

Development staff must vigilantly monitor new trends to assess how they will affect their institutions. But even as state-of-the-art technology increases our fund-raising effectiveness, the people side of the equation remains crucial. People give to people, and the successful development campaign will always hinge on the dynamic interaction—solicitor talking to donor. School development officers must be familiar with the latest techniques while retaining the generalist characteristics that enable them to communicate with donors.

Chapter 31

Raising Funds for Community Colleges

Nanette J. Smith

Community colleges have become the largest single sector of higher education in the United States. Nearly half the nation's undergraduates are enrolled in two-year institutions, but according to the Council for Aid to Education (CFAE), two-year colleges receive only about 2 percent of the private financial support given to American higher education.[1]

As the 1980s ended, 1,224 community colleges enrolled approximately 43 percent of the nation's undergraduates, including 51 percent of all first-time entering freshmen. Since World War II, the number of public two-year colleges has doubled, with enrollments multiplying nearly tenfold to more than five million students studying for credit. An additional four million are in non-credit and continuing education programs.

Most two-year institutions are public colleges, receiving funding primarily from state and local governments plus student fees. Federal assistance for college facilities, programs, and student aid was readily available at the zenith of the "Great Society" in the 1950s and 1960s, and these new "people's colleges" multiplied throughout the nation, bringing higher education opportunities to cities, towns, and rural areas.[2] The priority of these institutions was to extend access and opportunity; few sought to build private financial support.

With the 1970s came the realization that public funding would not long suffice to meet the capital, program, and student needs of the colleges. The American Association of Community and Junior Colleges (AACJC) encouraged member institutions to diversify development efforts. Meetings of AACJC and its National Council for Resource Development (NCRD) began to feature sessions on college-related foundations, private grantsmanship, and corporate giving. The 1974 merger of two advancement associations to form the Council for Advancement and Support of Education (CASE) made it possible for two-year colleges to participate with other sectors of higher education to develop fund-raising expertise. During the 1980s CASE began targeting programs and publications toward the two-year market, and two-year institutional membership in CASE increased 160 percent.[3]

THREE CHALLENGES TO COMMUNITY COLLEGES

Two-year colleges find their fund-raising results lagging behind their four-year counterparts for three major reasons.

1. *Image and identity.* Community colleges are "new kids on the block" in higher education. The community college is the only uniquely American educational invention, developed during the Depression era to provide financially and geographically accessible higher education. Business, professional, and community leaders might be primarily alumni of four-year colleges and universities, who may not have developed an appreciation of the quality or value of community college programs.

   In contrast with many large universities, community colleges do not have highly visible research programs that attract widespread media attention. Nor do they have professional schools such as medicine, law, and engineering, or Nobel-winning faculty members who keep the institution's name in the headlines. Two-year colleges must capitalize on their unique assets, develop their own approaches, and maximize effectiveness of their appeals to prospective donors.

2. *Constituencies and connections.* Development programs at most four-year institutions rely on the continuing loyalties of older and financially successful alumni. Alumni often form strong bonds based on memories of dormitory life, sororities or fraternities, and football weekends. Community colleges rarely have dormitories or extensive social organizations, and few states permit football on community college campuses.

   Nor do community college students match the traditional image of the carefree undergrads at State U. Their average age is 29. Three-fourths of them are part-time commuter students. Two-thirds work to support themselves and perhaps families. Many community college students who eventually transfer to upper-division colleges also transfer their alumni loyalties, giving to the four-year institution in later years. Even so, increasing numbers of community colleges are establishing alumni organizations or activities tailored to their own situations and are finding some unexpected benefits.[4]

3. *Organizing and investing.* Because private fund raising is a relatively recent development on two-year campuses, programs are generally newer, smaller, and sometimes less sophisticated than at the more experienced senior institutions. Token commitments to development may take the form of a part-time assignment or a "one-person shop." This may whet institutional appetites for a productive development effort. Often, however, the lack of adequate staff and technical support may frustrate expectations of success, resulting in institutional disillusionment with the entire development idea.

With increasing demands on colleges for programs and services, competition for resources within institutions is increasing. Community college presidents and senior administrators, products of higher education administration programs a decade or more ago, frequently must develop new philosophies that encourage investing scarce institutional resources in the future of the college. This requires patience and courage on the part of the president, who must be willing to defend the advancement outlay while waiting months or even years until the investment begins to produce returns.

Many community college trustees and presidents are not aware of the potential of private fund-raising programs or what is required for success. Professional organizations such as CASE, NCRD, and the Association of Community College Trustees (ACCT) are helping college boards, presidents, and staffs to close the gaps in philosophy, skills, and experience. Such organizations frequently structure workshops so that teams of trustees, administrators, and foundation board members can learn and plan together. The body of literature on community college development is expanding, and CFAE reports indicate that private gifts and endowments are growing each year.

FOUNDATIONS FOR PROGRESS

Because of its image, as discussed earlier, the community college frequently must work harder to gain and maintain credibility with the community and with donors. If the college has been in existence only a few years, its alumni may not yet have gained positions of community power and leadership. Politically appointed or elected board members may not have the connections that could assist the college in securing individual, foundation, or corporate gifts.

Increasing numbers of two-year colleges have found that by establishing a separate foundation, they can enlist an entirely new base of community leaders to support and speak for the institution.[5] A foundation, incorporated and approved under Section 501(c)(3) of the Internal Revenue Code as a recipient of tax-deductible contributions, can be a vehicle not only for generating funds but also for involving corporate leaders, influential community members, and donors in the life of the college.[6]

The foundation board should represent the key geographic and economic sectors of the college district, with members who provide access to all facets of community leadership. The board should also represent individuals and viewpoints new to the community and reflect a mix of ages to ensure continuity. And it should include professionals with expertise in tax law and financial planning who can assist the college in securing planned or deferred gifts.

A properly structured board will have the credibility, access, and influence needed to assist the interests of the institution more effectively than those on the college's payroll can. Foundation board members can be the college's advocates in board rooms, professional offices, and corporate headquarters. They may speak for the college to government or political leaders.

To earn and maintain the trust and involvement of a high-caliber foundation board, the college must provide the necessary organization and continuing support.[7] College trustees and administration must commit adequate facilities, staff, and equipment to see that the foundation's business is conducted properly and promptly.

COMMUNITY COLLEGES HAVE AN EDGE

Although conventional wisdom has long suggested that community colleges lack many of the marketable appeals necessary for successful fund raising, recent history has demonstrated that a well-organized development effort, when firmly grounded in the mission of the college, can significantly enhance college life and programs.[8]

By their nature, community colleges are organized within a community to meet local needs. They are designed not only to serve students directly but also to promote the economic well-being of the community through service to business, industry, agriculture, and the professions. Many colleges are discovering the potential of financial participation by businesses and other organizations that receive valuable services from the college. Although companies are not in business to give money away, colleges that successfully show how their success serves a company's interests—for instance, in providing skilled personnel or services that the company needs—can frequently persuade the company to provide funds, equipment, or facilities in exchange.[9] Capitalizing on their local presence, visibility, and reputation for quality, community colleges can often negotiate cooperative efforts that benefit both parties.

For example, in the mid-1980s, we at Edison Community College in Fort Myers, Florida, received corporate funding to initiate a respiratory therapy program. Local hospitals had found it difficult to recruit respiratory therapists; the average cost of recruiting one therapist from outside the area was $20,000, and those who were hired tended to move on as better opportunities arose elsewhere. Cooperating with the college, the hospitals were able to ensure a continuing local supply of these vital technicians. The hospitals funded the program for its first three years, with each hospital giving according to its size. The cost to each hospital was less than recruiting costs had been. In short, everyone benefited: the health-care system gained a stable supply of trained technicians, students learned marketable skills, and the college enjoyed an expansion of its curriculum.

Proximity to a donor base that is mostly local also gives community colleges an edge in fund raising. Local pride and identity can be great assets to the institution as area residents come to view it as "our college." Students come from the community and most often stay in the community. Prospective donors almost always know people who have attended the college or who work there. And the appeal of improved quality of life in the hometown can be a powerful motivation for giving.

The nearness of the institution and its products also enables staff to follow up with donors and demonstrate the results of their gifts. This can contribute greatly to the effectiveness of the fund-raising program. For example, development officers can easily arrange meetings between donors and their scholarship recipients, and these meetings seldom fail to produce additional gifts.

In any institution, donors develop trust and confidence in development staff as they work together over time. At a community college, this relationship becomes even stronger as donors see their development contacts more frequently, both through the institution and in the community. Regular visits, telephone calls, or luncheons with donors keep the college in their minds and on their contribution lists. Ongoing, consistent communication is especially important to the success of planned giving programs; colleges may work for years to arrange a bequest of money or property, but without continuing communication and reinforcement another charitable organization may take the college's place in the will.

PERCEPTION IS FUND-RAISING REALITY

Effective fund raising in the community college setting depends on potential donors' perceptions of the college, its performance, and its products. Community colleges are in unique positions to attract corporate gifts and, as noted above, are ideally situated for maintaining personal contact with donors. But the challenge of the perception of the two-year college, as compared to its four-year counterparts, requires continuing attention. We must constantly reinforce the image of the community college as an attractive higher education option.

The image begins with the college's people: The reputation and credibility of the trustees, the president, faculty and staff, and students all contribute to the public's perception. They are *in* the community and *of* the community, and community members generally form their initial impression of the institution's quality through these personal contacts.

Of all these individuals, the president, the board or key volunteers, and the chief development officer are perhaps the three elements most important to the success of a community college development program.[10] The president is the pivotal point of the effective program. The president is highly visible in the local community and demonstrates his or her commitment to local betterment through leadership roles on community boards and projects. The president's personal, enthusiastic involvement in the college's fund-raising and donor relations programs is essential to acceptance and success.

The college campus also contributes powerfully to public perception. An attractive campus, well-groomed grounds, and well-maintained buildings greatly enhance the impression of community members and potential donors. Well-instructed campus public safety officers and switchboard personnel can add greatly to the public's positive perception of the college's effectiveness.

The bottom line, however, is the quality of the college's product; community members know of successful students, effective programs, and respected faculty members. Regardless how visible and positive the key personnel are, and regardless of the appearance of the campus, the institution's academic reputation finally determines its credibility.

Demonstrating the institution's quality to parents, community members, and business leaders requires well-developed communications and marketing plans. Although professionals have long recognized that college communications and marketing efforts can enhance development, only recently has placement of college relations and development together within the organization made this cooperation practical.[11] In many community colleges today these functions are allied within the area of "institutional advancement," working together to multiply the effectiveness of both staffs.

Adding college relations expertise to the development effort can help target appropriate communications to donor audiences;[12] likewise, the development professional can give input from the donor community that can assist the overall communications program. Frequently special events can help accomplish the goals of both areas cost-effectively.[13] Cooperation between the college relations and development staff is necessary if the institution is to compete successfully for community support.

ALUMNI AND COMMUNITY COLLEGES

Although four-year colleges have depended heavily upon alumni as a major funding source, traditional alumni associations with class reunions, class campaigns, and annual class gifts are rare at community colleges. For a variety of reasons, alumni have not been major donors to community colleges, and two-year colleges expecting former students to produce major gifts have frequently been disappointed.

Community colleges that have viewed alumni as a different type of resource, however, have been successful.[14] Many colleges see alumni as potential college volunteers and advocates and have cultivated former students to provide valuable input to the institution. More and more colleges are systematically organizing groups of alumni, carefully formulating goals and objectives, and working with alumni to improve communication with the college district. The large numbers of community college alumni can be of great assistance when political advocacy is needed, and alumni can help students and faculty by providing links with local business and professional groups.

Most successful have been "affinity groups" of college alumni: graduates of nursing programs, engineering programs, arts programs, and others get together for picnics, reunions with faculty, professional workshops, or other events of particular interest. Special newsletters or direct mail pieces keep them in touch with each other and with their college. These groups might conduct fund-raising projects to provide scholarships for students in their programs or to pay for new equipment.

Some colleges with a philosophy of "lifelong learning"—that is, of providing educational experiences throughout the lives of their constituents—view the entire community as the alumni association. They treat the community at large as advocates, supporters, and beneficiaries of college services and expect that many residents will respond with gifts and support. Ideally, successful community residents who have no college affiliation develop the same relationship they might have with their alma mater, supporting the local community college, attending its events, and providing financial assistance.

LEARN FROM THE BEST

The differences between two-year and four-year institutions, and between private and public colleges, dictate the necessity for tailoring strategies to meet institutional needs. But the differences do not preclude two-year colleges benefiting from activities and programs that are effective for very different types of institutions.

Human appeals are universal, and some theories work equally well (but in different ways, or on different scales) for all of higher education. Principles of good donor relations, fund-raising ethics, and sound financial investment and management practices are generic. But the institutions that employ them must adapt each to their own needs and situations.

For example, a two-year college in New York successfully adapted capital campaign strategies from the University of Michigan. A development officer from a private university in California offered a solution that aided a technical college in South Carolina with its annual fund. And at Edison, we scaled down Duke University's planned gift program to meet our own needs, and the program has paid dividends ever since.

Such is the success that comes of sharing ideas through professional workshops and through books such as this. As more and more community college fund raisers take advantage of these opportunities to grow professionally, perhaps the next decade will report that two-year colleges have significantly increased their share of voluntary support of higher education.

NOTES

1. *Voluntary Support of Education 1988-89* (New York: Council for Aid to Education, 1990), 5.

2. Edmund J. Gleazer, Jr., *The Community College: Values, Vision, and Vitality* (Washington, D.C.: American Association of Community and Junior Colleges, 1980), 7.

3. Nanette J. Smith, "Organization of the Successful Advancement Office," in *Marketing and Development for Community Colleges*, eds. G. Jeremiah Ryan and Nanette J. Smith (Washington, D.C.: Council for Advancement and Support of Education, 1989), 2.

4. Richard J. Pokrass, "Alumni Programs," in *Marketing and Development for Community Colleges*, eds. Ryan and Smith, 195.

5. So many community college trustees and administrators are working to begin foundations that CASE's Commission on Two-year Institutions, together with representatives from AACJC and the League for Innovation, received a grant from the Exxon Educational Foundation to publish a step-by-step guide, *Initiating a Fund-raising Program: A Model for the Community College* (Washington, D.C.: Council for Advancement and Support of Education, 1989).

6. Kenneth B. Woodbury, Jr., "How to Establish a College Foundation," in *Building Voluntary Support for the Two-year College*, ed. John E. Bennett (Washington, D.C.: Council for Advancement and Support of Education, 1979), 14.

7. Smith, "Organization of the Successful Advancement Office," 9.

8. James L. Wattenbarger, "The Case for the Community College Foundation," in *The Community College Foundation*, ed. W. Harvey Sharron, Jr. (Washington, D.C.: National Council for Resource Development, 1982), 20.

9. M.F. Luck and D.J. Tolle, *Community College Development: Alternative Fund-raising Strategies* (Indianapolis: R&R Newkirk, 1978), 79.

10. Danette L. McNamara, "Characteristics of an Effective Two-year College Private Fund-raising Program" (Ph.D. diss., Oklahoma State University, 1988).

11. Donna Shoemaker, *Greenbrier II: A Look to the Future* (Washington, D.C.: Council for Advancement and Support of Education, 1985), 5.

12. Elaine B. Ironfield, "Marketing and the Development Officer," in *Resource Development in the Two-year College*, ed. David P. Mitzel (Washington, D.C.: National Council for Resource Development, 1988), 232.

13. Marjorie M. Davidson and Stephen R. Wise, "Fund Raising—The Public Two-year College," *Advancing the Two-year College*, eds. Peter S. Bryant and Jane A. Johnson, New Directions for Institutional Advancement no. 15 (San Francisco: Jossey-Bass, 1982), 62.

14. Pokrass, "Alumni Programs," 197.

Part Eleven

Special Considerations for the Fund-raising Profession

Terms like "fund-raising profession" and "development professional" appear throughout this book, including in the title of this section. Used loosely, the term "profession" is interchangeable with "field" or "area" or "activity." But the term also has a more precise definition, based on several criteria.

One particularly important mark of a profession is an accepted code of ethical conduct. While there have been various attempts to prescribe such a code for fund raising, none has earned universal agreement. Indeed, it may be difficult for any code to cover all the possible issues that may confront the college or university development officer. The most useful standard may be that proposed by Jake Schrum in Chapter 32: that development officers make decisions as if everything they do will be subject to public scrutiny and judgment. Schrum also proposes that development officers see ethical dilemmas as opportunities to teach donors about higher education's values.

In Chapter 33, Peter McE. Buchanan addresses directly the question of whether fund raising is a profession. He concludes that by most standards educational fund raising is still "emerging."

One such standard is whether a field has an established body of specialized knowledge, based on research. In Chapter 34, Judy Grace outlines current trends in fund raising and advancement research. While she points out that the volume of advancement research continues to grow, she also notes some of the obstacles to this important work and describes efforts by CASE and others to encourage and support it.

Finally, educational fund raising in the future will be greatly influenced by the law—both by tax laws affecting charitable giving and by the increasing collection of statutes that seek to regulate fund-raising practice. In Chapter 35, Norman Fink outlines recent trends and possible future developments. Fink's chapter brings this part of the book full circle, since it is clear that only by adopting professional standards of ethics and practice can educational fund raising hope to avoid its own undoing through punitive legislation.

Chapter 32
Ethical Issues in Fund Raising

Jake B. Schrum

We in educational fund raising face one essential task that extends far beyond our striving toward monetary goals. As those goals rise ever higher, and as fund-raising activities reach more and more of our fellow citizens, we must endeavor as never before to protect and maintain our own and our institutions' credibility and integrity. We must also protect our donors' interests and make every effort to enlighten as well as cultivate them.

To meet these fundamental goals, we must make professional ethics a basic component of our philanthropic work. If we bring to our work a broad understanding and deep appreciation of the true values that philanthropy represents—concern for others and for the community, respect for truth and for fairness—then ethical decisions and actions will tend to follow naturally. Even so, we will inevitably find ourselves face-to-face with ethical dilemmas that challenge our best thinking.

Several people have made significant contributions to the study of ethics in fund raising. My favorites include Derek Bok, former president of Harvard University, and Robert Payton, director of the Center on Philanthropy in Indianapolis. CASE, in concert with the Institute for the Study of Applied and Professional Ethics at Dartmouth College, has also been doing important work on behalf of fund-raising practitioners.

In this chapter, I will examine fund raising from three different perspectives—the institution's, the fund raiser's, and the donor's—and try to address the ethical issues that we increasingly face in the course of ensuring the honor and integrity of our work. There is, of course, a fourth perspective, one we must always bear in mind: the public's view of our enterprise. As our institutions set higher and higher goals for campaigns, for example, we run the risk of appearing avaricious. And if in pursuing campaign goals we depend too heavily on deferred gifts that may not be realized until long after the campaign's completion, we run the risk of appearing deceptive.

In discussing the first three perspectives, I have chosen ethical issues that many of us have faced through the years—ones common to almost all institutions engaged in fund raising: (1) issues linked with institutional mission and integrity, (2) issues of the fund raiser's personal and professional ethics, and (3) issues involving donors and the opportunity for enlightenment. Most often these issues present us with dilemmas—uneasy conflicts between values, rights, and interests. We can best resolve them if we believe in fundamental principles, such as truth and fairness, and if we have at hand some basic definitions and standards for applying these principles.

THE INSTITUTION'S MISSION AND INTEGRITY

Fund raisers for institutions that have ill-defined missions and ill-stated purposes are most susceptible to recurring ethical dilemmas in the quest for financial support. Those whose institutions have clearly defined and well-charted courses will, conversely, find it easier to understand and resolve questions of fund-raising ethics.

Take, for example, the small private college approached by an alumna who wants to give $20 million to create a law school that would bear her name. As a successful lawyer and a distinguished federal judge, she desires a legacy tied to her chosen field. The law school that she attended, at the state's flagship public university only thirty minutes away, is already named for someone else. So she has turned to her undergraduate alma mater, and has asked the president if he will accept her $20 million to build and endow a new law school with her name.

This college is just ending the fourth year of a five-year, $50 million capital campaign. The campaign is at a standstill with only $25 million raised. Most of the campaign goals related to support of facilities and students have yet to be met. On the one hand, accepting the gift would have immediate major monetary benefits for the fund-raising campaign; the gift would not only bring the campaign within reach of its overall dollar goal but might revitalize pursuit of its other goals. On the other hand, what are the long-term implications for the college and its institutional integrity?

Here is where the institution's mission statement becomes crucial. A mission statement for such an institution might read, "The mission of our college is to educate students to live fuller lives and gain a lifelong appreciation for the pursuit of knowledge."

Or then again, it might read: "We are committed to providing a superb undergraduate education within a residential community that values the intellectual, spiritual, and physical growth of the whole person."

Does the president have an ethical dilemma? If he does, how do these two mission statements help or hinder finding a solution?

A mission statement as loosely defined—and thus almost meaningless—as the first one gives the president and his board much flexibility. They might take the gift in good faith, build the law school, cause irreparable damage to the faculty in arts and sciences, and then have trouble securing law students because of overwhelming competition from the nearby public university. If they refuse the gift, they might be declining an exciting opportunity for the college to expand its academic frontiers as well as achieve the campaign's financial goal.

With the second statement, the decision is simple. The statement is very clear about the institution's central educational purpose. It is an undergraduate institution, exclusively. This does not mean that the president should not be open to new opportunities—even those that change the institution's purposes and priorities. The institution can always amend its own mission. However, in this case it would be clear to all of the college's constituents that grafting a professional faculty and curriculum onto the comprehensive undergraduate program would alter the institution's educational course significantly. The president in this instance would almost certainly refuse the gift.

Other offered gifts pose dilemmas for the institution. Take the donor who wants to endow a professorship in the economics department—but also wants to control the faculty appointment. This would put at risk the institution's academic freedom and autonomy. Or consider the contractor who expects his gift will bring university business to his firm; the uncle who wants assurance that his niece will gain admission to next fall's freshman class; the entrepreneur who hopes some well-publicized generosity will offset his reputation as a white-collar criminal.

In such instances as these, accepting the gifts could diminish or seriously damage the institution's integrity. As Derek Bok reminds us, some gifts should best be refused:

> In some situations, donors seek to attach conditions to their gifts that invade Justice Frankfurter's "four essential freedoms of the university"— "To determine for itself on academic grounds, who may teach, what may be taught, how it shall be taught, and who may be admitted to study." Since these freedoms are central to the university, a president or dean must constantly work to protect them against encroachments, whether the incursions come in the form of government regulations or in the more seductive guise of restricted gifts. Accordingly, an institution must reject donations that would require it to deviate from the normal standards of admissions, or give a donor the power to appoint a professor, or restrict a chair to persons advocating a particular set of values or beliefs.[1]

THE FUND RAISER'S PERSONAL AND PROFESSIONAL INTEGRITY

The nature of fund-raising work often places us in situations involving personal ethics. Let me suggest one question that fund raisers should ask in such situations: "If my behavior were open to public scrutiny, would anyone have cause to believe that I had compromised my personal integrity?"

Individuals often confront ethical dilemmas brought about by conflicting pressures and expectations. Fund raisers who are expected to meet unrealistic goals may consider taking liberties in how they count gifts—or may be directed to do so by others whose performance is also on the line. Under deadlines, they may be tempted to secure million-dollar gift commitments today from donors who might have made $5 million commitments if properly cultivated over a longer period. The proposal writer pressed to secure a grant may be tempted—or told—to stretch the truth about the institution's potential to use the grant effectively.

Such situations place fund raisers at odds with others at the institution—and sometimes at odds with the best interests of the institution itself. They may also pit the fund raisers' personal interests in keeping their jobs or enhancing their "track records" against their own standards of professional behavior.

Other conflicts of interest may arise in relationships between fund raisers and donors whom they cultivate for gifts. Donors may ask fund raisers for advice in estate planning—but should fund raisers get themselves into positions where they might be advising donors not to make particular gifts to the institution? And what about donors who offer fund raisers special favors—"I can see you're exhausted; why don't you and your family use our beach house for a week?"

While such donors may intend no wrong, they place the fund raisers in conflicts between various personal, professional, and institutional interests. Donors may also unwittingly ask fund raisers for special favors that would compromise the fund raisers' own integrity as well as that of their institutions.

Major fund-raising campaigns, increasingly common today, multiply the opportunities to engage in ethically questionable behavior—particularly in the area of counting gifts. Campaign score-keeping offers many temptations when fund raisers are under intense pressure to reach goals. Fund raisers may be tempted to include gifts dating back several years in the tally for the early, or "nucleus," phase of a campaign. Or they may count in campaign totals some bequest commitments from alumni whose life expectancies extend well into the next century.

Today's multi-purpose mega-campaigns also run the risk of focusing attention more on attaining the total dollar goals than on fulfilling the purposes for which the funds are sought. If the fund raisers count all the gifts that are received during a campaign—regardless of what the gifts are for—they may attain the campaign's dollar goal without fulfilling its purposes. If, for example, the president of the college we described above accepted the judge's $20 million gift and counted it toward the campaign goal, the campaign would have become only $5 million short of its $50 million goal. Yet it still would have remained $25 million short of the funds it needed to meet the campaign's original purposes. Similarly, if fund raisers rely too heavily on deferred gifts in a campaign, they may attain the campaign's dollar goal—even after discounting those gifts—yet have far too little money actually in hand to realize the campaign's announced purposes.

The best way to prevent such problems is for all concerned to agree on ground rules before a campaign starts and then follow those rules once the campaign is under way. This can ensure that fund raisers and their institutions are honest with themselves and their constituents.

A panel of professionals, the Campaign Reporting Advisory Group, has worked long and hard to draft standards for conducting campaigns and reporting results. The panel represents CASE, which established the group, and three other organizations: the Association of Governing Boards, the National Association of College and University Business Officers, and the American Association of Fund-Raising Counsel. The panel's final report, expected in early 1993, should provide us all with a basic rulebook to ensure credibility and public acceptance of fund-raising campaigns and greatly reduce the risks of any ethically dubious behavior in counting gifts.

Another ethical issue facing fund raisers involves confidentiality in research on potential donors, especially in today's world of increasingly sophisticated research techniques and technologies. How much should we seek to know about our donors, and how should we use that information in formulating our approach to them? My guideline is simple: Do not acquire, maintain, transmit, or otherwise use any information about your donors unless that information comes from public sources or has been knowingly provided by the donors themselves.

Suppose your institution's financial aid director tells you that the parents of an incoming freshman have submitted family financial information to determine whether their child is eligible for any type of scholarship or financial aid. The parents, who appear from this information to be better prospects for future major gifts than for financial aid, assume the information will be held in a confidential file in the admissions office. Should it be shared with the development office—or any other office in the university? The answer is clearly "no." The information does not come from public sources, and the parents did not intend for it to be shared with other offices within the university.

We must each protect our personal integrity and self-worth. The continuous questioning of the motives of our minds and our hearts enhances our ability to know when our integrity is at risk. Moreover, if our decisions and actions can pass public scrutiny as well as our personal test of moral responsibility, we should find ourselves in fewer ethical compromises.

THE DONOR'S RIGHTS AND REASONS

Most donors want to be helpful to the institution they intend to support. As mentioned earlier, however, educational fund raisers must be wary of some donors, even the best-intentioned, who in their zeal may offer contributions that would cause the institution more harm than good.

How often have you heard a president, dean, department chair, or development officer say to a colleague, "That donor just does not understand academic freedom—or higher education, for that matter." Sometimes we uneasily accept gifts despite ethical concerns, or refuse gifts because we suspect the donor intends to compromise the institution's integrity. But must such situations be compromising or confrontational? I maintain that they can provide us one of the most significant opportunities we may ever have to stretch beyond our ivy-covered walls and enlighten those who say they want to support education.

It is possible that some educators may not understand the intricate values and motives at work in our nation's economic system. It is equally possible that some business people who want to be donors may not fully understand the philosophy and reasoning underlying our respect for academic freedom. If a donor wants to make a gift that might muddle the institution's mission or compromise the integrity of the academic community, we have an obligation to explain to that donor why such a gift would be harmful. After all, donors' reasons for giving are important to them. We should be sensitive to the history, philosophy, and emotions that lead them to want to share their resources in certain ways.

As educators, we should welcome the opportunity to interact with our donors in ways that allow them to teach us about their goals and perspectives while we enhance their understanding of the intricacies of the academic community. As we learn about them, so too can they learn about us. Our willingness to understand their needs will, in many cases, encourage them to understand ours. If we handle these situations sensitively and openly, we can contribute to greater understanding on both sides of the table.

After all, we call ourselves educational fund raisers. That can simply mean that we raise money for education. But it can also mean that we have an educational role to play as well as a fundraising role. Why not try to enlighten such donors, and then try to negotiate terms that would allow our acceptance of their gifts after all—with institutional integrity intact? Once again, fund raisers who represent an institution with a well-defined mission and who have a solid grasp of the underlying principles of institutional integrity will be best equipped to resolve whatever ethical dilemmas they face in working with donors.

For example, the college president whom I described earlier might suggest to the benevolent judge that she consider endowing a program of scholarships for female undergraduates who plan to enter law school after getting their bachelor's degrees. A $5 million gift would fund a significant scholarship program—and another $5 million could finance development of a special pre-law curriculum. That way, the judge could memorialize her own career by making it possible for other women to follow in her footsteps and by funding an important addition to the curriculum—without compromising the college's integrity as an undergraduate institution.

Unfortunately, sometimes neither educators nor donors are willing to make the necessary effort to understand each other. Sometimes too, even after much discussion and explanation, deeply held values, reasons, or attitudes prevent the two sides from coming to terms. In the end, the fact remains that we must refuse some gifts, and some donors will conclude the academic community cannot fulfill their philanthropic needs.

Nonetheless, donors and educators should welcome opportunities for mutual enlightenment, and such interaction should become a routine part of the fund-raising process. If we ignore or reject these opportunities, one might well wonder about our commitment to education for enlightening and possibly inspiring others. Indeed, one might argue that donors who approach us to make gifts that we consider inappropriate have a right to expect us to enlighten them and show them how they can make their gifts acceptable.

We must recognize, in fact, that donors do have certain rights of their own in the philanthropic process—rights that we satisfy as we ourselves behave ethically toward them. They have the right to expect that we will be truthful with them, both in presenting our need for their gifts and in reporting our use of the gifts entrusted to our stewardship. If they restrict their gifts to certain purposes, and we accept the gifts with those restrictions, we must abide by them. They rightfully expect us to be accurate in counting campaign gift totals and equitable in recognizing donors. That is, if we have a policy that donors must contribute 50 percent of the construction cost of any new facility in order to have the right to name that facility, we should not make an exception to let a donor name a building for only 30 percent of its cost.

Donors should also certainly expect us to respect their privacy when we gather information about their resources and philanthropic interests. And we should take donors' own needs and those of their families into account before we accept unusually generous gifts.

CONCLUSION

Fund raisers, their colleagues in education, their institutions, and their donors will continue to face ethical dilemmas—often ones with no easy answers. All of us must squarely recognize and answer difficult questions before making decisions that affect—sometimes for several generations—individual lives and institutions.

In making these decisions, however, we should always bear in mind these three fundamental questions: Does the proposed gift conform to the mission of our institution? Do the circumstances jeopardize our personal integrity? Are the donor's rights being respected?

NOTE

1. Derek Bok, *Beyond the Ivory Tower: Social Responsibilities of the Modern University* (Cambridge: Harvard University Press, 1982), 266-267.

Chapter 33

Educational Fund Raising as a Profession

Peter McE. Buchanan

Even a cursory review of the literature about the meaning of the word "profession" will persuade most readers that deciding how to class a given human occupation involves myriad choices along a wide continuum. That continuum might range from a complex set of tasks, to what one calls a job, to a vocation, and then finally to a profession. Webster's dictionary includes the following (though not preferred) definition of the word "profession": "a principal calling, vocation, or employment." If one accepts that definition, then educational fund raising certainly qualifies as a profession. Yet few could find satisfaction in such a glib and barren conclusion.

It is important to decide whether educational fund raising, as distinguished from other kinds of fund raising, is significant to this discussion. Since this chapter is principally devoted to an analysis of the meaning and importance of the word "profession," I will take the author's privilege to say that while my own professional engagement in fund raising came solely from my commitment to education, and not vice versa, I believe the following commentary is perfectly appropriate to fund raising, to "development" as practitioners use the term today, to "advancement" in its broadest application in education, and to all stops in between.

One caveat, however. I do not believe that fund raising, or educational fund raising, in its narrowest conception will ever be considered seriously as a profession. On the other hand, advancement in its broadest conception is already considered a profession by a precious few, whose numbers will grow rapidly as that broader conception is better defined and more widely communicated to the public. As one advancement officer wrote in a recent informal survey of trustees of the Council for Advancement and Support of Education, "Advancement is the answer." I think and hope she will be right.

THE VALUE OF PROFESSIONAL STATUS

Perhaps the most important question to address is why worry about whether advancement is or is not a profession in the first place. I can just hear several of the best practitioners in the country saying, "You are wasting your time and mine with this discussion, when that time should be devoted to getting the job done, out there where our prospects are."

The answer to the question seems at first bipolar. On one hand, the determination of professionalism is self-serving. Harland Bloland and Rita Bornstein wrote in 1989 that "all occupations are interested in increasing their legitimacy, defining their jurisdictional boundaries, [and] gaining control over their work circumstances."[1] On the other hand, occupations are also interested, and we hope principally so, in increasing the effectiveness and efficiency of their services to the institutions that employ them. On examination, however, it is clear that legitimacy and control over work circumstances are essential ingredients to the effectiveness and efficiency that spell success for the institutions educational fund raisers serve.

Two simple illustrations make the point painfully clear. If those managing an advancement program do not have sufficient legitimacy in their institutions to enforce a prospect control procedure, it makes no difference whether the prospect control system is well designed and fairly administered. It still will not work. Or, take the circumstance of the fund-raising executive who is denied authority over the means of communication with his or her constituency of potential supporters or the wherewithal to communicate directly with them. Such work circumstances prevent a practitioner from working effectively and, hence, of being fairly evaluated and held accountable for results. Yet both these illustrations are real; they occur in all kinds of institutions. Therefore, regardless of whether one approaches this subject from a skeptical or supportive perspective, moving toward the professional end of the spectrum has significant benefits as well as some admitted self-serving characteristics.

Bloland and Bornstein also explain succinctly why educational fund raisers should be interested in professional status for their occupation: "Most of the time, the term profession refers to a high-status occupation that commands respect, admiration, and trust and is associated with contributing to society's needs, as well as affording its practitioners comfortable and often high incomes."[2] Who among us would not wish to be so described?

Bloland and Bornstein provide perhaps the most realistic, as well as the most encouraging, view of professions in recent literature: "There is no point at which an aspiring [vocation] can be assured that it has become a profession and that its place in an occupational status hierarchy is permanent. Occupations are not headed for the same destination, nor is the place they occupy at one time secure."[3] While the older professions, medicine and law, are viewed by the public as having positions high in the status hierarchy of occupations, this pluralistic power approach accounts well for the ebb and flow in these professions' status and economic well-being, as well as for the future prospect that advancement and other aspiring occupations may become members of society's more highly valued professions.

Recent studies on professionalization have concentrated on a broader framework of cultural studies in which institutional theory "focuses on the processes by which work is legitimately organized and comes to be taken for granted (institutionalized)."[4] How often over the years have senior advancement practitioners commiserated with one another about institutionalizing their functions within their schools, colleges, and universities, so that staff and programs would not be decimated in times of economic austerity or changes in institutional leadership. Most serious difficulties with development in its broadest definition—advancement, if you will—come from the fact that only in a relatively small percentage of U.S. institutions has the practice been truly embraced or institutionalized by the academy. The professionalization of advancement is one strategy by which that may be achieved.

CHARACTERISTICS OF A PROFESSION

Most critics and scholars would agree that at least three characteristics are essential if a vocation is to be considered a profession. They are (1) a high level of expertise in a well-grounded field of knowledge, (2) the development of a strong theoretical base for that field, and (3) ongoing research in the field.[5] While there is considerable activity on the part of advancement practitioners, educational institutions, and professional associations in all three areas, rapid progress is inhibited by unclear definitions of the field(s) of knowledge advancement represents, the related difficulty of developing theory for ill-defined or disputed fields of knowledge, and the paucity of both practitioners and academics interested in and capable of doing sophisticated, significant research.[6]

Many critics and scholars would add to the above characteristics the following: a full-time activity, a code of ethics, a professional association, professional training in higher education, and certification of expertise.[7] One might argue that however difficult the definitional problems, all of these characteristics are in ample supply. Yet, consider the following:

There are probably thousands of part-time development officers across the country who feel—and no doubt are—highly qualified professionals. Are we to exclude them from practice?

Multiple codes of ethics have been put forth in the advancement field, but none have sanctions. More troublesome, some do not agree. (Perhaps most important, provisions advising institutions against the use of commission-based compensation for raising money or recruiting students are considered by some as a restraint of trade, though I strongly disagree.)

The country has several professional associations relating to advancement, differently financed, organized, and in varying degrees of institutional health. There is no single all-encompassing American Bar Association for educational advancement, though the Council for Advancement and Support of Education (CASE), of which I am president, is the strongest candidate.

Training in higher education in advancement-related fields is multiplying across the country, yet there is no established professoriate for the field.

The National Society of Fund Raising Executives (NSFRE) has created a certification program, but some development officers—including some so certified—view it with disdain, and to my knowledge no employer has ever insisted upon it as a condition of employment.

In summary, the existence of these traits in the advancement field clearly does not easily or persuasively translate it into a profession. The difficulties should be seen only as temporary obstacles, not crippling and irremedial ones. The existence of the traits and the evidence of the functional stages of a profession in advancement give credence to Robert Carbone's 1989 claim that educational fund raising is an emerging profession. It should be lost on no one that the growing importance and stature of the advancement field has triggered an explosion of initiatives designed to bring the practice as rapidly as possible to that status.

The challenge that lies ahead is to focus the energies and intellects of practitioners, academics, and association leaders on those particularly knotty problems that impede progress on the road to professional status. Six areas require urgent attention: (1) definition, (2) integration, (3) theory formulation, (4) professional education, (5) the endorsement of educational leaders, and (6) commitment to service.

DEFINITION

Often in an effort to be inclusive rather than exclusive, practitioners have extraordinary difficulty defining what words are used to describe what activities. In the current jargon of educational advancement, the accepted disciplines or functional areas of expertise are fund raising, alumni administration, and institutional relations. Institutional relations is said to include public relations, communications (including periodicals and publications), and community and government relations. There is not yet widespread agreement about whether or not student recruitment and retention is to be considered a part of advancement. As difficult as the task is, advancement leaders must come to agreement about definitions before much more progress can be made.

I believe that the first agreement must be about the umbrella term for these functions. It has been six years since the landmark Greenbrier II conference—high time for everyone to adopt the term "advancement" and use it in every speech, communication, and utterance. The profession is not named for its subspecialties; it is a broad, inclusive field, just as the profession of law includes estate law or corporate law. If we are to have a profession, then first we must name it. Then, we can go on from there to resolve the more difficult questions of definition.

It is also high time that advancement make use of the term "marketing" in order to discriminate where its true boundaries lie. Two examples suffice to make the point. In the area of student recruitment, the use of the term "marketing" helps make advancement's boundaries clear by focusing on the communications and programming necessary to attract prospective students and their families to the institution—not on the formulation of admissions policy, which most assuredly is not advancement's province. Marketing also makes clear that advancement is responsible for the communication with and solicitation of prospective donors, but does not include the formulation of the institution's needs that will be presented for those donors' consideration. That is not to say that marketing considerations should be ignored by institutional leaders, or that advancement officers should be reluctant to provide a marketing perspective for major institutional decisions. It is only to say that one way to determine advancement's boundaries is to use marketing to define what territory falls within the field.

INTEGRATION

The rapid expansion and sophistication of the advancement field has created specialization in many different ways and at different levels. The responsibilities of the president of a private foundation of a public institution, the president or executive director of an independent alumni association, the chief advancement officer of an independent school or college, or the senior government relations officer of a private university may have substantial similarities. But the differences are also staggering.

Countless trades and vocations have separate national associations, and fund raisers have more than a handful. The proliferation of organizations is as American as apple pie, but often it has occurred because existing organizations were not sensitive enough to the different needs of small groups of individuals with unique but pressing needs. Examples of this phenomenon are the formation of the Council of Alumni Association Executives (thankfully now being served by CASE but nevertheless independent) and of the American Prospect Research Association. I believe further splintering of those involved in advancement will make the field's professionalization increasingly difficult to achieve.

Another characteristic of specialization in the field tends to drive people with similar personal and professional objectives in different directions. In some cases, conflict among these practitioners erupts in both institutional and association settings, without almost any direct professional contact between them. The result is that the finest practitioners in the country meet in their own particular affinity groups, and have almost no contact of any kind with one another.

For example, of the 53 individuals in two outstanding senior professional groups, representing the finest development officers and communication officers in the United States, only one person is a member of both groups. The overwhelming majority of members of each group have not met a single person in the other group in their lifetimes, except for people who have worked at the same institutions. After a recent CASE conference, I reviewed the registration list of executives of 48 institutionally related foundations from around the United States and found the same startling pattern: Only one such executive was a member of either professional affinity group I mentioned earlier.

If advancement is to become a profession, the leaders must not only come together, but work together to give it shape and direction. The plain reality is that academics and association leaders, no matter how effectively they work together, cannot travel the road to profession without the practitioners in the driver's seat.

THEORY FORMULATION

There are now at least six centers for philanthropic study in the United States: the Mandel Center for Nonprofit Organizations at Case Western Reserve University; the Center for the Study of Philanthropy at the Graduate Center of the City University of New York; the Center for the Study of Philanthropy and Voluntarism at Duke University; the Indiana University Center on Philanthropy; the Institute for Policy Studies at Johns Hopkins University; and the Program for Nonprofit Organizations at the Institution for Social and Policy Studies of Yale University. This gives advancement a beginning foothold in the difficult terrain of theory formulation, so important to the formation of a profession.

Only two chief advancement officers attended the 1990 annual conference on philanthropy in Indiana. If there is to be progress in this arena—one of the most difficult obstacles we face—then practitioners must participate and help shape the research agenda with the most promising academic allies advancement has.

PROFESSIONAL EDUCATION

The recent multiplication of graduate degree programs in fund raising and philanthropy is one of the most positive signs of the growing importance of advancement in the country. At the same time, Bloland and Bornstein document carefully the lack of consensus among advancement leaders about the value and the utility of professional training in higher education for the field.[8]

I believe a substantial segment of advancement executives agree that an undergraduate liberal arts education is the best possible preparation for the field. There seems to be no agreement about what would be the most valuable type of graduate or professional training, but value is attached to graduate or professional training in general, especially a terminal degree.

While curriculum design should properly be in the hands of the appropriate graduate faculty, I believe a carefully designed program that would encompass the heart of the MBA; the estate and trust courses of the LL.B.; the theoretical material of the centers of philanthropy around the country; and courses in curriculum, student personnel, finance, and the study of academic constituencies would provide the kind of practical and theoretical training that would contribute mightily to making advancement a profession. While it may be a more difficult road to travel, pursuing such professional graduate education will be more valuable in the long run to the individual and contribute more to the effective practice of advancement than will current programs of certification.

THE ENDORSEMENT OF EDUCATIONAL LEADERS

Appearing in virtually every written statement about professions is the word "autonomy," a reference to the professional's control of the work and the workplace. While the place for advancement work is often the development or institutional relations office, historically advancement was the president's work, and therefore first took place in the president's office.

A recent study on public relations activities of presidents of colleges and universities shows once again that as much as things seem to change, much remains the same. Presidents' work is still largely advancement work—no matter how large and complex development, alumni relations, and institutional relations offices may be, or how far distant physically from the president they are.

The survey garnered a 55 percent response from a random sample of 300 presidents across the United States and Canada. Of those replying, 66 percent said they would spend between 21 and

61 percent of their time on public relations activities during the 1990s; most narrowed that estimate to 21 to 41 percent of their time.[9] If one adds fund raising and some alumni relations activities to the president's time clock, today's leaders probably spend not less than one third and probably about half of their time leading, shaping, and participating in advancement activities.

It is little wonder, therefore, that James Fisher, former president of CASE, offered lengthy advice to presidents about the appropriate relationship with the chief advancement officer:

> You must *sincerely* include your fund-raising vice president in all substantive discussions about the institution and its affairs. . . . This vice president should be perceived as your surrogate. . . . You can delgate this much responsibility only to an exceptional person, and so you must invest a great measure of presidential trust and confidence therein.[10]

While the commentary concerned the chief fund-raising executive, it could and should hold for other advancement executives reporting to the president as well.

Any senior advancement practitioner will tell you that such relationships are the exception rather than the rule. Why so? The answer lies in a combination of at least four factors. First, there are too *few* well prepared and experienced advancement practitioners in education. Second, there is no existing pool of such qualified people to which our institutional leaders have access. Third, there is rapid turnover of both presidents and chief advancement officers throughout education. Fourth, there is ambiguity in how advancement activities should be organized and directed.

Some amplification of the last point may be useful. Today, some large universities have advancement officers in public relations, fund raising, and alumni administration who report separately but directly to the president. In many other institutions, these functions are combined, or one reports to another. Regardless of the pattern of reporting, each field is of overriding importance to a successful advancement program. Institutional leaders need an in-depth understanding of how these fields reinforce one another and how they can best be organized to yield optimum results.

At least three initiatives would help address the difficulties listed above.

1. Establish a national—indeed, international—registry of *qualified* senior advancement practitioners. That one does not currently exist should be no obstacle to its creation.
2. Provide new means of evaluating institutions' existing advancement programs and personnel at reasonable cost. Advancement consultants provide this service for many institutions; other institutions simply cannot afford it, or think they cannot. Perhaps a joint venture between the educational associations and the consultant community could provide less expensive ways of institutional evaluation to benefit all concerned.
3. The nation's educational associations must join together to provide education and training sessions for new presidents and new chief advancement officers. These sessions should continue until the extraordinarily high turnover of both presidents and senior advancement officers recedes.

Concrete steps of this kind can help create the strong relationship about which Fisher writes. Without them, the firm endorsements of the chief executive officers of the nation's schools, colleges, and universities are not likely, and advancement will not achieve professional status where it needs it the most—within the academy itself.

COMMITMENT TO SERVICE

Robert Carbone writes that members of a profession are thought to be motivated primarily by the desire to serve clients and, in a larger sense, to serve society.[11] It is often true that those whose work is based upon a strongly held personal and professional philosophy of public service are valued more highly than those who hold no such view, even when the work itself is comparable. Carbone's study and recent interviews with development practitioners conducted by Bloland and Bornstein make clear that most advancement leaders talk about the importance of service in their work and many believe deeply in such a view, but others consider it only a secondary or peripheral matter.

In a 1990 article, Harvey K. Jacobson points out, "Observers have noted that institutional advancement is unlikely to achieve professionalism until practitioners genuinely internalize an intellectual and moral commitment."[12] The importance of one's personal assessment of what one does and why has never been more significant for the field of advancement than it is today. Are people principally motivated to serve education, or are they motivated by increased status and high income?

Judith T. Shuval (1990) suggests that the process of professional socialization is a powerful means of converting an occupation into a profession. She writes, "Professional socialization concerns the transformation of laymen into professionals through a process of learning to abandon old roles and self-conceptions and acquiring new ones. This is accomplished by a process by means of which people selectively acquire the values and attitudes, the interests, skills, and knowledge—in short, the culture—current in the group in which they seek membership."[13]

This is, it seems to me, the ultimate challenge to advancement leaders everywhere. Will they take responsibility for the professional socialization of those in their charge? What beliefs will, in fact, drive that socialization? CASE already has spent several years working on the definition of the skills, knowledge, and attitudes every advancement officer must adopt as a senior practitioner in each of the related advancement specialties; therefore, the foundation of professional socialization is in fact now being constructed. The question is whether or not a philosophical commitment to service will or should undergird that work. Those in advancement will eventually produce the answer.

In the meantime, I would submit that at the heart of educational advancement must be an unshakable belief that its effective practice is a moral commitment in service to education, and hence to society. Only with such a central belief can advancement be a full-fledged family member in its own house and have its practice fully accepted as a profession by the public.

NOTES

1. Harland G. Bloland and Rita Bornstein, "University Fund Raisers at the Academic Table: Diners or Waiters" (presentation at the annual meeting of the Association for the Study of Higher Education, Atlanta, 1989), 28.

2. Ibid., 6.

3. Ibid., 11.

4. Ibid., 12.

5. E. Greenwood, "Attributes of a Profession," *Social Work* 2 (July 1957):24-55.

6. W.J. Goode, "The Theoretical Limits of Professionalization," in *The Semi-professions and Their Organizations: Teachers, Nurses and Social Workers*, ed. A. Etizoni (New York: Free Press, 1969), 266-313; and H.J. Wilensky, "The Professionalization of Everyone," *Journal of American Sociology* 70 (September 1964):137-58.

7. Robert F. Carbone, *Fund Raising as a Profession* (College Park, Maryland: University of Maryland, Clearinghouse for Research on Fund Raising, 1989), 10.

8. Bloland and Bornstein, "University Fund Raisers," 31ff.

9. Kenneth J. Kerr, "Survey of College and University Presidents' Perceptions of the Public Relations Function" (University Park, Pennsylvania: Pennsylvania State University, Division of Planning Studies, February 1991), 6-7.

10. James L. Fisher and Gary H. Quehl, eds., *The President and Fund Raising* (New York: American Council on Education/Macmillan, 1989), 11.

11. Carbone, *Fund Raising as a Profession*, 19.

12. Harvey K. Jacobson, "Research on Institutional Advancement: A Review of Progress and a Guide to the Literature," *The Review of Higher Education* 13 (Summer 1990):465.

13. Judith T. Shuval, "The Pharmacist: Processes of Becoming," excerpted in *Becoming a Profession: Readings for Fund Raisers*, ed. Robert F. Carbone (College Park, Maryland: University of Maryland, Clearinghouse for Research on Fund Raising, 1990), 21.

Chapter 34

Trends in Fund-raising Research

Judy Diane Grace

Institutional advancement activities on campuses have accelerated greatly over the past decade. Research to support these efforts, however, has not kept pace. This has been particularly noticeable in fund raising. For both the research community and the educational fund-raising office, the need for immediate results has sometimes eclipsed the broader view. Expediency has overridden effectiveness.

Much of past research has been institution-specific and oriented toward short-term goals. Fund-raising studies have consisted of, for example, descriptions of alumni donor behavior at one institution at a particular time, rather than longitudinal examinations from several campuses using multiple factors.

In the past decade, however, fund-raising administrators have made research a higher priority. They are becoming convinced that using research in a broader sense, and understanding the parameters of social-science research, will benefit the profession and individual institutions. This increased emphasis on research has taken several distinct directions. These trends involve not only the content of research, but also the people who conduct it, the data on which it is based, and the means by which it is disseminated.

DEFINING A BASE OF KNOWLEDGE

Research on fund raising—and in the other areas of institutional advancement—received its greatest boost at Greenbrier II, a 1985 colloquium of advancement professionals and researchers who examined the status of the profession. From this introspective meeting came a recommendation for developing a formal knowledge base in advancement. Greenbrier participants recognized that such a knowledge base—including a description of what is known and what remains to be learned about fund-raising effectiveness—is one of the characteristics that define a profession.[1]

But most of what was known about fund-raising effectiveness was mythological, and research supporting the myths had been fragmented and fugitive at best. Practice often consisted of reliance on past successful techniques, not reflective use of research findings.

The first trend in research on fund raising, then, is a distinct effort to describe, in a reliable way, "what works." While fund raising may still be regarded as an art, for which some people have a talent, effective techniques can be identified, analyzed, and replicated.

The Council for Advancement and Support of Education (CASE) has taken on the task of identifying existing research and encouraging research in needed areas. Through its professional development efforts, CASE teaches its members the knowledge, skills, and attitudes essential to successful professional practice. While the content of this curriculum for training is essentially time-tested techniques, provided by successful practitioners, it is increasingly based on research done in conjunction with the academic community, much of it under CASE sponsorship and encouragement. This research enhances practice and establishes baselines for comparative data used in policy and resource allocation decisions.

ACHIEVING ACADEMIC ACCEPTANCE

CASE and other groups interested in fund-raising issues—such as the Center on Philanthropy at Indiana University-Purdue University at Indianapolis, the Center for the Study of Philanthropy and Voluntarism at Duke University, and the National Society of Fund Raising Executives (NSFRE)—have provided grants for studies in the field. Many of these go to dissertation work. And most of the research has been associated with academic centers with strong programs in educational leadership or nonprofit management.

Still, the area of educational fund raising has long been of only small interest to traditional academic researchers. Since the field lacks a unique set of conceptual frameworks, it is often regarded at best as interdisciplinary, and more typically as not suitable for legitimate research. To pursue research in this area can be challenging for the young academic seeking tenure. Applying accepted social-science methodologies to a field not well understood by most graduate faculty leads to findings not always useful to practice.

But as voluntary support for education becomes more important to colleges and universities, and to elementary and secondary schools, research in this area is finding more encouragement and approval. This is the second trend in fund-raising research: the increased acceptance of research-based information on educational fund raising within the academic community and among practitioners.

The rewards for pursuing fund-raising research are increasing and the importance of the studies growing. And, as research is completed, it is entered into major collections (such as UMI and ERIC) from which it may be disseminated. What is known—the knowledge base—broadens and becomes more visible. As researchers test conclusions and verify findings, their efforts bear fruit: Institutions use their results to set policies and gain resources.

TURNING RESEARCH TO PRACTICE

Many obstacles still exist to acceptance of fund-raising research by both academics and professionals. Some reluctance reflects problems of vocabulary. Academic researchers and development officers often speak different languages. The result is a lack of "technology transfer"; that is, researchers fail to communicate their results in ways useful to practitioners. Since advancement is an emerging field, with a malleable vocabulary, time and maturation will eventually close this gap.

But proactive steps are needed. The third trend in fund-raising research, then, is increased activity in translating research into practice.

This activity has taken many forms. Faculty and deans, increasingly aware of the need for voluntary support of their efforts, are becoming more involved in fund raising. Development offices are offering internships to expose students to concepts and practical problems. Several national-level fellows programs are providing practitioners the opportunity to study practice from a broader perspective; for example, four Fulbright awards have gone to advancement practitioners.

And at its annual national meeting, CASE sponsors a Research Forum, modeled on that of the American Association for Higher Education, during which senior advancement professionals work with academic researchers to develop fund-raising research topics. The result will be research that is more focused and applicable to general practice.

COLLECTING DATA ON DONORS

Many researchers cite the lack of usable data as the main obstacle to productive, broad-based research. While the Council for Aid to Education publishes a yearly survey of fund-raising results titled *Voluntary Support of Education,* researchers also need concrete information on the traits of donors and potential donors, including current students. On the national level, these data are meager.

Even on the institutional level, systematic reporting and standard definitions—essential conditions for reliable research—do not always exist. Databases on individual campuses are rarely interconnected, and administrators are sometimes reluctant to share information across administrative lines. These barriers make sophisticated analyses impossible.

This is the fourth trend: the continued struggle of researchers—both academics and practitioners—against the lack of standardized data and other technical obstacles.

In 1987, CASE, the Center on Philanthropy at IU-PUI, and the University of Arizona began a pilot national database study on donor characteristics. The project's main finding was that donor files at individual institutions were so idiosyncratic that they could not be used for general analyses.[2] Existing data files are not comparable; many lack basic characteristics such as gender.[3]

Without a broad-based effort to build a standardized national database, research is inevitably limited. Several groups of researchers are broadening their samples,[4] but fund-raising studies generally have yet to meet standards acceptable in social science research.

STANDARDIZING REPORTS

The lack of a database on donor characteristics is not the only data challenge in fund-raising research. The costs of fund raising continue to be of interest to campus administrators and government policymakers. As fund-raising efforts consume more resources, record-keeping and results will receive more scrutiny. Reporting standards and definitions are of concern both to development professionals and to the Internal Revenue Service.

The fifth trend, therefore, is the increasing internal and external pressure to report fund-raising costs and results in standardized formats, allowing for comparisons among institutions and over time. The adoption of uniform definitions and reporting standards is essential to research by economists and public-policy scholars as well as to credibility within and outside the field.

In 1990, CASE and the National Association of College and University Business Officers issued the results of a survey on college and university expenditures for fund raising, alumni relations, and public relations.[5] The effort to establish uniform reporting guidelines and definitions for this study moves the fund-raising research agenda forward.

APPLYING THEORY FROM OTHER FIELDS

The sixth trend is the growing use of established theories and frameworks from other fields to examine issues and problems in fund raising.

An increasing amount of literature looks at fund raising as an organizational issue—for example, the advantages of centralized or decentralized models; the reporting relationships of development officers; the roles of foundations, trustees, and other advancement administrators in the administrative hierarchy.

Another set of questions involves the role development plays in the institution's relationships with its constituencies. These issues concern image and marketing; social, economic, and political contexts; "shops" and "sales"; planning; assessment; accountability; costs; and other concepts based in management or communications theory.

The study of fund raising as a unique enterprise has come into its own. An increasing amount of time and resources is being devoted to study the structure of fund raising as an administrative activity: to describe and determine effective patterns of organization and management;[6] to develop donor profiles using market segmentation patterns;[7] to weigh the ethics of various practices;[8] to evaluate the impact of tax laws and legal concerns. The richness in these areas from the researcher's perspective is the connection of an emerging field to an established set of theories and conceptual frameworks.

ESTABLISHING ACADEMIC CENTERS

The research tasks outlined above are accomplished more easily where there is a critical mass of students and faculty—and practitioners. While there are several centers for the study of nonprofit management, such as at Yale, and some specifically for philanthropy, notably at IU-PUI, students elsewhere who seek course work and concentrations in educational advancement often find it difficult to put together a program and a committee to oversee their dissertation research.

The seventh trend is the genesis of academic programs in fund raising and advancement at research universities. Various foundations, including Lilly and Exxon, have encouraged and supported these centers, and other organizations, such as NSFRE and the American Association of Fund Raising Counsel, have supported work by faculty and students associated with them. The establishment of educational fund raising as a scholarly activity associated with such academic centers will further enhance and encourage research in this field.

RETRIEVING RESEARCH

As the body of literature in a field expands, the need arises for categorizing publications so that they can be retrieved. The eighth trend is the development of collections dealing specifically with fund raising and philanthropy, which will become available to practitioners and researchers through existing information sources. Access to collections is essential if the field is to evolve.

Various researchers have made attempts to name and describe the elements of voluntary support in the nonprofit sector and in education specifically.[9] But national reference databases still contain very few descriptors that afford practitioners or researchers any help in looking for fund-raising information in library collections. As late as 1989, for example, the widely used ERIC catalog used only four terms to classify fund-raising research. At the national offices of CASE and NSFRE, the two major professional associations for fund raisers, research-based information is filed under practitioner vocabulary. But access to these collections can be difficult for researchers who cannot travel to the association offices.

Under a grant from the Lilly Foundation, the Center on Philanthropy at IU-PUI has developed a master plan to collect and catalog historical materials on philanthropy. The archivists at the Indiana University libraries will catalog materials from NSFRE and CASE. These records will then be available to a wide audience through sophisticated electronic systems.

DEVELOPING QUESTIONS

The ninth trend is the expectation of "outcome-specific" research. The best research questions give practitioners immediate answers. Most research provides mere evidence, not proof.

Informal catalogs of existing research are already available. The task now is to organize that information to form the outline of the profession's "knowledge base"—the research-based information that informs practice. Research advisory groups for both CASE and NSFRE have generated catalogs of specific research questions. These questions show a clustering of topics; definite patterns reveal areas in which information and evidence is missing. Several researchers have offered ways to classify this knowledge. The following examples are not comprehensive, but they do give us a sense of the direction future research might take.

John A. Dunn, Jr., suggests that fund raisers might be most helped by research in three areas: prospect identification and information, the management of fund raising, and environment enhancement.[10] Barbara E. Brittingham and Thomas R. Pezzullo suggest further research on consistency of college mission, spending and effectiveness in fund raising, the roles of governance and trustees, attitudes of alumni, segmented markets, and the evaluation of fund-raising research.[11] Robert F. Carbone makes the case for predictive generalizations on the philanthropic environment, the work and career of fund raisers, and the management of fund raising.[12]

EXAMINING OUR KNOWLEDGE

The tenth trend in fund-raising research is reflective: the development of a framework in which fund-raising professionals can study the knowledge base of their profession. We need to use consistent vocabulary both in practice and in research. The wide acceptance of definitions and concepts is the beginning of systematic examination of the knowledge base.

In a 1986 article, Harvey K. Jacobson discussed the barriers to applying fund-raising research to professional practice. He focused particularly on the inconsistencies in reporting and evaluating fund raising from both the philosophical and technical viewpoints. He encouraged researchers to develop a strategic plan for research in fund raising. Specifically, he suggested that they:

- build a network to collect, evaluate, and distribute research results, both to the research community and practitioners;
- accept a working conceptual framework for theories of fund raising;
- identify and use the principal players on campus and elsewhere who are interested in educational fund raising—those who make policy and those who control the databases—in encouraging research-based practice; and
- bring researchers and practitioners together regularly for ongoing interaction and evaluation.[13]

The trends we have reviewed in this chapter show that we are well on the way to accomplishing many of these tasks. Each of these steps enables us to better use a formal knowledge base in our professional practice.

NOTES

1. See Judy Diane Grace and Larry L. Leslie, "Research on Institutional Advancement: Emerging Patterns and Parameters," *The Review of Higher Education* 13 (1990):425-32; and Harvey K. Jacobson, "Research on Institutional Advancement: A Review of Progress and a Guide to the Literature," *The Review of Higher Education* 13 (1990):433-88.

2. Larry L. Leslie, Judy Diane Grace, Kenneth Brown, and Jeff Rapp, "Progress Report on a National Donor Database" (presentation at the annual meeting of the Association for the Study of Higher Education, Atlanta, November 1989).

3. Larry L. Leslie, "Information, Please," *CASE Currents*, January 1990, 80.

4. For examples, see Margaret A. Duronio and Bruce A. Loessin, "Fund-raising Outcomes and Institutional Characteristics in Ten Types of Higher Education Institutions," *The Review of Higher Education* 13 (1990):539-56; and John A. Dunn, Jr., "Research on Fund Raising: What Are the Next Questions?" (presentation at the Annual Assembly of the Council for Advancement and Support of Education, Washington, D.C., July 1989).

5. Council for Advancement and Support of Education and National Association of College and University Business Officers, *Expenditures in Fund Raising, Alumni Relations, and other Constituent (Public) Relations* (Washington, D.C.: Council for Advancement and Support of Education, 1990).

6. Margarete R. Hall, "A Comparison of Decentralized and Centralized Patterns of Managing the Institutional Advancement Activities at Research Universities" (Ph.D. diss., University of Maryland, 1989).

7. Gerlinda S. Melchiori, ed., *Alumni Research: Methods and Applications*, New Directions for Institutional Research no. 60 (San Francisco: Jossey-Bass, 1988).

8. Barbara E. Brittingham and Thomas R. Pezzullo, *The Campus Green: Fund Raising in Higher Education*, ASHE-ERIC Higher Education Report no. 1 (Washington, D.C.: George Washington University, 1990); and Harlan Stelmach and Mark A. Holman, "Institutional Advancement: Survival with Integrity," in *Ethics and Higher Education*, ed. William W. May (New York: American Council on Education/Macmillan, 1990).

9. Jon Van Til, "The Shifting Boundaries of the Independent Sector," in *Looking Forward to the Year 2000: Public Policy and Philanthropy* (Washington, D.C.: Independent Sector, 1988), 57-66; Jacobson, "Research on Institutional Advancement"; Dunn, "Research on Fund Raising"; and Robert F. Carbone, *An Agenda for Research on Fund Raising* (College Park, Maryland: University of Maryland, Clearinghouse for Research on Fund Raising, 1986).

10. Dunn, "Research on Fund Raising," 5.

11. Brittingham and Pezzullo, *The Campus Green*, 87-99.

12. Carbone, *An Agenda for Research*, 8.

13. Harvey K. Jacobson, "Toward a Network: Problems and Opportunities in Fund-raising Research," in Carbone, *Agenda for Research*, 37-40.

Chapter 35

Legal Trends Affecting Philanthropy

Norman S. Fink

In this last decade of the millennium, the ever-changing landscape of economic, political, and social commitments of American society includes both horizons and minefields for philanthropy. Since it is the legal system that holds society together and charts its course, one must look to the laws regulating the nonprofit sector for guidance to avoid the minefields and attain the horizons.

As to the horizons, Judge Benjamin Nathan Cardozo wrote in 1924:

> Existing rules and principles can give us our present location, our bearings, our latitude and longitude. The inn that shelters for the night is not the journey's end. The law, like the traveler, must be ready for the morrow. It must have the principle of growth.[1]

When it comes to the minefields, it was Judge Roscoe Pound who said, "The law of each age is ultimately what that age thinks should be the law."[2]

This chapter will discuss three basic topics relevant to the work of colleges and universities (and their satellites, such as libraries, hospitals, museums, and research institutes). These topics are (1) tax-exempt status, (2) the charitable deduction, and (3) regulation. These topics share common threads of history, and one must look to the past to forecast the future. The trends for the future do indeed have their seeds in the past.

TAX-EXEMPT STATUS

Although the practice of charity has been chronicled from the beginnings of recorded history, the modern law of charity began with the enactment in 1601 of the English Statute of Uses. Significantly, this statute defined charitable causes, but did not include "religion" in those causes, only "the repair of churches." All church holdings had been taken over by the Crown during England's Reformation.[3]

The nonprofit laws of England were part of the cultural background of the people who colonized our nation. It is not by accident that the Crown charters that established our earliest colleges and universities provided both property tax exemption and perpetual life to these institutions.

The formation of charitable organizations in the early years of the United States was a state-by-state matter, and special acts of the legislatures determined applicable government policy. The tradition has continued, with but a few charities receiving congressional authority.

Accordingly, the tradition of exemption from property tax has a long and varied history in the United States. As the objects of taxation expanded—for example, inheritance, gift, income, and sales, as well as real and personal property—so have the laws of exemption for charities; however, the state laws are not uniform. For example, the New York statute lists more than twenty different specific charitable purposes eligible for organization and exemption, while Pennsylvania refers only to religious, charitable, and educational institutions.[4]

Tax exemption on a national level was first expressed in 1894 with the passage of the first federal income tax law on income and profits of corporations. The exemption provision was declared unconstitutional a year later, but since the exemption was to recur in subsequent federal income tax legislation, the language is relevant:

> That nothing herein contained shall apply to . . . corporations, companies, or associations organized and conducted solely for charitable, religious, or educational purposes . . . nor to the stocks, shares, funds, or securities held by any fiduciary or trustee for charitable, religious, or educational purposes.[5]

It took the 16th Amendment to the Constitution in 1913 to remove obstacles to a federal income tax law, and, in the same year, such a law—with the tax exemption provisions—was enacted. Subsequent income tax laws added exempt purposes, but the die for federal tax exemption had been cast in 1894. The development of the exemption was a natural progression from colonial and individual state laws rooted in the English legal tradition.

Limits on Tax Exemption

Encroachment on the concept of tax exemption by the federal government began seriously in the 1950s, culminating in the 1969 Tax Reform Act, and it continues. This trend calls for constant and vigilant attention.

The motivations for legal limits on tax exemption are often the same as the arguments for limits on tax deductions. Perhaps the two principal motivations, stridently repeated each decade since the 1950s, are the need for revenue and the public reaction to abuses by charities. Penalties may be imposed for such actions as self-dealing—that is, using one's position for personal financial gain—imprudent investment, unreasonable accumulations of income, excess business holdings, delayed distribution of income, expenditure of funds for prohibited purposes, and misrepresentation.

A separate but important intrusion was the imposition of excise taxes on tax-exempt private foundations in 1969. This precedent could well be perceived to establish a basis for such taxes on other types of nonprofit institutions.

The recent and well-publicized debate on unrelated business income tax (UBIT) is an outgrowth of this evolution. This tax affects nonprofit organizations that engage in income-producing projects that bear little relation to their statutory tax-exempt charter. An institution, no matter how well-meaning, that wanders from its defined mission in the search for revenue can find itself in commercial competition with taxpaying businesses that pursue identical activities. While somewhat latent now, this issue can be expected to reappear as federal, state, and local tax authorities seek new sources of revenue. Television revenues and commercial sponsorship for athletic events, admission charges, dormitory rents, and royalties are vulnerable to challenge.

The practice of some institutions of paying fees-for-service to local government in lieu of taxes runs counter to concept. Such practices, no matter how well intentioned, are what lawyers call an "admission against interest"—in other words, an acknowledgment that a tax might be valid. And, of course, these payments establish precedents.

Exemptions are at stake not only from federal and state income and excise taxes, but from local real estate taxes as well. Real estate taxes support, among other public services, public primary and secondary education, and local communities facing crises in this area have called for expanding the tax base to include college property whose direct relevance to education is suspect, such as the president's house or the football stadium. The devastating financial impact of this trend upon charities cannot be overestimated. Governing boards must tread carefully to avoid the characterization of abuse and to counteract revenue demands by demonstrating that their institutions' services are of overcompensating value to the community.

In a January 1991 speech to the American Hospital Association, Congressman Charles Rangel, a senior member of the House Ways and Means Committee, expressed the current climate well:

> Like it or not, the tax exemption granted to hospitals comes out of the computer as a revenue loser, and when revenues are at issue, it will come down to who presents the best argument. . . . Everything comes in one pot and when there is need for money, good causes will compete with good causes. Nonprofit hospitals need to be aware that members of Congress will consider whether their constituents are receiving appropriate benefits in exchange for the tax exemption provided.[6]

While these remarks focus on hospitals, it takes little stretch of the imagination to forecast an extension of this debate to other institutions favored with tax-exempt status.

Meanwhile, restrictions have tightened the criteria for tax-exempt status as an IRS 501(c)(3) organization. For example, such organizations are now prohibited from engaging in political activity. Cases in which tax exemption—and therefore deductibility of gifts—has been denied to institutions that fail to comply with antidiscrimination statutes represent another inroad into these broad-based criteria. As more such cases occur, questions must be answered: How serious must the noncompliance be in order to result in a loss of tax-exempt status? Should there be penalties other than the draconian withdrawal of tax exemption for lesser infractions?

THE CHARITABLE DEDUCTION

In 1917 Congress provided the first federal income tax deduction for charitable contributions by individuals.[7] In 1919, Congress authorized the estate tax deduction for charitable bequests.[8] The gift tax deduction in favor of gifts to charity was included in the 1926 tax laws.[9] In 1935, corporations received the right to income tax deductions for charitable contributions.[10] Since those early statutes, the history of the charitable deduction—whether income, gift, or estate—reflects a wide panorama of change. It is not the purpose of this chapter to explore or even recite all the changes, but to seek trends.

The Changing View of Charitable Giving

At the root of the issue of tax incentives to charitable giving in the United States is the question of whether philanthropic institutions and agencies are providing and performing in the country's highest interests.

The answer is not all that clear. Some people see philanthropy as pure, epitomizing the golden rule. Others see philanthropy as an unjust method for the gathering and distribution of funds and services dictated by the wealthy, who are "the establishment" and resistant to the dynamics of a changing society. The debate is not new. It applies to both the funds that charitable institutions receive and the funds that they disburse.

We are concerned with the funds given to charitable institutions. Charitable giving predated taxes; it is an unquestionable act of virtue in every culture. Those involved must struggle with the question of how to reconcile this virtue with the Internal Revenue Code and its state and local counterparts.

As individual participants in this society, more citizens are vitally affected by the Internal Revenue Code than by any other statute in this land of laws. The Code has come to be the reflection of the "social compact" of the American public—our unwritten expectations of our government. In this context, it represents a unique form of representative democracy in social, political, and economic terms. *Across the board,* it is the Internal Revenue Code that purports to reflect the societal *values* of the time. Where the majority of elected representatives have found "good," they have provided incentives, and where they have found "bad," they have instituted penalties.

It was and still is argued that tax incentives for charitable giving favor the rich—as indeed they do, for those who give. The elimination of the above-the-line-deduction for nonitemizing taxpayers reinforced that contention. Now, the 80 percent of all Americans who file simplified federal tax returns cannot itemize charitable deductions. This Act of Congress would appear to suggest that the federal government does not perceive that nonprofit institutions are acting in the nation's highest interest, nor does it choose to encourage this virtue with the great majority of taxpayers.

The populist contention that tax incentives to charitable giving serve the process of "elitism" rather than the cause of "democratic pluralism" is demonstrably false and without merit. One need only look at the wide range of philanthropic endeavors across the nation that respond to community demands and needs. The diversity of the nonprofit community bespeaks "democracy" in a dramatic people-to-people effort that is more responsive to date than legislation that follows laboriously on the demands for social welfare, educational reform, and cultural literacy. Volunteerism is the heartbeat of philanthropic institutions, and happily, there are no legislative penalties for this virtue—nor, it must be noted, are there any substantial tax incentives.

The notion of charitable giving as a "tax expenditure" has, in my opinion, been the root cause of what has become an increasingly strident conflict between governments and charity. The assumption of lost revenue for government in every deductible gift to charity belies the purpose of the gift. We have seen the cost of health and welfare to government. Can anyone imagine the cost to government of all the service that the nonprofit community provides? Study after study has shown that dollars given to the nonprofit sector—allegedly "lost" revenue—produce a greater return of service than those revenue dollars retained by government for equivalent services.

But the harsh reality is that in the foreseeable future, tax legislation will be revenue-driven. The ground rules have changed. The nonprofit sector—for all its good work and high purpose—has lost its status as the sanctified "vestal virgin" and has been thrust out of the temples and into the marketplace. Nonprofits had been creeping in that direction already, with their ardent solicitation of federal and state funds, their partnerships with private industry, and their quiet but persistent moves into profit-making endeavors.

These are some of the facts and circumstances inherent in the rationale behind recent legislation severely curtailing federal income tax incentives to charitable giving. Public perception often becomes reality in politics.

To say the nonprofit community has brought its house down on its own head may be too strong an indictment. But nonprofits are in the marketplace, and for some, that is hard to swallow. Attempts to reconcile nonprofits to the differing cultures and rules of the for-profit world affect what nonprofits do and those they serve.

Threats to the Charitable Deduction

Recent efforts to protect and expand the charitable deduction have focused on the following issues:

- preserving the full fair-market deductibility of gifts of appreciated property;
- maintaining the deduction for charitable gifts as opposed to a tax credit;
- defeating efforts to impose a floor on the amount that must be given in order to claim a charitable deduction;
- maintaining the unlimited, 100 percent estate tax charitable deduction;
- making a full charitable deduction available to all taxpayers; and
- eliminating appreciated property gifts from the alternative minimum tax (AMT) computation.

The success of these efforts has, at this writing, been notable, except for the AMT and the above-the-line deduction for non-itemizers.

In a 1990 conference presentation, Bonnie Brier, general counsel of Children's Hospital of Philadelphia, reviewed the unsympathetic treatment of charities by Congress in the 1980s and forecast that in the 1990s this congressional attitude was unlikely to change. She cited as targets for further restrictions such activities as the use of subsidiaries for profit-making ventures, the use of mailing lists for cause-related marketing, the use of proceeds from tax-exempt bond financing, the taxability of scholarships and fellowships, increased disclosure requirements and auditing, and requirements for donors about the deductibility of their contributions and how the collected funds will be used. In addition, she raised the awesome specter of whether the conferral of noneconomic benefit, such as the naming of a building or a scholarship fund, would be sufficient "consideration" in the eyes of the law to defeat a deduction for a charitable gift.[11]

In summary, allowing taxpayers to deduct the full amount of gifts to charitable causes continues to be desirable public policy, so long as that privilege is not abused. In the debate on the Revenue Act of 1915, concerning whether to allow deductions for charitable bequests, Senator Boies Penrose, the ranking Republican on the Senate Finance Committee, expressed the principles that can still apply in future debates on the efficacy of the charitable deduction:

> In this country educational and charitable institutions carry on in a large measure what essentially is public work. That our educational and charitable institutions have been largely founded and maintained by individual gift and bequest has been widely commented upon by publicists in every land. In this respect we differ much from older countries where state appropriations have largely aided this work. That in the United States they have been built by private enterprise furnishes a peculiar illustration of the qualities in American civilization which have made our country great. Contributors to these institutions have been remarkably loyal but under war conditions and with the high rates of income tax they could hardly have been expected to have done as well as in times of peace. The provision of the committee inheritance tax amendment [to the House version] exempting from tax transfers to the government or for any religious, charitable, or scientific purpose is to be commended particularly.[12]

REGULATION

Like the mountain to be climbed because it is there, the size of the nonprofit sector invites the attention of regulators. In his book *The Third America,* Michael O'Neill describes its scope:

> Nonprofits employ more civilians than the federal government and the fifty states combined. The yearly budget of the American nonprofit sector exceeds the budgets of all but seven nations in the world. Seventy million American adults and teenagers do volunteer work in nonprofit organizations. Seventy percent of American households donate to charity.[13]

In 1988, the voluntary support of private organizations serving a public purpose exceeded $100 billion for the first time, reaching $103 billion. In 1990, it came to $122.57 billion.[14] According to the latest IRS Annual Report, 464,138 organizations are classified as tax-exempt under Section 501(c)(3).

Nearly every aspect of Americans' lives has spawned nonprofit organizations. That is our history, and we are ennobled by it. Whether measured by their size, economic impact, cultural role, effect on personal and social values, or influence on public policy, private nonprofit organizations play a highly visible and important role in the life and times of the United States.

Nonprofits also engage in activities to spur government action—sometimes in ways incompatible with the political agendas of some office holders. This characteristic provides an additional incentive for lawmakers to increase regulation. As Alan Pifer recites, the nonprofit community has traditionally taken a role in:

- monitoring government to prevent abuses,
- shaping public opinion to effect social change,
- serving as an effective critic of business excesses,
- providing a sanctuary for unorthodox opinion and freedom of expression,
- providing variety and choice in the arts and education,
- providing a margin for experimentation, innovation, and research, uncontaminated by the political process, and
- encouraging the growth of self-help groups.[15]

Each of these functions, has, within recent memory, sparked congressional anxiety and proposals for legislative regulation.

Finally, the third factor that has dramatically attracted the attention of the regulators is abuse and private inurement—that is, personal gain. The recent excesses of the United Way management and of Reverend Jim Bakker—now in jail for appropriating church funds for his extravagant personal use—have drawn the eyes and ire of both the public and the regulators.

The interaction between government and nonprofits has yet to be fully analyzed, and it is worthy of a treatise unto itself. But for now, a few prominent trends are worth noting. Not necessarily in order of importance, they include the following:

- Regulators are examining nonprofits' revenues, distinguishing between gifts and fees, to determine "tax-exempt" qualification. We have seen this occur with hospitals, and one wonders how tuition-dependent colleges would fare in such analyses.
- Investment policies and financial management of nonprofits are being questioned. For example, is it appropriate for nonprofits to invest in leveraged buyout financing with tax-exempt funds?
- The search for taxable activities attributable to nonprofits is intensifying through increased requirements for disclosure and audits.

- More agencies are becoming involved in regulating nonprofits. On the federal level, the Commissioner of Internal Revenue determines appropriate activity for nonprofits falling under section 501(c)(3). But other federal agencies, such as the Justice Department and the Federal Trade Commission, have severely circumscribed tuition and financial aid policies of private colleges and universities— activities heretofore considered free of regulation or indictment by reason of those institutions' tax-exempt status.
- Privileges accorded nonprofits by the Postal Service are being scrutinized as never before, not only to increase postal revenue but also to narrow the criteria for eligibility.
- Research institutions are facing congressional and administrative censure and penalties for what appear to be excessive overhead charges on research grants. A public perception of abuse is sure to lead to increased regulation as well as a diminution of allowances.
- Federal regulation may expand to encompass fund raising. At present, the oversight on fund raisers for nonprofits has been within the jurisdiction of the states, and each year, as new abuses appear, the states add to the regulations. State regulation has been directed primarily at independent fund-raising consultants and paid solicitors, rather than at fund raisers employed by institutions. But with so many nonprofits engaged in interstate charitable solicitation, the call for federal regulation has been repeated over the years, and is likely to become more strident.

THE CHALLENGE TO NONPROFITS

The legal trends affecting philanthropy are as broad-based as those affecting society, for in the United States the two are vitally intertwined. A few have been discussed; there are many more. What is needed is national leadership in the nonprofit community to go beyond crisis management and to develop a consensus on what is right and what is wrong in the sector.

To avoid onerous regulation by government, the community of nonprofits needs to define its common characteristics while at the same time preserving its vibrant diversity. Bad apples need to be routed out of the barrel and exposed before they become national scandals. Professional fund raisers must undertake stricter self-discipline. Nonprofits must become more efficient and effective in management planning and communications. The commercialism that has seduced many nonprofits into cause-related marketing, aggressive direct-mail solicitations, commission fund raising, and inappropriate leveraging of tax-exempt funds has made it difficult to argue for legal incentives to giving or to defend against more regulation.

The fabric of charitable giving and volunteering is interwoven with our society's broader values of selflessness. The energy and resources committed to charitable endeavors is perhaps the single most visible characteristic of American society as a whole. It needs to be nourished and encouraged, not stifled and degraded.

NOTES

1. Benjamin Nathan Cardozo, *Growth of the Law* (New Haven, Connecticut: Yale University Press, 1924), 19-20.

2. R. Pound, *People ex rel Durham Realty Corp v. La Fetra*, 230 N.Y. 429, 450 (1921).

3. John P. Persons et al., "Criteria for Exemption Under 501(c)(3)," *Research Papers Sponsored by the Commission on Private Philanthropy and Public Needs, Vol. IV* (Washington, D.C.: Department of the Treasury, 1977), 1912-1913.

4. Ibid., 1923.

5. Revenue Act of 1894, Ch. 349, Sec. 32, 28 Stat. 556 (1894).

6. Charles Rangel (presentation at the annual membership meeting of the American Hospital Association, Washington, D.C., January 30, 1991).

7. Revenue Act of 1917, Ch. 63, Tit. XII, Sec. 1201(2), 40 Stat, 300 (1917).

8. Revenue Act of 1918, Ch. 18, Tit. V, Sec. 403(a)(3), 40 Stat. 1057 (1919).

9. Revenue Act of 1926, Ch. 20, Tit. 26, Sec. 1095, 44 Stat. 835 (1926).

10. Revenue Act of 1935, Ch. 829, Sec. 102(c), 49 Stat. 1016 (1935).

11. Bonnie Brier, "Coping with the Contribution/Consideration Problem from the Standpoint of the Charitable Institution and Personal Comments on a Failing System," in *New York University: Eighteenth Conference on Tax Planning for 501(c)(3) Organizations* (New York: Matthew Bender, 1990), chapter 10.

12. Quoted in Norman S. Fink, "Taxation and Philanthropy—A 1976 Perspective," *Journal of College and University Law*, June 1976, 1-14.

13. Michael O'Neill, *The Third America* (San Francisco: Jossey-Bass, 1989), 1-2.

14. *Giving USA: The Annual Report on Philanthropy for the Year 1990* (New York: American Association of Fund Raising Counsel Trust for Philanthropy, 1991), 8.

15. Alan Pifer, "Philanthropy, Voluntarism, and Changing Times," *Daedalus*, Winter 1987, 130-131.

Part Twelve

Current Issues and Perspectives

Michael J. Worth

There is great reason for optimism concerning the future of philanthropic support for our colleges, universities, and schools. It is a tradition deeply embedded in our history and culture. Significant philanthropic support for education preceded the introduction of the income tax and has continued to grow despite repeated changes in tax incentives. It has continued through wars and recessions. It has survived the cynicism of the 1960s, the "malaise" of the 1970s, and the "me decade" of the 1980s.

Moreover, our colleges and universities have never been more important to the achievement of our national goals and the personal goals of Americans. Higher education has been under attack in recent years from critics both outside and within. This widespread concern and attention, while presenting real dangers and threats, is also evidence of just how important higher education has become in our society. The demonstrated durability of our philanthropic tradition combined with the central importance of our colleges and universities gives us every reason to believe that the future of educational philanthropy is bright.

However, some writers—including several authors in this collection—have identified disquieting trends that must give us cause for concern. My purpose in this concluding essay is to bring these issues together and suggest how we as development professionals, educators, and citizens can help to preserve some of our most vital traditions. I will consider these trends at three levels: first, those in educational fund raising and the development profession itself; second, those in the broader field of higher

402 PART TWELVE: CURRENT ISSUES AND PERSPECTIVES

education that we serve; and third, those in the society of which our traditions and institutions are a part.

EDUCATIONAL FUND RAISING AND THE ISSUE OF CREDIBILITY

As Rick Nahm and Bob Zemsky say in Chapter 7, educational fund raising is at a crossroads. Critics increasingly question whether our priority is to raise money for bona fide institutional goals or whether we are engaged in smoke-and-mirror accounting that emphasizes the bottom line and fund raising for its own sake. Much of this criticism has been provoked by the "mega-goal" campaigns that combine the results of ongoing fund raising and new gifts under one overall goal, in effect counting everything as part of the campaign.

Some writers are concerned that widely publicized mega-campaign goals, combined with public resistance to rising tuition levels, will add to the public's perception of institutional greed and increase the pressures for punitive laws and regulations like those mentioned by Norman Fink in Chapter 35.

Other critics of such campaigns maintain that they put the emphasis in the wrong place—on the bottom line, rather than the academic needs to be met. This may encourage liberal accounting practices, such as counting pre-campaign gifts and bequest expectancies from young donors toward the campaign goal. Counting every gift toward the campaign goal may encourage gifts that bear no relationship to the institution's needs or that may even cause it additional new expenses; the fund-raising tail wags the academic dog.

Although there may be a few instances of outright abuse, I do not believe that most campaign accounting has been intentionally misleading or truly dishonest. And, as this chapter is being written, CASE is circulating for comment draft guidelines on campaign accounting that would standardize practices. This is an important step, but problems of perception and image may well remain. The accounting involved in mega-goals is complex and may not be clearly understood by the institution's constituency, which remembers only the one big number associated with the overall goal. Faculty, in particular, may gain the impression that campaign gifts are all new money. When they learn that most of the campaign income consists of annual gifts that already have been spent or bequests that will not be received for many years, leaving little for immediate new initiatives, disillusionment is the understandable result. This disillusionment is even more severe if the announcement of a successful campaign is combined, as it has been in some institutions, with budgetary problems and cutbacks.

One solution, of course, is simply to communicate better what the campaign includes and how various kinds of gifts count toward its goal. But, in practice, we may be asking too much of those not directly involved in campaign management to expect that they will understand and remember the fine points of "expendable" and "nonexpendable" gifts, the discount rate applied to certain kinds of planned gifts, and the exact accounting period included in the campaign. And if our campaign communications place too much stress on establishing such understanding, they may detract from the emphasis that should be given to the academic needs that the campaign addresses.

Some of the most respected professionals in the development field have expressed concern, even alarm. Since these criticisms come from friends, we should take them all the more seriously. Writing in the March 12, 1991, *Chronicle of Philanthropy,* fundraising consultant Robert Roche urged that campaign goals be based upon incremental money and exclude the results of ongoing programs such as the annual fund. "We need a frank debate about campaign goals, and we need it now," he said.[1] Charles Lawson, the chairman of Brakeley, John Price Jones Inc., wrote in the Winter 1990 *NSFRE Journal,* "The time has come to dismiss [the mega-goal] approach to capital campaigns and to adopt realistic goals within achievable time frames against supportable needs. Unless our not-for-profits act more responsibly in this area, I truly believe we will experience a very real donor backlash."[2]

As I mentioned above, campaign reporting standards may address some of the criticisms. And it may turn out that economic conditions in the 1990s will, at least temporarily, limit campaign goals, making the matter less relevant. At root, however, the issue is not these specific practices but the larger question of fund raising's role in the institution and its relationship to institutional mission and academic goals. And, as I will discuss more fully below, the question even goes beyond educational fund raising as a specific activity of colleges and universities to the issue of how institutions define their missions and measure their success.

The Trend Toward Commercialism

Other trends in educational fund raising threaten to undermine our tradition of volunteerism and philanthropy. They include the increasing use of paid solicitors, the payment of commissions and bonuses based on fund-raising results, and the blurring of business and philanthropy represented in cause-related marketing. Each of these trends runs contrary to our traditional view of philanthropy as something more noble than simply business and of fund raising as an endeavor motivated more by commitment than pecuniary reward.

Especially discomforting is the increasing acceptance of fund raising as a form of "marketing." This concept of fund raising is based on erroneous definitions and offers some real dangers. As Kathleen Kelly points out in an article in the Summer 1991 *NSFRE Journal,* marketing implies a *quid pro quo* in which the donor exchanges money for some product or benefit. Donors may receive something intangible in return for their gifts, such as satisfaction and recognition, but the primary benefit of their gifts is to society, not to themselves.[3]

Philanthropy is, by definition, altruistic, not the purchase of a product or service to meet some personal need or desire. Indeed, as Kelly points out, "an intention to exchange money for benefits of equal or greater value for oneself is, by legal definition, a nongiving behavior."[4] The use of a commercial term and concept like "marketing" to describe fund raising implies a *quid pro quo* similar to that in commercial exchanges. Such an implication diminishes our institutions, demeans our donors, and invites the eye of government on our tax-exempt status.

Second, the essence of marketing is, very simply, to "find a need and fill it." It implies a willingness to produce almost any product that consumers demand or desire, with the singular purpose of maximizing the bottom line. If a pharmaceutical company surveys the public and discovers a growing concern about wrinkled skin, a new soap advertised to "cure your wrinkles" will surely appear soon after. If the public wants smaller cars, or larger ones, Detroit will respond.

Certainly, colleges and universities must be responsive to their external environments. The concept of marketing may, in fact, have some relevance to student recruitment, which does involve a payment (tuition) for service (education). We do not offer academic programs in which no students wish to enroll. And no amount of persuasion will convince donors to support projects for which they can perceive no need. But we cannot imply that we stand ready to provide *any* product the market will buy; nor can we suggest that we seek gifts toward *any* purpose donors will support. To do so would be to undermine our integrity as educational institutions, and ultimately to lose the confidence and support of both the public and our benefactors. Our colleges and universities are not ivory towers, but neither are they Ivory Soap.

The Fund-raising "Profession"

In his essay mentioned above, Lawson says "the most troublesome trend . . . lies within the minds and hearts of those of us who have become so consumed with the trappings of professionalism and personal advancement that the reason for serving philanthropic causes is largely forgotten." He warns that "professional 'egomania' in the fund-raising field is rapidly growing beyond acceptable boundaries and its basis is largely unjustified. The role of the fund-raising executive is important, but it is that of a facilitator in a process that will continue with or without us."[5]

Based on those in my acquaintance, the overwhelming majority of my development colleagues are not personally guilty of egomania and are in fact sincere, thoughtful individuals who try to serve their institutions well. I would have difficulty accepting Lawson's criticism as applying generally or even widely to development officers as individuals. But it is possible that despite the best intentions and efforts of individual practitioners, the profession itself has evolved in a way that creates at least the image of the "professional egomania" Lawson sees.

In Chapter 3, I briefly traced the historical evolution of the development profession. Following the early days of paid "agents," there arose in the early twentieth century a new breed of fundraising "professionals." Their prototypes were individuals such as Ward and Pierce, whose role was that of facilitating the work of committed fund-raising volunteers. Today's trend away from the use of volunteers and toward solicitation by development staff and paid solicitors, some even receiving commissions and bonuses, is in a sense a regression to the earlier model. But, as I point out in Chapter 3, the paid agents of the early colleges usually were creatures of their own institutions, often motivated more by belief in its mission than by money. It is sobering to wonder if we risk creating a situation that combines the worst of both worlds:

"professionals" who work for the money, but without substantial interest or commitment to their institutions or their missions.

We have come to view professionalism in fund raising as a good thing. And, surely, if by that we mean adherence to high standards of ethics and performance, it is. But we have seen in other fields that an increased professional consciousness also can be to the detriment of institutions. It has happened with faculty in many fields, who gain their identity and recognition more through their association with colleagues in the same discipline nationwide than within their individual institutions. This focus on professional field rather than institution, combined with high mobility, has been widely observed as diminishing institutional loyalty and faculty participation in institutional concerns. If this tendency is troubling with regard to professors, it is potentially disastrous with regard to development officers, whose responsibility and sole purpose is the advancement of the college or university.

There undoubtedly are some in the development profession who place personal advancement and the trappings of professionalism ahead of service to the institution. But there also are an ample number of counterexamples to be offered, both in defense of our field and as models against which all of us can compare our own perceptions of our role.

I would encourage all of my development colleagues to read the wonderful autobiography of John Dolibois, who served 34 years as vice president at Miami of Ohio. *Patterns of Circles* recounts Dolibois' entire career as a soldier, an ambassador, and a development officer, but the part I found most poignant was his account of a comment by his son. Asked by his mother what he wanted to be when he grew up, the son replied that he wanted to follow in his father's line of work. "You want to be a fund raiser?" his mother asked. "Dad's not a fund raiser," the son replied. "He's a builder. When he goes to the office in the morning he passes the Sesquicentennial Chapel, one of the first projects for which he raised money. His office is in Murstein Alumni Center, next to Climer Guest Lodge, both of which his efforts made possible. From his window he looks down on Peffer Park. It's there because Dad had the vision to develop it. . . . One out of every twenty students he meets on campus has a scholarship, a loan, or a grant, for which Dad's activities are responsible. He's building a better university, not just raising money."[6]

I believe that the future of our profession and our institutions requires that we learn to blend our increasingly professional skills with such a sense of calling. As Peter Buchanan writes in his conclusion to Chapter 33, "At the heart of educational advancement must be an unshakable belief that its effective practice is a moral commitment in service to education, and hence to society. Only with such a central belief can advancement be a full-fledged family member in its own house and have its practice fully accepted as a profession by the public."

HIGHER EDUCATION AND THE MEANING OF EXCELLENCE

The issues I have identified above for educational fund raising are merely the shadows of related questions facing all of higher education. For example, as I noted, the increasing professional consciousness and concomitant decrease in institutional identity and loyalty affects professors as well as development officers. And as I will discuss below, it has a larger counterpart in our society.

The much-criticized mega-campaign likewise reflects a broader issue in higher education, one that goes to the heart of what we mean by educational "excellence." In 1985, Alexander Astin, a professor of higher education at the University of California, Los Angeles, described "a folklore about our higher education system in which the different institutions are organized hierarchically into a kind of pecking order." Astin noted that this hierarchy is determined primarily by reputation and financial resources. Institutions that rank high on these counts are defined to be "excellent" and other colleges and universities seek to emulate them. Astin cites David Riesman, who described this phenomenon as "a kind of snakelike procession, in that each institution follows the path taken by the head."[7]

In this environment, two-year colleges strive to expand to four-year, colleges seek status as universities, and good teaching universities aspire to significance in research. Because they are the best-known and command the most resources, the research universities become everybody's model for "excellence," as if a nation of 3,000 Harvards would really meet the educational needs of a diverse citizenry.

As Astin says, "According to the reputational view, excellence is whatever people think it is."[8] This leads colleges and universities to pursue the perceived correlates of quality—reputation and resources. And, in this conception, reputation and resources interact—more of the latter automatically provides more of the former. Indeed, even the *perception* of greater resources can enhance prestige.

In this concept of excellence, I suspect, lies at least one explanation for the much-criticized mega-campaign goals. The college's fund-raising goal is set to be greater than that of some rival college or university, probably one perceived as being just a bit higher in the institutional pecking order. Decisions about the campaign's length and types of gifts it will include then follow to produce the desired dollar result. Institutions that proceed in this way say their campaigns are designed to achieve educational "excellence." And they are sincere in making that connection. But they are operating under the mistaken definition of excellence that Astin describes.

This is not to say that colleges and universities do not need the dollars represented by large campaign goals. They surely do, and indeed, it is unlikely that any campaign ever meets all the bona fide needs of the institution. The issue is rather the conceptual starting point in linking mission to needs to goal, within a realistic and credible assessment of the institution's true fund-raising capacity.

Astin offers an alternate definition of educational excellence that is worth considering. He calls it "excellence as the development of human talent" and describes it as follows:

> The talent development view of excellence emphasizes the educational impact of the institution on its students and faculty members. Its basic premise is that true excellence lies in the institution's ability to affect its students and faculty favorably, to enhance their intellectual and scholarly development, and to make a positive difference in their lives. The most excellent institutions are, in this view, those that have the greatest impact—"add the most value," as the economists would say—on the student's knowledge and personal development and on the faculty member's scholarly and pedagogical ability and productivity.[9]

This view of excellence would permit institutions to be true to their missions. A fine community college, providing opportunity to less-well-prepared students, could be just as "excellent" as a selective four-year liberal arts college, which could be just as "excellent" as a major research university. If excellence depends on value added and defined mission, then these institutions are not better or worse; they are merely different.

If this view of excellence prevailed, matching the dollar goal of some "better" institution's campaign would not be the primary concern. Rather, the essential consideration would be the campaign's relevance to the identified needs of the institution in terms of its own mission and educational purposes. Campaigns would then start with needs rather than goals. This would enhance their credibility and that of the institutions they support.

Until the debate about campaign goals broadens to a discussion of how we view our institutional missions, development officers cannot solve the problem through mere accounting reform. The responsibility for defining educational excellence and setting institutional goals lies primarily with boards of trustees, presidents, and faculties. But the issues facing fund raising and philanthropy are so inseparable from those of higher education as a whole that development officers must participate in the wider debate.

It is interesting to note that the alarms concerning campaign goals have come first from the development profession itself. Motivated perhaps by what they see as unrealistic pressures, and concerned by the challenges to campaigns' credibility, development officers and fund-raising consultants have been the first to speak out for change. So far, their recommendations have been directed primarily to their colleagues and are essentially technical in nature, such as the standardization of campaign accounting rules. The development community has sought solutions within its own sphere, seeking to change the practices it controls. But development officers' concerns also reflect their implicit understanding of the nature of their institutions in the context of society and its philanthropic tradition. This understanding offers a valuable perspective that can contribute greatly to our institutions and to all of higher education.

In the past twenty years, development officers have achieved enhanced standing within their institutions. The vice president for development now sits alongside the vice president for academic affairs at the president's cabinet table in most colleges and universities. More and more of us hold advanced degrees, teach, do research, and serve on institutional committees. An increasing number follow the development track to the college or university presidency. We have a greater opportunity than ever before to join the larger discussion about the substantive higher education issues to which our own work is inextricably related.

SOCIETY AND THE FOUNDATION OF PHILANTHROPY

I write this concluding chapter amid discussion of a "new world order" in the era following the Cold War. Unprecedented international cooperation in the Persian Gulf War is cited by some as evidence that this new world order, based on cooperation among nations and respect for international law, is indeed emerging.

At the same time, there are disturbing signs, in the world and in our own country, of a regression in human affairs to an older, less hopeful order. In Quebec, Northern Ireland, Yugoslavia, South Africa, and elsewhere in the world, people remain bitterly divided along lines of language, religion, ethnicity, and race. The Soviet Union has broken up along the lines of ancient ethnic and economic rivalries. Cultural and religious antagonisms too intense and complicated for most Americans to even understand make the Middle East an ever-boiling cauldron. In our own country, stories of racial, ethnic, and religious tension fill the daily news and too often emanate from the campuses of our colleges and universities, presumably institutions devoted to reason and tolerance.

Identity with and loyalty to traditional institutions appears to be diminishing. This is reflected not only in a real shortage of volunteer leadership for nonprofit organizations, but also in new patterns of professional and political organization. I have mentioned above the increasing pattern of various professional groups subdividing into narrow specialties rather than looking to their home institutions as sources of recognition and reward. In the political realm, the growth of associations (lobbies) in Washington reflects our increasing tendency to relate to government professionally—as farmers, educators, and tire manufacturers—rather than as simply Americans through the traditional channels of our elected representatives.

At times, it appears that our society and the world are retreating into ethnic, religious, racial, and economic "tribalism," with a narrower and narrower definition of who is "us" and increasing hostility toward those who are "them."

But the history of philanthropy over the centuries reflects the *broadening* scope of the human community, from tribes to kingdoms to nation-states. Ever-larger numbers of individuals have been willing to find shared identity and to link their personal fates with one another and to the common good.

The remarkable history of American philanthropy reflects our particularly generous perceptions in that regard. It has demonstrated our willingness to accept other Americans, different from us and even unknown to us, as nevertheless part of the "American family" and to put the common good ahead of our own self-interest, economic or otherwise. Through our giving we have accepted personal responsibility not only for those less fortunate, but also for the welfare of our future generations and the institutions intended to serve them.

The greatest threat to the future of philanthropy and volunteerism would be an erosion of this sense of community and commitment to the common good—a descent into unbounded self-interest, in which the "us" becomes ever smaller and the "them" includes almost everyone else. At its ultimate extension, the "us" becomes only "me," and the basis for philanthropy is lost.

I have suggested ways in which we in the development field can make positive contributions both to our profession and to higher education. We also can bring our insights to our role as citizens. By valuing, demonstrating, and advocating the qualities of community and public responsibility in our own lives, we can help ensure a future society in which our work will be both possible and well-regarded.

Despite the disquieting issues I have discussed above, I will conclude this chapter as I began it, on a note of optimism. It is characteristic of humans, and especially of Americans, to engage in self-analysis, to identify disturbing trends and correct them to preserve our most cherished values. Indeed, our capacity and willingness to do so proves our continuing concern for the common good, and thus a continuing foundation for philanthropy.

I once heard John Gardner tell a story about an abandoned house in a decaying neighborhood. It was, he said, easy to make a list of the specific repairs needed, but to do so missed the fundamental issue. The real question, Gardner said, was this: Why is there not a caring family living in the house and tending to needed repairs as they arise? If we could answer that larger question, the specific defects of the house would be of secondary concern, because we could be sure that they would be addressed.

Likewise, it is easy to make a list of the specific problems in our society and world that need to be addressed. But to do so misses the fundamental issue: How can we ensure a continuing supply of moral, caring, intelligent people prepared to address these issues and other issues as they arise in the future? The answer lies, of course, in the continuing strength of our educational institutions. The fact that those of us who work in colleges and universities and schools continue to discuss and debate their futures should be our reassurance of their continued vitality and our greatest source of optimism about the future of society.

Unfortunately, the world is still the same as Francis Pray described it in the closing passages of his 1981 *Handbook*—"a world in which greed and need and want and misery are still all too dominant." But fortunately, it is also, as Pray found it, a world "in which some of the more decent of human institutions—those devoted to education—and some of the more decent of human urges and needs can come together with some hope of making a significant impact on the future." And, as Pray reminded us about our own professional work, "To be a part of the line of contact between the institution and the better impulses of humanity outside is a privilege we share with relatively few others."[10]

NOTES

1. Robert P. Roche, "Huge Fund Drives May Not Be Worth the Cost in Ill Will and Unfulfilled Expectations," *Chronicle of Philanthropy*, March 12, 1991, 40.

2. Charles E. Lawson, "The Nineties: Worrisome Trends in Fund Raising," *The Journal* (National Society of Fund Raising Executives, Washington), Winter 1990, 11-12.

3. Kathleen S. Kelly, "Marketing: A Flawed Approach to Fund Raising," *The Journal* (National Society of Fund Raising Executives, Washington), Summer 1991, 31.

4. Ibid., 31.

5. Lawson, "The Nineties," 9-10.

6. John E. Dolibois, *Patterns of Circles: An Ambassador's Story* (Kent, Ohio: Kent State University Press, 1989), 237.

7. Alexander W. Astin, *Achieving Educational Excellence* (San Francisco: Jossey-Bass, 1985), 11.

8. Ibid., 25.

9. Ibid., 60-61.

10. Francis C. Pray, ed., *Handbook for Educational Fund Raising* (San Francisco: Jossey-Bass, 1981), 403.

Glossary

Terms mentioned in a definition that have their own full entry elsewhere in the Glossary are italicized.

Alternative minimum tax (AMT). A provision in the federal income tax law intended to ensure that all income earners pay some tax. Under certain circumstances, the AMT may affect the deductibility of a charitable gift.

American Alumni Council (AAC). An organization of professionals in development and alumni relations, established in 1913. The AAC merged with the *American College Public Relations Association (ACPRA)* in 1974 to create the *Council for Advancement and Support of Education (CASE)*.

American Association of Fund-Raising Counsel (AAFRC). An organization of fund-raising consulting firms. Member firms subscribe to a code of ethics.

American College Public Relations Association (ACPRA). An organization of college and university communications professionals. ACPRA merged with the *American Alumni Council (AAC)* in 1974 to create the *Council for Advancement and Support of Education (CASE)*.

Annual gift. Gifts donors make in response to yearly requests to support the institution's current operating needs. Annual gifts are usually solicited through an organized program involving direct mail, organized telephone campaigns, and personal solicitation.

Ask. The point in a *solicitation* at which the solicitor explicitly requests a gift.

Bequest. A gift made through the donor's will, becoming effective on the death of the donor.

Capital campaign. An intensive, organized fund-raising effort to secure major gifts and pledges toward specific capital needs or projects within a finite time period, usually one or more years.

Capital gift. A gift that adds to the institution's long-term assets, usually designated for a facility or equipment (physical capital) or for addition to endowment funds (financial capital).

Case statement. A thorough and definitive written description of the institution and its plans, including the justifications for needs addressed in a campaign. The case statement is a master document from which various other campaign communications, including brochures and proposals, ultimately derive.

Cause-related marketing. Activities undertaken by companies for profit with some financial benefit going to a nonprofit institution or organization. For example, a company may promise to "contribute" a certain percentage of every sale of a product.

Centralized development program. A pattern of organization in which all development staff in an institution report, through channels, to a single chief development officer. The central office maintains authority over all fund-raising policy decisions, approves fund-raising priorities, and coordinates prospect assignments. (See *Decentralized development program.*)

Class agents. Alumni volunteers who take responsibility for soliciting gifts from the members of their graduating classes.

Community foundation. A foundation that limits its grantmaking to its local community. Community foundations generally receive their assets through contributions from donors in the community and are governed by boards representing local constituencies and interests.

Comprehensive campaign. An intensive, organized fund-raising effort similar to a *capital campaign* but encompassing a broader range of needs, often including annual giving as well as facilities and endowment. These campaigns usually have larger overall goals than capital campaigns, encompassing these various types of support, and usually extend over a longer period of years.

Constituent alumni associations. Organizations for alumni who attended a particular school or college within a university or who have a particular interest in a specific area (for example, the performing arts). Constituent alumni associations often are sub-groups of the institution's general alumni association and are often represented on the larger association's governing board.

Corporate foundation. A foundation that receives its funding from a parent corporation and whose grants reflect the interests and priorities of that corporation in their giving. The boards and staffs of corporate foundations typically include corporate officers.

Council for Advancement and Support of Education (CASE). An organization of professionals in all institutional advancement specialties, created in 1974 through the merger of the *American Alumni Council (AAC)* and the *American College Public Relations Association (ACPRA)*.

Cultivation. The process by which an institution develops a relationship with a prospective donor by providing information and involving the individual in the institution's planning and life, with the goal of engendering that person's commitment and support.

Decentralized development program. A pattern of organization in which individual schools, colleges, and other units of a large university directly employ and supervise development officers. These units have considerable autonomy in setting fund-raising policies and priorities. (See *Centralized development program.*)

Deferred gift. A gift made by bequest, insurance, or a life income arrangement or trust, with the institution's access to the principal being "deferred" until the death of the donor or another beneficiary. The term "deferred gift" has for the most part been replaced by the broader term *planned gift.*

Development. A process that includes the identification of institutional needs and priorities; the identification, *cultivation,* and involvement of prospective donors; the *solicitation* of gifts; and *stewardship* intended to continue the donor's interest and involvement. The term is generally used synonymously with *fund raising* today, but has been used more broadly in the past to mean the activities now encompassed by the term *institutional advancement.*

Direct mail. The solicitation of gifts with a mailed "package," usually including a letter, brochure, and response device designed to encourage the recipient to send a gift by return mail.

Donor research (or **prospect research**). The identification of potential donors, the gathering of background information on their interests and giving capacity, and the development of *cultivation* and *solicitation* strategies tailored specifically to the individual prospects.

Donor-driven. A fund-raising campaign or program that is primarily responsive to the interests of prospective donors. (See *Need-driven*.)

Endowment. Funds invested for the long term, with principal remaining intact and only income being available for expenditure. Income from endowment funds may be earmarked for specific programs or activities or may support general institutional needs.

Family foundation. A foundation established and controlled by the members of a family as a vehicle for their philanthropy. Family foundations are typically small, and their grants reflect the personal interests of family members.

Feasibility study. A market survey to determine the potential level of support for the institution and its needs from among its identified constituency. Feasibility studies are usually conducted prior to a campaign as a guide to goal-setting and campaign planning, and usually involve confidential interviews conducted by an outside consultant.

Fund raising. Programs and activities involving the solicitation of gifts to the institution. The term is generally used synonymously with *development*.

Fund-raising pyramid. A graphic device used to illustrate the way in which *annual gifts, major gifts,* and *ultimate gifts* relate to each other. A large base of donors, giving relatively small gifts, form the bottom of the pyramid, and the largest portion of total gift revenue comes from a much smaller group of donors at the top.

Gift club. A technique for recognizing donors by granting them membership in various club levels according to the size of their annual or capital gift.

Gift-in-kind. A gift of physical property intended for use by the institution in its educational or research programs (for example, books, equipment, or art works).

Independent foundation. A foundation that makes grants in predetermined areas of interest and priority and uses formal procedures for assessing funding proposals. Independent foundations are typically governed by boards more diverse than those of family foundations, usually have larger assets, and often employ professional staff.

Institutional advancement. Defined by A. Westley Rowland as "All activities and programs undertaken by an institution to develop understanding and support from all its constituencies in order to achieve its goals in securing such resources as students, faculty, and dollars." The term usually includes the professional specialties of educational fund raising, alumni relations, public relations and publications, student recruitment and marketing, and government relations.

Institutionally related foundation. A foundation that exists solely for the purpose of raising, managing, and disbursing funds to support the programs of a specific (usually public) college or university.

Kickoff. The point at which a campaign and its goal are made public. The kickoff usually includes an announcement of the *nucleus fund* total and is usually marked by a highly visible public event.

Life income gift. A gift made to the institution with the provision that the donor and/or other beneficiaries receive income for their lives.

LYBUNT. An acronym used in annual giving programs to describe individuals who gave "last year, but unfortunately not this (year)."

Major gift. A gift larger than an *annual gift*, often paid in installments over a period of years and usually designated for a capital purpose. The dollar level at which a gift is considered "major" depends upon the needs and fund-raising history of the institution.

Mega-campaign. A term coined in the 1980s to describe college and university comprehensive campaigns with very large goals, typically in the hundreds of millions of dollars (and in some cases, more than $1 billion).

National Association of College and University Business Officers (NACUBO). A professional organization that, along with CASE, developed reporting standards for the accounting of voluntary support. (See *Council for Advancement and Support of Education.*)

Need-driven. A fund-raising campaign or program whose primary focus is to raise gifts for specific, predetermined needs of the institution. (See *Donor-driven.*)

Nucleus fund. The total of gifts and pledges made during the initial "quiet period" of a campaign, after the institution's internal approval of a campaign but before the public announcement or *kickoff.* A nucleus fund totaling 30 to 40 percent of the campaign goal is generally recommended as the minimum necessary for campaign success.

Operating foundation. A foundation that develops, supports, and manages its own programs or activities and generally does not accept outside proposals.

Philanthropy. A tradition in which individuals contribute, for reasons of altruism, their time and financial resources to nonprofit institutions, with the goal of improving society.

Phonathon. An organized program of telephoning, either by volunteer callers or paid professionals, to solicit gifts from a large number of donors. Phonathons are commonly used in annual giving programs.

Planned gift. A gift made in the context of the donor's total financial and estate planning. Planned gifts often involve a bequest, trust, or annuity arrangement and usually provide tax benefits or other financial advantages to the donor as well as benefiting the institution. (See *Deferred gift.*)

Premium. A token given to donors (such as a decal, a pin, or a coffee mug with the institutional seal), either with a direct mail solicitation (front-end premium) or after a gift has been received (back-end premium.)

Proposal. A formal, written solicitation for a gift or grant, typically used when approaching corporate or foundation donors.

Prospect. An individual or organization confirmed as having the capacity to make a gift to the institution and some existing or potential interest in doing so. (See *Suspect.*)

Prospect management and tracking. An ongoing process including the matching of prospect interests to institutional needs, the development of *cultivation* and *solicitation* strategies, the assignment of responsibility for the prospect to staff and volunteers, and the systematic monitoring of activity undertaken with the prospect.

Prospect research. See *Donor research.*

Regional campaign. An intensive effort to secure gifts and pledges from donors in a specific region or city, usually as a component of a larger overall campaign.

Resident management. An arrangement through which a consultant works at the institution full-time for a finite period to direct a specific campaign.

Rule of thirds. A long-held and widely accepted axiom, originated by Harold J. Seymour, that states that for any campaign, the 10 largest gifts will account for one-third of the goal, the next 100 gifts will account for another third of the goal, and the rest of the gifts will account for the final third. Many writers contend that these proportions have changed over time, as an ever-higher proportion of campaign funds come from a smaller number of top donors.

Screening (or **rating**). A technique whereby staff and volunteers review lists of potential donors and offer judgments, based on personal knowledge, as to the prospects' ability and inclination to support the institution. Many institutions now use computerized screening programs, which rely primarily on demographic data, to tentatively rate prospects' financial capacity.

Solicitation. The process of asking a donor to make a gift. The solicitation visit, or "call," includes various elements of communication or conversation leading up to, or following after, the *ask* itself.

Special gift. A gift made toward some specific, nonrecurring need of the institution. Some writers use the term interchangeably with *major gift*. In a formal campaign, the term "special gift" is sometimes used to distinguish capital gifts at some arbitrary intermediate level (for example, $10,000 to $99,999) from "major gifts" at a higher level (for example, $100,000 and up).

Sponsored research. Specific research studies undertaken by faculty or staff and paid for by a donor (or "sponsor") who often has an interest in the results.

Stewardship. Activities designed to keep donors informed and involved regarding the use and benefits of their past gifts. Stewardship is often seen as an aspect of *cultivation* for donors' future support. The term also is used more broadly to include the institution's careful management of the gift and the activities it supports in order to keep faith with the donor's intentions and confidence.

Suspect. An individual or organization identified as a potential donor for the institution but whose financial capacity or interest remains undetermined. (See *Prospect.*)

SYBUNT. An acronym used in annual giving programs to describe individuals who give "some years, but unfortunately not this (year)."

Telemarketing. A sales technique developed by for-profit firms involving the use of direct mail and organized phone calling by trained callers. With modifications, these techniques are used by many colleges and universities to solicit both annual and capital gifts.

Ultimate gift. A term coined by David Dunlop to describe the largest gift of which a donor is ultimately capable. Ultimate gifts are often, but not always, given through a planned giving device such as a trust or bequest.

Unrelated business income tax (UBIT). A federal tax on income that colleges, universities, alumni associations, and other nonprofit organizations receive from activities not directly related to the educational, research, or charitable purposes of the organization.

Voluntary support. All gifts and noncontractual grants to colleges and universities, defined in accordance with accounting standards established by the Council for Advancement and Support of Education and the National Association of College and University Business Officers.

For Further Reading

BOOKS FOR GENERAL REFERENCE

Brakeley, George A., Jr. *Tested Ways to Successful Fund Raising*. New York: AMACOM, 1980.

Brittingham, Barbara E., and Thomas R. Pezzullo. *The Campus Green: Fund Raising in Higher Education*. ASHE-ERIC Higher Education Report No. 1. Washington, D.C.: School of Education and Human Development, George Washington University, 1990.

Broce, Thomas E. *Fund Raising: The Guide to Raising Money from Private Sources*. Norman, Oklahoma: University of Oklahoma Press, 1979.

Dolibois, John E. *Patterns of Circles: An Ambassador's Story*. Kent, Ohio: Kent State University Press, 1989.

Duronio, Margaret A., and Bruce A. Loessin. *Effective Fund Raising in Higher Education: Ten Success Stories*. San Francisco: Jossey-Bass, 1991.

Fisher, James L., and Gary H. Quehl, eds. *The President and Fund Raising*. New York: American Council on Education/Macmillan, 1989.

Gurin, Maurice G. *What Volunteers Should Know for Successful Fund Raising*. New York: Stein and Day, 1981.

Lord, James Gregory. *The Raising of Money: Thirty-Five Essentials Every Trustee Should Know*. Cleveland, Ohio: Third Sector Press, 1984.

Panas, Jerold. *Born to Raise: What Makes A Great Fundraiser: What Makes A Fundraiser Great*. Chicago: Pluribus Press, 1988.

Payton, Robert L. *Philanthropy: Voluntary Action for the Public Good*. New York: American Council on Education/Macmillan, 1988.

Pocock, J. W. *Fund-Raising Leadership: A Guide for College and University Boards*. Washington, D.C.: Association of Governing Boards of Universities and Colleges, 1989.

Pray, Francis C., ed. *Handbook for Educational Fund Raising*. San Francisco: Jossey-Bass, 1981.

Rowland, A. Westley, ed. *Handbook of Institutional Advancement: A Modern Guide to Executive Management, Institutional Relations, Fund-Raising, Alumni Administration, Government Relations, Publications, Periodicals, and Enrollment Management*. 2d ed. San Francisco: Jossey-Bass, 1986.

Seymour, Harold J. *Designs for Fund-raising*. 2d ed. Rockville, Maryland: Fund Raising Institute, 1988.

Warner, Irving R. *The Art of Fund Raising*. New York: Bantam Books, 1988.

Willmer, Wesley K. *A New Look at Managing the Small College Advancement Program*. Washington, D.C.: Council for Advancement and Support of Education, 1987.

PERIODICALS ON FUND RAISING

CASE Currents, monthly magazine (Council for Advancement and Support of Education, Washington, D.C.).

Chronicle of Philanthropy, biweekly newspaper (Washington, D.C.).

Foundation News, bimonthly magazine (Council on Foundations, Inc., Washington, D.C.).

FRI Monthly Portfolio, monthly newsletter (Fund Raising Institute, Rockville, Md.)

Fund Raising Management, monthly magazine (Hoke Communications, Long Island, N.Y.).

Taxwise Giving, monthly newsletter (Conrad Teitell, Old Greenwich, Conn.).

BOOKS AND ARTICLES ON SPECIFIC TOPICS

Giving Patterns and Donor Behavior

American Association of Fund Raising Counsel. *Giving USA: The Annual Report of Philanthropy* (annual statistical report). New York: AAFRC.

Cialdini, Robert B. "What Leads to Yes: Applying the Psychology of Influence to Fund Raising, Alumni Relations, and PR." *CASE Currents*, January 1987, 48-51.

Council for Aid to Education. *Voluntary Support of Education* (annual statistical report). New York: CFAE.

Duronio, Margaret A., and Bruce A. Loessin. "Fund-raising Outcomes and Institutional Characteristics in Ten Types of Higher Education Institutions." *Review of Higher Education* 13 (1990): 539-556.

Hodgkinson, Virginia A., and Murray S. Weitzman. *The Charitable Behavior of Americans: A National Survey*. Washington, D.C.: Independent Sector, 1986.

Leslie, Larry L., and Garey W. Ramey. "When Donors Give: How Giving Changes in Good and Bad Economic Times." *CASE Currents*, October 1985, 25-26.

Leslie, Larry L., and Garey W. Ramey. "Donor Behavior and Voluntary Support for Higher Education Institutions." *Journal of Higher Education* 59 (March/April 1988): 115-132.

Lindenmann, Walter K. "Who Makes Donations?" *CASE Currents,* February 1983, 18-19.

Loessin, Bruce A., Margaret A. Duronio, and Georgina L. Borton. "Finding Peer Institutions for Fund-raising Comparisons." *CASE Currents*, September 1988, 37-40.

Loessin, Bruce A., Margaret A. Duronio, and Georgina L. Borton. "Questioning the Conventional Wisdom: Do the Rich Get Richer?" *CASE Currents*, September 1988, 33-36.

Nichols, Judith E. *Changing Demographics: Fund Raising in the 1990s.* Chicago: Bonus Books, 1990.

Willmer, Wesley K. "Preventing the No: How to Spot—and Work With—a Donor's Mental Anchors, Rubber Bands, Boomerangs, and Caterpillars." *CASE Currents*, January 1987, 52-54.

Annual Giving and Direct Mail

Benson, Richard V. *Secrets of Successful Direct Mail.* Savannah, Georgia: Benson Organization, 1987.

Clark, Constance L. *25 Steps to Better Direct Mail Fund Raising.* Alexandria, Virginia: Clark Communications, 1988.

"Gathering More Givers: How to Get More Alumni to Give to Your Annual Fund" (special section). *CASE Currents*, April 1989, 25-44.

Gayley, Henry T. *How to Write for Development: Better Communication Brings Bigger Dollar Results.* Rev. ed. Washington, D.C.: Council for Advancement and Support of Education, 1991.

Gee, Ann D., ed. *Annual Giving Strategies: A Comprehensive Guide to Better Results.* Washington, D.C.: Council for Advancement and Support of Education, 1990.

Hodgson, Richard S. *Direct Mail and Mail Order Handbook.* 3d ed. Chicago: Dartnell, 1980.

Lautman, Kay Partney, and Henry Goldstein. *Dear Friend: Mastering the Art of Direct Mail Fund Raising.* Rockville, Maryland: Taft Group, 1984.

"Pull in a Profit: Making Direct Mail Work" (special section). *CASE Currents*, May 1988, 14-28.

"State-of-the-Art Phonathons" (special section). *CASE Currents*, March 1991, 18-42.

Williams, M. Jane. *The FRI Annual Giving Book.* Ambler, Pennsylvania: Fund Raising Institute, 1981.

Major Gifts and Planned Gifts

Arthur Anderson & Co. *Tax Economics of Charitable Giving.* 10th ed. Chicago: Arthur Anderson & Co., 1987.

Ashton, Debra. *The Complete Guide to Planned Giving: Everything You Need to Know to Compete Successfully for Major Gifts*. 2d ed. Cambridge, Massachusetts: Jeffrey Lant Associates, 1991.

Clifford, Denis. *Plan Your Estate*. Berkeley, California: Nolo Press, 1990.

Conrad, D.L. *How to Solicit Big Gifts*. San Francisco: Public Management Institute, 1978.

Hopkins, Bruce R. *The Law of Fund Raising*. Somerset, New Jersey: John Wiley & Sons, 1991.

"The Major Gift Difference: How Staff Can Add the Personal Touch" (special section). *CASE Currents*, November/December 1990, 32-57.

National Committee on Planned Giving. "Bibliography and Resource Guide." Indianapolis, Indiana: NCPG, 1991.

"The New Planned Giving Landscape" (special section). *CASE Currents*, June 1987, 22-40.

Panas, Jerold. *Mega Gifts: Who Gives Them, Who Gets Them*. Chicago: Pluribus Press, 1984.

"What's New in Planned Giving: Donor Clubs, Small Shop Strategies, and the Surge of Interest in Canada" (special section). *CASE Currents*, May 1990, 22-40.

Williams, M. Jane. *Big Gifts: How to Maximize Gifts from Individuals, With or Without a Capital Campaign*. Rockville, Maryland: Fund Raising Institute, 1991.

Campaigns

Bayley, Ted D. *The Fund Raiser's Guide to Successful Campaigns*. New York: McGraw-Hill, 1988.

"The Campaign Nucleus Fund" (special section). *CASE Currents*, June 1989, 16-56.

Dove, Kent E. *Conducting A Successful Capital Campaign*. San Francisco: Jossey-Bass, 1988.

Gearhart, G. David, and Roger L. Williams. "Do Mega-Campaigns Make Us Look Greedy?" *AGB Reports*, January/February 1991, 16-19.

Quigg, H. Gerald, ed. *The Successful Capital Campaign: From Planning to Victory Celebration*. Washington, D.C.: Council for Advancement and Support of Education, 1986.

Worth, Michael J. "The Challenge of Mega-Goal Campaigns." *AGB Reports*, March/April 1989, 18-22.

Corporations and Foundations

"Business Sense: Making Corporate-Campus Partnerships Work" (special section). *CASE Currents*, March 1988, 6-32.

Foote, Joseph. "The Name of the Game is Change." *Foundation News*, March/April 1987, 51-53.

Foundation Center. *America's New Foundations*. 5th ed. New York: Foundation Center, 1991.

Murphy, Mary Kay, ed. *Cultivating Foundation Support for Education*. Washington, D.C.: Council for Advancement and Support of Education, 1989.

Ross, J. David, ed. *Understanding and Increasing Foundation Support*. San Francisco: Jossey-Bass, 1981.

Saario, Terry. "Redirecting Corporate Giving." *AGB Reports*, September/October 1985, 32-33.

"Writing Proposals That Get the Grant" (special section). *CASE Currents*, October 1988, 6-22.

Managing the Development Program

Council for Advancement and Support of Education. *Management Reporting Standards for Educational Institutions: Fund Raising and Related Activities*. Washington, D.C.: CASE, 1982.

Council for Advancement and Support of Education and National Association of College and University Business Officers. *Expenditures in Fund Raising, Alumni Relations, and Other Constituent (Public) Relations*. Washington, D.C.: CASE, 1990.

Drucker, Peter F. *Managing the Nonprofit Organization: Practices and Principles*. New York: HarperCollins, 1990.

Hall, Margarete R. "A Comparison of Decentralized and Centralized Patterns of Managing the Institutional Advancement Activities at Research Universities." Ph.D. dissertation, University of Maryland, 1989.

Heeman, Warren, ed. *Analyzing the Cost Effectiveness of Fund Raising*. New Directions for Institutional Advancement, no. 3. San Francisco: Jossey-Bass, 1979.

Leslie, John W. *Focus on Understanding and Support: A Study in College Management*. Washington, D.C.: American College Public Relations Association, 1969.

Loessin, Bruce A., and Margaret A. Duronio. "The Role of Planning in Successful Fund Raising in Ten Higher Education Institutions." *Planning for Higher Education* 18 (1989-90): 45-56.

"Managing the Demands of Development: A Guide to Planning, Computers, and Small Shop Strategies" (special section). *CASE Currents*, March 1990, 26-42.

Murray, Dennis J. *How to Evaluate Your Fund-raising Program: A Performance Audit System*. Boston: American Institute of Management, 1985.

"Training an A-Plus Staff" (special section). *CASE Currents*, July/August 1989, 26-44.

Prospect Research

American Prospect Research Association. *The American Prospector: Contemporary Issues in Prospect Research*. Rockville, Maryland: Fund Raising Institute, 1991.

Henderson, Emily Pfizenmaier. "Proactive Prospecting: A Modest Proposal for a New Approach to the Role of the Prospect Research Specialist." *CASE Currents*, March 1987, 28-34.

Jenkins, Jeanne B., and Marilyn Lucas. *Fund Raising Research*. Ambler, Pennsylvania: Fund Raising Institute, 1986.

McNamee, Mike. "Privacy and the Prospect Researcher: How to Draw the Line between Uncovering Useful Donor Data and Digging up Dirty Little Secrets." *CASE Currents*, June 1990, 10-17.

Strand, Bobbie J., and Susan Hunt, eds. *Prospect Research: A How-To Guide*. Washington D.C.: Council for Advancement and Support of Education, 1986.

Worth, Michael J. "Prospect Research: A Tool for Professionalism in Fund Raising." *Fund Raising Management*, June 1991, 43-44.

Development and Other Advancement Fields

Kotler, Philip, and Karen Fox. *Strategic Marketing for Educational Institutions*. Englewood Cliffs, New Jersey: Prentice-Hall, 1985.

Roehr, Robert J., ed. *Electronic Advancement: Fund Raising*. Washington, D.C.: Council for Advancement and Support of Education, 1990.

Topor, Robert S. *Institutional Image: How to Define, Improve, Market It*. Washington, D.C.: Council for Advancement and Support of Education, 1986.

Webb, Charles H., ed. *Handbook For Alumni Administration*. New York: American Council on Education/Macmillan, 1989.

Williams, Roger L. "They Work Hard for the Money: An Informal Poll Reveals That PR Officers Play a Major Role in Supporting Capital Campaigns." *CASE Currents*, June 1989, 36-41.

Special Constituencies

Brooker, George, and T.D. Klastorin. "To the Victors Belong the Sports? College Athletics and Alumni Giving." *Social Science Quarterly* 62 (1981): 774-750.

"Direct to Deans: The Dean's Guide to Fund Raising, PR, and Alumni Administration" (special section). *CASE Currents*, June 1988, 16-52.

Frey, James H. "The Winning-team Myth: Studies Say Top Teams Don't Automatically Bring in Top Dollars." *CASE Currents*, January 1985, 32-35.

Gaski, John F., and M. Etzel. "Collegiate Athletic Success and Alumni Generosity: Dispelling the Myth." *Social Behavior and Personality* 12 (1984): 29-38.

Weiss, Larry J., ed. *Parents Programs: How to Create Lasting Ties*. Washington, D.C.: Council for Advancement and Support of Education, 1989.

Special Types of Institutions

Bryant, Peter S., and Jane A. Johnson, eds. *Advancing the Two-Year College*. New Directions for Institutional Advancement, no. 15. San Francisco: Jossey-Bass, 1982.

Council for Advancement and Support of Education. *Initiating a Fund-raising Program: A Model for the Community College*. Washington, D.C.: Council for Advancement and Support of Education, 1989.

Mitzel, David P., ed. *Resource Development in the Two-Year College*. Washington, D.C.: National Council for Resource Development, 1988.

Reilly, Timothy A., ed. *Raising Money Through an Institutionally Related Foundation*. Washington, D.C.: Council for Advancement and Support of Education, 1985.

Ryan, G. Jeremiah, and Nanette J. Smith, eds. *Marketing and Development for Community Colleges*. Washington, D.C.: Council for Advancement and Support of Education, 1989.

Sharron, W. Harvey, Jr., ed. *The Community College Foundation*. Washington, D.C.: National Council for Resource Development, 1982.

Worth, Michael J., ed. *Public College and University Development: Fund Raising at State Universities, State Colleges, and Community Colleges*. Washington, D.C.: Council for Advancement and Support of Education, 1985.

Professional Issues and Trends

Astin, Alexander W. *Achieving Educational Excellence*. San Francisco: Jossey-Bass, 1985.

Bok, Derek. *Beyond the Ivory Tower: Social Responsibilities of the Modern University*. Cambridge, Massachusetts: Harvard University Press, 1982.

Brakeley, George A., III. "Ethical versus fraudulent fund raising: A synopsis by the AAFRC." *Giving USA Update*, May/June–July/August 1989, 1.

Burlingame, Dwight F., and Lamont J. Hulse. *Taking Fund Raising Seriously: Advancing the Profession and Practice of Raising Money*. San Francisco: Jossey-Bass, 1991.

Carbone, Robert F. *An Agenda for Research on Fund Raising*. College Park, Maryland: University of Maryland, Clearinghouse for Research on Fund Raising, 1986.

Carbone, Robert F. *Fund Raising as a Profession*. College Park, Maryland: University of Maryland, Clearinghouse for Research on Fund Raising, 1989.

Carbone, Robert F. *Becoming a Profession: Readings for Fund Raisers*. College Park, Maryland: University of Maryland, Clearinghouse for Research on Fund Raising, 1990.

Council for Advancement and Support of Education. *Asking the Right Questions: Ethics and Institutional Advancement* (report of the CASE Ethics Colloquy, December 3-5, 1985). Washington, D.C.: CASE, 1986.

"Do You Lie, Cheat or Steal? Even If You Don't, You Face Tough Ethical Choices" (special section). *Case Currents*, January 1987, 8-42.

Grace, Judy Diane, and Larry L. Leslie. "Research on Institutional Advancement: Emerging Patterns and Parameters." *Review of Higher Education* 13 (1990):425-32.

Gurin, Maurice G. *Advancing Beyond the Techniques in Fund Raising*. Rockville, Maryland: Fund Raising Institute, 1991.

Jacobson, Harvey K. "Research on Institutional Advancement: A Review of Progress and a Guide to the Literature." *Review of Higher Education* 13 (1990):433-88.

Lawson, Charles E. "The Nineties: Worrisome Trends in Fund Raising." *The Journal* (National Society of Fund Raising Executives, Washington, D.C.), Winter 1990, 11-12.

May, William W. *Ethics and Higher Education*. New York: American Council on Education/Macmillan, 1990.

Melchiori, Gerlinda S., ed. *Alumni Research: Methods and Applications*. New Directions for Institutional Research, no. 60. San Francisco: Jossey-Bass, 1988.

Powell, Walter W., ed. *The Nonprofit Sector: A Research Handbook*. New Haven, Connecticut: Yale University Press, 1987.

Shoemaker, Donna. *Greenbrier II: A Look to the Future*. Washington, D.C.: Council for Advancement and Support of Education, 1985.

Smith, Joel P. "Professionals in Development: Dignity or Disdain?" *CASE Currents*, March 1981, 10-13.

Index